The

Ancient

World

in the

Cinema

Jon Solomon

The

Ancient

World

in the

Cinema

REVISED AND EXPANDED EDITION

Yale University Press New Haven and London

Designed by Sonia Shannon.

Set in Adobe Garamond type by Running Feet Books.

Printed in the United States of America by Sheridan Books, Chelsea, Michigan.

Library of Congress Cataloging-in-Publication Data

Solomon, Jon, 1950–

    The ancient world in the cinema / Jon Solomon. — Rev. and expanded ed.

      p.   cm.

    Includes bibliographical references and index.

    ISBN 978-0-300-08337-8

    1. Historical films—History and criticism.   2. Civilization, Ancient, in motion pictures.   I. Title.

PN1995.9.H5 S6 2001

791.43'658—dc21   00-044915

A catalogue record for this book is available from the British Library.

The paper in this book meets the guidelines for permanence and durability of the Committee on
Production Guidelines for Book Longevity of the Council on Library Resources.

10 9 8 7 6 5

To Lois, *quasi quasar universi mei*

contents

preface

When I began the first version of this book in 1976, there was little interest in the genre of films that I ironically and intentionally labeled "ancient." Not only were most scholars in the field of classical studies uninterested in the application of the classics to popular culture, but the film world itself had abandoned the production of "ancient" films, which since the beginning of the century had made a significant impact on the development and continued success of the film industry. Since 1976, however, hundreds of classical scholars in America and Europe have turned their critical trainings to a variety of popular-culture genres, giving professional papers, publishing articles and books, and teaching classes on the influence of the classics. In addition, the film world itself was in 1976 just about to experience a renascence—predicted in the first edition of this book—that began with such television productions as the BBC's *I, Claudius* and had by the end of the second millennium produced more than a half-dozen feature films, animated features, and television series, as well as scores of classical allusions in contemporary Hollywood films.

What originally inspired the writing of this book was my preteen screening of such films as *The Ten Commandments, Ulysses, Solomon and Sheba, Jason and the Argonauts,* and, of course, *Ben-Hur,* films that, along with several fine Latin teachers, helped to inspire my lifelong interest in classical studies. Nearly two decades later I was in graduate school at the University of North Carolina, equipped with newly acquired research skills, close enough to the Library of Congress and New York's Museum of Modern Art to do film research, and invigorated by a flurry of coffee-table books about film genres and well-known actors. Because this was just before the video and cable revolutions and all my film viewing was performed at institutions, I was at the mercy of the limitations of their holdings, opening hours, and equipment—except for the 16mm copies of films I rented and had shipped to my apartment. (My landlady suspected me of running a pornographical business under her roof.)

Two decades later, not only do we all have the opportunity to study a video copy of almost every film in the genre—whether purchased or taped from one of the dozens of cable channels available—but a number of new reference options are available, including online databases that allow one to cross-reference names and titles in seconds rather than having to search manually through books with incomplete indexes, or none at all.

All these advances make this a more complete and more accurate book. More films are now available for examination, and more information is available about them. The status of the database is not perfect, however. There are still lost films (Theda Bara's 1917 version of *Cleopatra*), ineptly edited films (Fox's 1963 version of *Cleopatra;* Bob Guccione's *Caligula*), and many insecure dates and multiple titles—most of them originating in Italy in the spans 1908–1916 and 1959–1964. The scholar awaits more memoirs and autobiographies from and biographies about actors, directors, and producers, and it is a realistic hope that the e-revolution might soon place unexpected resources in our hands.

In revising this book I left intact the Musaic order of the chapters and the arrangement of the films discussed, inserting in their proper positions discussions of and references to films produced after 1977. As best I could stomach I left intact also much of the "charm" I was more capable of exuding as a young man unaware of life's many potholes, though it was now proper to edit out the unintentional political incorrectnesses that my original 1970s-style pronouns betrayed. Of course I added data and corrected mistakes, but I also changed my opinion about some of the films: twenty years of maturation and accumulated knowledge allow me to appreciate better the position of such films as *Fabiola* (1948), *Two Nights with Cleopatra,* and DeMille's *The Sign of the Cross* in the history of cinema.

In revising the book and reviewing the films I found that films of the 1950s and 1960s that were nostalgically interesting in 1976 had become, forty years after their production, virtual antiques nearly as old as films of the 1930s had been to me while writing the first edition of the book. As a result I revised my estimation of the genre, from genuine admiration to a gratitude that these films had been made and have continued to be made—albeit in different formats—for nearly a century. The genre of films about the ancient world tells us much about our own century, and now that scholars are more frequently turning their attention to the contributions of twentieth-century culture, the following pages provide an interesting method of surveying our modern view of antiquity and ourselves. As Marie Wyke pointed out in *Projecting the Past: Ancient Rome, Cinema, and History* (Routledge, 1997), it is virtually impossible to look at Hollywood's treatments of Romans in films like *Quo Vadis?* (1951), *Ben-Hur* (1959), and *Spartacus* (1960) without comparing the Romans to Nazis and Communists. No longer are we examining just a sometimes brilliant, sometimes profound, sometimes campy genre of films; we are now looking at a century's worth of international cinematic production that reflects how the modern creative artist and our common populace perceive the ancient world.

preface to the first edition (1978)

Millions of filmgoers have been enjoying large numbers of films about the ancient world for more than seventy years now, and part of the reason for antiquity's cinematic attraction is simply its colorful costumes, classical architecture, and military heroics—the vaguely familiar trappings of our past. For some of these viewers it can be enough, besides the robes and columns and swords and chariots, to know that Cleopatra loved Antony, that Hercules was strong, and that David slew Goliath. True popular entertainment needs no explanatory introduction. But a considerably large segment of the filmgoing populace realizes that a film about antiquity often demands years of research, millions of dollars, and an epic scope. They realize that the Herculean effort represented by the "ancient" film's production should encourage a minimal effort by the audience, too. And they realize that the more one knows about antiquity, the more one should be able to appreciate a film about antiquity. One can certainly enjoy film classics such as *Ben-Hur, The Ten Commandments, A Funny Thing Happened on the Way to the Forum, Fellini Satyricon,* and *The King of Kings* as "pure entertainment," but one should also be able to view them in light of ancient history and literature. Why? Because these films can be excellent entertainment, yet they can be much more. My intentions in this book are by no means strictly academic, however. I examine all of these films first as pure cinematic entertainment; then I examine them as cinematic renderings of history; and I also examine them as cinematic adaptations of ancient, biblical, or modern literature. Ultimately, what I find is that those "ancient" films which first glean from historical and literary authenticity the power, complexity, and excitement of ancient life, and then respect a money-paying audience as well as the heritage of mankind, those "ancient" films become the most successful. Success usually necessitates historical authenticity *and* cinematic entertainment.

Unfortunately, when some people think about the ancient world in the cinema they immediately conjure up visions of ridiculously ketchupy and muscular sword fights, unconvincingly lionized Christian martyrs, and thinly tunicked slave girls. In this book I never deny their frequent presence amidst the genre's four hundred titles. But the genre also proudly claims many mature, powerful, artistic films. In addition, many "ancient" films have served as critical turning points in the cinema's overall development, so any serious film watcher risks becoming a hypocrite by uniformly panning the entire "ancient" genre. It is an unforgivable crime worthy of death in the crocodile pit to lump all four hundred "ancient" films together under the cloud of "schlocky costumer." Hopefully, the remainder of this book will help to dispel such a misconception, on both historic and cinematic grounds.

Since there are so many films in the genre, it will be impossible to discuss all of them, or even any one of them, in all the historical, literary, archaeological, theological, psychological, and cinematic detail that might be necessary. Consequently, one or two most noteworthy aspects of each film will be discussed in detail—be it the scenery of *The Greatest Story Ever Told,* the special effects of *The Ten Commandments,* the muscular heroics and cinematic influence of *Hercules* or *Cabiria,* the "meta-historical" approach of *Medea,* or the scandal behind *Cleopatra* (1963).

I must make several apologies before signing off and letting that faceless third person narrate the rest of the book. To classicists I apologize for not citing more ancient sources and for not delving into all the intricacies of each film's specific historical authenticities. But I never meant this book to be a multivolumed, thickly annotated, academic work; its rather popular nature does not allow for very frequent and detailed excursions into the pages of Livy, Josephus, Homer, or Tacitus. Moreover, no one knows everything about antiquity, and this certainly includes this writer; so professional classicists are invited to use the information and photographs in this book as a basis for their own investigations, judgments, and analyses. It was absolutely mentally and physically impossible to investigate all of the historical authenticities and inauthenticities. I hope the work I have done here will at least inform you about "ancient" cinematic history, techniques, and intentions and thereby lay down an inchoate methodology for approaching this most relevant humanistic progeny of antiquity—the "ancient" cinema.

To nonclassicist laymen, those who have quite understandably spent their lives in the present, I apologize for not including more frequent rudimentary explanations of things ancient and for perhaps occasionally assuming too much knowledge of antiquity on the part of all my readers. But specific analyses of the ancient toga, sandal, chariot, hairstyle, sword, military procedure, political complexity, and the like inevitably lead to controversy. Hopefully, the amount of basic historical, archaeological, and biblical information in the text and captions of this book will prove helpful and instructive without being too technical.

To film scholars I should apologize for omitting the titles of some two dozen silent films, but I cannot really apologize for assuming these four hundred "ancient" films to be an heretofore unrecognized filmic genre. Some "ancient" films are historical films, some pure costumers, some epics, some adventures, some comedies, some romances, some novel-based, some Bible-based, but not one of these established film genres actually includes all of these "ancient" films. The importance and periodic return of this film genre will be made evident in Chapter 1 and throughout the book.

Lastly, to devout and/or sensitive Jews and Christians I apologize for often treating divinities such as Yahweh and Jesus as mere cinematic "characters," but this is a book about cinema and antiquity, not a book about religion. Old Testament and New Testament generalities, indelicacies, and flippancies are by no means intended as slurs against anyone's religion. My concern is how to depict God on the screen, not how to worship him. Render unto cinema what belongs to cinema. My apologies in this regard must also apply to followers of Zeus, Ishtar, Isis, and Baal-Marduk, if there are any of you still hidden behind the faded idols or in the crumbled temples of yesteryear, whither we now proceed.

Orators are indeed permitted to lie about historical

matters so they can speak more subtly.

(Quidem concessum est rhetoribus ementiri in historiis,

ut alizuid dicere possint argutius).

— CICERO

Since the popularization of theatrical film in the first decade of the twentieth century, the wide-reaching world of the cinema has incorporated many different artistic genres, geographical localities, and historical eras, none of which have been any more recurrent, significant, or innovative than the genre of films set in the ancient Greco-Roman and biblical worlds.

Some four hundred feature films set in the ancient world have made familiar to many hundreds of millions of modern people an alluring, historical world well-marbled with graceful columns, gently folded togas, wine-filled goblets, racing chariots, divinely inspired prophets, golden idols of pagan gods, Christian-devouring lions, scantily clad slave girls, and brawny heroes. Classical Greece and Rome, in spite and because of their antiquity, create a popular and inimitable atmosphere on the screen, and biblical Palestine is as much a part of filmdom as it is of Western Civilization and its Judeo-Christian substructure.

Quo animo? Why has the ancient world had such appeal for the cinema? There are several reasons. Ancient warfare with its clashing chariots and hand-to-hand combat provides magnificent spectacle, as do glorious triumphal processions and fiery pagan rites. Seductive royalty like Cleopatra and Salome, powerful historical figures like Julius Caesar and the pharaohs, biblical revolutionaries like Jesus Christ and Moses, and complex mythological demigods and demimortals like Hercules and Helen of Troy are figures whose names are familiar and whose images are impressive to almost everyone. Old Testament patriarchs and the Passion of Christ have always

1   Richard Egan, portraying the Spartan King Leonidas, posed in silhouette for this publicity shot for *The 300 Spartans* (1962). Without action, color, narrative context, dialogue, or even an actor's face, this martial image, with its crested helmet, round shield, and thrusting spear, is immediately recognizable as belonging to the ancient Greco-Roman world.

challenged filmmakers to re-create on the silver screen what their millions of viewers have long since created deep within their own minds. The profoundly human yet ultimately divine plays of Sophocles and Euripides have contributed their own attraction. And the fantastical surroundings of ancient myths—surroundings that belong less to us than to an extinct branch of mankind—allow adventurers, escapists, visionaries, romantics, and intellectuals to lose themselves temporarily in that lost world of classical antiquity. Humans fill the screen, yet they wear different clothes, use different utensils, ride different transportation, pronounce pithy maxims, practice primitive religions (or complex religions in their primitive forms), employ different methods of warfare, order half-naked slaves to do their bidding, and view life and even death with different attitudes: unlike our highly developed modern civilization, biblical and classical antiquity were recently civilized forms of humankind and offered humankind newly conceived approaches to divinity.

Yet after all, the ancient world was of course the very source of our own world. Our modern culture owes its very existence to antiquity. And though the ancient world, like almost every aspect of human life, looks different on the screen, viewers can still see that the ancient world was inhabited with people who acted very much like people in our own world.

Along with these visual and cultural reasons for antiquity's popularity in the cinema is a historical reason: the ancient world never really released its grasp on Western civilization. From before the Renaissance to the last quarter of the twentieth century, through all the postantiquity ages of man, Greek sculpture, philosophy, poetry, comedy, and drama, Roman architecture, language, and historiography have continued to be the roots from which their modern descendants have grown. Whether it be the mundanity of the sandal, sword, and spear or the profundity of Christianity, Judaism, and Socratic wisdom, antiquity's legacy is an inherent, perpetuating part of modern life.

One of the reasons the young cinema immediately adopted antiquity as one of its favorite subjects was that antiquity was already quite popular in the contemporary theatrical, literary, and educational worlds at the end of the nineteenth century. *Ben-Hur, Quo Vadis?* and *The Last Days of Pompeii* were already best-selling novels; Shakespeare's *Julius Caesar* and Sophocles' *Oedipus Rex* were perennial favorites on the stage; the Bible was the basic core of almost everyone's education; and Latin texts were familiar not only to the elite but to the growing middle class. When the pioneers in the cinema looked for filmable subjects and themes, the ancient world was an obvious choice. As early as 1897, Thomas Edison filmed a brief, nonnarrative *Cupid and Psyche,* and overseas cameras captured the theatrical Passion of Christ at Oberammergau in 1897 and Luigi Topi's religious ten tableaux in 1900. Among his early films the French director Georges Méliès filmed a charming *La Sibylle de Cumes* (*The Sibyl of Cumae,* 1898), *Cléopâtra* (1899), *Neptune et Amphitrite* (1899), *Le Tonnerre de Jupiter* (*Jupiter's Thunderbolts,* 1903), *Pygmalion et Galathée* (1903), and *L'île de Calypso* (1905, entitled *Ulysses and the Giant Polyphemus* in English). Other early French films included Pathé's *Samson and Delilah* (1903), *Belshazzar's*

Feast (1905), and *Moses* (1907). Italy produced *Giudetta e Oloferne* (*Judith and Holofernes,* 1906), *A Modern Samson* (1907), and *The Rivals; a Love Drama of Pompeii* (1907). The British director Robert William Paul offered the first film version of *The Last Days of Pompeii* (1900), though this was merely eighty feet of film showing a volcano erupting and people fleeing from a collapsing ceiling. A few sources also report a British *The Sign of the Cross* (1904), supposedly made by the same Sigmund Lubin who directed *The Great Train Robbery* that year.

Although this respectable number of films based on ancient characters or themes was produced in the last years of the nineteenth century and the first years of the twentieth, the virtual birth not only of the ancient world in the cinema but also of the epic cinema as we know it occurred in 1908. That year, Arturo Ambrosio, an Italian optician turned camera enthusiast, produced his first overwhelmingly successful feature film at his Turin studios, *Gli Ultimi Giorni di Pompeii (The Last Days of Pompeii).* With its intriguing plot, classical setting, Egyptian twists, and holocaustic Vesuvial climax, director Luigi Maggi's film became a smashing success for the fledgling industry. In the ensuing so-called Golden Age of Italian cinema, dozens of costume epics set in ancient times were filmed. Ambrosio continued with *Nerone* (*Nero; or the Burning of Rome,* 1909), directed by Maggi, as well as *La Vergine di Babilonia* (*The Virgin of Babylon,* 1910), *Ero e Leandro* (*Hero and Leander,* 1910), *Lo Schiavo di Cartagine* (*The Slave of Carthage,* 1910), *The Queen of Nineveh* (1911), and the partially ancient *Satan* (1912). Ernesto Pasquali produced or directed *Teodora, Imperatrice di Bisanzio* (*Theodora, Empress of Byzantium,* 1909), and *Spartaco* (*Spartacus,* 1913); Giuseppe De Liguoro directed *Martire Pompeiana* (*The Martyr of Pompeii,* 1909), *Sardanapalo Re dell' Assiria* (*Sardanapalus, King of Assyria,* 1910), *Edipo Re* (*Oedipus Rex,* 1910), and *L'Odissea* (*The Odyssey,* 1911); Enrico Guazzoni directed *Brutus* (1910), *Agrippina* (1910), *I Maccabei* (*The Maccabees,* 1910), *Quo Vadis?* (1912), *Marcantonio e Cleopatra* (1913), *Caius Julius Caesar* (1914), and *Fabiola* (1916); Mario Caserini directed *Catilina* (*Catiline,* 1910), *Gli Ultimi Giorni di Pompeii* (1913), and *Nerone e Agrippina* (1913); and Giovanni Pastrone directed *Giulio Cesare* (*Julius Caesar,* 1909), *La Caduta di Troia* (*The Fall of Troy,* 1911), and the immortal *Cabiria* (1914). Other Golden Age Italian sword-and-sandal films featured more tales based on Roman history, the Old Testament, and the passion of Christ: Cines's *Amor di Schiave* (*Love of the Slaves,* 1910), *Rameses, King of Egypt* (1912), *Spartaco* (1914, starring Antony Novelli), and *Christus* (1915); Itala's *Una Vestale* (*One Vestal Virgin,* 1909); Latium's *Spartaco* (1909) and *Poppea ed Ottavia* (1911); Febo Mari's *Attila* (1916); Savoia's *The Triumph of the Emperor* (1914); Pathé's Italian production of Racine's *Phèdre* (1910); and *In Hoc Signo Vinces* (1913), *David* (1912), and *Salambo* (1914).

In these works the cinema overcame the limitations of the stage, which had been so confining to early French and Italian films. They necessitated the replacement of the indoor stage with outdoor location shooting. Gigantic sets began to fill the screen, and hundreds of extras were hired to re-create realistic crowd and battle scenes. The greatest successes after Ambrosio's *Gli Ultimi Giorni di Pompeii* were Guazzoni's *Quo Vadis?* (1912) and then Pastrone's *Cabiria* (1914). For *Cabiria,* whose story concerns Rome and its second confrontation with Carthage, four cameras, one of them movable, were used to shoot thousands of feet of film on location in Rome, Sicily, and North Africa. Of all the Italian epics of the silent Golden Age, *Cabiria* best demonstrated to subsequent filmmakers how to make a successful, full-length, visually crowded, narratively energetic film sprinkled liberally with bits of historical detail and special effects.

With their early epics Ambrosio, Guazzoni, and Pastrone established an association between the ancient world and films of lavish, gigantic scope, impressive prototypes that subsequent directors and producers often attempted to equal or surpass even decades later. In addition, Pastrone's *Cabiria* inspired a clutch of popular "Maciste" films. Nearly a dozen spin-offs involving *Cabiria*'s strongman Maciste (played by Ernesto [Bartolomeo] Pagano) were produced between 1915 and 1927. This was the first such brood of popular strongman films, the forerunner of *Hercules* and the dozens of sequels, imitations, and combinations that that 1957 film spawned.

American filmmakers, too, had begun making films set in antiquity or alluding to ancient subjects. In 1907 the director Sidney Olcott grabbed an armload of Metropolitan Opera costumes to outfit his limited cast at Manhattan's Battery Park for the first film version of *Ben-Hur,* which he followed with the ambitious *From the Manger to the Cross,* shot on location in the Holy Land in 1911 and released by Kalem in 1912. Soon after Olcott's neonatal version of *Ben-Hur,* Edison in 1908 produced *The Star of Bethlehem, Aida,* and, in seven scenes, *Nero and the Burning of Rome.* Vitagraph, an aggressive company formed in Brooklyn in 1908, immediately responded with *In Cupid's Realm,* Oscar Wilde's *Salome,* and *Julius Caesar,* which, with fifteen scenes, was even more luxurious than Edison's *Nero.* Vitagraph's *Antony and Cleopatra,* also made in 1908, starred such luminaries as Maurice Costello and Florence Lawrence. The next year the studio produced and released *Saul and David, The Way of the Cross,* in which a converted Roman and his Christian sweetheart are thrown to Nero's lions, and a five-reel, hand-tinted *The Life of Moses,* which the Patents Company insisted be released in serial fashion, one reel per week. Then followed Richard Strauss's *Elektra* (1910), *The Minotaur* (1910), *Cain and Abel* (1911), and *The Deluge* (1911). Most of these Vitagraph films were directed by J. Stuart Blackton, the British pioneer and a former collaborator with both Edison and Olcott.

Other early American production companies produced additional titles. In 1908 Kalem issued its *David and Goliath* and *Jerusalem in the Time of Christ,* Selig produced *The Christian Martyrs* (1910), with an arena sequence, and Essanay created *Neptune's Daughter* (1912), in which mortal Francis X. Bushman marries Undine (Martha Russell), the daughter of Neptune. Important individuals also produced "ancient" films: D. W. Griffith created the first of several entries with *The Slave* (1909) starring Mary Pickford and Florence Lawrence, and Helen Gardner produced and starred in *Cleopatra* (1912).

No early national cinema was as prolific as the French, no doubt inspired by the

2/3   Maciste (Bartolomeo Pagano), left, stands with Fulvius Axilla (Umberto Mozzato) before the entrance to the temple of Moloch in Carthage, in the groundbreaking *Cabiria* (1914). The huge oral entrance in the background, which stems from medieval visions of Hell, was much imitated, as were Maciste's muscles and chains, in scores of sword-and-sandal films of the early 1960s. The medieval portal to Hell is from Paris, Bibliothèque Nationale, ms. fr. 143 (*Le Livre des échecs amoureux*).

more than five hundred short films made by Georges Méliès from 1895 to 1913. Following the success of Ambrosio's *Gli Ultimi Giorni di Pompeii* in 1908, the next few years brought a spate of "ancient" films from French filmmakers who had a particular preference for mythological subjects. In rapid succession Parisians viewed Neptune and Cupid in Le Lion's *Goddess of the Sea* (1909), the Hydra and the divine Greco-Roman thunderer in Gaum-Kleine's *Hercules and the Big Stick* and *Jupiter Smitten* (1910), and a series of mythological struggles in Emile Cohl's animated *Les Douze Travaux d'Hercule* (*The Twelve Labors of Hercules,* 1910). At the same time Pathé released a series of films based on ancient subjects, including *Hercules in the Regiment* (1909), in which bullets bounce off the modernized Theban's chest, and the color-tinted *The Legend of Orpheus* (1909). Charles Pathé, whose lengthy, four-reel *Les Miserables* advanced the cause of the historical epic in Europe, also satisfied the French audiences' preference for films set amid the noble and antinoble polarities of ancient Roman history with such releases as the color-tinted *Caesar in Egypt* (1910), *The Justice of Claudius* (1911), *Nero and Britannicus* (1913), and a non-Shakespearean *Antony and Cleopatra* (1913), as well as a farce entitled *Back to Life After 2000 Years,* in which an ancient Roman comes to life in modern Rome. Pathé's biblical entries included *The Birth of Jesus* (1909), *The Slave's Revolt* (1911), which takes place in Egypt under Pharaoh Rameses, the color-tinted *Joseph's Trials in Egypt* (1914), and *The Life of Our Saviour* (1914), an expanded, color version of their *Life of Christ* (1910). All of C.G.P.C.'s releases were biblical: *Cain and Abel* (1911), a color-tinted *Infancy of Moses* (1911), *Abraham's Sacrifice* (1912), and *Saul and David* (1912). Henri Andréani directed a series of both historical (*Antony and Cleopatra, Messalina* [both 1910]) and biblical (*Caïn et Abel* [1911] and *Esther, La Mort de Saül, Rebecca,* and *La Reine de Saba* [all 1913]) films as well.

The largest output was by Gaumont, whose productions of 1910 included *Cain and Abel, Herod and the Newborn King, Esther and Mordecai, Jephthah's Daughters, The Marriage of Esther,* and *Pharaoh, or Israel in Egypt.* In 1911 the studio released *Saul and David; The Christian Martyr,* which includes an arena sequence à la *The Last Days of Pompeii; In Ancient Days,* about an Egyptologist dreams of a Pharaoh who causes his daughter's suicide; *The Son of the Shunamite,* which tells the story of Elisha and his raising of the dead; *In the Days of Nero,* a color-tinted story of palace intrigue and poisoning; *The Hour of Execution,* based on a Damon and Pythias motif set during the reign of Emperor Tiberius; *The Maid of Argos,* in which some romantic hanky-panky gets the better of the High Priest; and another romance, *A Priestess of Carthage.* After 1911 Gaumont produced only one "ancient" film, *Belshazzar's Feast* (1913).

Other early French films include Film d'Art's *The Kiss of Judas* (1909), a Shakespearean *Cleopatra* (1910) in eight scenes, and, most notably, Charles Le Bargy's *The Return of Ulysses* (1908), Hecla's *Oedipus Rex* (1912), Eclair's *The Sacking of Rome* and *The Resurrection of Lazarus* (both 1910) and *Herodias* and *The Prodigal Son* (both 1911). Urban-Eclipse also released a scenario set in Roman occupied Gaul — *The Gaul's Honor* (1910) — as well as *St. Paul and the Centurion* (1911).

The French cinema was negatively affected by the early successes of the Italian *Quo Vadis?* and *Cabiria:* almost no "ancient" titles appeared after 1914. The same is true in England, where after a burst from Dutch director-actor Theo Frenkel in 1911–1912 (*Oedipus Rex, The Modern Pygmalion and Galatea, The Lust for Gold, Esther: A Biblical Episode, Caesar's Prisoners, Telemachus, Samson and Delilah, The Fall of Babylon, Julius Caesar's Sandals, Judith,* and *Herod),* no further titles appeared there either. The positive impact of *Quo Vadis?* and *Cabiria* on the American film industry, however, was considerable in terms of scope, even if the American predilection for biblical fare still predominated. In 1913 audiences could see such films as Vitagraph's *Daniel;* Eclair's *The Holy City* and *The Crimson Cross,* a twenty-scene biography of Jesus; Famous Players' *The Daughter of the Hills,* in which a gladiator and his wife are converted by St. Paul; Powers's *In a Roman Garden,* where an affluent Roman falls in love with a Christian girl; the American Film Company's drama about the Huns entitled *In the Days of Trajan;* Helen Gardner's *The Wife of Cain,* in which Cain and his wife live in the land of Nod; and Thanhouser's *The Star of Bethlehem* and *Joseph in the Land of Egypt.* In the following year Universal released *Samson* as well as *Damon and Pythias,* and the American Film Manufacturing Company released *The Last Supper,* directed by Lorimer Johnstone and starring Sydney Ayres, which may have been as long as two thousand feet. Paramount's first version of *The Sign of the Cross* appeared in 1914.

None of these films had an impact on the development of the American film industry comparable to D. W. Griffith's two "ancient" spectacles, *Judith of Bethulia* (1913) and *Intolerance* (1916). Hollywood legend has it that after seeing Guazzoni's *Quo Vadis?* Griffith sat in a New York hotel room thumbing through the Scriptures to find the biblical and narrative inspiration for *Judith of Bethulia,* and the influence of *Cabiria*'s set decorations on *Intolerance* is clear. But whereas *Cabiria* and *Quo Vadis?* had been huge popular successes, *Intolerance* was ultimately a financial disaster, preaching untimely peace and tolerance to a bellicose world on the eve of its huge war. Only years later would the film be vindicated, even praised by a small cadre of critics as the greatest film ever made in America.

Often the zenith of a film genre's popularity invites the creation of animated imitations or satires. This period of "ancient" epics was no exception, for Windsor McCay produced his animated *Centaurs* in 1916.

Discouraged by the financial disappointment of *Intolerance* and distracted by the war in Europe, American studios produced few "ancient" films over the next few years. Notable exceptions to this period of relative dormancy include Theda Bara's *Cleopatra* (1917), which displayed the rolling-eyed vamp in fifty costumes, and *Salome* (1918). Also released in 1918 were Victory Films' *The Triumph of Venus,* which domesticizes the gods of Homer's *Odyssey* and focuses on the goddess's marriage to Vulcan and her affair with Mars, and Triangle Films' *The Golden Fleece,* whose protagonist Jason lives in a modern setting.

By the conclusion of the First World War the Golden Age of Italian epics set in ancient times had all but run its course. There were admirable offerings produced in 1919, including Pineschi's version of *Spartaco* and *Fedra (Phaedra),* and in 1921 Unione Cinematografica Italiana-Ambrosio filmed Victorien Sardou's *Teodora.* A minor resurgence took place in the 1920s, as several films displayed a brighter, more contemporary sophistication and grandeur. Guazzoni's *Messalina* (1922), Ambrosio's *Quo Vadis?* (1924), and

4   Theda Bara in *Cleopatra* (1917). This pose with diaphanous veil, split dress, and floral ornament
hardly stems from ancient Egypt, but Bara's audiences did not pay money to see authenticity.
There are no remaining prints of *Cleopatra,* so the American Film Institute has ranked it among its
top ten missing films. Check your attic and basement.

Amleto Palermi's *Gli Ultimi Giorni di Pompeii* (1926) were three of the costliest and most ambitious Italian films ever made. The last of these films, Palermi's *Ultimi Giorni,* starring Maria Corda and Victor Varconi, was a spectacular in more than the long-running, multi-extra, history-sweeping cinematic sense. It was a spectacular financial disaster as well, and it can fairly be blamed for the demise of the "ancient" film in Italy. One last *Giudetta e Oloferne* appeared in 1928, but this biblical film was a mere ghost of past Italian glory and a silent film world which was soon to be forgotten almost entirely. Not until the early 1960s would the country's film industry again match the frequency with which such films had been produced in the first years of the century.

America and transalpine Europe produced more successful and artistic films in the 1920s, particularly J. Gordon Edward's *Queen of Sheba* (1921) and *Nero* (1922), the latter in turn inspiring a comical takeoff by Universal in 1925, Alla Nazimova's curious *Salome* (1922); Korda's biblical romance *Samson and Delilah* (1922) and comical romance *The Private Life of Helen of Troy* (1927); Fox's *The Shepherd King* (1923); F.B.O.'s romance about Pharaoh Tutankhamen entitled *The Dancer of the Nile* (1923); the fledgling MGM's *Ben-Hur* (1925), starring Francis X. Bushman and Ramon Novarro; and Raoul Walsh's *The Wanderer* (1925).

The genre now spilled over into Germany as well. Two German films—*I.N.R.I.* (1923) and an updated *Passion Play* (1924), filmed at Oberammergau and Freiburg—continued older traditions, but Germany at this time was also a training ground for a number of filmmakers who soon flocked to Hollywood. Ernst Lubitsch, for example, directed *Das Weib des Pharao* (1922), which was later released in the United States as *The Loves of Pharaoh.*

Coming to the fore in the 1920s was the "ancient" moralizing film, which included both ancient and modern sequences. Several examples of modernized ancients had been produced in the previous two decades, but now more elaborate feature films regularly employed ancient sequences to provide a moral applicable to the modern sequences. Korda's *Samson and Delilah* experimented with this technique, as did *Queen of Sin* (also known as *Sodom and Gomorrah,* 1923), Michael Curtiz's Austrian-produced *Die Sklaven-königin* (*Moon of Israel,* 1924), and Robert Leonard's *Circe the Enchantress* (1924). Warner Brothers ventured into this style of moralizing film while introducing Michael Curtiz to America in *Noah's Ark* (1929). Another directorial giant had already established his unique feel for the genre with *Manslaughter* (1922), *The Ten Commandments* (1923), and *Made for Love* (1925). The director was Cecil Blount DeMille, the man who was to develop, dominate, and in many ways symbolize the entire corpus of ancient films. His next "ancient" film, *The King of Kings* (1927), was shown, if one includes Sunday morning and weekday evening church viewings, more often than any other movie in that era.

The 1930s added sound to the cinema, and films like Universal's *The Mummy* (1932) and United Artists' Busby Berkeley musical *Roman Scandals* (1933), starring Eddie Cantor, ushered a new era of "ancient" films into the theater. Films that had been made in the silent era were now fair game for the microphone and speaker. Working for Paramount, DeMille first directed a low-budget version of Wilson Barrett's 1895 play *The Sign of the Cross* (1932), which Paramount had first filmed in 1914. For nearly twenty years DeMille had been thumping the Bible while titillating his audiences, but this "talkie" version of *The Sign of the Cross,* with its infamous "lesbian dance" scene, became the focus of an attack on the sinful Hollywood film industry by the Catholic press.[1] DeMille followed the financially successful release of *The Sign of the Cross* with a lavishly impressive version of *Cleopatra* (1934), which had already been filmed in at least nine European and American, Shakespearean and non-Shakespearean versions between 1899 and 1917. DeMille's *Cleopatra* included still another exotic scene in which the Egyptian queen takes a milk bath, but other filmmakers were wary of the Hays Commission and the Production Code: RKO complied with a drastically rewritten, emasculated sound version of *The Last Days of Pompeii* (1935), and Warner Brothers put the inoffensive African-American biblical farce *The Green Pastures* on film in 1936.

For the most part the 1930s belonged to Hollywood itself. There was no need to set romance, hatred, heroics, or decadence in the ancient world because the modern Californian "Babylon" supplied all the wonder and awe that antiquity used to supply. And with renewed moral pressure from the Catholic press in the wake of *The Sign of the Cross,* there was little incentive to make films set in antiquity. One antiquarian film that *was* made in Hollywood, in fact, was actually the product of an Italian film company, La Itala Film Company di Hollywood, which moved to California and produced a film about Helen of Troy, *La Regina di Sparta* (*The Queen of Sparta,* 1931). Europe, meanwhile, produced a few gems: *Golgotha* (1932), *Anna und Elisabeth* (1933), and *Amphitryon* (1935). Perhaps the grandest of all would have been Alexander Korda's ambitious *I, Claudius* (1937), but filming was never completed.

The Second World War reinforced the relative indifference toward antiquity; a historical fantasy world of plastic swords and mock chariots must have seemed absurdly ineffective in a real world menaced by tanks, planes, and aircraft carriers. The only "ancient" films to be made during the war were either light-hearted or inspirational fare: the Three Stooges' comedy two-reeler short *Matri-Phony* (1942); another comedy styled after *Roman Scandals, Fiddlers Three* (1944); and Fox's pseudobiblical *The Great Commandment* (1942).

The end of the war brought a period of economic recovery and a refocusing of film audiences' attentions, two elements that were required to revive the "ancient" genre. Initially, following the lead of Laurence Olivier's production of Shakespeare's *Henry V* (1944), "ancient" cinematic interest focused on dramatic adaptations or farces about ancient subjects—for example, the Stooges' *Mummy's Dummies* (1948), RKO's adaptation of Eugene O'Neill's *Mourning Becomes Electra* (1947), George Bernard Shaw's *Caesar and Cleopatra* (1946), Universal's musical *Night in Paradise* (1946), Columbia's musical *Down to Earth* (1947), in which Rita Hayworth plays the muse Terpsichore helping a Broadway producer, Wiener Mundus's Austrian adaptation of Aristophanes' *Lysistrata* (1948), and

5/6   These two sequential production shots from RKO's *The Last Days of Pompeii* (1935) demonstrate how the cinema magically mimics antiquity. A once static water tank and prop boat with fresh paint and "gilded" oar portals explodes with action as disturbed waters, dense smoke, and a multitude of panicked citizens try to escape Pompeii, re-creating that fateful night in August, A.D. 79. Marcus (Preston Foster) stands on the right of the static photo and heroically helps the lad in the center of the action photo.

Cocteau's *Orphée* (1949), yet another French film based on a mythological subject. But by 1949, a whole new Golden Age of antiquity on film was about to be molded and cast.

If the one acorn from which the mighty oak grew can be singled out, DeMille's *Samson and Delilah* (1949) deserves leading credit for reinvigorating the "ancient" genre. True, the film followed on the heels of the postwar films in the genre, but the overwhelming success of *Samson and Delilah* fostered imitations, adaptations, and re-creations throughout the next decade and well into the 1960s. No doubt motivated by Paramount's success with DeMille's film, MGM celebrated its fiftieth anniversary with its version of *Quo Vadis?* (1951), the third major film version of Henryk Sienkiewicz's Nobel Prize–winning novel. Almost ten years earlier MGM had planned a version starring Orson Welles and Marlene Dietrich, but the project had been shelved; now it was revived and utterly reconfigured for this expensive version starring Robert Taylor and

Deborah Kerr. In the wake of its multimillion-dollar success, Columbia released *Salome* (1953), *Serpent of the Nile* (1953), and *Slaves of Babylon* (1953). Columbia set even a Ray Harryhausen horror film, *Twenty Million Miles to Earth* (1957), amid the ruins of Rome, and later a Pompeian "mummy" appeared in United Artists' release *The Curse of the Faceless Man* (1958). Universal answered with *Sign of the Pagan* (1954), and RKO with a Shavian *Androcles and the Lion* (1952). United Artists visited its cameras upon the expeditions of *Alexander the Great* (1955), and Warner Brothers offered *The Silver Chalice* (1954) and *Helen of Troy* (1955). MGM reentered the fray with *Julius Caesar* (1953), *The Prodigal* (1955), and *Jupiter's Darling* (1955), Fox *David and Bathsheba* (1951), and Lippert with *Sins of Jezebel* (1953). Even cartoons and animated features joined the party: Popeye appeared as Hercules in *Greek Mirthology* (1954), and Bugs Bunny "starred" in *Roman Legion-Hare* (1955).

Beyond the successive successes of *Samson and Delilah* and *Quo Vadis?* two other factors spurred on the revival of the genre. The first spur was an important economic one—television. Television had begun drawing customers away from the box office by the millions in the early fifties, and Hollywood desperately needed a gimmick with which to bring back its paying customers. The gimmick was wide-screen projection, and the first CinemaScope film was Fox's *The Robe* (1953). As with *The Last Days of Pompeii* in 1908,

Cabiria in 1914, and *Intolerance* in 1916, when cinematic frontiers were to be crossed, an ancient subject was called upon to provide the weighty narrative and a familiar, absorbing spectacle. What better narrative was there than *The Robe,* a best-selling novel about Rome and Christ? Fox followed this huge success with *Demetrius and the Gladiators* (1954), *The Egyptian* (1954), and *Queen of Babylon* (1956). The revival's second spur was an archaeological one, the widely publicized discovery in Egypt of Khufu's solar boat in the spring of 1954. Just as Howard Carter's 1920s excavation of the tomb of "King Tut" inspired Karl Freund's *The Mummy* in 1932, the discovery of this Fourth Dynasty relic redirected film producers' attentions across the ancient Mediterranean from Rome to ancient Egypt. Within a year, *The Egyptian* (1954), *Valley of the Kings* (1954), and *Land of the Pharaohs* (1955) had made their respective attempts at capturing the aged Nilotic zeitgeist.

Not all imitations of a successful artistic prototype are necessarily of lesser quality, the complaints of film critics in the mid-1950s to the contrary. In the face of calls for a halt to the flood of mediocre cinematic antiquity, Paramount, exploiting CinemaScope, revived interest in Egyptology, and the impassioned vision of Cecil B. DeMille brought the "ancient" film to new heights in 1956 with the still venerable *The Ten Commandments.* But if the recent success of *Quo Vadis?* had inspired a new flurry of "ancients," the moguls of Hollywood recognized that DeMille's expensive and lavish production would be difficult to equal. Only those of vision and fat wallets could successfully rival Paramount's second gigantic "ancient" success in a decade. United Artists released *Solomon and Sheba* in 1959, but it was *Ben-Hur,* MGM's answer to *The Ten Commandments,* that swept triumphantly through box offices that year, reaped eleven Academy Awards, then spawned a whole new cluster of historical and biblical epics.

MGM followed *Ben-Hur* with *King of Kings* (1961) and *Atlantis, the Lost Continent* (1961), the latter borrowing the fire sequences from *Quo Vadis?*. Among the other films of the post-*Ben-Hur* era were Warner Brothers' *Hannibal* (1960), Columbia's *Barabbas* (1962) and *Jason and the Argonauts* (1963), United Artists' *The Big Fisherman* (1959), Universal's *Spartacus* (1960), Paramount's *The Fall of the Roman Empire* (1964), and Fox's *The Story of Ruth* (1960), *Esther and the King* (1960), *The 300 Spartans* (1962), *Sodom and Gomorrah* (1963), *The Bible* (1966), and the controversial and extravagantly expensive *Cleopatra* (1963). Even *The Mummy* (1959) returned to the screen in a Hammer Productions version. Brazil made its contribution to the genre with *Black Orpheus* (1959), and a few years earlier Sweden released an unheralded *Barabbas* (1952) based on Par Lagerkvist's Nobel Prize–winning novel.

And Italy kept its once prolific hand in the newly inspired ancient pie. Even in the politically war-stormed 1930s, Mussolini had created *Scipio l'Africano* (1937) as ancient "proof" that Italy was historically the rightful owner of North Africa—ancient Carthage. In the 1950s a number of Italian films were seen in the United States, notably *Fabiola* (1948, 1951 U.S. release), *Queen of Sheba* (1953), *Two Nights with Cleopatra* (1953), *Sins of Rome* (1954), *Attila* (1954), and *Ulysses* (1955); Hedy Lamarr's Italian *The Face That*

Launched 1000 Ships (1953) was itself never launched. All these films were partially inspired by MGM's location shooting of *Quo Vadis?* in Rome, and such later films as *Sign of the Pagan* and *Ulysses* used Italian crews and cast but featured such American stars as Jack Palance, Jeff Chandler, Kirk Douglas, and Anthony Quinn.

A year or two later, after the American success of *The Ten Commandments* in 1956, Italy was ready to reclaim its ancient cinematic heritage, for from the lofty walls and ketchupy flesh of Cinecittà, *Hercules* (1957) was about to burst boldly into American theaters. Here was a film that earned anywhere from one-eighth to one-third as much as either *Ben-Hur* (1959) or *The Ten Commandments* (1956) yet cost less than 1 percent as much to produce. It offered simple entertainment, lots of action and adventure, hokey romance, half-naked women, and the biceps and sharply defined chest of Steve Reeves. The Italian sword-and-sandal epic was born again, and more than 180 neohistorical and neomythological films would be among the progeny of *Hercules*.

The post-*Samson*, post–*Quo Vadis?* trend was born in the mind of DeMille, grew up with the invention of CinemaScope, and matured in 1956 and 1959 with *The Ten Commandments* and *Ben-Hur*. It then received a mortal wound with the multimillion-dollar failure of *Cleopatra* in 1963. A few years later, after Anthony Mann's *The Fall of the Roman Empire* (1964) and John Huston's *The Bible* (1966)—both of which were already in production before the *Cleopatra* catastrophe—were released, the American four-hour, multimillion-dollar ancient spectacle had for the most part had its last "Hail!" The few films which were still set in antiquity were such foreign productions as the elaborate Polish *Faraon* (1966), based on Bolesław Prus's 1897 novel; *The Viking Queen* (1967), which was the lone British sword-and-sandal film of the era; *Kureopatora* (1972), a somewhat scandalous animated Japanese rendition of the Cleopatra story, and the quintessentially American Roger Corman offspring, *The Arena* (1973), which matched Margaret Markov and Pam Grier as Spartacus-like gladiatrices.

As often happens at the end of a popular film era, the "ancient" genre had become so commonplace, wearisome, and ripe for ridicule that even a satire of ancient films could be put into an ancient setting, so Richard Lester directed a film version of the hit Broadway musical *A Funny Thing Happened on the Way to the Forum* (1966). Two years earlier, the British *Carry On* team, which had already made nine farces, produced one set in the ancient world, *Carry on Cleo*.

In continental Europe the emphasis was entirely changed. So great was public indifference toward spectacle and ancient swordplay that Italian muscleman films were immediately succeeded by the newly trendy "spaghetti Westerns" of Sergio Leone, who recently had directed *The Colossus of Rhodes* (1961) and had earlier gained valuable experience working on the second unit of *Ben-Hur*. Leone championed popular films, but many of the European masters of late 1960s and early 1970s cinema produced and directed an abundance of artistically and intellectually provocative films based on ancient literature, films like Federico Fellini's *Fellini Satyricon* (1969); Pier Paulo Pasolini's *The Gospel*

7   Arnold Schwarzenegger hoists an Olympian goddess on his newly immigrated, Mr. Olympia–
winning shoulders in this publicity shot from his first film, *Hercules in New York*. His voice was
dubbed, and his improbable last name was discarded in favor of Strong. Atop the steps is Hercules'
father, Zeus (Ernest Graves).

According to Saint Matthew (1964), *Oedipus Rex* (1967), and *Medea* (1970); Rod Whitaker's
Thyestes (1968); Michael Cacoyannis's *Electra* (1962), *The Trojan Women* (1971), and *Iphigenia*
(1977); Roberto Rossellini's *Acts of the Apostles* (1969), *Socrates* (1970, TV), and *Agostino
d'Ippona* (*Augustine of Hippo,* 1972); and Luigi Magni's *Scipione Detto Anche l'Africano* (*Scipio,
Also Called Africanus,* 1971), starring Marcello Mastroianni and Silvana Mangano. So preva-
lent was this new European emphasis that Universal's release of *Oedipus the King* (1967) featured an almost entirely British cast and crew, and Charlton Heston had to go to Britain to
costar with Jason Robards in *Julius Caesar* (1969) and to direct and play the lead in *Antony
and Cleopatra* (1973), which was barely even given an American theatrical release.

    Another aspect of the 1960s that stretched into the 1970s was the reemergence of
modern adaptations—ancient tales, predominantly Greek myths, retold in modern settings. These productions include such clever contemporary adaptations of Greek tragedies

as Jules Dassin's *Phaedra* (1962) and *A Dream of Passion* (1978)—both starring his wife, Melina Mercouri—the Greek *Aphrousa* (1971), a modernized *Antigone* in *Year of the Cannibals* (1971), Giorgos Zervoulakos's *Lysistrata* (1972), and Costas Ferris's dreamlike *Prometheus, Second Person Singular* (1975). Even behind the Iron Curtain, Czechoslovakia produced a short *Metamorfeus* (1969), which offered a retelling of the story of Orpheus and Eurydice. Less reverent and catering more to the pop-art culture that was developing in the mid- to late 1960s were the film versions of Andrew Lloyd Webber's musical *Jesus Christ Superstar* (1970) and of *Godspell* (1973), as well as Russ Meyer's pop-art setting of Aeschylus's *Eumenides* in *Faster, Pussycat! Kill! Kill!* (1966). Then there was a British horror film, *The Gorgon* (1964), set in modernity but based on the ancient mythological character Medusa, and Americans were offered an updated version of Hercules set in the contemporary United States, *Hercules in New York* (1970), which starred a champion Austrian immigrant bodybuilder with such an improbable name—Arnold Schwarzenegger—that original prints of the film billed him as Arnold Strong.

Perhaps the most significant popular development during the 1960s and 1970s was not in theatrically released films but in made-for-television films aimed specifically at American television audiences. The film and television industries had been merging since the late 1950s, when film studios began to open subsidiary television production companies and then lease out many of their old Hollywood films for television broadcast. In the mid-1960s some films considered unworthy of risking theatrical release—like Joseph E. Levine's *Hercules,* or *Hercules and the Princess of Troy* (1965)—were premiered instead on television. Soon other projects were developed specifically as television pilots: William Shatner's *Alexander the Great,* for example, aired on ABC television in January 1968. At this time Shatner was riding the crest of his popularity on television's *Star Trek* (1965–1968), and a decade later it became common practice for the networks to produce inexpensive formula films featuring second-tier or aging box-office stars. Initially all the entries in the ancient genre were biblical: *The Story of Jacob and Joseph* (1974); *Moses, the Lawgiver* (1975), starring Burt Lancaster; *The Story of David* (1976); and Franco Zeffirelli's *Jesus of Nazareth* (1977).

Zeffirelli's lavish *Jesus,* which ran eight hours, was in the vanguard of the multi-part made-for-television movie (or "miniseries," as the subgenre was styled) that proliferated in the late 1970s in the wake of the wildly successful *Roots* (1977). Inspired by the Public Broadcasting System's successful importation of the British Broadcasting Company's production of *I, Claudius,* television producers created other lengthy explorations of antiquity—*Masada* (1981), *The Last Days of Pompeii* (1984), and *A.D.* (1985)—most of them aired during Holy Week. *A.D.,* like Fox's *Cleopatra* two decades earlier, was so costly and so unremarkable to both critics and contemporary audiences that it discouraged subsequent productions set in antiquity for nearly a decade. Italy produced one of these, too, a made-for-television *Quo Vadis?* (1985) that featured international stars Klaus Maria Brandauer and Max von Sydow.

Television miniseries were so visible and so financially successful in the mid-1970s

8   Malcolm McDowell recalls an infamous moment in history in Bob Guccione's X-rated
Caligula (1980). Suetonius (*Calig.* 46) reports that Caligula invaded Britain but abruptly ordered his
soldiers to "gather sea shells." Notice that around his neck the mad emperor wears the "little boots"
(*caligae* in Latin) for which he was nicknamed as a child. His own gold boots and short tunic are
intentionally suggestive of his odd sexual cravings.

that they encouraged producers to make a handful of theatrically released feature films set
in antiquity. The first release of this modest renascence in the late 1970s and early 1980s
was Ray Harryhausen's *Sinbad and the Eye of the Tiger* (1977), soon followed by his *Clash
of the Titans* (1981). Both these films were aimed at the young-teen and preteen *Star Wars*
generations, as were the Italian-produced *Hercules* (1983), which attempted to put the
bodybuilder Lou Ferrigno, television's Incredible Hulk, into an ancient setting enlivened
by special effects à la *Star Wars*. Ferrigno starred in two other films with ancient settings,
The Seven Magnificent Gladiators (1983) and *The Adventures of Hercules* (also called, as was
the fashion at the time, *Hercules II,* 1985).

         These films targeted demographically preselected audiences. Comedian Mel
Brooks's *The History of the World, Part I* (1981) was specifically aimed at his eager fans, just
as the irreverent British ensemble Monty Python satisfied theirs with *Life of Brian* (1979),

which was so controversial that its opening was boycotted by a number of religious groups. The same fate befell a film that dealt much more seriously with the same themes, Martin Scorsese's screen adaptation of Nikos Kazantzakis's *The Last Temptation of Christ* (1988), which portrayed Christ (Willem Dafoe) as a mortal living a genuinely earthly existence. In the film's most controversial sequence, Christ envisions himself making love to a woman. Even "adult" audiences were offered *Penthouse* magazine publisher Bob Guccione's X-rated *Caligula* (1980). And for younger audiences there was a Japanese animated feature, *Winds of Change* (1978), based on Ovid's *Metamorphoses.*

The same period produced a handful of films that contained individual ancient characters or scenes set in antiquity. The early Michael Crichton project *Westworld* (1973) included a Roman environment filled with vacationers acting out orgy fantasies. The same rock-nostalgia crowd that had flocked to see *Grease* in 1978 was offered Olivia Newton-John playing a Greco-Roman Muse in *Xanadu* (1980). And like Brooks's *History of the World,* both *Time Bandits* (1980) and *Bill and Ted's Excellent Adventure* (1988) contained one sequence each set in ancient Greece.

This brief revival in theatrically released feature films was followed by a second wave of made-for-television films. The waters were first tested by *Goddess of Love* (1988), a vehicle created for television game-show celebrity Vanna White, and the BBC's *Chimera* (1991), a political thriller involving a half-man, half-ape beast. Then Turner Broadcasting, a pioneer in made-for-cable programming and an advocate of "family viewing," commissioned and broadcast a series of four-hour films about the lives of the patriarchs and other Old Testament figures: *Abraham* (1994), *Jacob* (1994), *Joseph* (1995), *Moses* (1996), *Samson and Delilah* (1996), *David* (1997), and the Italian-German-produced *Solomon* (1997). Turner's success ultimately inspired NBC's *The Odyssey* (1997), an Emmy Award–winning project that had been initially planned by David Wolper *(Roots)* in the mid-1980s, and *Cleopatra* (1999).

During this same period in the early 1990s, the universe of cable television expanded considerably, creating the opportunity for a wide spectrum of new kinds of television offerings. At the same time satellite technology was expanding international markets, so in the wake of the alluring, body-focused *Baywatch,* a new brood of syndicated television adventure series aimed at the teen audiences spread over the globe. The most successful of these was a concept initiated by the innovative filmmaker Sam Raimi with five made-for-television films starring Kevin Sorbo as Hercules and Anthony Quinn as Zeus: *Hercules and the Lost Kingdom, Hercules and the Amazon Women, Hercules and the Circle of Fire, Hercules in the Underworld,* and *Hercules and the Maze of the Minotaur,* all in 1994. The resulting series, *Hercules: The Legendary Journeys,* was so successful that after one season it spawned a spin-off, *Xena: Warrior Princess,* which was in turn followed by *Young Hercules,* a daily syndicated television adventure drama introduced for the 1998 season by a prime-time pilot film. Completing the 1990s parallel to the Hercules boom of the late 1950s and early 1960s, the revitalized Disney Corporation made the Theban hero the

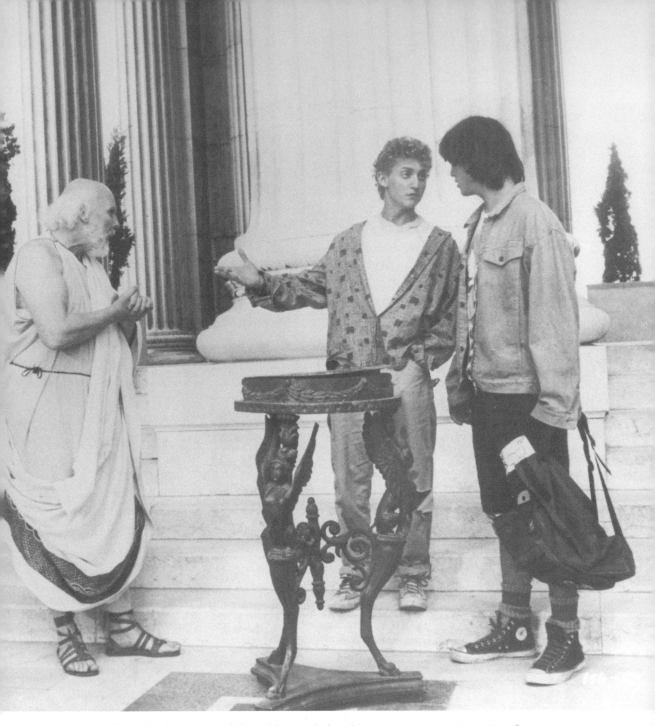

9   In the 1980s it became fashionable to include at least one sequence set in ancient Greece or Rome. Here Socrates ("sow-crates") discusses the meaning of life with two teenage California time-travelers (Alex Winter and Keanu Reeves) in *Bill and Ted's Excellent Adventure* (1988). The philosopher (Tony Steedman) speaks a bit of ancient Greek before the teens tell him: "The answer is blowin' in the wind."

subject of a major animated feature film release, *Hercules,* in 1997; and this in turn inspired DreamWorks' animated adaptation of the story of the Ten Commandments, *The Prince of Egypt* (1998).

This crop of new films and television programs set in antiquity may signal still another renascence in the genre as a result of the high-tech revolution of the past two decades. Two ingredients are in place: the public is no longer weary of epic "ancient" films, as it was in the late 1960s, and the prohibitive costs of mounting ancient spectaculars have been significantly reduced by the use of computerized animation. That technique not only offers the breathtaking visual and aural effects expected by today's new generations of moviegoers, it costs much less than building monumental sets in foreign locations and insuring film stars and casts of thousands of extras. Films have continued to join the genre in 1999 and 2000. Universal's *The Mummy* (1999), standing on the shoulders of 1994's *Stargate,* puts the ancient Egyptian spoken language into the mouth of several frightening versions of the revivified mummy. Ridley Scott's *Gladiator* (2000) is set — coincidentally, like *The Fall of the Roman Empire* (1964), one of the last major "ancient" films of its era — during the second-century A.D. reigns of Marcus Aurelius (Richard Harris) and Commodus (Joaquin Phoenix).

Julie Taymor, who utterly reformatted Disney's animated *The Lion King* for the Broadway stage, created *Titus* (1999)—an Americanized version of Shakespeare's fictitious, Roman revenge tragedy *Titus Andronicus.* Disney itself revived a classic in *Fantasia/2000* (1999), which included an Old Testament sequence, with Donald Duck playing Noah's assistant. And there were several made-for-television films as well: NBC's *The Odyssey* (1997), ABC's *Cleopatra* (1999), NBC's *Mary, Mother of Jesus* (1999), CBS's *Jesus* (2000), and NBC's *Jason and the Argonauts* (2000).

Besides the hundreds of films that have been set in antiquity or that offer modern adaptations of ancient myths, hundreds of films set in the modern world and based on new stories make references to antiquity. Most often they appear in an isolated but memorable line of script or a single piece of visual decoration. Remarkably, some three hundred such references are to be found in films made from 1986 to 2000, although the tradition goes back to the early days of sound films. In 1929 *Broadway Melody* contained a musical number with a Roman galley scene à la *Ben-Hur,* and *The Hollywood Revue of 1929* placed Neptune amid several underwater effects. In *Start Cheering* (1938) Jimmy Durante puns with a college librarian about a book on the Roman Empire by asking, "Who wants a book about baseball?!" In the noir film *Dark City* (1950), Lizabeth Scott asks Charlton Heston, "Where are we?" while gazing at an urban river. "Across the Styx," Heston replies.

Many filmmakers are well aware of film history, and whatever traditional education they might have had is supplemented by their familiarity with films set in antiquity several decades ago. Some make references to such well known mythological characters as Helen of Troy: *Highlander II: The Quickening* (1991), *Night and the City* (1993), and *Switch* (1991). Some invoke Hercules: *Bad Boys* (1995), *The Nutty Professor* (1996),

The Phantom (1996), and *Paradise Road* (1997). Still others allude to such famous historical personages as Julius Caesar: *Conquest of the Planet of the Apes* (1972), *JFK* (1991), and *National Lampoon's Loaded Weapon I* (1994). But a variety of classical allusions are used in different ways, some with great effect. Horace's well-known poetic admonition *carpe diem* from his first book of *Odes* is the motivating philosophy taught by Robin Williams's character to his students in *Dead Poets Society* (1989), and the truth about the mysterious but educated Richard Gere character in *Sommersby* (1993) is deduced from his several references to the *Iliad*. In these instances and in many others, screenwriters employ classical allusions at poignant moments, and usually they are the only literary allusions in the films.

The ancient Greek language itself appears only occasionally, as in *The Thin Red Line* (1998) and even *Bill and Ted's Excellent Adventure* (1988), but a number of films employ Latin. Sometimes the purpose is etymological, as in *Malcolm X* (1993), where Elijah Muhammad explains the original sense of the word *adorare*. Elsewhere Latin is used as a motto, as in Ovid's *amor vincit omnia,* quoted in *The Fisher King* (1991), or to describe a character's feelings: in *Fat Man and Little Boy* (1989), Robert Oppenheimer describes the confusion he feels about the atomic bomb by reciting (while on horseback) Catullus's "Odi et Amo." Often Latin is used to humorous effect, as in the verbal duel in *Tombstone* (1993) or on the tombstones in *The Addams Family* (1991). In the ever-inventive Zucker-Abrahams-Zucker team's *Top Secret!* (1984), a priest reads the Latin rites to a prisoner on death row ("*Gallia est omnis divisa in partes tres . . . corpus delicti, habeas corpus . . . hic haec hoc, huius, huius, huius . . .* ") and finishes in pig Latin. Latin also suggests an attitude: in *National Lampoon's Loaded Weapon I* (1994) Charlie Sheen uses the phrase *quid pro quo;* asked what the Latin means, Sheen responds, "It means I'm pretentious."

Allusions to ancient history appear frequently as well, be it a mobster's conscious, vivid re-creation of the suicide of Seneca in *Godfather II* (1974), Robert Duvall's statement that "I am at Thermopylae and the Persians shall not pass" in *Rambling Rose* (1991), Harrison Ford's brief Annapolis lecture on ancient Athenian naval power in *Patriot Games* (1992), or *The Warriors* (1979), a film based on Sol Yurok's novel about New York gangs clearly modeled on Xenophon's *Anabasis*.

There have also been a number of conscious visual references, even in earlier periods. In the height of the 1950s epic era, Audrey Hepburn's character in *Funny Face* (1957) models a dress with a flowing scarf in front of the Louvre's Nike of Samothrace. A few years later, in Alfred Hitchcock's *Psycho* (1960), when Norman Bates (Anthony Perkins) talks with Marion Crane (Janet Leigh) in a room off the lobby of the now infamous hotel, the instant the conversation turns to the subject of Norman's mother the camera angle changes dramatically to focus on his face in the foreground and a reproduction of Titian's *Venus at Her Toilet* in the background. This painting, which depicts Venus with her doting son Cupid, sits on the wall that separates them from the room that Norman, dressed as his mother, will enter to stab Marion to death. Hitchcock himself highlighted the poignant

10   A handful of Greco-Roman monuments are so widely recognized that a film can use them to make compelling visual statements. Here Audrey Hepburn in *Funny Face* (1957) models a gown and scarf in sharp perspective with the Hellenistic Nike of Samothrace ("Winged Victory") along the Louvre's broad marble stairway leading up to the Gallerie d'Apollon.

11/12   Janet Leigh shares her last meal with Norman Bates in Alfred Hitchcock's *Psycho* (1960). As soon as she begins discussing Norman's mother, she strikes this odd pose. The next shot reveals Norman sitting in front of a copy of Titian's *Venus at Her Toilet* (1552–1555), which portrays the goddess in a similar pose. The keen viewer suspects immediately that Norman Bates and his mother have as irregular a love relationship as Cupid and his mother. The painting is used again in Gus Van Sant's 1998 remake of the film.

parallel here between Norman, his mother, and Cupid in a trailer to the film. Gus Van Sant's 1998 remake of *Psycho* featured Titian's painting again, though hanging on a different wall, and the temptation to use ancient images in films has flourished in the 1990s. After Meryl Streep shoots Goldie Hawn with a shotgun and blows a four-inch hole clear through her abdomen in *Death Becomes Her* (1992), Hawn falls into a modernized *impluvium* decorated with a Venus *pudica* statue. Hawn has already drunk a magic potion, however, and as she rises from the waters "born again," we see the statue of her classical exemplar directly through the hole in her belly. The next year in *Boxing Helena* (1993), a replica of the Venus de Milo ironically falls on Julian Sands after he has surgically removed the arms and legs of Sherilyn Fenn. Filmmakers also employ some of the darker visual images from antiquity. One of the initial images of *Flatliners* (1990), the story of daring medical students who are "flatlining" and then resuscitating each other for several minutes to achieve a temporary death, is a colossal bust of Hermes Psychopompos set beneath the dark rotunda of their medical school (actually Chicago's Museum of Science and Industry).

Classical themes abound. There is Homeric imagery in *The Natural* (1984), Land of the Dead imagery in Mary Lambert's *Siesta* (1987), and a clever modernization of the Platonic "split-aparts" in *The Butcher's Wife* (1991), to name just a few. Oedipal themes are important elements in *The Empire Strikes Back* (1980), *Voyagers* (1991), and Woody Allen's "Oedipus Wrecks" in *New York Stories* (1989). Allen often uses classical imagery; he even had an ancient Greek dramatic chorus make Greek-choruslike commentary intermittently throughout *Mighty Aphrodite* (1995), and included a blind Teiresias character (Jack Warden) as well. Jon Voigt also played a Teiresias-like prophet in Oliver Stone's *U Turn* (1997).

One of the most interesting methods of adding a classical allusion to a contemporary film is via reference to older, easily recognized films set in antiquity. *The Crimson Permanent Assurance,* a short subject preceding *Monty Python's The Meaning of Life* (1983), opens with a sequence clearly modeled after the galley scene of *Ben-Hur.* When Paul Hogan dies and goes to the gates of heaven in *Almost an Angel* (1990), none other than Charlton Heston is there to greet him. Henry Wilcoxon—Cecil B. DeMille's son-in-law and Rameses' general in *The Ten Commandments* (1956)—plays a miraculous round of golf to the music of *The Ten Commandments* in *Caddyshack* (1980), and, similarly, in David Zucker's *The Naked Gun 2½: The Smell of Fear* (1991), when Leslie Nielsen is having sex, among the assemblage of relevant film clips is the erection of the obelisk for Sethi's jubilee in *The Ten Commandments.* The most frequently used reference to a film set in antiquity is the "I'm Spartacus" sequence from *Spartacus* (1960), used in *Monty Python's Life of Brian* (1979), *Punchline* (1988), *That Thing You Do* (1996), *In and Out* (1997), and *The Mask of Zorro* (1998); additional notable *Spartacus* references occur in *The Bird Cage* (1996) and *Clueless* (1995).

Another iconic scene from the genre is the chariot race in the 1959 *Ben-Hur.* But because this scene would be so prohibitively expensive to reproduce, there are only rare adaptations. There were two in the film's fortieth anniversary year: one was the stunning, wide-screen film-within-a-film sequence at the home of a cunning football coach in Oliver Stone's *Any Given Sunday* (1999). The other was a veritable homage—the pod race in George Lucas's *Star Wars: Episode I, The Phantom Menace*—which included echoes not just in the lap counters and crowd scenes but in the climactic struggle at the end of the race in which the Messala figure is destroyed while trying to destroy the Judah figure.

In making the hundreds of films set in the ancient world, the producers, directors, and their staffs have confronted challenges that do not so consistently face films in other genres, especially noncostume films. Most important, when the film's subject is a character with whom the viewer might be familiar (Julius Caesar, Spartacus, Hercules) or a story the viewer may know intimately (the Passion of Christ, stories from the Old Testament), the film has to find a delicate balance between historical authenticity and dramatic effectiveness. "Historical authenticity" may necessitate a reverent depiction of the Christ, a carefully delineated, complex political character such as Caesar or Cleopatra, or an architectural setting that actually belongs to the period being filmed. Unless the film is a comedy or a farce, Julius Caesar should not be a romantic fool, nor should Bronze Age Greek settings have classical-era, linear vase paintings on the walls, as is the case in many Italian muscleman films. Dramatic effectiveness, on the other hand, demands a dynamic film portrait of the Christ, a lively, emotive, and even romantic Caesar and Cleopatra, and

13 Kiefer Sutherland stands in front of a colossal head of Hermes in *Flatliners* (1990). The plot takes young medical students into the Land of Death, and Hermes Psychopompos (Leader of Souls) is the appropriate Greek god to guide the journey.

14 A snake-goddess from Knossos, Crete. Made circa 1600 B.C., this faience idol's garb is highlighted by tight sleeves, open chest, and segmented dress. The fashion was imitated precisely in the costumes for *The Warrior Empress* (1960) and *Ulysses* (1955), except for certain adjustments to the bustline.

an architectural setting that is pleasing or interesting to look at and creates the general atmosphere desirable for a particular scene.

Some of the films about the life of Christ lean too much toward historical authenticity or aim at an uncinematical reverence. Zeffirelli's *Jesus of Nazareth* (1977) and the otherwise magnificent *Golgotha* (1932) are typical examples, and *Sodom and Gomorrah* (1963) makes the same mistake. The inevitable result is cinematic boredom and—even more detrimental to the intended effect—the type of cheap piety at which many people in a crowded theater are apt to laugh. Then again, a total lack of reverence or historical accuracy is no more desirable. *Solomon and Sheba* (1959), *The Fury of Hercules* (1960), and *Cleopatra* (1999, TV) turn the Old Testament, Greek mythology, and Roman history for the most part into romantic and military mishmash, erasing the historicity of the characters. This in turn takes away our centuries-old admiration for them, and ultimately the drama becomes a mere pageant of unheroic characters. The costumes begin to look silly, and the whole film leans toward absurdity—more absurdity than one could achieve in a bad noncostume film.

The balance between historical authenticity and dramatic effectiveness is not an easy one to find. The critical viewer has almost as much responsibility as the director in establishing this balance; some viewers might be more critical than others. For example, the great Babylonian banquet hall in Griffith's *Intolerance* includes Assyrian, Persian, and ancient

15   The Roman *testudo* (turtle). A well-trained group of soldiers held their shields above their heads and around the sides of the rectangle they formed. Moving in unison, the formation was completely covered by this "shell" of shields. This particular testudo was carved in Trajan's column about A.D. 100, and the maneuver was reenacted for the battle of Alexandria in Fox's 1963 *Cleopatra*.

16   Caligula (Emlyn Williams), Messalina (Merle Oberon), and Claudius (Charles Laughton) in
Alexander Korda's unfinished *I, Claudius*. The costumes and decor are a fine blend of authenticity
and cinematic license. The chairs in the background are absolutely authentic in design, while the
whip in Caligula's hand is a fitting attribute for an emperor who would make his horse a consul.

Indian architectural motifs in addition to the proper and authentic Babylonian art. But at
least Griffith remains within the ancient Orient, and the viewer who can distinguish between
Assyrian, Babylonian, and Persian decor is a rare one indeed. Griffith's set shows a workable
balance between historical authenticity and cinematic atmosphere, and it should be accepted
as such. Only in very rare cases is letter-perfect authenticity either possible or desirable.

　　DeMille was another director who often found the correct balance. His special
talent was the exploitation of historical possibility. His temple of Dagon in *Samson and
Delilah* (1949) was decorated with Minoan and Sumerian paintings. DeMille's research department would have told him that Delilah's Philistines were historically "sea peoples,"
whom scholars believe to have come to Philistia from Minoan Crete, and they would have
told him that the Sumerians had a strong influence on all of the ancient East. DeMille
therefore combined Minoan and Sumerian decor in recreating a Philistine temple about
which scholars otherwise know very little. Though the decor of such a temple would have
been neither purely Minoan nor purely Sumerian, DeMille's combination of the two styles
has a historical basis. More important, DeMille's temple creates an atmosphere that is vivid
and pleasing to look at, yet plausibly authentic.

DeMille occasionally emphasized this plausible authenticity by focusing on a particular object. In his 1956 version of *The Ten Commandments* he focuses on a scale: first he has young Rameses (Yul Brynner) put weights on a scale as he details Moses' crimes—feeding the Hebrew slaves and giving them a day of rest; then Moses explains that this makes the slaves stronger so they can make better bricks, and he places a brick on the scale, clearly outweighing Rameses' accusations.

Finding this balance does not result from accident. Griffith, DeMille, Fellini, Pasolini, John Huston, and many other directors of "ancient" films were well read in the subjects they filmed, and Griffith, DeMille, and Fellini especially provided themselves with tomes of historical and architectural research before embarking on their respective works. Mervyn LeRoy began *Quo Vadis?* (1951), his lone venture into the genre, by reading Hugh Gray's specially prepared volumes of research about Neronian Rome and its appearance, customs, and eccentricities. Robert Rossen spent three years preparing his *Alexander the Great* (1955), and the same emphasis on historical accuracy was essential to Josef von Sternberg's unfinished *I, Claudius* (1937). Even cheap Italian productions like *Hercules* (1957) and *Ulysses* (1955) have properly inverted Mycenaean columns, and Fox's *Cleopatra* (1963), for all the scandalous hullabaloo about the torrid on-set love affair between stars Elizabeth Taylor and Richard Burton, offers the most authentic ancient naval battle in filmdom and a marvelous re-creation of a Roman army's *testudo* ("turtle") formation. In brief, it is rare that a film director has not delved into the history, architecture, dress, jewelry, artifacts, and customs of the period that is to be filmed. If a film does not reveal some evidence of careful historical research, the chances are excellent that the dramatic aspects of the film received just as little care.

The balance is most delicate. When directing *I, Claudius,* Josef von Sternberg asked his costume designer to create costumes for the Vestal Virgins of ancient Rome. The designer proceeded to several libraries and museums ("musea," as long as the discussion is about historical authenticity) and found that the half-dozen priestesses of Vesta were cloaked in thick capes and crowned with tiaras. When he conveyed this information to von Sternberg, the director weighed the merits of historicity and dramaturgy and then admonished his cautious designer, "This won't do; I want sixty of them! I want them naked! And I want them on the set tomorrow morning!"[2] Films about ancient history must consider current events as well—specifically, such matters as shooting schedule, budget, and the ultimate financial consequences of each decision on the set. Von Sternberg ended up with a large group of diaphanously veiled females carefully positioned on a flight of steps; they created a soft, mysterious atmosphere for the rest of the set, which already included authentic reproductions of Augustus's Ara Pacis, a marvelously decorated Roman audience hall (on matte), and authentic characterizations of stuttering Claudius, wicked Caligula, and the aging Livia—or if not authentic, at least faithful to the portrayals by the novelist Robert Graves and his Roman source Suetonius. Thanks to these prevailing authenticities, a few extra lightly clad Vestal Virgins did not undermine credibility. After all, a film like *I, Claudius* is art, not document.

Sometimes a director purposely avoids an historical reality either for dramatic effectiveness or to please a misinformed audience. George Stevens planned to shoot *The Greatest Story Ever Told* (1965), his version of the life of Christ, in the authentic Holy Land. When he flew to Lebanon and Israel to survey the Levantine topography, he found it disappointingly dull, dry, and unimpressive. He chose instead to shoot the film in Utah, where the magnificent sandstone mesas would create a staggering backdrop for the Passion. Whether his decision was valid is completely a matter of personal judgment. But critics should at least acknowledge that Stevens was aware of the actual locale and that he had his reasons for disregarding the authentic scenery and moving to scenery that *looked* more authentic.[3]

As for pleasing a misinformed audience, biblical scholars are reasonably sure that in Roman crucifixions the convicted criminal carried only the cross-beam *(patibulum)* to the place of execution. The vertical part of the cross was permanently installed at the site of execution. Once the convict arrived at the site, the cross-beam would be fitted to the vertical beam, and the criminal would be tied and/or nailed to the already erect cross, there to suffer through the agony and asphyxiation of crucifixion. But throughout the history of European painting almost every pictorial representation of Christ bearing his cross shows him dragging the whole cross, so movie directors, hesitant to contradict the age-old iconography, generally feel compelled to show Christ dragging the whole cross. It might be more authentic to have him drag only the cross-beam, but the shock or uneasiness that this change in iconography might cause among the movie audience would undermine the advantage in authenticity. In fact, some viewers would no doubt claim immediately that the film was inauthentic.

Similarly, Old Testament priests going authentically barefoot inside their temples would strike many moviegoers as silly and "inauthentic." A potentially shocking authenticity avoided studiously by filmmakers is the nose-ring often worn as jewelry by Old Testament–era women. D. W. Griffith dealt with the problem of "inauthentic authenticity" in a characteristically distinctive fashion. In filming the fall of Babylon for *Intolerance* he was so worried about audience reaction to his use of obscure but authentic cuneiform documents instead of the less accurate but widely read *Book of Daniel* that he included explanatory footnotes.

Historical authenticity should never be the sole factor in evaluating a film about the ancient world. Even if it were, authenticity is not always a clear-cut matter, but is often open to judgment and relative values. As with DeMille's temple of Dagon, for example, even the most dedicated historians and archaeologists can be quite ignorant of how a particular monument looked. Most historians, archaeologists, Egyptologists, classicists, or biblical scholars who have made a careful study of the everyday life of the ancients have encountered many dead ends. One may know much about the philosophy of Plato or the theology of Sophocles but have little or no idea what color or style of *chiton* (tunic) or what style of sandal Plato or Sophocles used at the Academy or at the theater, what type of paper, pen, desk, or lighting they used while composing dialogues or poetry. Similarly, the garment Julius Caesar wore at leisure: was it a toga? a tunic with a leather girdle? The exact type of table at which Christ ate his Last Supper—did he sit or recline? These are lost historical facts about which the most highly educated scholars can only speculate.

But the director, the set decorator, the costume and art designers of a film about the ancient world must make exactly the sort of "certain" judgments unavailable to those scholars. In this difficult task they usually turn to historical advisers, who may be classicists or historians such as Hugh Gray *(Helen of Troy, Ulysses, Quo Vadis?)* or Will Durant *(The Fall of the Roman Empire),* and may use primary and secondary literary and archaeological sources, paintings and renditions by the European masters, or the advice of colleagues. When they are "wrong" about something and the movie seems inauthentic, the "error" may be merely a matter of judgment and not of fact. Knowledgeable movie viewers must remember that the historical adviser or the director has generally tried to make a thorough investigation of the relevant historical material. More than once, a Ph.D. has scoffed at an "inauthenticity" in a film only to find later that it indeed *was* authentic.

Perhaps the most vital concept to keep in mind when viewing a film about antiquity is that film directors are artists, and as artists they have every right to adapt, change, or eliminate matters of history in deference to their cinematic art. In this sense, DeMille's fondness for exploiting the slightest thread of historical possibility, Griffith's occasional insistence on the most specifically footnoted historical reality, and Pier Paolo Pasolini's creation of his own world of "meta-history" instead of authentic history, are all possible approaches to cinematic antiquity. Cinematic antiquity belongs first to the demands of film, and second to the demands of history.

Cicero's statement cited as the epigraph for this chapter should be applied to this context. It indeed is "permitted" for film directors, as for "orators," to "lie," if that is what the art behind their "ancient" film demands. The essential question must be: "What are the directors trying to do, and are they succeeding?" If historical authenticity is part of what they are trying to achieve, then it must be factored into the equation; if not, then in all fairness, dramatic criteria alone must be used. But when directors look in both directions and achieve that delicate balance between historical authenticity and dramatic effectiveness, then they have indeed produced a brilliantly artistic re-creation of history, overcoming the greatest difficulties and transfigured historical problems and dramatic pretense into "ancient" cinema at its grandest.

Examining the balance between historical authenticity and dramatic effectiveness is only one method of evaluating an "ancient" film. But measuring the success of "ancient" films with other methods is no easier than evaluating the success of films in other genres. The corpus of work is large and varied. Clearly, most of the post-*Hercules* Italian muscleman epics of the early 1960s are of a lower standard and should not be weighed against expensive Hollywood studio productions. Other films of the genre are virtual milestones in the history of the cinema: *Ben-Hur* (1907, 1925, and 1959), *The Last Days of Pompeii* (1908), *Quo Vadis?* (1912 and 1951), *Cabiria* (1914), *Intolerance* (1916), *The Ten Command-*

ments (1923 and 1956), *The King of Kings* (1927), *The Sign of the Cross* (1932), *Samson and Delilah* (1949), *The Robe* (1953), *Cleopatra* (1963), and, broadening the perspective, *I, Claudius* (1976), *Caligula* (1980), *The Last Temptation of Christ* (1988), and the made-for-television Hercules films of 1994.

Despite the importance, innovation, and influence of these films, there are viewers who despise the entire genre. They cringe at the belabored historicity as well as the in-authenticities, the costumes, the pageantry, the grandeur, the maxims, the portrayals of religious icons, and the relative lack of psychological relevance for the modern world, not to mention the three- or four-hour running times. This is no surprise. "Ancient" films usually offer a lot to swallow, and some viewers decline to immerse themselves in the reconstructed waters of the past. *De gustibus non disputandum est.*

But a number of films about the ancient world have been adored by audiences. Nine films about the ancient world used to rank among the top money earners of all time: *The Ten Commandments* (1956), *Ben-Hur* (1959), *Cleopatra* (1963), *The Robe* (1953), *The Bible* (1966), *Spartacus* (1960), *Quo Vadis?* (1951), *Hercules* (1957), and *Samson and Delilah* (1949). Each earned over $11 million, an enormous gross if we take into account inflation and several decades of population growth. *Ben-Hur* (1959), budgeted at $15 million, was the top moneymaker of 1959, grossing $70 million during its theatrical release. And then there is DeMille's unique *The King of Kings* (1927), which in addition to its paid admissions was shown free—and without rental charge—to millions of churchgoers.

But the industry changed drastically in the 1970s. Filmgoers, particularly teenagers, began to see popular films two, three, or ten times, the number of screens in theaters mushroomed, and there were new aftermarkets in satellite, cable, and home video. To illustrate the contrast between films made before and after *Jaws* (1975), Disney's animated *Hercules* (1997) earned $245 million worldwide—more than three times the amount *Ben-Hur* earned—and yet its earnings paled in comparison to the top three films of 1997 (*Titanic, The Lost World: Jurassic Park,* and *Men in Black*), which earned approximately $3 billion combined. Of the top 133 money-making films, only two were made before *Jaws*—Disney's animated *Bambi* and *101 Dalmations,* both of which have been rereleased since 1975. Still, if it is any consolation to those who yearn for earlier days, *Ben-Hur* has subsequently earned another $37 million in video rentals.

If critics' awards are valuable criteria, "ancient" films earned nine berths on the *New York Times* annual "ten best" lists: *Ben-Hur* (1925), *The King of Kings* (1927), *The Green Pastures* (1936), *Julius Caesar* (1953), *Ben-Hur* and *Black Orpheus* (1959), *Electra* (1962), *Cleopatra* (1963), and *The Gospel According to Saint Matthew* (1966). *Ben-Hur* (1959) won eleven Academy Awards, including the major Oscars for best picture, best director (William Wyler), best actor (Charlton Heston) and best supporting actor (Hugh Griffith), as well as awards for color cinematography, color art direction, sound, film editing, music, color costume design, and special effects. No film has ever won more Academy Awards. Another seventeen Oscars have been claimed by *Spartacus* (1960: best supporting actor [Peter Ustinov], costume design, art direction), *Cleopatra* (1963: special effects, costume design, art direction, cinematography), *Black Orpheus* (1959: foreign-language film), *The Ten Commandments* (1956: special effects), *The Robe* (1953: costume design, color set decoration), *Julius Caesar* (1953: black-and-white set decoration), *Samson and Delilah* (1950: art direction, set decoration, costume design), *Cleopatra* (1934: cinematography), and *The Prince of Egypt* (1999: best music, song). Most of these are technical "minor" Oscars, but costume design, art direction, set decoration, special effects, and cinematography are in one sense the most important awards an "ancient" film can win: they create the atmospheric essentials that can convincingly reproduce the "antiquity" in a film about antiquity. To our preconditioned modern eyes—so conditioned since 1907—an "ancient" film often needs the pictorial splendor and broad scope in order to look as if it is really taking place in antiquity. Not all "ancient" films are or should belong to the epic genre, but vivid and effective visual and aural enticements are certainly part of the attraction of antiquity in the cinema. Six "ancient" films also received Oscar nominations for best film—*Cleopatra* (1934 and 1963), *Quo Vadis?* (1951), *Julius Caesar* and *The Robe* (1953), and *The Ten Commandments* (1956)—another five actors and actresses were nominated for best actor or best actress, and Martin Scorsese was nominated as best director for *The Last Temptation of Christ* in 1989. Still another eight films set in antiquity were nominated for various Academy Awards—*Electra*, *The Gospel According to St. Matthew*, *The Fall of the Roman Empire*, *The Greatest Story Ever Told*, *The Bible*, *Jesus Christ Superstar*, and *Hercules* (1997)—as were another twenty-two films set in the modern world but containing important classical allusions, two of which—*The English Patient* and *Braveheart*—won the best picture Oscar. In addition, of the made-for-television films and miniseries, *I, Claudius, The Last Days of Pompeii, Joseph,* and *The Odyssey* each won at least one Emmy award.

In general, "ancient" films have always demanded special care, huge costs, and top-rate actors and directors. In terms of cost, *Quo Vadis?* (1912), *Cabiria* (1914), *Intolerance* (1916), *Quo Vadis?* (1951), *The Ten Commandments* (1956), *Ben-Hur* (1959), *Cleopatra* (1963) were, at their specific eras, the costliest films ever made, and the same can be said of *Masada* (1981) and *A.D.* (1985) among television films. The names of directors that worked on "ancient" films themselves make up an epic list: Academy Award winners William Wyler, George Stevens, Joseph L. Mankiewicz, John Huston, Michael Curtiz, Robert Wise, Martin Scorsese, and Frank Borzage, as well as King Vidor, Raoul Walsh, Howard Hawks, Stanley Kubrick, Cecil B. DeMille, D. W. Griffith, Federico Fellini, Pier Paolo Pasolini, and many others. Academy Award–winning actors who have starred in films about the ancient world include Marlon Brando, Ernest Borgnine, Charlton Heston, Peter Ustinov, Hugh Griffith, Yul Brynner, George C. Scott, Anthony Quinn, Charles Laughton, Burl Ives, Rex Harrison, Broderick Crawford, Dean Jagger, George Sanders, Sir Laurence Olivier, Fredric March, H. B. Warner, Anthony Hopkins, Anne Bancroft, Sophia Loren, Elizabeth Taylor, Susan Hayward, Vivien Leigh, Claudette Colbert, and Jessica Lange.

Ultimately, considering the massive historical material that directors of "ancient" films must digest, the weighty, maxim-filled scripts they often must use, the popular expectations and hoopla that they must satisfy, the religious and theological parameters that they must respect, and the complex decisions about decor, properties, costumes, and settings that they must make, not to mention the multimillion-dollar corporate investment for which they are responsible, it is clear why "ancient" films are rarely if ever perfect. An ancient film inherently presents a greater challenge than most other films; so much can go wrong in a large costume production with lions, elephants, horses, thousands of extras, huge sets, and location shooting, in addition to all the human and historical problems. The handful of triumphant ancient films that have succeeded in overcoming these Herculean challenges and presenting realistic and powerfully dramatic re-creations of the ancient world truly belong on the lofty and ratified heights of filmdom's Olympus.

How many ages hence

Shall this our lofty scene be acted over,

In states unborn, and accents yet unknown.
.

— S H A K E S P E A R E ,

J u l i u s   C a e s a r ,   3 . 1 . 1 1 1 − 1 1 3

History has always fascinated humans. Before people could write, they told their history in legends; before they invented drama, they wrote their history on tablets and stone; and before they invented the cinema, they acted out their history on stage.

Then came film. Since 1900 every major historical character and epoch has been captured on film, and the ancient world has had more than its share. From the archaic age of Greece, in which Sappho, the Lesbian from whom lesbians got the name, wrote her poetry, to Attila's barbarian invasions of Rome, nearly all of the major personalities of the ancient world have been honored with a celluloid portrait. And what personalities! The energetic Alexander, the reservedly regal Julius Caesar, the treacherous Nero, the alluring Cleopatra, as well as Hannibal, Spartacus, Constantine, and other historical giants — their legacy still lives though their lives were spent some two thousand years ago.

The quality of these historical films varies widely. They range from the multimillion-dollar spectacle of *Cleopatra* (1963) to the low-budget black-and-white *Julius Caesar* (1951), from a script by George Bernard Shaw to poorly dubbed Italo-English dialogue, and from the carefully researched historical accuracy of *Alexander the Great* (1955) to the delightfully absurd fabrications of *Son of Spartacus* (1962). But neither expense nor historical accuracy is the one ultimate criterion for evaluation of these films. Each film should be judged according to its aims, execution, and periods — the period *in* which the film is made and *about* which the film is concerned. It would be unfair, for example, to criticize both the spectacular silent *Cabiria* (1914) and the low-budget sound *Hannibal* (1960) with the same standards even though both movies are set in the Second Punic War. One might as well compare Eisenstein's *October* with *Dr. Zhivago*. It would be just as unfair to praise *Alexander the Great* because of its historical accuracy and simultaneously to pan *The Fall of the Roman Empire* (1964) because it makes some academic errors; in terms of dramatic achievement *The Roman Empire* rises and *Alexander* is not so great.

Some historical filmmakers defeat their very *raison d'être* by ignoring historical details that would have made the film better drama. *Constantine and the Cross* (1962) portrays one of the most able and shrewd politicians in history as a one-dimensional, whitewashed holyman (Cornel Wilde); this cinematic portrayal of Constantine flattens the historically complex character of a pagan general who connived his way to the Roman Empire's throne by publicly (and calculatingly) embracing the growing subversive Christian movement. Believe it or not, *The Fall of the Roman Empire* depicts the insane emperor Commodus (Christopher Plummer) too temperately. Our historical sources tell us that while personally participating in gladiatorial battles, he wore a lion skin over his head and carried a club in imitation of Hercules, a harmless eccentricity that a filmmaker might have used as an early clue to Commodus's delicate emotional balance. Later, to reveal the worst of the insane emperor's character, the film could have alluded to his sleeping with his sister and then having her put to death for trying to assassinate him because he was not showing her enough affection. These bizarre idiosyncrasies were omitted from the film even though they are historically documented. In contrast, Alexander Korda's unfinished production of *I, Claudius* (1937) re-created one of the early Roman Empire's most interesting moments, when mad Caligula (Emlyn Williams) presented his horse as a government official to the Roman Senate. This historical detail added much to the film's fine characterization of the demented Caesar Caligula.

Films of Ancient Greece

Because the Romans etched so indelibly on the tablets of history such vivid images as bloody gladiatorial spectacles and seductive Oriental queens, their history has offered Hollywood and Cinecittà more material than Greek history. Yet some of the better-known memories of ancient Greece—Sappho, the Persian Wars, Socrates, Damon and Pythias, Alexander the Great, and the Colossus of Rhodes—have found their place in film. A survey of these films follows, in order of historical, not cinematic, chronology.

Sappho, one of archaic Greece's finest poets, appears as the graceful heroine of the Italian-made *The Warrior Empress* (1960). Never judge a book by its cover, and never judge an Italian movie about the ancient world by its English title. In this case, the original Italian title was a less bellicose *Saffo, Venere di Lesbo* (Sappho, Venus of Lesbos). A lovely Tina Louise portrays the poet of the Greek island of Lesbos, who falls in love with the (masculine) rebel hero Phaon (Kerwin Matthews). The flowery wall frescoes and light interior decor give an appropriately archaic sixth-century B.C. impression, though the tantalizing costumes of some of Sappho's fellow Lesbians are closely modeled after the dress of the Bronze Age Minoan "Snake Goddess" of Knossos. The plot generally follows the stories told in the poems of Sappho, her fellow Lesbian Alcaeus, and other archaic Greek poets of a civilian revolt, a love triangle, and a personal vendetta. The pace of the film drags while the insipid romantic plot develops, but at least *The Warrior Empress* made an attempt at re-creating an otherwise fairly obscure historical character on the screen. Sappho's brother Larichus, the rebel leader Pittacus, and the revolt against Melanchrus are all historical, as is Sappho's lover, Phaon. The poet, a Lesbian geographically, was not exclusively so sexually. Our sources tell us that she had a husband and bore him a child, and that she ultimately threw herself over a cliff on the island of Leukas because of her unrequited love for Phaon.

Two films take place in the era of the Persian invasions of Greece, 490–479 B.C. In *The Giant of Marathon* (1959) the main character Philippides (Steve Reeves) runs from the battle of Marathon to Athens at the instructions of the Greek leader Miltiades. Meanwhile the Persian forces, aided by the Athenian traitor Hippias, invade Athens by land and sea. There follows a macabre naval battle typical of director Jacques Tourneur's work *(Berlin Express, Cat People)*. Shot with frequent underwater photography, the climax of the operations focuses on a Persian ship with movable wooden jaws at its prow that crush Greek ships in their crunching grip. The film is based on the story of the famous historical character Pheidippides (or Philippides [Herodotus 6.105]), who ran from Marathon to Athens to bring news of the Greek victory. After running the twenty-six miles, he collapsed and died, his legendary fatal run immortalized in the name of our long-distance run. In the film, Philippides—out of breath, perhaps, but still breathing—takes his girl Andromeda into the sunset in the final reel. The light, romantic mood, the athletic heroics of Philippides, and the despicable encroachment of the Persians and evil Greek traitors, all displayed in cheap costumes and brought to the inevitable happy conclusion with a Persian defeat, assure us that this is a pretty typical *peplum*—an enjoyable early-1960s romantic, heroic, Italian muscleman film without pretenses, subtleties, or sophistication.

In producing and directing *The 300 Spartans* (1962), Rudolph Maté chose one of the most glorious moments in human history: the Spartan defense against the Persian advance through the central Greek pass of Thermopylae in 480 B.C. He wisely chose to film not a whole war, nor one general's career, but one classic battle that became legendary within a generation of its waging. Maté carefully characterized the three essential historical figures—the brave King Leonidas of Sparta (Richard Egan), the cruel, megalomaniac Persian King of Kings, Xerxes (David Farrar), and the Athenian admiral and political wizard, Themistocles (Ralph Richardson). Besides the character development, the focus on a single battle gave Maté a ready-made climax: the famous clash and the poignant death of all three hundred Spartans. The entire film builds up to this crescendo, and the slain heroes meet a compellingly tragic end.

Early in the film Xerxes' aide Hydarnes warns Leonidas that Persian arrows will "blot out the sun." In response, Leonidas coolly squints, looks at the sun, and says, "Then we'll fight in the shade." When Leonidas falls in the last desperate defense of Thermopylae, the Spartans are surrounded by Persian archers, and their whizzing arrows do indeed blot out the sun as the handsome and brave red-cloaked Spartan warriors succumb to one of the largest armies ever assembled in ancient times. We remember the Spartan scout's quaint description: "For six days I watched them pass; I ran out of numbers and still there were more of them!" The music suddenly strikes a screeching and mournful strain, and within seconds the small band of heroes that had impressed us through the entire film is wiped out.

Lifting many lines directly from the Greek historian Herodotus, George St. George's screenplay usually rises above clichés. Themistocles recites the immortal warning of the Delphic Oracle that the Athenians should "hide behind wooden walls." Then a hen-pecked shepherd speaks amusing lines of St. George's own creation: "Who can understand the ways of the gods; they create lovely girls and then turn them into wives." The ancients loved their aphorisms, and a generous sprinkling of them — whether genuinely venerable or crafted to seem so — helps create "ancient" atmosphere on film.

The pleasant, foot-tapping music of the thematic Spartan march turns dissonant as the Persian "Immortals" (Xerxes' bodyguard) make their way into the pass of Thermopylae; they are led by a Greek traitor, the gold-worshiping Ephialtes, the Judas of Greece. Then in three classic Persian assaults, Spartan cunning and training perform miracles. They surround the black-cloaked Persians with fire; they box the enemy in with a phalanx of hoplites; and they wedge their way through the Persian line. Using a cast of a few thousand (modern Greek soldiers) and covering them well with a panning CinemaScope lens — angling alongside the straight rows of Spartan spears and shields, and rising to include the massive numbers of Persians — Maté created one of the most exciting and authentic ancient battles ever put on film.

From the opening shot of the film, in which thousands of black-cloaked, conical-helmeted, and wicker-shielded Persian soldiers march and shout "Xerxes! Xerxes!" to that last shot of the three hundred horse-crested Spartans falling in a heroic heap, the film moves insistently toward the tragic climax. The unflinching determination of the Spartans is an inspirational contrast to the whimpering of the Oriental tyrant Xerxes. As he sits proudly on his colored marble throne covered in thick, rich, embroidered cloth, Xerxes angrily declares "I shall capture them alive, put them in cages, and exhibit them all over Asia!" The audience appreciates the irony: the Spartans, we know, will lose the battle, but the Greeks will win the war. Interrupted only occasionally by a formulaic young-lovers motif that runs sporadically through the story, *The 300 Spartans* sings the fame of the legendary Lacedaemonian warriors while tragically sacrificing them in the name of freedom before our admiring eyes.

Unfortunately, culturally brilliant fifth-century Athens has been ignored by the

17/18   Most Greek hoplites, like the Spartan soldiers in the production photo from *The 300 Spartans* (1962), wore short tunics and carried round shields, long spears, and short swords. Notice how the shields overlap in the flying-wedge phalanx formation. The Persians have conical helmets, black robes, and wicker shields. The Greeks' nose-guarded Corinthian helmets, also used in *Alexander the Great*, were made of bronze and characterized by the nose piece; they came with or without a crest. In a relief from Delphi's Siphnian Treasury (525 B.C.), the soldiers have discarded their spears.

cinema. No one has thought Pericles, Alcibiades, or the Peloponnesian Wars worthy of the modern cinema. Even wise and ironical Socrates was the focus of only one feature film—a 1970 Italian television movie by Roberto Rossellini. But although Rossellini uncompromisingly re-creates Plato's *Euthyphro, Apology, Crito,* and *Phaedo,* the film never rises above its quasi-documentary form; it remains a mere subtitled dialogue on film. More interesting by contrast is Maxwell Anderson's less reverent Hallmark Hall of Fame television production of *Barefoot in Athens* (1966), starring Peter Ustinov. And more fun by far is the role of Socrates in *Bill and Ted's Excellent Adventure* (1988). Here the philosopher, whose named the dimwitted title characters pronounce as a bisyllabic "sow-crates," actually speaks a few syllables of ancient Greek and time-travels to contemporary California to help the two dudes pass their history class.

Fourth-century B.C. Greece has four entries in the film world: two versions each of *Damon and Pythias* and *Alexander the Great.* Like its 1914 Universal predecessor, the 1962 Italian/American coproduction of *Damon and Pythias* concerns the immortal tale of a friendship set in the Greek colony of Syracuse, on Sicily. Their friendship was strong enough to cause Damon to offer his own life to save Pythias's and vice versa, but ultimately neither has to die at the hands of the tyrant Dionysius. (This is the same Dionysius who invited Plato to visit him, but this historical event was overlooked in the film.) The sprightly and lively acting by Guy Williams (Damon) and the almost profound, speculative conversations about the (historically authentic) secretive Pythagorean philosophies help elevate *Damon and Pythias,* as does the directing by German-born Curtis Bernhardt, best known for his 1953 Rita Hayworth vehicle, *Miss Sadie Thompson.* Incidentally, Damon's friend was actually named Phintias, but the better-known if erroneous name was used to avoid confusing the audience. Popular misconceptions about history are often best left undisturbed in film.

Alexander the Great (1955) is one of the most historically faithful of all movies about the ancient world and perhaps one of the most intelligent, too. It was written, produced, and directed by Robert Rossen, who was between his Academy Award–winning *All the King's Men* (1949) and his Academy Award–nominated *The Hustler* (1961). *Alexander the Great* does not idle in meaningless physical combat, nor does it excessively glorify or whitewash Alexander. Instead, the most intriguing episodes in his fascinating life that were passed down from ancient times (mostly in Plutarch's *Life of Alexander*) appear in the film—Alexander's semidivine birth, the burning of the temple of Ephesus, his admiration for the mythical Achilles and his love for Homer's *Iliad* (he always kept a copy, just as Napoleon would keep a copy of Plutarch's *Alexander* with him), his years with Aristotle at Mieza, his power-hungry mother and his drunken but shrewd father, his throwing the spear to claim Asia, his cutting of the Gordian knot, the destruction of Persepolis, his murdering his best friend Cleitus, his marriage of ten thousand Greeks and Orientals at Susa, and his early death at Babylon.

Richard Burton does an admirable job in acting the part of the energetic, visionary Alexander. He portrays a young man displaying constantly changing moods and qualities of anger, reverence, courage, collapse, energy, fever, idealism, practicality, shrewdness, hot temper, and intelligence. His short stature and smooth, handsome, blond appearance contrasts well with the dark, hairy, and frightening look of his barbaric father, Philip (Fredric March). March's imposing characterization of Philip imbues the most haunting scene in the film: after Philip has won the battle of Chaeronea against the united cities of Greece, he gets drunk and mocks the famous Athenian orator Demosthenes for calling him a barbarian; in an echoing voice he shouts, "Philip the barbarian, Philip the barbarian," and dances precariously and clumsily on top of a rocky cliff. His voice has a curious sound of alcohol-induced self-pity, and although Philip dies early in the picture, his vivid memory lives on in Alexander's mind (and ours) for the rest of his life.

Their father-son relationship is complicated by the fact that Alexander may have had a hand in Philip's assassination. History is unsure about the affair, so Rossen cleverly leaves the blame ambiguous. Alexander hears his mother, Olympias (Danielle Darrieaux), "suggest" to a young Macedonian to kill Philip. Rossen does not hint at any other involvement until after the young man has stabbed Philip on the palace steps at Pella; Alexander then runs after the assassin and kills him—ostensibly for revenge, but perhaps so the young man cannot announce that Alexander was privy to the plot. Even more difficult than putting historical fact on film is putting historical controversy on film, and Rossen accomplished this nicely here. Confining himself to what the consensus of our historical sources tell us, Rossen neither accuses nor acquits Alexander.

Alexander the Great offers a realistic portrayal of a historical legend. Alexander never has superhuman strength, and he suffers personal defeats and setbacks despite his youthfully glorious conquest of the Persian Empire. At the zenith of his conquest of Asia, Alexander's boyhood companion, "black" Cleitus, warns him that he is getting too much like an Oriental potentate—like the pampered Darius (Harry Andrews) he just conquered. In his drunken anger Alexander throws a spear into his friend's back. He hugs Cleitus's corpse and weeps; this is no plastic, one-dimensional, unerring, cinematic conqueror. Surrounded by able actors playing the full complement of Macedonian and Greek generals— Attalus (Stanley Baker), Parmenio (Niall MacGinnis), and another Greek traitor, Memnon (Peter Cushing)—Alexander and his staff are emotive, energetic, and rational soldiers who live war, friendship, and politics on a most realistic scale.

The battles in *Alexander the Great* are brief but effective. The battle by the river Granicus in Turkey (shot by the Jarama River in Spain) consists of a splashing-through-the-river charge by Alexander, surrounded by six thousand extras dressed as Macedonians and Persians. The battle culminates quickly as a Persian raises his sword to slice at Alexander but soon sees his own bloody arm fall into the river from Cleitus's saving swoop; shocking, momentary, and vivid, this authentic scene is directly from the pages of ancient history. Some of the other panning military shots of the Macedonian troops carrying their

19   The magnificent Alexander mosaic from Pompeii (above). Executed some time before Pompeii's destruction in A.D. 79, this mosaic depicting Alexander, left, and the Persian King Darius, right, uses the long Macedonian pikes *(sarissae)* for angular emphasis.

unique eighteen-foot pikes *(sarissae)* are artistically arresting.

Still, *Alexander the Great* demonstrates one of the problems inherent in making a historically accurate film about a historical character. Literary accounts of history cannot be easily translated into cinematic accounts, and a penalty is paid in dramatic energy for progressing intelligently through Alexander's life. The film sometimes drags while Burton's monotonic words are thrown instead of spears. But $4 million and three years of Rossen's planning and research otherwise produced an excellent filmic document about a most complex and interesting young general. Our curious fascination with Alexander the Great lives on in this authentic biopic.

A second attempt at a biography of Alexander was filmed nearly a decade

20/21 Albrecht Altdorfer's 1529 painting of Alexander's battle of Issus against the Persians (facing page, bottom) again uses the angling spears to highlight Alexander (labeled as Alexander Magnus) and to create a swirling motion throughout the painting. The sixteenth-century painting conventionally dresses Alexander in contemporary armor. Robert Rossen's *Alexander the Great* (1955, above) maintains the artistic tradition by surrounding Alexander (Richard Burton) with long Macedonian pikes. The other soldiers have round or trapezoidal shields, pikes or swords, Corinthian or Macedonian helmets, and military cloaks.

later—an unsold 1964 television pilot starring William Shatner, who, after establishing his

reputation as a young Shakespearean actor in the 1950s, was at the time (1960–1968) establishing his own eternal fame as Captain Kirk in the television series *Star Trek*. The hour-long film also featured John Cassavetes (General Karonos) and Joseph Cotten (Antigonus).

As the historical Alexander lay on his deathbed, his generals huddled around him to hear who would be designated his successor; Alexander curtly said, "To the strongest." Three hundred years of war, political marriages, and assassinations were spent deciding the designee of these words. This period of history between the death of Alexander and the rise of Rome, called today the Hellenistic Era, was a period of commercial expansion and modernization. This was the period in which Sergio Leone set his *The Colossus of Rhodes* (1961), an excitingly gruesome and creatively bizarre movie that anticipated the "spaghetti Western" and the end of the linguini cloak-and-sandal film.

Leone, the son of the director Vincenzo Leone and the actress Francesca Bertini, both prominent figures in Italian cinema, had recently refined his directorial skills working on such overseas American productions as *Ben-Hur*. He began writing and directing action films in 1958 with *Nel Segno di Roma* (released in the United States as *Sign of the Gladiator*) and *Afrodite, dea dell'amore (Slave Women of Corinth);* he then continued with a new version of *The Last Days of Pompeii* in 1960 and *Romolo e Remo (Duel of the Titans)* and *The Colossus of Rhodes* in the following year. He became internationally recognized for his next few films, casting Clint Eastwood as the Man with No Name in the quintessential "spaghetti Westerns" *A Fistful of Dollars, For a Few Dollars More,* and *The Good, the Bad, and the Ugly.*

The plot of *The Colossus of Rhodes* is the standard stuff of *peplum:* in another typical early-1960s revolt of the masses, the macho hero Dario (Rory Calhoun) challenges another Snidely Whiplash–like ancient tyrant. But the gloomy atmosphere and the magnificent bronze (actually plastic) colossus that looms gigantically over the harbor make the film at once artistically engaging and visually bizarre. The colossus straddles the harbor and drops deadly bowlsful of hot oil on helpless enemy ships below. The inner wooden and metal machinery inside the colossus provide a curious setting for the few sword duels inside its head, on its arms, and through its three-foot ear canals. True to history the colossus is ultimately destroyed by an earthquake at the end of the film.

The tense, brutal style made famous in Leone's Western trilogy is already in evidence in *The Colossus of Rhodes:* at one juncture Peliocles (George Marchal) and his men are tortured with bubbling hot oil dripping through sieve-holes in a stone roof onto their backs; in another excruciating scene, Peliocles suffers excruciating pain when placed inside an eight-foot iron bell, which is then rung around him, sparkling blood pouring from his numbed ears. With ominous, windblown shots setting up desolate exteriors similar to those to be seen in *The Good, the Bad, and the Ugly, The Colossus of Rhodes* offers

22   The great Syracusan naval battle in one of the most influential movies ever made, *Cabiria* (1914). Under the direction of the ancient scientist Archimedes, the Syracusans remove a cloth covering from a huge mirror. Within minutes the reflected sunlight has the Roman fleet in flames. Three decades ago, a historian took three hundred mirrors to the Greek coast and proved that such an ancient flame thrower could actually work.

the same savage naturalistic ambience that would soon remove Italian cinema from B.C. to the wild West.

Films of Ancient Rome

The same expansive Hellenistic period that produced the famous colossus of Rhodes also introduced a new power into the Mediterranean—Rome. Led by its famous general Scipio against Carthage, with its equally renowned quarterback Hannibal, Rome eventually wiped its foe off the map for a few generations. Five movies have been made about these Punic Wars, including the finest spectacular production of the silent era in Europe. *Cabiria* (1914) is the story of a young Sicilian girl who has been taken to Carthage as a slave. There she is rescued twice by a Roman spy and his faithful, muscular servant, Maciste (Bartolomeo Pagano). Meanwhile, the Romans attack Syracuse and Cirta while Queen Sophonisba falls into an ill-fated love that causes her death. The romantic plot rests on a structure of historical fact; Livy (29.23–30.15) and other Roman historians tell us about Scipio's attack on Cirta and Rome's famous naval assault on Syracuse, where the Hellenistic genius Archimedes instructs the defenders to aim a huge reflecting glass at the Roman fleet to burn it to a soggy crisp. The Romans eventually win the war, of course, and Cabiria and the Roman spy, Fulvius Axilla, set a dubious film precedent by riding off into the sunset with a superimposed circle of angels fluttering around them.

Cabiria is a classic. The whole silent spectacle exudes an unequaled charm. The cheerfully innocent Cabiria and the strong-willed, dark, and heroically chiseled form of mighty Maciste provide us with two lovable characters set in striking contrast to the spectacles of Archimedes' mirrors, Hannibal crossing the snow-covered Alps, Mount Etna erupting in fiery furor, Roman soldiers forming a testudo, and the child-devouring furnace in the forty-meter-high Carthaginian temple of Moloch. The elegant suicide of Queen Sophonisba, who had been introduced while luxuriously stroking the backs of her two pet leopards, and the lightly cunning and deceiving antics of the little Carthaginian man called "la Scimmia" (the monkey) broaden the human elements of the plot.

Shooting *Cabiria* at the Turin studios of Itala Films as well as on location in the Alps, Sicily, and Tunisia (Carthage), director Giovanni Pastrone revolutionized filmmaking with his technical innovations. He was the first to use the camera dolly, which he patented. He was the first to use extensive artificial lighting—hence the eerie atmosphere inside the massive and fiery temple of Moloch and at the burning of the Roman fleet in the harbor. He was one of the first to edit extensively; he shot some 20,000 meters of film, which he cut to 4,500 meters—approximately three hours' running time. These techniques and the finished film itself influenced the directors of film spectaculars who followed. De-Mille learned his concept of gigantism from *Cabiria,* and it is no accident that Griffith's *Intolerance* was shot in the two years that followed the American release of *Cabiria;* some critics at the time even claimed that Griffith owned his own print of *Cabiria* and looked at it in secret. Whatever the truth of this rumor, Griffith's elephant-tid columns, massive stairways, and panning camera were all preceded by Pastrone's masterpiece.

But if *Cabiria* influenced later spectacles, it borrowed from its predecessors as well. Maciste, the muscular protector of the young girl, is influenced by the character Ursus in the novel and early film version of *Quo Vadis?* "La Scimmia" originates in *Quo Vadis*'s Chilon. The volcanic eruption in Cabiria's Sicilian homeland was a motif central to the novel and early film versions of *The Last Days of Pompeii.* Pastrone himself had used massive crowds a few years before in *La Caduta di Troia* (1911). But the blend of effects is part of the unique charm of *Cabiria.*

The impact of *Cabiria* on audiences in Europe and America in 1914 is difficult to imagine now, for this extraordinarily long and spectacular movie was often shown with the accompaniment of a large chorus and orchestra—the Sensurround equivalent of the age. In its rerelease in New York in 1921 it was hailed as "the greatest picture in memory," and it was rereleased again in 1929.[1] Inspired by the 1911 Turkish invasion of Tripolitania, which was part of the ancient Carthaginian and Roman empires, Pastrone used an adventure story set in ancient times to pursue a politically volatile issue: the foreign invasion of traditionally Roman territory. He added an innocent and sympathetic heroine, spectacular special effects, technical innovations, and an unforgettable hero named Maciste. He even gave the film a literary seasoning by hiring poet Gabriele D'Annunzio to write some of the titles. (The poet was broke at the time and living in exile to avoid paying his massive debts.) So with gimmick and art, with borrowing and innovation, with contemporary and ancient politics, and with charm and spectacle, Pastrone gave birth to *Cabiria* —a delightful monument in the history of the cinema.

Wary of professional actors, Pastrone found his muscular Maciste working on the docks in Genoa. Pagano was so well received that he went on to make several more "Maciste" films; he helped to establish a new word for the English language and set the precedent for the muscleman epics that made international movie heroes of Steve Reeves and his eventual successor, Arnold Schwarzenegger.

Rossano Brazzi and Tina Louise were not quite so fortunate in their roles in *The Siege of Syracuse* (1962). Brazzi played the part of Archimedes in this unremarkable film that, thanks to *Cabiria,* highlights the famous mirror battle waged by the Syracusan scientist. Another film about the Carthaginians and Romans, *Carthage in Flames* (1960), has an interesting sea battle that uses real ships rather than the usual models. A highlight is a flaming confrontation between a large Phoenician-type ship, fitted with an open mouth at the bow, and a high-decked Carthaginian trireme. This vivid naval battle, the special effects during the burning of Carthage, the noble attempt at historicity, the frequent references to the Goddess Tanit, the exciting music of Mario Nascimbene *(Alexander the Great),* and the experienced directing of Carmine Gallone (*The Last Days of Pompeii* [1926]) combine to produce an exciting adventure film, even if entertainment substitutes for art.

If the idea of *Cabiria* was suggested by contemporary political maneuvers in 1911 and their relation to ancient Italian sovereignty in North Africa, Mussolini's propaganda film *Scipio L'Africano* (1937) was a full-scale cinematic justification for his African campaign. The dialogue, filled with Fascist rhetoric, bogs down the film and undermines its grand design, and today it is rarely screened, even in Italy. But the large sets of the Roman Forum built in Il Duce's colossal new studios at Cinecittà were epic indeed, as were the life-sized galleys shot at the port near Ostia. The battle scenes are memorable, particularly in director Carmine Gallone's *(Carthage in Flames)* use of Hannibal's historic bevy of pachydermic tanks.

And speaking of pachyderms, we could hardly forget the opening scenes of *Hannibal* (1960), shot in the wintry Alps, where the Carthaginian general (Victor Mature) leads sixty elephants and forty thousand men from Gaul to Italy via a rocky, frozen, steep, and slippery path. The broad location shots are impressive: infinitely long lines of fur-bundled soldiers struggle against the blurred, white mountainsides. We see four or five elephants in close-ups, and an irritating corporal keeps hollering "Keep going" to the numbed Carthaginians and Numidian mercenaries. This opening scene, though crude in parts, certainly has scope, and if you think it incredible that elephants could climb a snowy mountain, you're in good company: the ancient Romans thought it incredible, too, until Hannibal caught them with their togas down in the autumn of 218 B.C. and slaughtered more than fifty thousand of them in three battles. Hannibal and Sylvia (Rita Gam) have the requisite inconsequential love affair, but the film also includes such historical details as the flinging into Hannibal's camp of his brother Hasdrubal's head, the clever battle plan of Hannibal at Cannae, and the immortal statement of Hannibal's cavalry commander, Maharbal: "You know how to win victories, Hannibal, but you don't know how to follow them up" (Livy, *Ab Urbe Condita,* 22.51.4). The interior set of Sylvia's house—a *peristylum* of white marble, fluted columns, graceful urns, and neatly arranged shrubbery, drapery, and sculpture—adds to the film's realism. Ultimately, however, *Hannibal* lacks both the vitality needed for a great adventure film and the intellect and grandeur needed for an epic.

From the long period of Roman republican power that begins with the Second Punic War in 218 B.C. and ends with Augustus's establishment of the rich and expansive Roman Empire in 31 B.C., we have appropriately derived some of our longest, most famous, richest, and most expensive movies. If numbers mean anything, the forty-three years between Spartacus's revolt and Cleopatra's asp are documented in sixteen films lasting more than thirty hours and costing about $100 million.

The first of these, gauged by historical chronology, is Stanley Kubrick's $12 million, 184-minute *Spartacus.* Hailed as "the thinking man's epic" before it was released in 1960, it afterward was criticized as a "spotty spectacular" and a "ragged toga saga."[2] But *Spartacus* deserves praise for its human sensitivity, sharp characterizations, visionary photography, and bold political realities. An impressive leading cast of Kirk Douglas (Spartacus), Laurence Olivier (Crassus), Jean Simmons (Varinia), Charles Laughton (Gracchus), and Academy Award–winning Peter Ustinov (Batiatus) is supported by an effective group of heavies led by towering Woody Strode (Draba), sadistic Charles McGraw (Marcellus), and eccentrically Oriental Herbert Loin (Tigranes). They present a wide range of well-developed and contrasting characters, and their individual talents are supplemented by Kubrick's meticulous direction (so meticulous that he even numbered "dead" men on the battlefield; by calling a dead man's number he could tell him to move into a more effective position before the next take). The whole cast deftly pronounces the rich and often witty lines of blacklisted Dalton Trumbo's script (based on the novel of the unofficially blacklisted Howard Fast), and the literate dialogue flows as easily as sweat on a slave's brow.

The action opens in 73 B.C. amid the arid desert mountains of Libya. On top of the chalky red, sulfuric mountainside, a slave is beaten, and then the squeamishly pretentious Batiatus enters on a litter. While choosing slaves to buy for his gladiatorial school, he carries on this uniquely Ustinovish, admirably despicable monologue:

"These? Carrion! The buzzards are late. . . . I don't like Gauls . . . hairy. . . . Be good enough to show me the teeth . . . yes, as the teeth go, so go the bones . . . this fellow is made of chalk." His unctuous cowardliness is most evident in a later response to Crassus, who has just insisted that Batiatus remain for the ensuing battle: "But you don't understand. I'm a civilian. I'm even more of a civilian than most civilians!"

Laughton's Gracchus is heroically unheroic and deliciously cynical. In one of the

23   Victor Mature in a process shot from *Hannibal* (1960) oversees his pachyderms crossing the snowy Alps.

film's finest moments, these two corpulent men, one a money-hungry member of the middle class, the other a land-wealthy aristocrat, sit at a feast with thinly clad *concubinae* on their laps. Gracchus gives this terse and accurate statement on Roman morality and imperialism: "I'm the most virtuous man in Rome. I keep these women out of my respect for Roman morality—that morality which had made Rome strong enough to steal two-thirds of the world from its rightful owners, founded on the sanctity of Roman marriage and the Roman family." Batiatus nods in amused agreement as he licks a thick brown gravy off his pudgy fingers.

Gracchus plays the self-aware, populist patrician, while the conservatives include young Julius Caesar (John Gavin) and Crassus (Laurence Olivier), the wealthiest man in Rome. They portray the Roman aristocracy as a cruel, shrewd, power-hungry, and treacherous mob who by the lucky graces of destiny happen not to be slaves but wealthy, educated, and powerful citizens. Trumbo's neo-Marxist characterization of the Roman aristocracy is epitomized by Crassus's remark to another patrician: "The unfortunate thing about being a patrician is that occasionally you have to act like one." Elsewhere, Crassus, cold and unmoved, watches Spartacus and Draba duel in deadly gladiatorial combat until a victorious but compassionate Draba leaps up from the sandy arena to kill Crassus. Cool

24   Batiatus (Academy Award–winning Peter Ustinov) and Gracchus (Charles Laughton) abound
in corpulent luxury in this scene from *Spartacus* (1960). The gourmet detail on the table and the
bathtub and Venus statue in the background are authentic. And notice the ram's-head table legs:
many pieces of ancient furniture had this sort of zoomorphic ornament.

as ice, Crassus slashes Draba's throat with his dagger without even rising from his chair.
The aristocratic women who accompany Crassus, meanwhile, examine the half-naked
gladiators with rolling eyes and lick their lips as if selecting slabs of ham from the butcher.
"A couple of capricious, overpainted nymphs," Batiatus calls them in private; when Crassus is present, Batiatus characteristically stoops to flattery of "those charming ladies."

  This is the insensitive, powerful Roman establishment against which Spartacus re-
volts. His misery is evident from that first scene with Batiatus in the Libyan mountains; in
frustration he bites through the ankle of a Roman guard and "hamstrings" him. He is
bought by Batiatus and taken to Capua in southern Italy to be trained as a gladiator by
Marcellus. The trainees are humiliated in every way—beaten, painted on, held in silence,
forced to train with imposing wooden machines. Batiatus and Marcellus leer and laugh at
Spartacus from a small cell window as he prepares to make love to Varinia. Prodded by
these humiliations and the unforgettably ghoulish sequence in which the gladiators
silently file past Draba's inverted and naked corpse, a rebellious instinct overpowers Spar-

tacus. After distinctively drowning Marcellus in a large pot of disgusting brown stew, Spartacus leads the trainees out of the school and into the hills of Italy, where they experience freedom at long last.

Spartacus might appear to be an otherwise unremarkable slave, an illiterate Thracian already defeated in the arena, but his ordinary physique and his limited intellectual capacity belie a splendidly rebellious spirit surpassed by few in history. One hundred thousand slaves follow him because he treats them like people instead of like animals. He has a naive confidence that endears him to his army and to us: "A free man dies and he loses the pleasure of life; a slave loses his pain. Death is the only freedom a slave knows. . . . That's why we'll win." The contrast between the simple humanity of the slaves and the shrewd cynicism of the Romans is the real essence of *Spartacus,* a contrast highlighted not only by Trumbo's incisive lines but by Kubrick's intimate shots of slaves huddled with their families, marching through rain and snow, milking their goats, telling folktales, and smiling with the contentment of freedom—even if just for the moment. The most poignant of these tableaux appear under the poetic voice-over by Antoninus (Tony Curtis), illuminating a world two millennia past but a nature identical to our own. Of all the films made about the ancient world, this is the only one that artistically, realistically, and sympathetically shows common people in a time when being common people was much worse than it is today. This emphasis on humanity perhaps suggests the exact opposite of "the thinking man's epic," but then again, the human condition is the very essence of thought.

Film critics and Ph.D.'d scholars bemoan the crucifixion that Spartacus receives in the film, for history tells us that he was hacked to pieces in battle. But while the quibblers reread their Plutarch's *Life of Crassus* to find other historical inauthenticities, the film lover watches with swelling emotion as Crassus, victorious in the final battle, offers amnesty to the defeated slaves if they will point out Spartacus to him; Spartacus rises to say, "I'm Spartacus," but he is instantly anticipated first by Antoninus and then by hundreds and then thousands of rising faithful coconspirators, each proclaiming, "I'm Spartacus! . . . I'm Spartacus!" To omit this scene—or the anguish of the crucified Spartacus, looking down from his cross at his wife Varinia and their infant child—would be a far graver histrionic error than the actual historical error. Those who demand pure history as the main course for their cinematic appetite can be assured that Thracian Spartacus, Gallic Crixus (John Ireland), Batiatus, Crassus, the Cilician pirates, Caesar, the decor, the uniforms, and the Capuan revolt are all historical; the historical meat of *Spartacus* may have some Hollywood sauce, but it is still meat.

And forty years later, the "I'm Spartacus! . . . I'm Spartacus!" scene is the film's best remembered and most imitated. In recent years it has been used in such films as *Life of Brian* (1979), *Punchline* (1988), *That Thing You Do* (1996), *In and Out* (1997), and *The Mask of Zorro* (1998).

In all of filmdom, there is no better exhibition of Roman military genius than the last battle in *Spartacus.* Shot (in Spain) in an effective wide-screen format (Super Techni-

25/26   Spartacus (Kirk Douglas) and Draba (Woody Strode) fight to the death in *Spartacus* (1960). Spartacus fights in the Thracian style, with short sword and shield (discarded), while the Ethiopian fights as a retiarius, with net and trident. The armor of mail for the thrusting arm was common to all styles of gladiatorial fighting in ancient Rome. A second-century A.D. mosaic from Leptis Magna in Libya shows gladiators in full dress. The gladiatorial scene in *Spartacus* lacks greaves and helmets because it is not a full-scale combat, but the short sword, mail arm protector, thick belt, and triangular loincloth were all re-created for the film.

27   The climactic battle from *Spartacus* (1960). The camera is set up behind the undisciplined rebellious slaves to give us their view of the organized Roman legions on the opposite hill. Roman legions of six thousand troops were arranged into centuries of one hundred and maniples of ten, and each unit was trained to move on signal. They usually intimidated and then outmaneuvered their opponents, as they did here. The historical Spartacus was killed in this battle of 71 B.C.

rama 70 with Panavision lenses), the scene places us within the rebellious hordes of slaves as a few thousand Roman soldiers gather on the long, rolling, green hill one-half mile in the gloomy distance. We are desperate and determined, dressed in dull leather and the odd piece of stolen armor; the Roman cohorts and maniples, machinelike and crimson-cloaked, maneuver efficiently into perfectly straight phalanxes of icy death. In ancient days, the sight of the Roman rectangular organization with its quick movements struck fear into the once bold spirits of non-Romans all over the Mediterranean and Europe. For almost a thousand years, this was the most formidable weapon on Earth. Contrary to most ancient battle sequences in films, Roman legions did not usually fight battles in mishmash affairs of independent shields and swords. They were as organized as the Stoic cosmos and as powerful and menacing as a colossal monster.

Despite his professional approach to *Spartacus,* Kubrick was disgruntled that he did not have total control over the making of the film. "I am disappointed in the film," he complained. "It had everything but a good story."[3] True, perhaps, but we should not give too much credence to Kubrick's self-criticism. After all, Vergil's last instructions are said to have been "Burn the *Aeneid*." Of all the ancient epic films of the period, only *Spartacus* was fully, digitally restored and rereleased in the 1990s. The 1991 version ran 198 minutes, 14 minutes longer than the premiere release, and some of this restored footage included the notorious sequence in which Crassus tries to seduce Antoninus with "oysters and snails." (Hollywood rumor has it that the sound track had been damaged, so Anthony Hopkins dubbed in some of Olivier's lines.)

The character Spartacus appeared in five other films set in antiquity. Our sources are vague or confusing regarding Latium's 1909 version of *Spartaco* and the 1914 Cines version starring Anthony Novelli. The former, no longer extant, was no doubt based on Raffaello Giovagnoli's much-adored 1874 novel *Spartaco*. Pasquali's 1913 version, starring Mario Guaita Ausonia and directed by Giovanni Enrico Vidali, is still available (albeit incomplete) for examination because George Kleine distributed it in the United States in 1914. Efficient and muscular acting by Ausonia and a fat, amusing Crassus convey the light style of this early costumer. Essentially a "gladiator film," *Spartaco* predictably culminates with some lion wrestling in Rome's famous Circus Maximus. The Circus sequence is well done, as are the exteriors at Vesuvius (including the famous scene in which Spartacus and his men lower themselves down the cliffs on ropes made of vines). The costumes are typical of the early Italian spectacles: full and dark, covered with excessive embroidery, and heaped up with double or triple mantling, they look operatic. But in this instance there was good reason to sacrifice historical accuracy in exchange for black-and-white chiaroscuro effect.

Sins of Rome (1954) is one of those movies that is so badly written, so terribly overacted, so sloppily dubbed that it is amusing to watch if one is in the right (silly) mood. It does offer some clever night photography and camera angles, and Renzo Rossellini's music can be stirring, but otherwise this Italian version of Spartacus is a slave to its own ineptness.

The Slave (1962), also released as *The Son of Spartacus,* picks up where Kubrick's film left off. A Roman soldier named Randis (Steve Reeves) finds out that he is the son of Spartacus. He proceeds to lead another revolt, seeing how the last one failed, and this time the poor folk win. *The Slave,* produced by the same crew that made *Duel of the Titans,* contains a satisfactory complement of competent action shots and creative photographic angles—for example, a crowd is seen through the diagonal support beams of a crucifix. There is Egyptian scenery, some exciting, urgent music, and the magnificent chest of Steve Reeves. Crassus, Caesar, and Clodia are the historical personages included here. Our historical sources make plausible the sequence set at Crassus's court at Zeugma complete with authentic-looking belly-dancers, but the villainous plutocrat receives an absurd method of execution reminiscent of the colossus sequences in Sergio Leone's *The Colossus of Rhodes:* molten gold is poured onto his face. "Gold was your life, now let it be your death," say the victorious rebels. The historical Crassus was beheaded. Either

28   Crassus (Laurence Olivier), the wealthy patrician, examines seven new slaves in the *peristylum* (courtyard) of one of his villas in *Spartacus* (1960). The Ionic columns, bronze and marble statuary, and mosaic floors all reflect Crassus's vast fortune. The Latin sign hanging from the neck of Antoninus (Tony Curtis) says, "Antoninus, Sicilian, age 21, player and magician, never ran away or went mad."

29   This ancient mosaic, made in Rome, was copied for *Spartacus* (1960); the replica can be seen on the floor of Crassus's peristylum. The original depicts a Nilotic scene complete with reed boats, pygmies, crocodiles, and hippopotamuses, but the *Spartacus* imitation omits the animals.

30   David Bradley's 16mm *Julius Caesar* (1951) was one of the few midcentury independent films to enter the commercial mainstream. This shot taken on the porch of Chicago's Museum of Science and Industry hides Cassius (Grosvenor Glenn) and Brutus (Bradley) in shadows while Caesar (Harold Tasker) and Antony (Charlton Heston) create a bold chiaroscuro effect against the dark columns.

method of execution must have been unpleasant, but cinematically the method chosen for *The Slave,* in which we see the gold poured onto the screen with the subjective camera angle, is more effective.

Julius Caesar has been honored twelve times with a film portrait. The finest of the early versions was Cines's 1914 *Giulio Casare,* starring Amleto Novelli. This semidocumentary film covers the life of the renowned soldier, author, and statesman from his marriage to Cornelia in 83 B.C. to his assassination on the Ides of March, 44 B.C. The most memorable sequences are those in tripartite Gaul, where Caesar's neatly armored legions battle Gauls who wear thick-strapped boots, bulky fur clothing, and spiked helmets. These proto-Frenchmen are led by the proud Vercingetorix. Defeated in battle by the Roman *ballista* (a type of catapult), the subjugated Gauls and Vercingetorix humbly bow and kiss Caesar's foot. Before the battle of Pharsalia between Pompey and Caesar, the forces of the two generals are contrasted: those of Pompey argue among themselves while Caesar's are disciplined and orderly; obviously, Caesar's troops will win the battle. Kubrick effectively used a similar contrast between Roman discipline and non-Roman disorder before the great battle scene in his version of *Spartacus.* The photography in the 1914 *Giulio Casare* displays some signs of precocious artistry. During the battle of Pharsalia, the camera frames a few dead men in the foreground while the infantry battles in the distance. Later, there is a fine shot of a silhouetted Caesar standing by the shore; maintaining a noble stance near a few men with dark Roman standards, he gazes out at Pompey's ships fleeing into the sunset. When Caesar returns triumphantly to Rome, we see a magnificent parade of fifteen lictors, Roman standards and eagles, eight *tubae* (horns), SPQR and legionary signs, infantry with spears, fifty senators, a horse-drawn float with Caesar on top, Egyptian priests with ostrich-feather fans, and cavalry, all in a Forum jammed with people waving in every portal and arcade. This magnificent scene helped to set the precedent for all the luxurious and expensive triumph scenes in films to come, *Quo Vadis?* (1951), *Ben-Hur* (1959), and *Cleopatra* (1963) among them.

The other three versions of *Julius Caesar* have the honor of having been written by the finest poet Hollywood ever used—Shakespeare. David Bradley's 1951 version betrays its amateur origin and its $10,000 budget with inexpensive costuming, bare scenery, and crude 16mm photography. Yet this artistic film made an indelible impression on audiences. It was one of the first amateur films to enjoy commercial success, a success owed in part to the fine acting of a young unknown named Charlton Heston as Antony, and in part to its shadowy settings and oblique camera angles. Shot near Lake Michigan's shores and among the neoclassical buildings on the South Side of Chicago (particularly the Museum of Science and Industry), this unprofessional film is transformed into an unique creative experience via heavy shadows, bold facial close-ups, and camera angles that exploit high columns and long shadows to the utmost. Black and white has rarely been used with such profound effect; Bradley achieved the perfect union of photography and classical architecture. One memorable scene is Cassius's soliloquy (1.2.305 ff.) during which the conspirator walks toward the camera between two sides of a long, eerie colonnade of Soldier's Field, as if emerging from the deep linear perspective of a Dürer etching.

Joseph Mankiewicz chose to film *Julius Caesar* (1953) in black and white as well. The MGM follow-up to the grand success of *Quo Vadis?* (1951) had a budget of only $2 million, but the resulting film remains one of the most faithful Hollywoodian renditions of a Shakespearean drama. Louis Calhern is fine in the title role, and John Gielgud and James Mason complement each other perfectly as the "lean and hungry"–looking Cassius and the stoical Brutus. But Marlon Brando as Antony provided the most rousing performance of the film with the famed funeral oration—once the bane of so many eighth-graders. In a well-paced speech building gradually to its climax, Brando's angry eyes pierce the crowd from under lowered brows; his jaws are clenched so firmly that the tendons bulge on his rounded forehead. Brando was an unconventional choice for the role; in fact, the young Heston had been considered for the part. But *Julius Caesar* established Brando's credibility among many doubting critics who had feared that he

31   Years after the die was cast and long after coming, seeing, and conquering, Julius Caesar
(Louis Calhern) desperately clings to Brutus, who has just stabbed him in *Julius Caesar* (1953).
Brutus (James Mason) evokes Shakespeare's immortal words, "Et tu, Brute? Then fall Caesar."
Caesar's ring is an authentic Roman design.

would act the part in a dirty toga and mumble "Fwens, Womans, countwymun." To the
contrary, he was featured in his (clean) toga on the cover of *Life* in May 1953 and was
nominated for an Academy Award.

As in all three screen versions of Shakespeare's play, the last two acts (which follow Caesar's assassination) of the 1953 version are extensively cut. The battle at Philippi is
brief and unremarkable, but Miklos Rozsa's score supplies it with some intensity.

While Bradley's version was amateurishly significant and Mankiewicz's faithful
and somber, Stuart Burge's 1969 version is the most cinematic of all. The film abounds
in pastel colors and makes full use of exterior shots in Acts 4 and 5. Even the opening of
the film is colorfully vivid: the camera pans the dead warriors on the battlefield of Mundae,
where Caesar has defeated Pompey's sons; vultures perch on overturned chariots; the cam-

32   Marcus Antonius (Charlton Heston) offers to read Caesar's will in the 1969 version of Shakespeare's *Julius Caesar*. The thick, cowled robes belong more to the Renaissance than to antiquity; but Shakespeare's antiquity can be performed in ancient, Renaissance, or modern dress.

era closes in on one skeleton seemingly gasping "Cae-sar, Cae-sar!" and his macabre voice soon blends into the deafening roar of thousands chanting the same syllables, initiating a rousing march that heralds Caesar's triumph in Rome and Act 1. The distinctive sound of a Moog synthesizer is frequently heard in the film, and costumes and decor combine Renaissance and Roman elements.

Charlton Heston, in reprising Antony, approaches the funeral oration magnificently. In a rendering grander than his interpretation in the Bradley version and more explosive than Brando's, Heston uses his unique ability to portray "the Heroic" in such a way that the crowd below him becomes part of his art. Brando's Antony was intense and subtle, but Heston's is overwhelming. He offers Caesar's will to the hungry desires of the Roman rabble as if offering Christians to salivating lions. His energy might have pleased even the Stratfordian himself. The rest of the cast performs admirably, although Jason Robards's philosophically stoic Brutus is a bit too linguistically stoic. John Gielgud is a consummate Caesar, while Richard Johnson plays an impressive Cassius, Richard Chamberlain a handsome young Octavian, and Diana Rigg a noble Portia. Casting horror-film icon Christopher Lee as the mysterious Artemidorus was a stroke of genius.

The scripts of all three sound versions of *Julius Caesar* maintain Shakespeare's original blank verse, although speeches are cut, edited, and rearranged somewhat. This use of centuries-old dialogue makes the films unrealistic and at best quasi-historical while at the same time elevating the language above that of the average prosaic script. The Bradley and MGM versions were essentially conceived of as plays on film. Special effects, especially double exposure, were used only for Calpurnia's dream and for Caesar's ghost. The Burge version, however, aimed at spectacle, as had *Henry V* some twenty years earlier. It is a tribute to the unparalleled dramatic brilliance of Shakespeare that three completely different versions of *Julius Caesar* have been put on film and that each is successful in its own unique way.

While an infamous number of jealous senators were attacking Julius Caesar in front of Pompey's statue on March 15, 44 B.C., two of the dictator's earlier acquaintances dwelled in other parts of the eternal city—his general and his mistress, Antony and Cleopatra. This most famous couple came together in the wake of mighty Caesar's death, and before they parted, they themselves were to be involved in the ultimate struggle for control of the massive Roman domain. Their lives centered around love, politics, and power, and for those glamorous few years they spent together, they became a legend. They have appeared on film at least fifteen times.

After Georges Méliès's 1899 version, the earliest feature film called *Cleopatra* was produced by the Helen Gardner Players in upstate New York in 1912. One of the first "full-length" American feature films, this primitive, one-hour movie seems crude to our modern eyes. A still camera views a cardboard barge "sailing" across a stage before a painted matte of the sea; a hefty Cleopatra (Helen Gardner) steps out and waves, gestures, pleads, embraces, faints, supplicates, and strokes a cumbersomely uniformed Antony. Gardner's acting is emotive and varied, but all else in this early American film lacks conviction. The sea battle of Actium shows Cleopatra and Antony ridiculously rocking back and forth while buckets of water are tossed at them. Nonetheless, this film was handsomely promoted as a "road show": several different groups were sent around the country to show a print of the film, lecture on its subject, and count the profits reaped from the various showings in opera houses, town halls, and theaters.

Cines produced *Marcantonio e Cleopatra* in 1913 starring Antony Novelli (Antony) and Giovanna Terribili Gonzales (Cleopatra). Displaying the same fine photography used in *Giulio Casare* the following year, Cines hit its creative peak with this spectacular and fascinating silent. Superbly acted dual scenes (Cleo and Antony, Antony and Octavia), quick-paced action, and large crowds were essential to all Cines films of the era, but *Marcantonio e Cleopatra* is distinguished by small touches as well: Charmian's bizarre death amid alligators, the Senate's declaration of Antony's treason, a lovely shot of Octavian's troops reflected in a pool of marshy water, the battle at Alexandria. Of special interest is the scene after Antony's death. In all the other film versions of the story, Cleopatra commits suicide immediately after Antony does so. Here, however, Cleopatra lives on for a little while. She stares longingly at her lover's throne; she even fondles his armor, and then she dreams of herself in Octavian's triumphal procession amid festooned balustrades and the people-filled porches of Rome (like the triumph in *Julius Caesar*). Rather than have this nightmare come true, she gives a poisonous asp a taste of her breast.

In 1917 Theda Bara vamped a version of *Cleopatra* directed by J. Gordon Edwards. From the opening shot, which espied the great Sphinx from a distance, then moved in to focus in on its face—that of Theda Bara—the film was purposefully dazzling, not to mention lucratively shocking. Bara wore several dozen costumes, most of them expensive looking—though one eyewitness account recalled that one particular costume "cost $1,000 a yard, and Theda seemed to be wearing only ten cents' worth."[4] Fox reported that the film cost $500,000 to produce and had a cast of several thousand, but Bara's screen presence and the controversy surrounding the film ensured a million-dollar box office. Several still photographs survive, but the film itself is lost; the last two known prints were destroyed by fires in the Fox studios and at the Museum of Modern Art in New York. Thousands of silent films have been lost because of neglect and the chemical deterioration and flammability of their nitrate base, but Theda Bara's *Cleopatra* is on the American Film Institute's list of Top Ten Missing films.

The first sound version of the story was Cecil B. DeMille's *Cleopatra* (1934). A Cleopatra who can speak can become a more complex character than a silent Cleopatra, and the charming, calculating, yet vulnerable chatter of Claudette Colbert's queen is as complex as the layered gauze wrapped around a mummy. She is matched with an unmovably haughty, veni, vidi, vici-ing Caesar (Warren William) and a hot-headed, wildly debauched Antony (Henry Wilcoxon). All the witty dialogue is spouted before delightfully lavish sets and able character actors (C. Aubrey Smith as Enobarbus, Joseph Schildkraut as Herod). The film also revels in the inimitable DeMillish combination of grand magnificence, wickedly cute dialogue, and forcefully climactic action.

The film opens with an exciting chariot run set to rousing music, and Cleopatra is deposited in the desert by her political enemies. Left alone to die with her aide Apollodorus, she hears his sage suggestion to ally herself with Rome. She replies with a regally childish pout, "Why do you talk about Rome and politics? I'm hungry!" Soon after, we see Julius Caesar in Alexandria testing a new siege engine. Enter a merchant with a rolled-up Persian carpet; impatient Caesar is not amused when Cleopatra is unrolled from the tapestry, but wily Colbert, about to win her Oscar for *It Happened One Night,* comments in a low, tempting voice,

> CLEOPATRA: It's strange to see you working. I've always pictured you
> either fighting . . . or loving.

CAESAR: I've had experience with fighting.

CLEOPATRA: But not with loving, I suppose?

CAESAR: Not with pretty little queens.

Such dialogue is only a small part of DeMille's attack on the legendary and historical story. Antony's visit to Cleopatra's elegant, swan-necked barge is DeMille at his most lavish. After Cleopatra wheedles Antony into drinking and having an enjoyable evening in spite of himself, she gives the signal: two flowing curtains are crisscrossed before our eyes, rose petals fall gently from the ceiling, and long festoons are raised; the camera pulls back to take in the lightly clad dancers, the graceful attendants, and the large Nubian slaves; the compelling music builds and builds while stylized animal-headed oars move in time to the crash of a huge drum; a muscular conductor *(hortator)* pounds out a throbbing beat in his angular attack on the drum as the music climaxes and the scene dissolves. The barge scene is without parallel in grandeur, grace, and romantic power, and its historical source is Plutarch's *Life of Antony*.

DeMille's court scenes entertain us with humorous cynicism; when Antony sees a slave's body carried out he hears that "the queen is testing poisons." And although the naval battle of Actium and land battle of Alexandria consume less than two minutes, these carefully edited sequences make an immediate and effective impact. With footage borrowed from *The Ten Commandments* (1923), a smoke-filled screen of Stygian gloom moves in rapid succession from Nubian to Roman tubae, marching spearmen and standards, deafening chariots, a gigantic battering ram, falling and grimacing faces, a huge rolling echinodermatous spike, catapults of fire, underwater shots of the dead, all ending in a large fireball shot right at the camera.

Twelve years later Gabriel Pascal followed up his screen versions of George Bernard Shaw's *Pygmalion* and *Major Barbara* with another Shavian masterpiece, *Caesar and Cleopatra* (1946). Spending just under $3 million to create lavish sets and splendid costumes, Pascal also captured the superficially silly yet intellectually challenging contexts that characterize most of Shaw's work. Shaw himself wrote the dialogue for the film. His genius combined well with the elegant continental music of Georges Auric and the fascinating sets by Oliver Messel and John Bryan. Claude Rains plays Caesar, the father figure, who tries to teach the young, giggly Cleopatra (Vivien Leigh) how to be a queen. Their relationship is a playful one amid the soft bluish cyclorama tint of the Egyptian sky and before a large, imposing sphinx. In her childlike simplicity, Cleopatra rues that "Julius Caesar's father was a tiger, his mother was a burning mountain, and his nose is like an elephant's trunk." She has heard that Caesar will "gobble me up in one bite." But the charming and kind "old" Caesar encourages her to act regally. Cleopatra asserts her newfound royalty by beating a helpless slave; "I'm a real queen, ooo!" The other two main characters are Stewart Granger as the Oriental swashbuckler from Sicily and Flora Robson as Cleopatra's humorless nurse, Ftatateeta, whose name Caesar repeatedly mispronounces, calling her "Teeta Tota," "Tora Teeta," and eventually an exas-

33/36   Claudette Colbert as Cleopatra in DeMille's 1934 *Cleopatra*. Her low, suggestive voice and her adaptability to comedy and drama made her perfect for the part. Her costume, hardly the Hollywoodian fantasy that might be expected, incorporates two bird-shaped earrings used as bracelets in the film, the crown of Isis-Hathor, and a vulture collar. The earrings and collar are from the renowned treasure of Tutankhamen. The Isis-Hathor crown has been modified for the film; the horns (Hathor was originally a cow) and the disk (symbolizing the goddess of the sky) have been shrunk, and most of the snake heads have been omitted. The feather-textured gilded cap and the frontal cobra head remain intact.

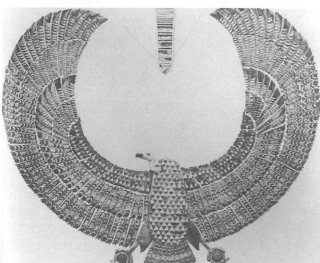

37/38   Britannicus (Cecil Parker), Caesar (Claude Rains), and Cleopatra (Vivien Leigh) talk politics and love in George Bernard Shaw's *Caesar and Cleopatra* (1945). The mixture of humor and epic sweep in this British film is unique; where else would Cleopatra say, "Oooo! the Romans will gobble me up in one bite"? Cleo's wig and the mosaic floor are authentic, and a helmet carved about A.D. 100 on the head of no less a warrior than the god Mars, shows the type used for Caesar's helmet. Claude Rains's version adds cheek pieces to the authentic visor, crest, sculpted reliefs, and frontal griffin. This helmet is the typical Italian type— very different from the Corinthian used in Greece some four centuries earlier (and in *The 300 Spartans*).

perated "Tota."

Some epic sweep appears in the battle at the film's end, but for the most part *Caesar and Cleopatra* concentrates on its unique synthesis of intellectual wit and mundane play. When Cleopatra and her effeminate teenage brother/husband, Ptolemy, contend for the right to the throne of Egypt, Cleopatra (whose sweet smile, batting eyelashes, and wily plans suggest Miss Scarlett vying for an Egyptian Tara and a Roman Rhett) runs into the room and ignobly pulls her brother from the throne onto the floor. After some silly verbal squabbling, Roman troops enter under Rufio's generalship. Suddenly the young Egyptian king and queen are "Roman guests." Ptolemy sticks his tongue out at his "mean" sister, while his regent, Pothinus, demands of Caesar, "Where is your right to do this?" Caesar replies in a superior tone, "In Rufio's scabbard, for the moment."

The next two versions of Cleopatra were cheap and disappointing. Columbia produced *Serpent of the Nile* (1953), which drastically changes the story of the two lovers so that Cleopatra (Rhonda Fleming) loves not Antony (Raymond Burr) but his best friend. In 1959 Vittorio Cottavafi directed *Legions of the Nile,* also entitled *Legions of Cleopatra,* a cinematic comic book containing brutal ruffians, sleazy or sassy girls, and overbold heroes, each cut from the thinnest cardboard. Thanks to some spirited action scenes and some amusing romantic play, the film becomes almost tolerable.

And then came the quintessential version of *Cleopatra.* What is there to write about a film that caused an international scandal and cost the studio president, the film's producer, two directors, and a clutch of scriptwriters their jobs? What can be justified about a film that cost more than $30 million to put on the screen and opened in six hundred theaters? What can be described about a movie that has over ninety-six hours of film in the cans (120 miles!) yet is shown in slightly more than three hours? And how many words can be used to analyze a film so hyped, talked about, and scandalous before its release that its advertisements did not even need to include the title?

Plenty. Filmmakers and critics alike still shudder when they think of one of the most expensive (allowing for inflation), longest, most publicized, and most controversial pictures ever made. Opinions range widely, but in one way or another, for better or for worse, the 1963 version of *Cleopatra* is undeniably one of the most spectacular movies that will ever be made.

It all started with Theda Bara in 1917. Fox had produced her successful version of *Cleopatra,* and throughout the resurgence of ancient films in the 1950s Fox had been considering a remake. But earthquakes start as small tremors, so at first Fox president Spiros Skouras and producer William Wanger—whose credits include such varied films as *Stagecoach* (1939), *Joan of Arc* (1948), and *Invasion of the Body Snatchers* (1956)—planned a modestly budgeted, $2 million film, with Joan Collins playing the title role. Soon Audrey Hepburn and Susan Hayward were being considered, but Elizabeth Taylor, fresh from her contract's termination at MGM, agreed to do the part for a few hundred thousand dollars. Skouras and Wanger knew that the big name in the title role would make the picture more successful, and Liz had just won her Oscar for *Butterfield 8*. Rouben Mamoulian was hired as director, and location shooting was planned for Egypt and Italy, then Turkey, then London —yes, definitely London. This was 1959.

By September 30, 1960, eight and one-half acres of ancient Alexandria had been built at Pinewood Studios outside of London. The first day of shooting was buried in fog, and the fog lasted all week. Liz contracted a fever. The delays continued. By November 1 the $2 million was spent. The cold and damp weather remained. Whenever someone spoke, frosty vapors accompanied the dialogue. This was Egypt? In mid-November, Liz's illness continued, so production was closed down until January 3. Soon a new scriptwriter, Nunnally Johnson, was hired, but Mamoulian quit on January 18. So far, the film had cost $7 million, taken sixteen months, and yielded twelve minutes of footage. Lloyds of London covered part of the losses, so Skouras splurged on a new director, Joseph L. Mankiewicz (*Julius Caesar* [1953]).

Within a week Elizabeth Taylor was in the hospital, near death with pneumonia and anemia; she underwent a life-saving tracheotomy. The director decided to shoot the rest of the picture in Hollywood—no, Rome. Meanwhile, Peter Finch had been replaced as Caesar by Rex Harrison, Olivier having declined. Richard Burton then left his Broadway role in *Camelot* to replace Stephen Boyd as Antony. Once Liz was healthy, they could shoot this picture.

By September 1961, only one of a planned forty-seven interior sets was ready; meanwhile, the costumes had been ripped. In November a sudden windstorm arose and shut down production for the day; cost: $75,000. That winter began "Le Scandale." Reportedly, Richard Burton's first words to Taylor were, "Has anybody ever told you that you're a very pretty girl?" Corny, but it worked. By the spring Liz and Richard were oppressed by *paparazzi* and Italian gossip hounds. Photographers came to the door of their $3,000-per-month house dressed as carpenters, servants, and priests.

Delays continued to abound. In April a cat and her kittens were heard meowing underneath *Cleopatra's* bedroom set. Shooting was interrupted while the set was dismantled, the cats were freed, and the set was reassembled; cost: $17,000. Production costs, including overtime for the stars, were now $500,000 per week. By March 2, 1963, the last day of shooting, Wanger had been fired, Skouras had been ousted, and Daryl Zanuck had taken over Fox. Zanuck sent Mankiewicz to the employment bureau with this announcement: "In exchange for top compensation and a considerable expense account, Mr. Joseph Mankiewicz had for two years spent his time, talent, and $35,000,000 of Twentieth-Century Fox's shareholders' money to direct and complete the first cut of the film *Cleopatra*. He has earned a well-deserved rest."[5]

Finally ready for release, the film was advertised in New York on the world's largest billboard. Newspaper ads showed a reclining Cleopatra with Antony standing above her. There was no title in the ad; the whole universe had been hearing about the film and its personalities for three years, so who needed a title?

On June 12, 1963, *Cleopatra* opened at the Rivoli Theatre at $100 a ticket amid a Manhattan street crowd of ten thousand. Postcards with "Cleopatra-scented" perfume were sold in the lobby. Before the premiere, *Cleopatra* was already the eighth-biggest box-office hit of all time, with $15 million paid in advance rental. On opening night the film was four hours, twenty-four minutes long. Within two weeks it was mysteriously four hours, three minutes. In a few months, it was being shown in just over three hours. *Newsweek* called the film "The Amputee."[6]

What happened? Skouras admitted that the film should have cost half as much as it eventually did (even more than the $35 million Zanuck had cited, including printing and distribution costs). Mankiewicz bemoaned that "this was a chance to flirt with disaster."[7] Taylor reluctantly viewed a print of the finished (and cut) movie, described it as "vulgar," and promptly ran to the powder room to throw up.[8] She called Zanuck and offered to redub some of her weaker voice parts. He would not spend a cent more on the monstrous enterprise.

Cleopatra suffered from poor planning and ill fortune. Gossip and adverse publicity blamed Liz's romance, overeating, and high living for the delay and expense of the film. This was cruel and untrue. Her illness was not her fault, and Mankiewicz contracted strep throat, Roddy McDowall (Octavian) had a skin ailment, Harrison suffered food poisoning, and Burton missed shooting one day thanks to an Antony-esque drinking bout the night before. He nobly offered to pay for the lost day. Any self-respecting Roman general would have done the same.

Bad weather in London and Rome, excessive prices charged by the Italian vendors, and other delays and costs added daily figures onto the growing budget. At one point, elephants were hired for the famous scene in which Cleopatra enters Rome in a magnificent show. The elephants ran loose and disrupted the shooting. Mankiewicz ordered the beasts off the set and called them "wild." Fox was then sued for $100,000 for slandering the elephants. To build the Alexandria exteriors, a beach at Anzio was rented, for $150,000. By the end of shooting, the weary production manager, who had become a laughingstock, turned frugal at the wrong time in the wrong way. He told the cast, "Save on the paper cups." Miss Taylor's hairdresser was earning $800 per week. Her chauffeur was similarly well paid. Rex Harrison complained that his chauffeur was making less: "Why the hell should Elizabeth Taylor's chauffeur get more than mine just because she has a bigger chest!"[9]

Another reason for the great expense was the panic caused by Twentieth-Century Fox management. "Hurry up," they insisted. Mankiewicz was forced to rewrite the script over the weekend and to shoot the film in historical sequence in the following week. Rarely is a film shot sequentially, and the inefficiencies of that method are magnified in an expensive extravaganza. Idle actors cost as much as busy ones, and 250 days of shooting add up; Taylor was receiving $50,000 per week, Harrison $10,000. Then one day, 1,500 spears were "lost" somehow. On another occasion Italian vendors

39   One of the many famous moments in Cleopatra's life: Julius Caesar (Rex Harrison) unrolls a carpet that conceals Cleopatra inside. This episode in *Cleopatra* (1963) derives from Plutarch's *Life of Julius Caesar* (49). Unlike many authentic historical events, this one works well on film.

delivered an $80,000 bottled-water bill to Fox. Liz calculated that the volume specified in the bill represented two and one-half gallons of water per person per day. Someone was outfoxing Fox.

But these are the extraordinary expenses that were invisible in the film itself. The luxury that pervades the screen reveals the vast expenditures for sets and costumes. Cleopatra's costumes and wigs (thirty) and jewelry (125 pieces) cost more than $130,000. Her twenty-four-carat gold-thread dress for the entry into Rome cost $6,500. A huge cast of extras for the battles of Pharsalia, Actium, Philippi, and Alexandria (including the historically authentic "turtle") needed twenty-six thousand costumes; that cost half a million. The extraordinarily beautiful barge that carried Cleopatra to meet Antony at Tarsus cost $250,000, and the entry into Rome another half million. Mankiewicz summarized the insanity best: "This picture was conceived in a state of emergency, shot in confusion, and wound up in blind panic."[10]

The film—ah yes, the film. *Cleopatra* has three serious faults that no one tries to deny: length, editing, and the thinness of Elizabeth Taylor's voice. Taylor herself bemoaned her occasionally shrill voice, and Mankiewicz knew that audiences would think four hours was too long; he originally wanted two films of two hours and twenty minutes each, entitled *Caesar and Cleopatra* and *Antony and Cleopatra*. Fox declined Liz's offer to redub and rejected Mankiewicz's two-for-one plan. And even critics who declared that the film "bumps from scene to ponderous scene on the square wheels of exposition" realized that this rough-flowing lethargy was largely a result of the extensive and detrimental cutting.[11] In fact, even before the cutting the film underwent after its initial release, the portrayal of Antony was demolished by the first bit of surgery. Mankiewicz later stated, "The person who suffered most in the cutting of the film was Dick Burton. He gave a brilliant performance and a lot of his most marvelous scenes were never shown."[12] In the released version, Burton plays a dissolute, weak, passionately amorous pawn who expectedly loses a battle to the severe Octavian and his most able admiral, Agrippa. What we do not see is that Antony was at one time Caesar's most trusted general, a fully competent strategist who had Octavian equally matched until Octavian's cheap, slanderous propaganda campaign turned all of Rome against him and his "Nilotic serpent." The Antony of history and the Antony of the unused portions of the film began as the competent military and political successor to the mighty Caesar; his fall could only be a tragic one. The Antony of the released *Cleopatra* cannot be the tragic hero that Antony really was; a tragic hero has to be an epic personage who is felled from the zenith of his pride by the cruel and inexplicable force of destiny. This cinematic Antony starts at the bottom and falls sideways.

Another example of the poor cutting is the scene in which Caesar is assassinated. Suddenly Cleopatra is seen gazing into an oracular fire, and through the flames she sees the assassination pantomimed to the tense succession of buzzing viola chords. Cut from the film was a scene detailing Cleopatra's dependence on fire-worship and oracles. The oracular scene as it stands is thoroughly bewildering. Then there is the scene in which Octavian reads Antony's "will" to the Senate. Cut from the film is the scene that explains how the shrewd Octavian obtained this fictitious document.

But enough of flaws. Rex Harrison well deserved his best actor award from the National Board of Review; he also earned nominations from the Academy and the New York Film Critics. He displays a smiling, Caesarian confidence in his worldly knowledge, practical wisdom, and aristocratic air, yet he allows himself to have a human love for his son and for the young Cleopatra. Like Warren William's Caesar in DeMille's version, Harrison's Caesar is not impressed with the lovely young queen at first. "Have you broken out of your nursery, young lady, to annoy us adults? . . . You are what I say you are, and nothing more." His sense of humor is splendidly controlled. When he sees Apollodorus carry in the famous Oriental carpet with the queen concealed inside, he knowledgeably quips, "This rug may require some cutting." When planning his battle at Alexandria, he omits some details from his explanation to Agrippa. When Agrippa asks what will happen at dawn, Caesar condescendingly answers, "I thought you knew. The sun comes up."

Cleopatra holds her own when quarreling with Caesar. Cleopatra, "Kindred of Horus and Ra, beloved of the Moon and Sun, Daughter to Isis, and of Upper and Lower

Egypt, Queen," reminds the haughty Caesar, "You Roman generals take on divinity so quickly—a few victories, a few massacres. Remember, yesterday Pompey was a god!" Earlier, Caesar had been offered Pompey's head in a jar.

The love scenes between Antony and Cleopatra do drag a bit, but the script is at least literate, if not particularly fluid. Taylor is convincingly matronly when she tells Caesar, "I am the Nile; I will bear many sons," and appropriately noble at Cleopatra's suicide. Her passionate side is revealed when she hears that Antony has left her and married Octavia, Octavian's sister. She grabs a sword and hacks apart his clothes and their bed with the greatest of furor. Like Burton in *Alexander the Great,* Taylor has a particularly difficult part to play. She must be a beautiful queen, an ambitious politician, a seductive woman, a determined mother, and a desperate snake. It is perhaps too much to ask of an actor that he or she hit every note of one of the most complicated characters in history. Legendary historical figures are legendary precisely because they are hard to pin down. That a "mere actor" be expected to re-create perfectly such a prodigy is asking the impossible.

Burton is a sprightly Antony. He characteristically fires off passionate bursts in an intense flurry, and his humor drips with sarcasm as he is about to stab himself with his sword, "I always envied Rufio his long arms." There can be no doubt, however, that the unkindest cut was administered by the editor at Twentieth-Century Fox; we may never know exactly how Burton played this role.

The supporting cast adds to the color and complication of the plot. Martin Landau (Rufio) plays Antony's faithful aide, and Gregoire Aslan (Pothinus) and Herbert Berghof (Theodorus) are perfect as the effeminate eunuch regents of young Ptolemy ("a high position ta'en not without, shall we say, certain sacrifice," remarks Caesar). Roddy McDowall as Octavian embodies, in a few brief scenes, one of the shrewdest politicians in the history of mankind. Key to this characterization is Octavian's decisive victory over Antony's fleet at the battle of Actium. Agrippa plans, directs, and fights the battle while Octavian lies ill belowdeck. Agrippa runs in to tell the man who would soon become Emperor Augustus that he has won a tremendous victory: Octavian weakly raises himself on his sickly arms, looks briefly at the spirited, bearded admiral, and collapses in nauseated apathy. This is right from the pages of history (though Octavian's sickness actually came at Philippi); the scene characterizes Octavian exquisitely without his speaking a line. The scene in which Octavian kills Sosigenes, on the other hand, is historically absurd, and it turns him into a savage murderer rather than an unscrupulous politician.

The great hullabaloo about Elizabeth Taylor's elegant costumes, wigs, and splendid jewelry was certainly not exaggerated; her wardrobe set fashion trends for months, and her makeup helped make eyeshadow an essential part of the sixties look. The costly sets of Alexandria's harbor, the queen's palace, and Rome were likewise worth the price. But two scenes, in terms of lavishness and cinematic spectacle, are unsurpassed: the barge and the entry into Rome.

The arrival of Cleopatra's barge at Tarsus (in Turkey) was calculated to make a gi-

41 The real Arch of Constantine copied for *Cleopatra*. Fox's arch left out some of the sculptural detail and the central inscription—not to mention portraying an arch that would not be built for three and a half centuries. But it is impression and atmosphere that the film world demands, not historical precision.

40 The most spectacular pageant sequence ever filmed, the entry of Cleopatra into Rome in Fox's 1963 *Cleopatra*. The Roman senators with their purple-striped *praetextae* (togas) sit in the foreground surrounded by marble herms. Caesar sits enthroned in their midst with Antony on his right. The Roman populace fills arcade, rooftop, and piazza as three hundred slaves pull Cleopatra's float through the arch. Notice the winged girls with the pyramids below the outer two arches of the huge triumphal arch. This entry into Rome alone cost one-half million dollars.

gantic impression on Antony. DeMille's splendid interior of the barge had to be equaled, if not bettered. DeMille's exterior shots had been of a mechanical model, but Mankiewicz decided to build a full-scale, working barge. Then he planned to shoot the scene in the Bay of Naples. One quarter of a million dollars later, the 250-foot barge with its 100-foot masts was ready for filming. Two linen sails rise from a gracefully curved hull. An exotic palm tree stands in its middle. Cleopatra waits underneath light curtains at the back of the barge, resembling Plutarch's description in the *Life of Antony* (26), "dressed as a painted Venus." Thirty-five handmaidens throw coins over the steep sides of the boat as young men swim alongside to retrieve the gold, and forty more lovely Egyptian maidens strew flowers into the bay. Antony must have been impressed if the real thing was as elegant and luxurious as this. In fact, Twentieth-Century Fox was so pleased with the appearance of the barge that studio executives considered displaying the vessel at the New York World's Fair.

The entry of Cleopatra into Rome might be the most spectacular pageant sequence ever filmed. Even in its truncated present form, the procession includes seven minutes of constant entertainment, dance, color, crowds, excitement, and grandeur. White horses bearing tubae-players in two rows enter a large square in Rome through a well-reconstructed (if anachronistic) Arch of Constantine. Rows of racing chariots crisscross, followed by slaves tossing red ribbons through the electric air. Fifty archers shoot colored streamers into the sky, and a yellow–caped and feathered African dance troop performs an undulating act intriguingly blurred by thick yellow smoke. Oxen, zebra, and the slandered elephants follow, and fifteen-foot sistra are carried and shaken. Choreographer Hermes Pan *(Top Hat, Silk Stockings)* deserves much of the credit for all the varied movement in the scene. Finally men enter carrying long white ostrich-feather fans, accompanied by winged and gilded women with a pyramid float that releases fluttering white doves. The crowd of senators, wives, and Roman rabble step back in awe-inspired unison. Alex North's rhythmic and penetrating score leads in three hundred dark slaves in six rows. They slowly sway from side to side as they pull the two-ton float behind them.

The camera views the crowded spectacle from all angles as the porphyry float enters the square. At the top of this huge *nemes*-headed pharaoh sit the incarnations of Isis and Horus—golden-robed Cleopatra and the young son of Julius Caesar, Caesarion. The crowd runs to her and cheers loudly. Caesar, the man of reality and vision combined, ignores the entire procession except for what concerns him most. "See how unafraid he is!" he says of his son. Antony is not listening; he has his eyes on a different Egyptian. The Senate of Rome rises, and a red carpet is rolled out. Stairs are miraculously unfolded from the float, and nine Nubians bear Cleopatra's litter. Cleopatra winks at Caesar; she and he know that Rome has been conquered.

When the scene was being filmed, 4,500 Italian extras filled the set. There had been a bomb scare the night before, and Taylor feared that the crowd would react angrily to the accounts of her affair with Burton. As the mob closed in on her float at the climax of the scene, they ignored their prescribed line of "Cleopatra, Cleopatra," and replaced it with a heart-warming "Leez, Leez." Amazingly, Leez, er, Liz, had survived some of the most vicious publicity any movie star had ever faced.

The battle at Actium, the massive sea engagement of September 2, 31 B.C., was unequaled in ancient history. Octavian, Antony, and Cleopatra each sent in a few hundred ships to decide who would rule Rome, but Cleopatra suddenly and inexplicably pulled out of the battle, and Antony suffered an ignominious defeat. The battle sequence in *Cleopatra* is frighteningly realistic. Cleopatra's flagship carries on its deck a memorable relief map on which we can follow the maneuvers of the conflict. Antony's men clash their spears against their shields in a deafening roar; urgent signals are flashed with mirrors in the sunlight; and heavy war ships are equipped with massive ramming spikes. Ballistas send roaring, smoking firebombs of pitch into the quickly obscured sky. Trails of smoke and thunder lead to blazing ships. Helpless men swim for their lives amid the flotsam and fiery waters. Superior to the slightly smaller-scaled naval battles in *The Colossus of Rhodes* and *Ben-Hur* (1925), and to the exciting model work in the naval battle of *Ben-Hur* (1959), *Cleopatra's* Actium brings the bitter struggle between Octavian and Antony to an appropriately horrifying conclusion.

The aftermath of *Cleopatra* was a bitter one. Elizabeth Taylor described its shooting as "a disease" and observed, "Surely that film must be the most bizarre piece of entertainment ever to be perpetrated."[13] Twentieth-Century Fox sued her and Burton for the adverse publicity they had stirred up, though the actors reportedly lost much of their money to taxes anyway. Hurt by severe editing, the film was savaged by most leading critics, and it suffered at the box office. But it did win four Academy Awards and was nominated for five others, and by the time ABC signed to show the film twice on prime-time television, Fox eventually broke even. (In any case, $160 million in profits from *The Sound of Music* more than made up for *Cleopatra's* temporary losses.)

In the final analysis, *Cleopatra* is a mighty and a mighty choppy spectacle, with serious flaws and magnificent moments. The first half is generally superior to the second, and Fox might have profited from spending a little more money still to put a corrective finish onto the second half. The leading characters are well-developed people for the most part. A living, breathing Caesar, Antony, Octavian, and Cleopatra seem to be inextricably involved in a desperate era of politics, war, and destiny; we could say much the same about the principals in the making of the movie.

Oddly, even though the financial scare of *Cleopatra* almost single-handedly killed a genre of film that had been thriving for fourteen years, two of the next major "ancient" artistic projects were again about the life and loves of Cleopatra. The first was Samuel Barber's opera *Antony and Cleopatra,* composed for the inauguration of the new New York Metropolitan Opera House and produced by Franco Zeffirelli in 1966. Although the work was musically and visually impressive, the critics, tired of the Cleopatra-Antony romance

43   The huge float on which Cleopatra enters Rome is shaped like a pharaoh wearing a *nemes,* the traditional squared headcloth. DeMille used this huge pharaonic background in his 1923 version of *The Ten Commandments,* and no doubt Fox's float originated in this particular bit of DeMillean grandeur.

42   Elizabeth Taylor as Cleopatra with her son Caesarion (Loris Loddi). Her headpiece consists of the *uraeus*—the band of snake heads symbolizing royalty—and the disk and tall horns with feathered filling. Her dress was made of actual gold thread at a cost of $6,500. Notice the authentic cobra design beneath her, and the pharaonic float behind her. The film follows ancient Egyptian tradition in presenting Cleopatra and her son (by Caesar) as the gods Isis and Horus incarnate.

44   This bracelet of gold and glass paste from the first century B.C. shows the winged goddess Isis. Cleopatra entered Rome as Isis incarnate, hence her dress of gold wings. The wings symbolize Isis's protection of the dead.

45   Pharaoh Tutankhamen's throne from c. 1340 B.C. The woman's crown is copied in *Cleopatra* (1963). This splendid piece of furniture is wood covered with gold leaf, and inlaid with faience, glass, and stone.

46   An ancient Egyptian canopic shrine with a cobra design in its upper half duplicated in the great float for Cleopatra's entry.

and its association with extravagance, panned the otherwise gala evening.

The second was Charlton Heston's 1973 film version of Shakespeare's *Antony and Cleopatra*. Heston featured himself as Antony, and his Cleopatra was the young South African Hildegarde Neil, who commands her Shakespeare but lacks the Nilotic allure commonly associated with the role. Like its predecessors, Heston's version is elaborate, making use of several exterior sets to enliven the bard's drama. At one point two gladiators battle each other during a critical meeting between Antony and Octavian, and elsewhere Cleopatra and her handmaidens lie leisurely about a river bier.

The most recent attempt at filming the tale is the 1999 television miniseries *Cleopatra,* which features the ingenue Leonor Varela in the title role, Timothy Dalton as Caesar, and Billy Zane as Antony. Compared with this romanticized nonsense, the Fox version of 1963 looks like a history course at Harvard. Caesar rises like Shamu from the rose-petal-strewn waters of Cleopatra's pool to shout about the glory of being named king for life. And when all goes badly for Antony at the battle of Actium, Cleopatra dons a helmet and sword and fights her own battle, eliminating one particularly ominous Roman by slashing him in the groin. Theda Bara never vamped any Roman so blatantly!

Octavian's victory over Antony and Cleopatra at Actium ended once and for all the Roman Republic and gave birth to the Roman Empire. The Senate "voluntarily" confirmed the appointment of the successors of Augustus, and the next four Julio-Claudian emperors—Tiberius, Caligula, Claudius, and Nero—have all found their way into film history. From what clues we have, *I, Claudius* (1937) might have become one of the finest films Joseph von Sternberg ever directed, but it was never completed. Based on Robert Graves's best-selling novel, the film contrasted the mysterious brilliance of Claudius (Charles Laughton) with the lasciviousness of his bride Messalina (Merle Oberon) and the wickedness of his predecessor Caligula (Emlyn Williams). Oberon barely appeared at all in the six weeks of shooting before her head went crashing through the windshield of her wildly chauffeured car; production of the film was immediately canceled. But surviving rushes that display Claudius's risible limp and stuttering tongue ("Nature never quite finished me!") and those that show him announcing to the shocked Senate that he will be their next emperor hint at how great this movie could have been. BBC brought the remarkable rushes out of obscurity in 1965 and featured them in a television program called *The Epic That Never Was.*

I, Claudius was produced by Alexander Korda, who was trying at the time to "out-Hollywood Hollywood" with his historical spectaculars *(Catherine the Great, The Private Life of Henry VIII)*. Magnificent sets—including a full-scale replica of Augustus's Ara Pacis—were nearly dwarfed by the titanic performances of the cast. Augustus's eighty-year-old widow, Livia (Flora Robson), shakes and quivers with every feeble movement, yet she accurately reviles the young, beastly Caligula, calling him the "vilest, most despicable reptile the gods ever created. He's unscrupulous, dishonest—" "Vain, spiteful, lecherous, and cruel," interrupts the amused Caligula. "You flatter me."

Claudius, the buffoon with natural deficiencies who makes buffoons of all who underestimate him, lives on his pig farm writing books. His nephew Caligula calls him to Rome. When the self-glorifying Caligula "discovers" that he is becoming a god, he says to the groveling Claudius, "I am being reborn; it is painful to be one's mother. Well, you idiot, can't you see any change in me?" Claudius stammers: "I was blind n-not to see it at first. I w-w-was overc-c-come. I've b-b-been used to p-pigs." Von Sternberg also preserved Graves's accurate portrayal of the fawning and decadent Roman Senate under the Empire—the same Senate that might have accepted Caligula's horse to its membership. When one senator mocks Claudius's stutter, the emperor's uncle gently remarks, "I did not know you could also stutter; I thought your talents were confined to neighing like a horse."

Claudius's wife, Messalina, is one of the most notorious aristocratic sluts in history, and so she was a cinematic natural, featured in films in 1910, 1922, 1953, and 1960. Enrico Guazzoni's 1922 *Messalina* had stupendous settings and an artistically spectacular atmosphere, while Carmine Gallone's *The Affairs of Messalina* (1953), a low-budget, dull, subpar romance, would have perhaps fared better as one of his silent films. Two years later, however, Messalina was played with great verve by Susan Hayward in *Demetrius and the Gladiators*.

The two imperial predecessors of Claudius and his successor have appeared in important roles in a number of movies dealing with Christ and early Christianity. Tiberius was emperor when "that carpenter was crucified in the troublesome province of Judea" (as cinematic Roman generals are wont to say). He appears in *Ben-Hur* (George Relph) and *The Robe* (Ernest Thesiger). His successor, Caligula, plays a major role in *The Robe* (Jay Robinson) and its sequel *Demetrius and the Gladiators*. These films will be discussed in Chapter 5, which focuses on films of the New Testament. Bob Guccione's *Caligula* (1980) gave Malcolm McDowell a starring role as the depraved emperor. The film was the *Penthouse* magazine publisher's bold attempt at a mainstream pornographic release. He attached Gore Vidal's name to the project, attracted plenty of press attention, and hoped that perhaps the world's multiplexes were ready for a sex film. But the film offered much more X-rated sexual activity than history, and it spawned no mainstream heirs. It did pave the way, however, for a number of hard-core videos with titles like *Venus of the Nile* (1995), *Cleopatra's Bondage Revenge* (1985), *Rise of the Roman Empress* (1987), and *Rise of the Roman Empress II* (1990). Even HBO focused on a pornographic film with a classical title ("Eat-a-Puss Rex") in a 1995 episode of *Dream On* entitled "Am I Blue?"

Claudius's successor was the great maestro Nero (whose mother, Agrippina, allegedly poisoned Claudius with a plate of toxic mushrooms to "make room" for her son). His central role in the three versions of *Quo Vadis?* and *The Sign of the Cross* belongs to the discussion of films about early Christianity. Most of these Julio-Claudians have roles in the interminable made-for-television miniseries *A.D.,* which features Anthony Andrews as Nero, Ava Gardner as Agrippina, James Mason as Tiberius, and John McEnery as Caligula.

47   Gladiators exercise in Carmine Gallone's *The Last Days of Pompeii* (1926). Gallone reconstructed many buildings found during the excavations at Pompeii. The wall paintings and foreground statuary in this shot of the gymnasium are based on ancient Pompeian originals.

Nero himself rated ten dramatic films, not to mention two comedies. The 1922 *Nero,* directed by J. Gordon Edwards (Theda Bara's *Cleopatra*), had impressive natural scenery, with massive crowds, chariots, and all the other elements that go into making a visual spectacle about the ancient world. Nero's most famous (if not factual) crime—his burning of Rome—is mightily reenacted, but flat acting and some uneven photography mar the film. Nero's infamous and sexy wife, Poppaea, whose name to this day in modern Italian means "chesty," is perhaps more evil that either history or drama demands. An earlier silent version by Ambrosio in 1909 has a smaller scope and is less historical: Nero suffers from a guilty conscience for executing the Christians! But the painted mattes are excellent pieces of trompe-l'oeil, and Nero's double-exposed "flights of fancy" are particularly entertaining. Poppaea herself was highlighted in Latium Film's *Poppea ed Ottavia* (1911), *Nero's Mistress* (1956), *Le Calde Notti di Poppea* (*The Hot Nights of Poppaea,* 1969), an Italian B-film by Primo Zeglio called *Nerone e Messalina* (1949), and Bruno Mattei's exploitation film *Nerone e Poppea* (1981), while Agrippina had her brief cinematic stardom in Guazzoni's *Agrippina* (1910).

Historical novels have supplied the story line for many of the more popular movies about ancient times. *Spartacus, Barabbas, The Robe, Cleopatra, Ben-Hur,* and *Quo*

48 The two prime ingredients in most of the early Italian spectacles about the ancient world—the arena and natural disaster. This is the amphitheater of Pompeii, with Mount Vesuvius in the background. Early Italian versions of *The Last Days of Pompeii* were actually shot here. Thought to be relatively safe today, Vesuvius has erupted in 1631, 1794, 1871, 1900, 1903, 1904, 1906, 1929, 1944, and, of course, 79 A.D.

Vadis? all had their origins in the literary world. One of the most successful novels of this type, and one of the first, was Lord Edward Bulwer-Lytton's *The Last Days of Pompeii.* Set just before the catastrophic volcanic eruption of Vesuvius in 79 A.D., this novel involves a handsome young Athenian named Glaucus who falls in love with the lovely patrician maiden, Ione, and who is in turn loved by the impoverished, blind flower girl Nydia. The insidious priest of Isis, Arbaces, falls in love with Ione and tries to take her away from innocent Glaucus. He cruelly dupes heartsick Nydia into giving Glaucus a magic philter. She thinks it will make Glaucus fall in love with her, but it actually makes him mad. Arbaces' scheme is that Ione will abandon the now-lunatic Glaucus in favor of the evil priest. Glaucus drinks the potion, raves all over the decadent city, and is arrested (at Arbaces' instigation) for the murder of Ione's brother. Glaucus must face the lions in the arena, but Nydia finds out about Arbaces' wicked machinations, reveals Glaucus's innocence, and turns the huge crowd at the arena against the priest. At this climactic point—Kaboom!—the volcano erupts. Nydia helps Glaucus and Ione to safety but kills herself when she realizes that she will never have Glaucus's love.

The first major screen production of *The Last Days of Pompeii* appeared in 1908; I have assessed its importance for the history of the cinema and this genre in particular in Chapter 1. Three more versions appeared in 1913, one of them starring Ubaldo Stefani as Glaucus. This version has a graceful pace not evident in most silent Italian epics. With some fine acting by Stefani and Fernanda Negri-Pouger (Nydia), the tale of magic and perfidy receives a charming interpretation. The special effects used for the rainstorm on Vesuvius, the dream of Arbaces, and the eruption are quite primitive compared with those in the Cines version of 1926.

Carmine Gallone directed that version; it starred an international cast of Maria Korda (Nydia), Rina De Liguoro (Ione), and Victor Varconi (Glaucus). Although both these versions take advantage of their Italian origins by shooting on location at the ruins of Pompeii, the later version actually displays some fine reconstructions of real Pompeian buildings. With a superabundance of minor properties—fountains, urns, statuary, bowls, tables, jars, jewelry, signs, wall advertisements, frescoes—and some impressive crowd scenes in the forum and arena, this late silent spectacular was unfairly labeled "The Last Days of Italian Cinema."[14] Costing more than seven million lire (Korda alone received six thousand lire per day), the film ran into financial and business difficulties that anticipated those of Fox's *Cleopatra.* And like *Cleopatra,* the movie discouraged most film companies from filming in the ancient-spectacular genre for a few years. The production includes an impressive and daring banquet scene with bare-breasted dancers, realistic special effects during the eruption, and a clever insanity scene: Glaucus stares at a fresco of Zeus and the dancing Muses, and the figures on the wall suddenly come alive!

Shortly after RKO had devastated much of Manhattan in *King Kong,* the studio turned to the destructive powers of Vesuvius. RKO's *The Last Days of Pompeii* (1935) was produced, written, and directed by the same group of artists that created *Kong,* Merian C. Cooper, Ruth Rose, and Ernest B. Schoedsack, respectively. The music borrowed heavily from Max Steiner's *Kong* score; a few motifs are directly copied. The special effects belong again to the technical wizardry of Willis O'Brien.

This RKO version changes the novel's narrative, as bulky Marcus (Preston Foster) loses his once-happy blacksmith's life and bitterly learns that money is everything. He becomes a gladiator, and with numerous *morituri te salutamus*es and many victories, he becomes famous and fabulously rich. He travels to Judea, where he meets Pontius Pilate (Basil Rathbone) and a certain bearded Healer from Bethlehem. (RKO used cinematic license to move the eruption of Vesuvius back a few decades.) This straightforward melodrama maintains its exciting pace from beginning to end. It is energized by the addition of a robust Burbix (Alan Hale Sr.) and an insensitive Roman prefect (Louis Calhern). In the climactic eruption scene, O'Brien conjures a frightening mix of deadly sparks and flames, crumbling buildings, catapulted embers, thick smoke and dust, molten lava, and human panic.

If it was filmed in Italy in the silent era, you can be sure it would be filmed again in the early 1960s. Right on schedule, a new version of *The Last Days of Pompeii* was released in 1960, starring Steve Reeves, Christina Kaufmann, and Fernando Rey (Arbaces). Sporting a funky temple of Isis, complete with a hidden treasure vault and trap door, this film combines the Christian theme of the 1935 version with the novel's emphasis on the evil of Arbaces. A muscleman epic from start to finish, with every character either angelic or devilish, this entertaining film concludes with Reeves's triumph in spite of the volcano. The 1984 made-for-television version directed by Peter Hunt featured Franco Nero as Arbaces and Olivia Hussey as Ione. Like most television miniseries of the era, this version of *The Last Days of Pompeii* has the filmmaker's most precious luxury: almost unlimited time. But also like most television miniseries of the era, this film demonstrates why most films are better off telling a story in two hours, before tedium sets in and the director's attention to detail replaces dramatic tension. Writer Carmen Culver *(The Thorn Birds)* also added a number of new subplots, defeating the purpose of having the extra time to tell the original story.

The second century A.D. brought the zenith of the Roman Empire, with relative peace presided over by sane, even excellent emperors, whose successions followed smoothly. Good governance, bad drama: few films. One cinematic representative from this pax Romana was another film adaptation of a Shaw play, *Androcles and the Lion* (1952). Based on the original story told in Aulus Gellius's *Attic Nights,* the film portrays a humble Christian sentenced to death by the cruel Romans. Androcles is saved in the arena when the lion sent out to eat him turns out to be the same one from whose paw Androcles had removed a thorn a few weeks earlier. Shaw treats the entire affair with his irreverent witticisms and comically bitter sarcasm. The quality of the farce is enhanced by the intentional overacting of its players, particularly Caesar (Maurice Evans), who is portrayed as a middle-aged, vain, intellectual fool; Androcles (Alan Young), who is portrayed as a naive, humanitarian clown; and Ferrovius (Robert Newton), who is a big, strong, dirty Christian fanatic who loves to give his fellow men the chance to turn *their* other cheek ("I broke his jaw," he recalls of one such encounter, "but I saved his soul"). Jean Simmons, Elsa Lanchester, Victor Mature, and Jim Backus round out the cast. Occasionally hilarious, and always light as a feather, *Androcles and the Lion* boasts a sprightly, sometimes silly atmosphere. Androcles' baby-talk to the thorn-troubled lion is characteristic: "Has the thorn made you too sick to eat the nice Christian man for breakfast, liony-piony?" Incidentally, some of the sets for this RKO production were taken from the studio's *The Last Days of Pompeii,* and even Preston Foster can be glimpsed in the short gladiatorial sequence.

Another film made about the glorious and relatively stable second century A.D. was, ironically, Samuel Bronston's *The Fall of the Roman Empire* (1964). Critics joked of the folly of cramming Gibbon's massive opus into 188 minutes, but in fact the film begins with the death of the philosopher-emperor Marcus Aurelius (Alec Guinness) and focuses on the brief reign of demented Commodus. Because it was released one year after *Cleopatra, The Fall of the Roman Empire* had little chance for praise from the public; ancient spectaculars had had their day. Bosley Crowther described it as "a mammoth and murky accumulation of Hollywooden heroics and history."[15] It is true that some of the characterizations are rather flat and that history is occasionally distorted to no evident purpose, but Bronston and director Anthony Mann, who directed *Spartacus* for one week until he was replaced by Kubrick, deserve commendation for choosing the contrasting periods of Marcus Aurelius and Commodus. They capture the frustration of a gentle, philosophical man of high virtue whose twenty-year rule was filled with little but bitter barbarian battles and frontier wars, and who leaves behind as son and successor a twisted, spoiled pervert who deserved the death by strangulation he historically received.

ROM-S-23

Much of the film's action is located not in the capital city of Rome but in the cold, isolated frontiers of Armenia and Pannonia (Austria and Yugoslavia). In Armenia we see a magnificent sandstone fortress of Oriental design, while the Pannonia scenes employ one of the most atmospheric sets ever used in an historical movie. Not made to impress with grandeur and richness, the icy winter fortress in the barbarized European province gives us the lonely sense of exile to the ends of civilization. Heavy wooden beams and

49/50 Alec Guinness as the Stoic emperor Marcus Aurelius in *The Fall of the Roman Empire* (facing page, 1964). His squared beard, curled hair, heavy robe, and somber countenance can be found in ancient depictions of Marcus Aurelius. In a relief from the second century A.D., for example, the emperor sacrifices before a temple in Rome.

thick, snow-covered stone walls remind us that ancient life was not all polished marble and eating grapes. Modeled after as lofty an artistic enterprise as Trajan's column and approved by consultant Will Durant, this authentic winter fortress serves as the perfect isolated background in which Marcus Aurelius the Stoic must meet his expected death. Although some of Aurelius's dying words might seem to contradict those in his *Meditations,* the calmness with which he meets death, his frustration that the Empire has not yet seen the true pax Romana, and the philosophical loneliness he feels form a screen portrait of the wise stoic sovereign that any historian should appreciate. And for the average moviegoer, there is the tremendous pathos of it all.

From the bleak Danubian frontier the film moves to a Rome glorying in its richest and most dominant era. Using much of his $16 million budget on sets, Bronston rebuilt a Roman Forum and Capitoline Hill that even Nero would have been reluctant to burn. Skillfully utilizing the panning camera of Robert Krasker, Mann directed Commodus's triumphal entry into Rome with an enormous breadth of scope. The procession

51   The cold, isolated Danubian headquarters of Marcus Aurelius in *The Fall of the Roman Empire.*
Tributary princes ride before the seated emperor (Alec Guinness), with Timonides (James Mason) at
one side and Livius (Stephen Boyd) on the other. Surrounding them are lictors bearing *aquilae* (eagle
standards) and *fasces* (symbolic bundles of sticks with axes). To both sides of these can be seen
Roman-numeraled legionary banners and standards.

passes a classically rounded temple of Vesta, a long aqueduct, horses with crisp red capes,
soldiers in a variety of uniforms from all the territories of the Empire, towering victory
columns, statue-filled archways, and a magnificent and lofty temple of Jupiter glistening
in the bright sunlight. A deafening crowd cheers "Hail Caesar" while a somber slave stands
behind Commodus and recites the traditional words "Remember, thou art mortal." Before
long, Commodus would forget, even renaming Rome "The City of Commodus."

Even more authentic than the magnificent exterior sets are the elegant interiors
with their delicate acanthus columns and hanging garlands; the walls have Pompeian-style
pastel-colored frescoes between, deeply coffered sculpted ceilings and richly colorful mosaic floors. In the Capitoline Jupiter temple the huge chryselephantine (gold and ivory)
cult statue sits amid rows of magnificently stout, fluted, marble columns.

The acting in *The Fall of the Roman Empire* is superior as well. James Mason is
cast well as the Stoic Timonides; confronted with a desperate barbarian chieftain (John
Ireland) who is about to plunge fire into his face, Timonides philosophically suggests,

52/53   Two scenes from Trajan's column (c. A.D. 106) served as models for the Danubian frontier fort reconstructed for *The Fall of the Roman Empire*. In one scene the emperor Trajan, seated on a podium and surrounded by legionary standards and aides, receives enemy chieftains. Another scene shows Roman soldier-engineers building a fort much like the one in the film. Walls of large rectangular stones, wooden hatchwork, and crenellated ramparts typify Roman frontier architecture.

"Let's look upon this logically." Christopher Plummer's Commodus is convincingly sinister and half-mad, and Sophia Loren (Lucilla) and Stephen Boyd (Livius) do the best they can with their disappointingly bland roles; the undeveloped love element between Lucilla and Livius pulls the picture down from the heights it might have otherwise reached. But all the technical elements of *The Fall of the Roman Empire*—sets, costumes, the fine second-unit work of Yakima Canutt, the photography, and Dmitri Tiomkin's elusively insistent score—make this picture an aesthetically impressive exposition. The impressive double-decked square of thick shields in which Commodus and Livius fight to the death, the gigantic hand of Sabazius in the Forum from which the "divine" Commodus emerges, the exciting chariot chase in the snow, and Commodus's lavish baths—all merit more appreciation than they received in the wake of the *Cleopatra* debacle.

The very last scene, in which relatively virtuous Livius, triumphant over Commodus, is offered the position of emperor, while fat, rich, ambitious senators offer millions and millions of sesterces to buy the Empire's highest office, demonstrates in a few seconds the lack of leadership, the decadent politics, and the wild inflation that gradually gnawed away at the backbone of Roman society and left its carcass for hungry hordes of barbarians. This brief moment of shocking historicity subtly reminds us that great civilizations rarely fall to foreign conquerors before they are first felled from within.

54   Part of the vast Roman Forum reconstructed for *The Fall of the Roman Empire*. Covering
acres of (Spanish) ground, this reconstructed Rome includes the temple of Saturn, upper left, and
temple of Jupiter, upper right. Emperor Commodus (Christopher Plummer) stands before the huge,
bronze hand of Sabazius. On the stairway are his guard in Armenian leopardskin dress. (Each
Roman legion dressed individually, according to locale, function, and tradition.) In the foreground
the legionaries wear the *lorica segmentata* (segmented breast-cover of leather or metal); between
them and the leopardskinned troops are several legionary officers in the more familiar anatomical
cuirass (chest armor).

55　The Maison Carrée in Nimes, France. Built about 9 B.C., this Roman temple survives intact. Like many temples of the Roman Empire, it stands on a podium above ground level, is surrounded by fluted, acanthus-leaved, Corinthian columns, and is topped with a triangular roof. Today it lacks the roof-top finials placed on most ancient temples.

56　These Roman soldiers from Trajan's column wear the *lorica segmentata*. Their shields are *scuta* (the curved, rectangular type). Their modern counterparts in *The Fall of the Roman Empire* wear leather lorica and hold red, curved shields.

The Fall of the Roman Empire was the twentieth century's final Roman history film. Thereafter the "ancient" genre entered an extended hiatus that lasted several decades. Curiously, Gladiator (2000), the first Roman history film thereafter, revisited some of the same events and characters—the death of Marcus Aurelius and the rise and fall of Commodus. Unlike his counterpart in The Fall of the Roman Empire, Gladiator's Commodus (Joaquin Phoenix) is a young man (age nineteen) when he accesses to the throne. His sister Lucilla (Connie Nielsen) is accurately portrayed as a politically determined imperial widow who plots a failed revolt against Commodus; in the film her father, Marcus Aurelius, (Richard Harris) admits to her, "If only you'd been born a man, what a Caesar you would have made!" Commodus's murder of Aurelius, while not attested in our sources, is not beyond the realm of conspiracy theorists, and his swift termination of the German wars, his subsequent grand triumph into Rome, his initial popularity with the people of Rome, his antagonism toward the Senate, and his fondness for the gladiatorial arena are all well documented. Phoenix seems to have been born for the part of Commodus. His cleft lip and slumped shoulders give him a slightly off-balance appearance that barely masks the pervasive evil within his tormented soul.

David Franzoni's script gives Commodus ample opportunity for tyrannical

57/58   The interior sets in *The Fall of the Roman Empire* are brilliantly planned and varied. Here Livius (Stephen Boyd) and Lucilla (Sophia Loren) stand in a detailed, architecturally busy room (facing page). The three-dimensional portal, acanthus columns, delicate finials, festive garlands, statuary, and late-period Pompeii-styled frescoes give the true baroque feeling of Roman imperial life in the second century A.D. Adviser Will Durant may have suggested a Roman architectural source like this highly ornate fresco. The image, found in Herculaneum, which was destroyed along with Pompeii in the A.D. 79 eruption of Vesuvius, includes acanthus columns, garlands, statuary, and trompe-l'oeil architectural painting, all evident in the home of Livius in the film.

59   Commodus (Christopher Plummer) and Livius (Stephen Boyd) fight to the death with
iron pikes in *The Fall of the Roman Empire*. Commodus's Praetorians form a double-decked square
with their rectangular, metal-bound *scuta*. Commodus's leopardskin boots (the *crepidae* with open-
toes and laced on the instep) perhaps suggest his obsession with the gladiatorial life. Livius wears
caligae—heavy marching boots that are secured by shin-wrapping thongs.

duplicity and cruelty. His own father remarks that "Commodus is not a moral man." But
more intellectually impressive is a verbal confrontation between Commodus and the philosopher emperor. Commodus laments that Aurelius admired the four Platonic/Aristotelian/
Stoic virtues—wisdom, justice, fortitude, and temperance—while ignoring the virtues
Commodus possessed, devotion to family and ambition for good purposes. This passage
cleverly sidesteps *Fall*'s technique of articulating Aurelian philosophical meditations via
Alec Guinness's voice-overs; Franzoni transfers Aurelian meditations into the mouths of
others and uses them to build powerful emotional tensions.

     Later in the film Franzoni features another Aurelian paraphrase just before the final
battle between Commodus and Maximus (Russell Crowe): "Death smiles at us all, and all
we can do is smile back." Indeed, the concept of death is ubiquitous in the film. The opening shot and its concluding echo show us Maximus's vision of the Land of the Dead, and

periodically we are reminded that Maximus's yearning for an eternal Elysium makes the danger he faces as both a Roman soldier and a gladiator immaterial. Death is ever-present in battle and in the arena, and—so long as Commodus is involved—in politics as well. This theme helps convey to us how relatively cheap life was in late antiquity, when so many different livelihoods courted death, but also how comforting it must have been to have a strong belief in the afterlife. This is most certainly a pagan film, not a Christian film.

As a film of the twenty-first century, *Gladiator* enjoys the economic and visual advantages not just of computer-generated special effects but of an entire generation's worth of developments in film technique. A model of the lower tier of the Roman Colosseum was physically constructed for the film, but the entire four tiers are re-created through computer generation, and the audience gets to look at this famous ancient monument from a variety of angles—an aerial shot and a selection of interior midrange and distance views, including the views from the imperial box and from the luxury box of the gladiator owner Proximo (Oliver Reed), as well as sweeping eye-level views, not to mention several views of the machinery below the sands of the arena. Several ground-level views create breathtaking impressions of the Roman arena in its heyday: the porphyry and black marble–faced interior Colosseum walls frame an arena floor strewn with fallen gladiators, their futile weapons, roaming tigers, and rose petals, all bathed in light either streaming through wooden latticework above the portals or diffused and mottled by the canvases drawn over the top of the Colosseum. These moments evoke the neoclassical nineteenth-century paintings of the sort that inspired Griffith and DeMille. In addition, the contemporary style of hyperrealism introduced in recent works by Oliver Stone and Steven Spielberg, accomplished mostly through rapid editing and variations in film stocks and developing techniques, creates dazzling moments of suggestive and intense but not overly grisly beheadings, amputations, and other mutilations that inevitably accompanied combat with swords.

The antiquity in *Gladiator* was not created from hard drives alone. Before shooting the introductory Germanic battle scene (in Surrey, England), director Ridley Scott ordered four hundred acres of forest burned, two thousand sets of armor constructed, and twenty-six thousand arrows prepared. The African provincial town of "Zucchabar" was constructed with tens of thousands of sun-dried mud bricks. And Scott's staff did its cinematic homework as well. Twice the *testudo* ("turtle") formation first used in 1963's *Cleopatra* is re-created; the Praetorians form the boundaries for the final battle between Maximus and Commodus as they did for the final battle of *The Fall of the Roman Empire;* the Minotaur gladiator is drawn from *Fellini Satyricon;* and the gladiatorial school owes much to that in *Spartacus.* Similarly, the idea of having an African slave (Djimon Hounsou) befriend the protagonist echoes both *Spartacus* and *Demetrius and the Gladiators.* The suggested incest between the Aurelian siblings no doubt owes its inspiration to television's *I, Claudius,* and the twirling airborn sword Maximus throws is a set piece of television's *Hercules: The Legendary Journeys.* The death of the film's hero, a plot concept rarely seen in Hollywood films since the 1960s, probably derives more immediately from the medieval

60   When portraying a mad Roman emperor the cinema can revel in his historically documented eccentricity. Compare this third-century A.D. imperial portrait of Commodus, complete with Herculean lionskin, club, and Golden Apples of the Hesperides, with the attire of Christopher Plummer's mad Commodus in *The Fall of the Roman Empire*.

epic *Braveheart* (1995), but *Spartacus* again is a likely source.

Gladiator reveals another twenty-first-century bias. Contemporary Hollywood family values interject themselves into the ancient Roman zeitgeist. Maximus is offered the throne of the empire but prefers to return home to his wife and son. Lucilla might also take the throne, but her main concern is for her son Lucius Veras (the younger). Commodus suggests that he would have been a better human if his father had loved him, and Marcus Aurelius admits that his son's faults are the failure of a neglectful father.

To emphasize this theme the film distorts history. The historical Lucilla was so ambitious of accession to the throne that she was exiled and then executed—not what one wants from one's mother. And Aurelius took Commodus with him on his most important campaigns and trusted his son with a series of titles, honors, and promotions toward assuming full imperial power. Maximus, who at one point calls himself an improbable "Maximus Decimus Meridius," is an invented character and therefore not subject to the same scrutiny. In fact, his wish to return not so much to his family but to his farm to harvest the crops recalls an early Roman exemplar of nobility—Cincinnatus, who rescued his country in a fifteen-day war and immediately retired back to his farm.

Such values of Republican Rome reverberate throughout the film. Derek Jacobi's character is named Senator Gracchus, recalling both the Republican Senator Gracchus (Charles Laughton) in *Spartacus* and the historical populist reformers Tiberius and Gaius Sempronius Gracchus of the second century B.C. Maximus and others repeat an army slogan "Strength and honor." And in three scenes, including the last scene of the film, we see that Maximus honors his household gods, the Penates, which represent traditional Roman familial morality. In *HBO First Look: Gladiator,* director Scott said, "Togas and sandals and wreaths—I've tried to avoid that. Nobody lies down in this on a couch and eats grapes." To achieve his vision, he superimposed both modern familial sensitivity and ancient Roman Republican virtues onto a fascinating transitional decade of the Roman empire.

Sign of the Gladiator (1959) tells the story of Queen Zenobia (Anita Ekberg) and her mighty Eastern Empire of Palmyra. Accurately set in the third century A.D. in what is now Syria, this film (shot in Yugoslavia) has many technical errors. Hollow dubbing and slow-moving action are off-putting. The plot is less interesting than the historical facts. In reality, Zenobia led her armies against the Roman provinces of Asia Minor (Turkey) and Egypt and then proclaimed her young son as Emperor of Rome. The Roman Emperor Aurelian defeated her in battle, led Zenobia in chains to a massive triumph through the streets of Rome, and then kept her as a hostage for the rest of her life. Instead, this romantic pseudohistory has Zenobia fall in love with a Roman general, break with him, and, you guessed it, fall back in love with him after Aurelian pardons her. For those with sharp eyes, a copy of the frieze of embassies from Persepolis can be seen in Palmyra's main temple.

Fabiola, a tale of Christian martyrdom set circa 300 A.D. from Nicholas Cardinal Wiseman's 1854 novel, has been filmed twice. The silent version of 1916 suffers from a long initial period of tableau after tableau of introductions as director Enrico Guazzoni tries to introduce too many of the novel's characters. Once the story gets rolling, however, fine acting, varied and clever photography, and some delicately painted interiors appear. Climaxed by a somber early Christian funeral in the Roman catacombs and the baptism of the aristocratic Fabiola, the film reaches an inspiring conclusion.

The 1948 version of *Fabiola* was one of the most ambitious releases of postwar Italy. The impoverished Italian film industry was not responsible for the English sound track, which sounds as if it were dubbed by Martians; this was added in 1951 when a script prepared in part by Marc Connelly was dubbed over a much edited version of the 150-minute original release. The dark visual tones of the film were typical of the Italian neorealism of the time. (The film was produced the same year as Vittorio de Sica's *The Bicycle Thief*.) Of the noirish sequences, the most effective is the nocturnal romantic beach scene, but for *realismo* nothing surpasses the shadowy, sanguinary sequence showing St. Sebastian's sagittary martyrdom. The climactic gladiatorial sequences create a complex collage enlivened by oblique camera angles, close-ups of hungry lions, and wide shots of the convex arena and its large, ebullient crowds.

61   Jack Palance (Attila) grimaces and threatens a Roman soldier in *Sign of the Pagan* (1955). Long hair, Genghis Khan mustache, and fur or skin clothing are the most obvious characteristics of a cinematic barbarian. The hide-covered wagons and standards of skulls and horns also differentiate Hun from Roman. The Roman soldier to the far left wears the *squamata,* or scale-armor. Palance played another barbarian—Alboin, king of the Lombards—in *Sword of the Conqueror.*

Constantine and the Cross (1962) takes place during the reign of the fourth-century emperor who first brought Christianity under the Empire's protection. The film keeps to the basic truth of how Constantine (Cornel Wilde) had to battle for the throne against numerous rivals, chief among them Maxentius and Licinius. Also of historical interest is Constantine's canonized mother, Helena. The emperor's romantic feelings toward his wife Fausta (Belinda Lee) seem exaggerated, given that the historical Constantine did not hesitate to put Fausta to death a few years into his reign. But on the whole, *Constantine and the Cross* contains enough sobriety to satisfy mildly demanding students of the era. The character of Constantine is one-dimensional, but Wilde has a noble bearing and a serious approach to his important position. He wears the uniform of a Roman general particularly well—a talent not shared by all actors. Mario Nascimbene's music carries many of the well-planned action scenes, and the evening sky over the famed Milvian Bridge has one of the richest Nile blues imaginable.

The script is well above average for an early 1960s Italian cloak-and-sandal film. Maxentius remarks wisely as he holds up a bust of Constantine, "Our descendants have a right to know the faces of the great heroes of the past. We mere thinkers and authors must stay in the shadows and let posterity guess what we look like. This is the age of soldiers and warriors." When Constantine's handsome friend Hadrian is offered a glass of milk, his refusal—"Give me wine, chicken, anything but that!"—is historical as well as comic: Romans thought only barbarians drank milk. Before Constantine discovers the meaning of Christianity, he hears Maxentius say these historically ironic words: "These Christians are great actors; if they played Seneca, they'd be a great success."

The final battle at the Milvian Bridge—the battle before which Constantine sees in the sky his famous vision "In Hoc Vinces" (In this [sign] you will conquer)—shows some very clever strategy, exciting action, well-angled photography, and an authentic Roman stockade. These capable outdoor scenes and some beautiful interior sets, especially the red-bricked Roman Senate, the high vaults of the basilica, Fausta's marble pool, and the simple but elegant temple at Trevia, set the background for a solid cinematic rendition of Constantine's early reign. Some sloppy editing and uneven scenes keep the film from achieving a superior estimation, but it certainly rests a noble notch or two above most films of its ilk.

In the two centuries that followed Constantine, wave after wave of marauding Mongolian, Germanic, and Asian tribes forced their way into the outer fringes of the Roman Empire and into the history of Western man. These "barbarians," many of whom would be known within the next few centuries simply as Europeans, came in many nations and generations. One group, the Huns, surpassed the others in fame, largely because of the terrifying reputation of its leader, Attila.

Attila has appeared in three movies, including Febo Mari's 1916 *Attila*. In the two modern films, not surprisingly, he has been played by the heavies Anthony Quinn and Jack Palance. In *Attila the Hun* (1954), Quinn looks the "typical" barbarian in pants, sleeveless vest, thick mustache, and an earring; his hair falls in a strangely ferocious looking pigtail. He leads his fur-clad Huns against a badly governed Roman Empire. "Today Rome, tomorrow the world!" Attila predicts. The effeminate and childish Valentinian III is nominally the Roman emperor in 451, but his mother, Galla Placidia (Colette Regis), really runs things. The labored plot has Attila secretly loving Honoria (Sophia Loren), a relation of the Roman court, while he himself is loved by a fellow barbarian named Grune (Irene Papas). Although most of this is twisted history (Galla Placidia, for example, was already dead), the impetuous Attila did, as in the film, murder his brother Bleda and lead his thousands of hungry nomads against the Roman forces led by Aerius (Henry Vidal). *Attila* presents rousing action and offers a poignant contrast between the dissolute Byzantine court, with its colorful mosaics, and the barbarian hordes in their earthy encampments. The film ends with Attila giving way before the white-robed Bishop of Ravenna. The filmmakers got the church right, but historically Pope Leo is credited with saving Rome.

Sign of the Pagan (1955) presents us with a similar impression of the "Scourge of God." The actual history of Attila's barbaric invasions is juggled a bit more, but Jack Palance presents us with a frighteningly brutal portrait of the Huns' leader. This time Attila's Roman adversary is the Emperor Marcian (Jeff Chandler), but exciting battle sequences are curtailed for too much exposition of the politics of the period—which were far more interesting than the moviegoer would guess.

Four versions of *Theodora* have been filmed. Ernesto Pasquali directed the first, in 1909, and twelve years later Arturo Ambrosio directed a silent version based on the drama written by Victorien Sardou. Justinian, emperor of the Byzantine Roman Empire in the sixth century, falls in love with a streetwalker named Theodora (Rita Jolivet) and legally commits himself to a mésalliance. As empress, Theodora is cruel and so impractical that she eventually lets the arena's lions loose on the populace. Her subjects understandably resent this feline emancipation and storm the palace in the rousing climax. The film impresses us even today with its colossal marble columns and statuary and its crowds of thousands. The 1955 version of *Theodora* also offers us some splendid shots of Constantinople's hippodrome, palaces, and marketplaces, but—as with many "ancient" movies made in Italy in the early 1950s—the acting is stiff, the pace dull, and the dubbing out of whack.

Although *Titus* (1999), a film adaptation of Shakespeare's *Titus Andronicus,* is set during the Roman Empire, the characters are not historical. There was no Roman emperor Saturninus, though the name and political status no doubt derive from Julius Saturninus, who claimed to be emperor in A.D. 281 but was quickly assassinated—by his own troops. The late-third-century date of the historical Saturninus seems about right as well, for the play's Roman Empire, in which the barbarian Gothic queen Tamora plays an important role, surely predates the institutionalization of Christianity. The Goths made their first significant contact with the Romans in A.D. 251. As for the name Titus Andronicus, the Bard had probably heard of the famous early Roman poet Livius Andronicus.

Because more than 110 films have developed or exploited events and characters from ancient history (not including Greek mytho-history), it would be impossible to discuss all of them in depth in one chapter. Final mention must be made, however, of the numerous "ancient history" films made in Italy during the sword-and-sandal flourish in the early sixties. Besides the previously mentioned films that were Italian-made yet widely released throughout the United States—*Damon and Pythias, The Colossus of Rhodes, Constantine and the Cross, The Giant of Marathon,* and so on—Italy also re-created the semilegendary battle between the triplet Horatii and the triplet Curiatii in *Duel of Champions* (1961) starring Alan Ladd; the Gallic attack on Rome and Camillus in 390 B.C. in *Brennus, Enemy of Rome* (1960); the exile of Coriolanus (Gordon Scott) in *Coriolanus: Hero With-*

out a Country (1962), the script of which is most definitely not from Shakespeare; the Roman sack of Corinth in *The Centurion* (1962); Lars Porsenna's attack on Rome in *Amazons of Rome* (1963) starring Louis Jourdan; Praxiteles' workshop in *The Gardens of Love* (1960); Alexander's capture of Sardis in *Goliath and the Rebel Slave Girl* (1963); Caesar's struggles against Vercingetorix in *The Giants of Rome* (1963) and *The Slave of Rome* (1960); Lucullus's Eastern expedition in *Rome Against Rome* (1963); the Druid opposition to Rome in *The Viking Queen* (1966), which follows the story line of the opera *Norma;* the gluttonous emperor Vitellius in the atrociously titled *Terror of Rome Against the Son of Hercules* (1963); Pertinax's accession to the throne in *A Sword for the Empire* (1965); Caracalla's reign in *Gladiator of Rome* (1962); Alaric's sack of Rome in *The Revenge of the Barbarians* (1960); Alboin's rule over the Lombards in *Sword of the Conqueror* (1961); and several other films that vaguely toss in crudely drawn characters with names like Spartacus, Nero, Diocletian, and Commodus. The historicity of almost all of these early-sixties Italian films is slight; most producers, directors, and writers thought it was enough simply to base the film's narrative on an historical event or character. For the most part, they were wrong. History's fascination belongs not so much in its names, dates, and events as in its vivid and credible re-creation.

Upon the all-bounteous earth

And across the endless sea

Walks the immortal brilliance

Of heroic deeds.

— PINDAR, *ISTHMIAN*, 4.40

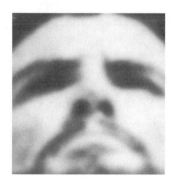

When the immortal Homer sang his glorious poems just shy of three thousand years ago, he could not possibly have imagined that someday his poems about Ulysses, Achilles, and the Trojan War would be re-created on something called a "silver screen." But the twentieth century A.D. still found the whole fabulous world of Greek mythology captivating, and it would have been unwise for movie producers to have left this magical source of heroes and monsters untapped. For centuries, the gloriously mysterious atmosphere surrounding such names as Helen of Troy, Perseus, Hercules, Jason, Orpheus, and Medusa created indelible impressions on the minds and eyes of artists. Those impressions were bound to emerge in the ultimate artistic medium of the Atomic Age. And so from the silent *Homer's Odyssey* (1911) to Pasolini's often strident *Medea* (1970), from the human reality of *Helen of Troy* (1955) to the magical land of *Jason and the Argonauts* (1963; TV, 2000), from Disney's pastoral centaurs in *Fantasia* (1940) to the destructive reptile in *Gorgo* (named for the Gorgons, 1961), Greek mythology has deservedly played its part in the history of the cinema.

Besides the numerous films that have used mythological names or characters— for instance, *The Andromeda Strain* (1971), *The Poseidon Adventure* (1972), *2001: A Space Odyssey* (1968), *Ulysses* (1967), *Penelope* (1966), *Kronos* (1957, 1973), *Neptune's Daughter* (1949), and *Black Narcissus* (1947)—approximately eighty films have been devoted entirely to Greek and Roman myths. The surreal stories, powerful heroes, primordial profundity, and pervading feeling of fantasy are four major elements that have made these vivid legends of ancient Greece popular enough to live on two

62   Most of what we see in the cinema is illusion, but Ray Harryhausen's films set in the ancient Greek mythical world require a number of extraordinary optical tricks. A sculptor by training, Harryhausen here puts the finishing touches on Kraken, the sea monster for *Clash of the Titans* (1981), which in the completed film seems to stand two hundred feet tall.

millennia after the peoples that fostered them have perished. In fact, Greek myth often thrives as a fascinating or profound cinematic source.

Generally speaking, most mythological films were produced either between 1897 and 1918 or between 1953 and 1981. Georges Méliès produced *La Sibylle de Cumae* (*The Sibyl of Cumae,* 1898), *L'Île de Calypso* (*Ulysses and the Giant Polyphemus,* 1905), and *Le Tonnerre de Jupiter* (*Jupiter's Thunderbolts,* 1903). *Le Tonnerre de Jupiter* shows a dwarfish Olympian throwing cardboard lightning bolts onto the stage. They explode, he does a few amusing flips, and the Muses appear behind him. Five more mythological films were made in France in 1909 and 1910: Emile Cohl's animated *Les Douze Travaux d'Hercule* (*The Twelve Labors of Hercules,* 1910); Gaum's *Hercules and the Big Stick* (1910), in which Hercules fights the Hydra, the Nemean Lion, and the Erymanthian Boar; Gaum's *Jupiter Smitten* (1910), with several metamorphoses; Pathé's *Hercules in the Regiment* (1909), in which bullets bounce off an invulnerable giant; and Le Lion's *Goddess of the Sea* (1909), which offers us Cupid and Neptune.

Because ancient history was not native to America as it was to Italy, most "ancient" films made by America's early cinematic imitators favored mythology over history. Following Edison's ballet *Cupid and Psyche* (1897), American audiences saw *In Cupid's Realm* (1908), *The Minotaur* (1910), *Neptune's Daughter* (1912), *The Story of Venus* (1914), *The*

Centaurs (animated, 1916), *The Golden Fleece* (1918), and *The Triumph of Venus* (1918). On the other hand, although Italy favored films based on its own ancient history, early Italian filmmakers still made a few mythological films, including Ambrosio's *Ero e Leandro* (*Hero and Leander,* 1910), and two Italian mythological silents became veritable classics: *La Caduta di Troia* (*The Fall of Troy,* 1911) and *L'Odissea* (1911).

Homer and the Trojan War has always been the best beginning. As early as 1911 a film version of the Trojan War had been produced in Italy, but *La Caduta di Troia* overemphasized the romance of the myth. First the Trojan Paris "steals" the beautiful Helen from Greece. We see the two lovers traverse the sea on a huge, Botticelli-inspired, scallop-shell bed pulled across the heavens by white-robed flying nymphs. After a brief battle before "the topless towers of Ilium," we see six hundred extras pull the famous Trojan Horse (a plywood cutout) into the doomed city. A model of the city burns in the finale while Menelaus, the Greek husband of Helen, slays Paris in a duel.

The advertising for this film's release in the United States was sheer genius. It broke all attendance records in Chicago, where some viewers paid again and again for repeat showings. A theater manager in Washington, D.C., somehow persuaded the local schools to teach Homer's epic that very month; when he showed the film during Easter vacation, his theater was filled with students. Although it was considered a "spectacular" in 1911, this primitive, brief, and low-budget film seems humorous and crude today. But at the turn of the century, when films about the ancient world were at one of the peaks of their popularity, the excitement of seeing the Trojan Horse, Helen, and Paris on the screen for the first time overcame the technical inadequacies of *La Caduta di Troia*. Within the next three years, director Giovanni Pastrone would expand and improve his technique for his spectacular *Cabiria*.

Alexander Korda's *The Private Life of Helen of Troy* (1927) is a satire set in a modern idiom and will be discussed in Chapter 8. *The Face That Launched 1000 Ships,* starring Hedy Lamarr, was an Italian production that was never released, though footage from it was used in *Loves of Three Queens* (1953). Lamarr took the title roles of Geneviève of Brabant, the Empress Josephine, and Helen of Troy in that film, the final third of which tells the story of Paris's abduction of Helen from Sparta, the war itself, the death of Achilles, and the death of Paris. Like most Italian productions in the immediate postwar era, *Loves of Three Queens* suffers from a low budget and low production values.

In 1956 Warner Brothers produced one of its few entries into the genre, *Helen of Troy,* an elaborate film retelling the same Greek myth. Director Robert Wise made his sole venture into the epic genre with this colorful spectacle; he said later that he would never do it again. The result has its merits, however, especially in retrospect nearly a half-century after its theatrical release. Like the Italian version of 1911, Wise's film overemphasizes the amorous qualities of heroine Helen rather than the heroic qualities of men like Achilles, Agamemnon, and Hector. This romantic concentration overshadows the martial and heroic themes immortalized in Homer's *Iliad;* perhaps Wise should have been reminded that Homer's treatment of the myth has lasted for millennia. The film becomes rather tedious when Helen (Rossana Podestà) and Paris (Jack Sernas) constantly talk love, eat love, sleep love, and make love. Neither the chemistry between the actors nor Hugh Gray's dialogue is strong enough to support these romantic scenes.

But the CinemaScope, WarnerColor, cast-of-thousands action scenes are terrific, if slightly anachronistic. The thinly clad Greeks with their stout, round shields march on the mighty bastions of Troy under the cover of tall, wooden siege towers and a huge battering ram. (The siege towers are un-Homeric, but they were used in other Bronze Age battles.) The Trojans desperately fight back with flaming arrows. The Greek attack suddenly bursts into flames and their long flight back to the ships is a memorable spectacle.

Hugh Gray, who was the historical adviser for MGM's *Quo Vadis?*, brought to *Helen of Troy* some of its more authentic moments. And some of the film's best scenes can be credited to Homer himself: Achilles (Stanley Baker) grovels in the dirt as he grieves for the dead Patroclus (*Iliad* 17, 18), Achilles quarrels bitterly with Agamemnon (*Iliad* 1), Achilles drags Hector's (Harry Andrews) body in the dust (*Iliad* 22), and Hector bids a touching farewell to his wife and infant child (*Iliad* 6). Massive amounts of props and extras magnify the effect of the sequence in which the Greeks unload all the supplies, cattle, carts, and horses from their numerous beached ships to prepare for the siege.

In the film's best scene by far, the Trojans bring the wooden horse into the city. The huge horse—one of the largest movable props ever built for a film—was made of balsa wood, and the actors reportedly had to pretend it was hard to pull. To the accompaniment

63/65   A court scene from *Helen of Troy* (facing page, 1955). Helen (Rossana Podestà) stands on the bottom step with Paris (Jack Sernas); to their right are Cassandra (Janette Scott), Hecuba (Nora Swinburne), and King Priam (Cedric Hardwicke). The inverted columns with their bulb-topped capitals do indeed belong to thirteenth-century Bronze Age Greece, as does Priam's throne. Two views from the palace of King Minos at Knossos on the island of Crete show the reconstruction of the grand staircase and the restoration of the stone throne. Paris's armor, however, is that of a sixth-century B.C. warrior. The delicate frescoes in the upper right are in Minoan-Mycenaean styles.

66 The throne at Knossos as excavated in 1900. It lacks most of the painting and finery of the throne as viewed today: it is not just the cinema that creates an illusion of historical accuracy.

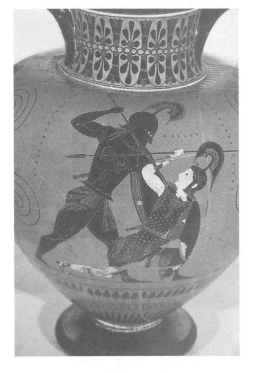

67 This vase from Athens, which shows Achilles slaying the Amazon Penthesileia, dates from the late sixth century B.C., six hundred years after the Trojan War, but Achilles' *thorax* (chest armor) served as a model for Paris's armor in *Helen of Troy*.

of Max Steiner's sharp, bold scoring, the fatal gift is pulled slowly past Troy's torchlit ramparts. Behind it frenzied dancers whirl. The whole scene creates the marvelously wild atmosphere that only sudden peace after ten years of war could produce. Throughout the center of the city soldiers drink wine from their helmets, red smoke eddies to the sky, festoons hang from every conceivable spot, and women are passed from man to man over the heads of the crowd, the hungry soldiers occasionally lowering a tempting women to kiss her passionately between her deeply cleft breasts. Cinecittà rarely looked so Dionysiac!

Some of the characterizations in *Helen of Troy* are equally convincing. Stanley Baker's Achilles presents an imposing, Homerically "dark" impression of awesome menace, and Sir Cedric Hardwicke's aged Priam and Janette Scott's fiery, prophetic Cassandra are true to images that have survived for nearly three millennia. On the other hand, other characterizations fall short of that standard: Paris fights too readily, courageously, and ably—not at all the coward portrayed in the *Iliad;* Menelaus (Niall McGinnis) and Agamemnon (Robert Douglas), the kings of Sparta and Argos, are too wicked and ignoble; and Helen lacks the complexity of the Homeric figure, who in the *Iliad* is torn between her love for Paris and for Menelaus. Here she curses Menelaus at every opportunity.

Helen of Troy was involved in a legal dispute and was not distributed or rereleased, shown on cable, or released in video format until 1996. Now viewers can appreciate how the film could have been improved if it had treated Homer's original story line with more respect, if it had swung the balance from vapid romance toward complex heroism. The film ignores the quintessential strength of the *Iliad*—the complex, catastrophic anger of Achilles—and turned a classical epic into 1950s romantic fiddle-faddle. Any film is the stylistic prisoner of the era or decade in which it is produced, so perhaps a more profound, less formulaic *Iliad* still awaits us.

In the Italian boom of ancient sword-and-sandal epics in the early 1960s, two new versions of the Trojan War appeared. *The Fury of Achilles* (1962) accurately follows the story of the *Iliad,* minus the divine interventions, from Achilles' quarrel with Agamemnon to the funeral of Hector. It suffers, though, as do most films of its type, from poor dubbing, mediocre acting, and perfunctory characterizations. *The Trojan Horse* (1962) rearranges the plot of the *Iliad* to put Aeneas (Steve Reeves)—best known for escaping from burning Troy and making his way to Italy, ultimately to found the city of Rome—at the center of the entire struggle. The titular vehicle of infiltration is here again, this time planned by a well-played Ulysses (John Drew Barrymore). The action in this muscleman epic offers the expected fun, particularly at the absurdly contrived funeral games of Patroclus.

While Homer's *Iliad* has earned four film treatments, his later work of adventure and fantasy, the *Odyssey,* has earned five. (This excludes, of course, the film of James Joyce's *Ulysses.*) Following Le Bargy's *The Return of Ulysses* (1908), *Homer's Odyssey* (*L'Odissea,* 1911) featured the company of Milan's La Scala. Less primitive than its Iliadic counterpart, the film includes surprisingly sophisticated special effects sequences in which the giant Cyclops eats one of Ulysses' men and throws a huge boulder at his ships. Many of the more

68   Despite the warning to "beware of Greeks bearing gifts," these Trojans in *The Trojan Horse* (1962) cheer their apparent victory as the wooden horse, pregnant with death, stands ominously in their midst. More Minoan-Mycenaean bulb-topped columns can be seen on the porch at the left.

popular episodes of Homer's epic are included—Penelope's unraveling her tapestry at night; Ulysses' encounters with the Sirens, Calypso, and Nausicaa; the suitor's throwing the stool at Ulysses; the bow contest; and the secret of Ulysses' bed. Most intriguing are the few shots of Ulysses' patron deity, Athena. She fades in and out and changes Ulysses' clothes with the magical powers available only to a goddess or special-effects technician. Rarely seen today, this silent version of the *Odyssey* still preserves the poem's original spirit of heroic fantasy.

The Lux–Ponti–De Laurentiis coproduction of *Ulysses* (1955) remains the finest of all film versions of the Homeric poems. Like the *Odyssey, Ulysses* begins in Ithaca, where faithful but ambiguously widowed Penelope (Silvana Mangano) awaits some news of her lost husband. Downstairs we hear a blind bard (shades of Homer) sing amid fairly authentic Mycenaean decor; he sings of the Greek exploits at Troy. This song produces the flashback of Ulysses (Kirk Douglas) at Troy; he is being cursed by Cassandra for violating Neptune's temple. The gloomy lighting and archaic flavor of these opening scenes in a Mycenaean/Geometric-period megaron dissolve into a grubby Ulysses sleeping on a sandy beach. Shipwrecked and lost in a storm, he has suffered a loss of memory. Beginning appropriately in medias res, *Ulysses* now places its hero at the colorful Phaeacian court of Alcinous. All the Phaeacians are dressed as Minoans, with tight-waisted pleated skirts for women and rich robes with long, curled and braided hair for the men.

Ulysses soon gets his memory back, and we relive with him the great adventures with the Cyclops Polyphemus, the Sirens, Circe, and Hades. Each adventure is treated with impressionistic brushstrokes that employ some of Homer's profound lines. Huge, hairy Polyphemus (played by the ex-Olympic wrestler Umberto Silvestri) is a perfect combination of the horrible, the grotesque, the clever, and the laughable. With realistic effects by the innovative Eugen Shuftan, Polyphemus grabs one of the little Ithacans and maws his bloody limbs. "These Greeks are stringy meat," he bellows in a deep voice. We laugh even as we are shocked by the gruesomeness. The audacious Ulysses soon makes wine for Polyphemus —a gift for which the grateful Cyclops "will eat Ulysses last" (*Odyssey* 9, 369–70). Never mind that wine needs fermentation; Ulysses leads his men in a feverish rhythmic chant as they stomp on basket after basket of purple grapes, and the gullible giant clumsily claps his hands in bizarre syncopation. The frenzied scene climaxes in the brutal blinding of Polyphemus. As Ulysses sails away to safety and Polyphemus randomly hurls gigantic chunks of cliff into the surf, the Greek brashly taunts the son of Neptune: "Remember the stringy Greeks! Who is mightier now—the god with his trident or the man with his grapes? Roar on, sightless drunkard, roar on! I am Ulysses, sacker of cities, destroyer of Troy, Son of Laertes, and King of Ithaca!" With his red beard and rugged chest, Kirk Douglas embodies the reckless yet crafty Ulysses: sometimes too bold, sometimes too cruel, not perfect, but human, Douglas is a Homeric Ulysses.

The siren episode also deserves the highest praise. To portray a music "so haunting that it led men to their death," director Mario Camerini put Alessandro Cicognini's intensifying choral music to the lamenting recitation by Penelope and Telemachus. Thus the Sirens lure Ulysses in the beckoning voices of his wife and son, exploiting the vulnerability of a man who has not seen his beloved wife and child in well over a decade. Lashed to the mast, he struggles against thick ropes while listening to the loud, tantalizing cries of wife and son; all this is set before the beeswax-eared sailors who row silently and swiftly behind him.

In contrast, the scene on Circe's island offers the amusing spectacle of Ithacans changed into pigs by a puff of smoke, then suffering the kicks of an uncomprehending Ulysses, who has called for his men doesn't recognize them in their porcine guise. "What are these pigs doing here?" he says, with comic frustration. Mangano plays Circe as well as Penelope, a cinematic strategy that accents the sorceress's mysterious power over Ulysses.

The Homeric enchantress Calypso is conflated with Circe for the sake of economy. Circe, like Calypso in the epic, offers Ulysses immortality, "the greatest gift offered to mankind," if he will stay with her. When Ulysses refuses, Circe raises the stakes by showing him the entrance to Hades. He does not descend to the edge of the Underworld as in the *Odyssey*, but several shades of past acquaintances appear to him in an effectively

69   Polyphemus, the monophthalmic carnivore, as portrayed by the ex-Olympic wrestler Umberto Silvestri in *Ulysses* (1955). His rough movements, gravelly voice, and bizarre humor ("These Greeks are stringy meat!") create an unforgettable impression.

smoky and deathly atmospheric tableau. Achilles' ghost moans one of the most profound lines in Homer: "I'd rather slave among the wondering barbarians than be king among all the dead" (*Odyssey* 11, 489–91). Ajax and Agamemnon rue their respective deaths by suicide and faithless wife. Death is horrible, yet Ulysses decides to remain a mortal—"I hope if men ever speak of me, it will be as one of them"—and prepares to sail home.

By telescoping the Hades, Circe, and Calypso sequences, the film adapts a broad range of Homer's dramatic and philosophical aims in an economical form appropriate to cinema. The strategy is artistically innovative yet true to the spirit of the source. Greco-Roman mythology has survived for so many years because it has always been flexible and allowed for artistic variation. *Ulysses* deserves to be appreciated with the same tolerance and understanding as Monteverdi's *Orfeo* or Chaucer's *Troilus and Criseyde:* all three works of art are entitled to the same mythopoetic license.

While no film should be expected to transfer a four hundred–page epic poem onto the screen, *Ulysses* preserves the archaic, mysterious aura of the *Odyssey,* along with the adventurous character of its hero and the fantastic oddity of his encounters at sea. Each of the famous episodes is rearranged slightly—the nature of the Sirens' music, for example, or the omission of the "No Man" ruse in the Cyclops sequence. But Ben Hecht,

70   This early-fifth-century
B.C. Greek vase depicting
Ulysses blinding the cyclops
Polyphemus contains a serious
narrative mistake: the cyclops
has two eyes! It is not just the
cinema that can be accused of
historical inaccuracies.

Hugh Gray, and Irwin Shaw combined to write one of the most entertaining and apoth-egmatic scripts of its kind. By no means a flawless film (the dubbing is weak, as are some of the minor characters), *Ulysses* still ranks high. A bit shallow on the surface and crude in realization, it captures the spirit of the earliest fantasy novel of Western civilization.

Mario Bava produced an Italian made-for-television film version of the *Odyssey* in 1969. Bava himself had long experience in the genre, starting simply as a crew member on the Steve Reeves *Hercules,* progressing to assistant director on the sequel *Hercules Unchained,* and then advancing to cinematographer and director on such other early Italian sword-and-sandal films as *Giant of Marathon, Esther and the King,* and *Hercules in the Haunted World.* His codirector was Franco Rossi, who later directed the Italian television version of *Quo Vadis?* (1985), *A Child Called Jesus* (1987), and a version of the *Aeneid.* In 1997 Francis Ford Coppola led a team of producers and created an ambitious made-for-television *Odyssey* that ran for four hours in May 1997. Directed by Andrei Konchalovsky, most of whose prior work had been in Russia and Europe, and starring Armand Assante, the film reverently works through episode by episode, ignoring the in medias res structure of the original and employing special effects that are only on occasion genuinely "special." For the voyage through Hades the television screen is filled with burning bits, but the scene is more a theme-park boat-ride through a fiery Christian Hellish inferno than the sobering gloom of the Homeric Land of the Dead. The brightest moment of the mini-series is the brief appearance by Hermes (Freddy Douglas), who, though the wings on his winged sandals do not move, let alone flutter, does hover nicely above Calypso's (Vanessa Williams) rock-top cavern, impudently delivers his message, then skyrockets back into the distance as quickly as he appeared from it.

The Homeric poems were part of a large epic genre that included other well-known ancient Greek myths. After the Trojan War cycle, the best known mythological

71/72   The *Argo* on
its way to find the
Golden Fleece in *Jason
and the Argonauts*
(1963). The ship is
actually a twin-engine
fishing barge with
ancient trappings. Aft
is the intentionally
misplaced figurehead
of Hera. A model for
the ship can be seen on
a fifth-century B.C.
vase painting: Ulysses
is lashed to the ship's
mast while the Sirens
swoop about the ship.
Jason and the Argonauts
copied the sail, mast,
apotropaic eye, prow
curve, rudder, railings,
oars, and rigging for
the *Argo*.

cycle concerned the romantic adventure tale of Jason, his quest for the Golden Fleece, and his encounter with the alluring sorceress Medea. An early Italian sword-and-sandal import, *The Giants of Thessaly* (1960) was the first sound film to retrieve the Golden Fleece from Colchis, but this Ricardo Freda import has little to do with the Greeks' legends, contaminating the original myth with such absurdities as talking sheep on the island of the Lemnian Women, the embittered hag/sorceress Gaia, and a stowaway named Atalanta, who is condemned to death until Orpheus—the expert in all matters of love—turns the condemnation to Love itself. The film even steals a page from Homer's (second) book, when a campily magnificent hirsute cyclops is killed by a toothpick-sized spear that Jason heaves into his lone eye.

By far the most profound film version of this myth is Pasolini's stark and symbolic *Medea* (1970), a metarealistic depiction of the struggle between a barely civilized Greek and a naturalist cult in Colchis. Appended to his film version of Euripides' play, this powerful mythological excursion will be discussed in Chapter 7, along with other ancient Greek dramas based on myths—*Oedipus Rex, Electra, Hippolytus, The Bacchae, Antigone, Iphigenia,* and *The Trojan Women.*

Columbia's *Jason and the Argonauts* (1963) is based on the *Argonautica,* by the Hellenistic poet Apollonius of Rhodes, but the famous story about the quest for the Golden Fleece is romanticized indiscriminately. The infamously cruel Oriental sorceress Medea (Nancy Kovack) is portrayed as a helpless, large-breasted, dancing Kewpie doll, and Jason (Todd Armstrong) is utterly colorless and physically unimpressive. But in spite of these severe flaws in characterization and casting, several aspects of the film excel in conception and execution.

The gods and goddesses of ancient Greece are shown in their lofty-columned palace on Mount Olympus. Bravo just for the attempt! The deities look down at the earth through a small pool of water, and they play chess with men's fates on a huge table. The treatment of these deities is tongue-in-cheek, an approach that offended many film critics, who apparently did not realize that the epic poets Homer and Ovid *(Metamorphoses)* depicted the gods with similar irreverence. Hera (Honor Blackman) and Zeus (Niall McGinnis) argue humorously as the bickering Mr. and Ms. Thunderbolt; their uppercrust British tone is appropriately haughty. Unfortunately, the only other Olympian god featured is Hermes (Michael Gwynn, who also played in *Barabbas, Cleopatra,* and *The Fall of the Roman Empire*). Among the mortals, Nigel Green (Hercules) and Lawrence Naismith (Argus) carry the transitional scenes.

Without question, *Jason and the Argonauts* is best known for the superb special effects of Ray Harryhausen. Thanks to him, the film surpasses all its predecessors in re-creating the fantastic aspects of Greek myth. With his unique SuperDynamation, Harryhausen brings to life such creatures as the huge, bronze, Cretan robotic Talos, who creaks with every move and metallically stomps after the Lilliputian Argonauts. When Jason loosens a bolt in the giant's bronze Achilles' heel and lets out his liquid *ichor,* Talos cracks

73   The unsurpassed Harpies from *Jason and the Argonauts*. Their eerie screech, slimy green skin, fluttering wings, and aggressive attacks on blind Phineus are representative of Ray Harryhausen's ability to create live images of Greek myth. The temple in the rear is the actual temple of Neptune (fifth century B.C.) at Paestum in southern Italy.

into pieces of patina and crashes to the earth. At the climax of the film Jason slays a writhing, hissing, seven-headed dragon, but King Aeëtes immediately sows its seven teeth in the earth and calls on Hecate, Goddess of the Night, to avenge the Hydra. Amazingly (and unmatched in any other version of the Jason myth), seven skeleton-swordsmen spring up. To the accompaniment of eerie woodwind music from Bernard Herrmann's score, this skeleton battalion marches on the stunned Greeks, attacking, hacking, and leaping with incredibly lifelike movements, until Jason leaps into the sea for safety. Earth-born men were part of Apollonius's poem, but they were flesh and blood, not skeletons; this was an idea that Harryhausen had conjured for an earlier film, *The Seventh Voyage of Sinbad* (1958). Apollonius himself, a master of scholarship and contrivance, would probably have borrowed these terrifying skeleton warriors from *The Seventh Voyage of Sinbad* if he had had the opportunity.

    Talos, the Hydra, and the skeletal warriors are the most famous of Harryhausen's creations in *Jason and the Argonauts,* but two horrible green Harpies convey the most vivid impression of any Greek mythological monsters seen on film. Shot before the mossy remains of the temple of Neptune at Paestum in southern Italy, this scene is memorable for the chaos created by the Harpies' bizarre screeching and their abrupt, irregular flying movements. Their skin is bumpy and slimy, their faces otherworldly, their voices thinner than paper. It took Harryhausen about two years to complete the SuperDynamation for *Jason and the Argonauts,* but the superiority of his fantasy creations are well worth the time and expense. Harryhausen's genius takes our impression of the Greek mythological world into a new dimension of visual reality. And he recognized his achievement with suitable pride: "Of the thirteen fantasy features I have been connected with, I think *Jason* pleases me the most."[1]

A timid update of the quest for the Golden Fleece is NBC's made-for-television movie *Jason and the Argonauts* (2000). Hallmark Entertainment, the production company responsible also for the network's *Odyssey,* again reduces Medea (Jolene Blalock), arguably the most dynamic and treacherous female character ever created in the history of Western drama, to a romantic wimp. She does not chop her brother to pieces, she is not responsible for Pelias's death, and, worst of all, the film concludes with her joyous marriage to Jason, with nary a hint of their infamous, infanticidal divorce. This grave omission negates the myth's great power and thereby reduces the film from mythological drama to happily-ever-after fairy tale.

Then again, as a fairy tale *Jason and the Argonauts* (2000) plays nicely. The quest for the Golden Fleece is by nature an episodic tale, and many of the episodes are imaginative and well executed. The poet Apollonius, in one of his sillier moments, tells us that while the other Argonauts slept, Hercules rowed the *Argo* by himself, using tree trunk–size oars. A clever variation in the film has the *Argo* appear to sail away to fool Aeëtes, but then we see Hercules at sea rowing the *Argo* all by himself—with regular-sized oars linked to all the other oars.

The serpent that guards the fleece was perhaps inspired by Disney's gigantic serpentine Hydra in *Hercules,* and the monstrous Neptune surely derives from the 1963 version of the myth. But thanks to *Hercules: The Legendary Journeys,* computer-generated monsters fare well in such made-for-television movies. The winged, grisly Harpies have the horrid countenances of gargoyles, and their shrieks mix beastly growls with bird-warblings. The latter are particularly appropriate, not just because the ancient Harpies were part woman and part bird but because the film's scene is set in a Mycenaean tholos tomb much like the one used for *Clash of the Titans:* any modern visitor to the "Tomb of Atreus" at Mycenae will hardly ignore the frequent and acrobatic entrances and exits of noisily warbling sparrows. Like its 1963 counterpart, this film eliminates the winged sons of Boreas, Zetes and Calais, who chase away the Harpies in Apollonius's epic, and replaces them with Hercules battering in the outer dome of the tholos and causing the falling ashlar masonry to crush the Harpies below. The computer-generated, bronze-hooved, fire-breathing bull offers some menacing moments to Jason, but the computer-generated earth-born warriors lack any personality at all. Jason makes quick work of them by bending over and letting them kill each other, as the ancient myth prescribes, and then it is on to the next commercial break.

74 Harryhausen's mytho-
logical beasts are often hybrids.
For *Sinbad and the Eye of the
Tiger* (1977) he created this
robotic Minotaur named
Minoton.

When the "ancient" film factory slowed to a crawl in the late 1960s, Harryhausen
pushed on, trusting in his art and the perennial support of children's audiences rather than
in market trends. In several Sinbad movies he inserted even more mythological creatures
from ancient Greece, including a Cyclopean Centaur in *The Golden Voyage of Sinbad*
(1973) and the robotic Minotaur ("Minoton"), as well as a voyage to the Land of the Hy-
perboreans, in *Sinbad and the Eye of the Tiger* (1977). Then, during the "ancient" renascence in the late 1970s, Harryhausen created his last hurrah, *Clash of the Titans* (1981),
which features the heroic myth in which Perseus beheads Medusa. Once again Beverley
Cross's *(Jason and the Argonauts)* screenplay focuses on a formulaic but engaging romance
between the hero (Harry Hamlin) and a princess, in this case Andromeda (Judi Bowker).

This time the star-studded cast of gods on Olympus—Sir Laurence Olivier as
Zeus, Claire Bloom as Hera, Ursula Andress as Aphrodite, and Maggie Smith as Thetis—
have exchanged their human-viewing pool for a cabinet filled with voodoo-esque statuettes
representative of the human race, and Burgess Meredith plays Perseus's delightfully impish but ever-irritated mentor Ammon. There is also a wonderfully devilish group of "Stygian Witches" (one of whom is played by Flora Robson), who are actually the ancient
Greek mythological *Graiai,* demon-women who were born so old that they have to share
their sole working eye, which Perseus ultimately steals from them.

Once again Harryhausen's creations carry the film. He begins with the giant merman Kraken (an inexplicably Teutonic beast), who rises from his underwater abode to destroy the city of Argos with a Hellenic tsunami. Then Harryhausen offers us the flying
horse Pegasus, a magnificent white winged stallion whom Perseus captures, tames, and
rides through the clouds to the uplifting strains of Laurence Rosenthal's ethereal music.
Along the way Perseus encounters the Stygian Witches and a superfluous limping, monstrous mute named Calibos (Neil McCarthy) before coming face-not-quite-to-face with

Medusa. Harryhausen's Medusa is an interesting creation. In ancient Greek art she is usually depicted as humanlike, save for a hideous face distinguished by a broad mouth and nose, swollen lips, fangs, and topped, of course, with a head full of snakes where hair belongs. In one famous archaic representation now in the Louvre she has the body of a horse. In *Clash of the Titans* she still has the requisite coiffure of snakes, but Harryhausen makes her an archer with a serpentine tail instead of legs.

In an interview in 1981 Harryhausen told me that he changed Medusa's appearance because the traditional Gorgon just did not look frightening enough; she needed to look more menacing and to be more terrifying. A similar cinematic imperative inspired Harryhausen to introduce Pegasus early in the film, even though our ancient Greek sources tell us that the winged horse sprang from the severed head of Medusa. He asked me whether I enjoyed seeing Pegasus on the large silver screen seemingly flying across the heavens. When I answered yes, he said, "That's why we used him all through the film!" What is particularly interesting about the liberties Harryhausen took with his sources is that all the great mythographers of antiquity—Hesiod, Homer, Pindar, Euripides, Vergil, and Ovid, among others—changed myths according to the requirements of their message, theology, or artistic style. Ancient Greek myths were not written in stone but were flexible, dynamic tales changed and adjusted by every storyteller, songster, and poet. That Harryhausen and Beverley Cross gave Pegasus birth before the death of Medusa—or, for that matter, that they had Perseus, rather than the hero Bellerophon, ride Pegasus at all—was an artistic decision guided by poetic license and aesthetic and narrative judgment.

After the success of *Clash of the Titans,* Harryhausen toyed with the idea of making a film about Hercules' labors. As it turned out, though, he opted instead to escape the pressures of filmmaking. After the Museum of Modern Art in New York honored his special-effects work with a retrospective, Harryhausen retired to become a full-time sculptor.

There were two earlier versions of the Perseus myth. *Perseus the Invincible* (1962; also released as *Medusa vs. the Son of Hercules* and under a number of other titles) faithfully if crudely presents the story of Perseus, Medusa, and Andromeda. *Winds of Change* (1978) is a childishly charming Japanese animated feature film enhanced by an international crew, including narrator Peter Ustinov. The film takes its newly invented hero Wondermaker through a series of adventures, including episodes illustrating the Ovidian tales of Acteon, Orpheus, and Phaethon. In the segment involving Perseus and Medusa, Pegasus is portrayed as part horse, part bird, and part dragon.

Perseus the Invincible was just one of scores of films that followed in the wake of *Hercules* (1959). In fact, no single film based on a Greek myth has been more influential than this Joseph E. Levine box-office smash of 1959. Raking in as much as $18 million (depending on whose figures you believe), thanks to a Herculean advertising effort, Levine metamorphosed his $120,000 investment in this 1957 Italian-made film *(Le Fatiche di Ercole)* into an overnight fortune. No one has ever denied that the film has serious

75/76   Harryhausen's mythical worlds depend not
only on special effects but on makeup and set design
as well. In the foreground of this interior photo from
Clash of the Titans (1981) are the long-haired
"Stygian witches" *(Graiai),* women born old. The
huge entrance stones formed into posts, lintel, and
relieving triangle are Mycenaean, as are the circular
colonnade with repetitive decoration above the thin,
inverted columns. Similar design can be seen in the
entrance to the Bronze Age tomb of Atreus at
Mycenae.

drawbacks—the long stay with the crescent-helmeted Amazons, the abysmal dubbing, the thin characterizations, the hokey atmosphere—but this film was the prototype for an entire genre. *Hercules* was the first neo-Italian cloak-and-sandal film that had no pretense except to turn historical action and romance into profitable entertainment—a dubious distinction, perhaps, but a distinction nonetheless. Eschewing the periodic profundity of *Ulysses,* the seriousness of *Fabiola* (1948), and the quasi-historicity of *Attila* (1955), the film focuses on gushy love and pure, exciting adventure, and the male stars have new requirements: eighteen-inch biceps and fifty-plus-inch chests.

Playing the title role was the most perfectly formed specimen of male musculature captured on film to date. Steve Reeves had broken into film in *Athena* three years before *Hercules* was filmed in Italy in 1957, but the new film vaulted him into fame and fortune. His smooth, sculptured, Hellenically proportioned physique stretched, pulled, grasped, and displayed itself on every page of the perfunctory screenplay, while American audiences argued nonstop about whether such a build was beauty or beast. In the meantime, there was a film going on, and the film had some worthwhile moments.

The story of *Hercules* is reasonably faithful to several ancient Greek myths about the demigod, son of Zeus and the human Alcmene. After tearing out a huge tree by its roots to stop the runaway horses of princess Iole (Apollonius, *Argonautica* 1.1180 ff.), Hercules comes to Jolco (Iolkos) to be Master of Arms. In the exercise yard he astounds everyone—including Aesculapius, Laertes, Orpheus, Argus, Castor, and Pollux—by throwing a discus beyond the horizon (to the effective warblings of a Moog). The scene reaches its climax when all the other Greeks back away from the mighty Theban. They are afraid because he has thrown the discus too far: he cannot be human; too strong for the rest of mankind, he stands alone. Although the philosophy behind the scene is treated in a shallow manner, it at least hints at the loneliness and isolation Hercules confronts in Euripides' *Heracles.*

Hercules then meets young and wily Ulysses. He ironically tells Ulysses (in a deep, dubbed voice), "Some day a bow and arrow may decide your fate." We must smile. But soon tragedy enters Jolco. Hercules kills a ravenous lion who has been terrorizing the countryside, but not before it kills the young prince Iphitus (Mimmo Palmara). Hercules, who had been Iphitus's guardian, is blamed for his death. To atone for his crime Hercules must serve as a vassal to the evil Eurystheus, who sets forth a series of seemingly impossible labors. All these events are more or less according to actual Greek mythology, though the chronology is somewhat confused. They give us the impression of a Hercules who is almost immortal, yet also a Hercules who suffers loneliness among mortals because of his share in divinity. As in the myth, Hercules' irrational passion causes the death of Iphitus, and leads to Hercules' travails. "Even the greatest strength carries with it a measure of mortal weakness," proclaim the opening titles of the film. In the early episodes, the film is a delightful combination of adventure, muscles, comedy, and mythology. Thereafter it falls apart.

Hercules begins his canonical labors by battling the Cretan Bull (a European Bison in the film). He goes with Jason on the quest for the Golden Fleece, and after encountering a gynarchy of warrior Amazons (Lemnian women) and some furry creatures (Apollonius 1.940 ff.), he returns to Jolco to find that Jason's uncle Pelias and Eurystheus have double-crossed him. Imprisoned via trapdoor in an underground cell, Hercules rips his chains from the wall, crashes through the door, and fights off one hundred armed soldiers by swinging the heavy iron chains around his head. He chases all the soldiers onto the porch of the palace, where he wraps each chain around a pillar. Flexing a magnificent, Mr. Universe–winning *V,* he yanks the supporting columns and crushes his enemies under the roof of the porch. *Vae victis!* Hercules and his girlfriend, Iole (Sylva Koscina), ride off into the sunset arm in arm.

The romance in *Hercules* is light, the action absurdly heroic, the evil characters without any redeeming characteristics, and the rest comically likable. Director Pietro Francisci, whose previous directorial work had been in such heavy-handed, historical films as *Queen of Sheba* (1952) and *Attila* (1954), develops his peculiar style of light-hearted adventure in this amusing production, the result of which is an uneven film of dubious merit. Nonetheless, there are several enjoyable and mythologically worthy sequences, and the film paved the way for the scores and scores of muscleman epics that followed in the next four years.

Following his successful *Hercules,* Joseph E. Levine defended his hard-sell tactics, announcing, "We are reminding everyone that this is a circus business."[2] To publicize the opening of the sequel *Hercules Unchained* (*Ercole e la regina di Lidia,* 1959), Levine threw a huge garden party in Hollywood, complete with a large statue of Hercules made out of ice, with variously colored light bulbs for muscles. To seven hundred press and movie people he gave four-pound chocolate statuettes of his mythological strongman.

As with its predecessor, the plot of *Hercules Unchained* is based in part on Greek mythology. The sequel begins where *Hercules* left off. In the Greek city of Thebes, Oedipus's semi-illegitimate sons, Eteocles and Polynices, are contesting the kingship. From the pages of Sophocles' *Oedipus at Colonus* comes the mysterious death of the blind widower and orphan, Oedipus. From the pages of Aeschylus's *Seven Against Thebes* comes the famous battle at the city's seven gates. Also mythologically sound is the movie's depiction of Omphale (Sylvia Lopez), the lascivious queen who keeps Hercules imprisoned against his will. We also see the mythological Antaeus (the ex-wrestling and boxing champ Primo Carnera), who is the child of Earth; he cannot be beaten in battle so long as he has contact with his alma mater, so Hercules kills him by lifting him off the ground with a bear hug. Francisci directed the film in the same light romantic style of the original, combining adventure and humor, mythology and complete fabrication. Very, very far from being a mythological masterpiece, *Hercules Unchained* employs its cheap sets and costumes, imaginative love triangles, and muscular feats to create another triumph of mundane entertainment.

77/78   In *Hercules* (1957) the Cretan bull (here a European bison) pins Hercules (Steve Reeves) against a hillside. The ancients had a different conception of how an ideal Hercules should look, as an early-fifth-century B.C. depiction of the demigod's seventh labor illustrates. This Hercules' girth and lack of proportion would prevent him from winning the Mr. Universe title claimed by modern Herculeses Steve Reeves and Arnold Schwarzenegger.

The mighty success of *Hercules* and *Hercules Unchained* gave birth to many feeble films in the next few years. Sequels to the sequel—*Ulysses vs. the Son of Hercules,* for example, and *Hercules, Samson, and Ulysses* (directed by Francisci), and even the quadruply implausible *Hercules, Maciste, Samson, and Ursus,* bringing out of retirement the stalwarts from *Cabiria,* the Old Testament, and *Quo Vadis?* to join the strongman of the hour—were produced ad infinitum and, inter alia, ad nauseam. In the next ten years, approximately twenty-five Hercules movies were released in bulging muscularscope. The quality of most of these *Hercules* sequels and imitations is generally poor, from both the cinematic and the mythological standpoint, but they have earned at least passing mention: *Ercole contro Moloch* (*Conquest of Mycenae,* 1963), in which Hercules, called "Glaucus" (Gordon Scott),

79   Hercules (Steve Reeves) exhibits a prize-winning V-shaped flex before Samsonesquely
destroying the palace of Jolco in *Hercules*. The gilded columns and mural-sized vase paintings are
absurdly inauthentic, but Reeves's well-proportioned musculature, a mythologically plausible plot,
and Herculean advertising earned this film $18 million and created a new genre of film—the
muscleman epic of the late 1950s and early 1960s.

battles against the tyrannical priests of Moloch in the city of Mycenae; *The Challenge of
the Giant* (1965), in which Hercules battles with Antaeus; *Hercules in the Haunted World*
(1961), in which Hercules' mythological paramour, Deianeira, is imprisoned by Lichas
(Christopher Lee), the agent of Pluto, so Hercules (Reg Park) and Theseus together venture
into the Underworld on her behalf to retrieve a magical flower; *Hercules and the Captive
Women* (*Hercules and the Conquest of Atlantis,* 1961), in which Hercules (Reg Park) visits
the mythical Atlantidean kingdom and there sees the ever-changing Proteus, the one-
man mythological zoo; *The Loves of Hercules* (1960), in which Hercules (Mickey Hargitay)
falls in love with Deianeira (Jayne Mansfield), the daughter of King Eurytus of Oechalia
(though mythologically this should be Iole), then fights Achelous and Queen Hippolyte's
Amazons; and *La Vendetta di Ercole* (*Goliath and the Dragon,* 1960), in which Hercules
(Mark Forest) battles against his mythological adversary Eurytus once again. This time
Broderick Crawford plays Eurytus, King of Oechalia, and his three-headed dog (that is,

Cerberus) gives Hercules a scare, though its barks are worse than its bites. Other Hercules films that make little pretense about re-creating Greek mythology include *Hercules of the Desert* (1960), a veritable Western; *Hercules Against the Mongols* (1960), in which Herc matches up with the three sons of Genghis Khan; *Hercules Against the Barbarians* (1964), in which Herc meets the great Genghis Khan himself; *Hercules Against the Sons of the Sun* (1963), in which Hercules battles against the Incas (!); *Hercules and the Giant Warriors* (1964), in which Hercules (Dan Vadis) must face ten bronze soldiers; *Hercules Against Rome* (1960), in which Hercules (Alan Steel) brings justice to the Caesars; *Hercules and the Black Pirate* (1962), set in sixteenth-century Spain; *Hercules, Prisoner of Evil* (1964), in which the strongman faces werewolves; *Hercules and the Masked Rider* (1963), set in the seventeenth century; *Hercules Against the Moon Men* (1964), which by now should not sound too surprising; *Hercules and the Tyrants of Babylon* (1964), which at least has something to do with antiquity; and *Hercules in New York* (1970), which starred another champion bodybuilder, one who barely spoke any English (Arnold Schwarzenegger, billed as Arnold Strong). Just a year later Adventure Cartoons produced *The Mighty Hercules* for Saturday-morning television.

Reeves and Schwarzenegger had made Hercules films the (dis)proving ground for would-be actor/bodybuilders, so Lou Ferrigno, whose film debut had been in Schwarzenegger's documentary *Pumping Iron* (1977), starred in two subsequent Hercules films, *Hercules* (1983) and *Hercules II* (1985), in the renascence of ancient films more than two decades after the original was made. When the Hercules juggernaut was in high gear in the 1960s, *Hercules and the Princess of Troy* (1965) was filmed as a pilot for a television series, but the Gordon Scott vehicle was never put into production. Apparently the time was not right. Almost thirty years later, with dozens of additional television networks and channels available through cable and satellite delivery systems, a series of 1994 pilot films starring Kevin Sorbo *(Hercules and the Lost Kingdom, Hercules and the Amazon Women, Hercules and the Circle of Fire, Hercules in the Underworld,* and *Hercules and the Maze of the Minotaur)* was much more successful. The essential formula in these films is to characterize Hercules as tall, handsome, and physically imposing—but not a bodybuilder. He is vulnerable emotionally because of the loss of his wife Deianeira, and he is always wary of Hera, his eternal celestial enemy. The special effects are usually computer generated: two fine examples in *Hercules and the Amazon Women* show a child morphing into Hera and the Hydra sprouting new heads. The fight sequences are choreographed according to practices well-honed during the kung fu era two decades earlier. The successful pilots led ultimately to four syndicated television series, one each for Hercules, "young" Hercules, a Diana-like warrior named Xena, and Sinbad. Sinbad's connection with Greek myth in the series doubtless owes more to Ray Harryhausen's work in the 1970s than to the influence of Greek myth on the medieval *Tales of the Arabian Nights.*

In the wake of this new Hercules mania among a mostly adolescent audience, Disney aimed at even younger moviegoers with its animated feature *Hercules* (1997).

Packaged with fast-food-restaurant purchase offers and a huge merchandizing campaign (which was simultaneously satirized and promoted in the film itself), the enterprise turned a $245 million profit as just one in a revitalized series of annual Disney animated features. Its success is no surprise, for in many ways the film is much more clever than its young audience (and many parents) could appreciate. The opening, in which the Motown Chorus of Muses comes to life from a vase painting to sing a prologue summarizing the Greek creation myth recounted in Hesiod's *Theogony,* is already beyond the youngsters. Later we see the three heads of Cerberus fight over a steak and the conflated Fates/Graiai (the *Clash of the Titans* influence again) predict, "Indoor plumbing: it's gonna be big!" The self-destructive power of blue-flame-headed Hades (James Woods), with his silly companions Pain and Panic, is similarly beyond the ken of the youngest viewers, and all these details depend on a thorough and irreverent rethinking of Greek myth.

On the other hand, in a nod to the young audience and the Disney image, the film softens the ancient confusion between Hercules' biological father Zeus and his mortal father Amphitryon. In this version, Pain and Panic steal Hercules from his Olympian crib, drug him with some "Grecian Formula" to make him mortal, and drop him to the earth, where Amphitryon and Alcmene adopt him. Hercules develops into a strong and unintentionally destructive teenager, who knocks down the columns of an entire stoa in one fell swoop. This creates the isolation that is so important in contemporary Herculean characterizations. Hercules tells his troubles to a statue of Zeus, which, as in Pausanias's ancient description of the image of the god at Olympia, comes to life and reveals Hercules' divine birth. Zeus promises that Hercules can become a god if he can prove himself a "true hero." Aided by the Yoda-like satyr Philoctetes (Danny DeVito: "Call me Phil"), Pegasus (thanks again to *Clash of the Titans*), and the Academy Award–nominated song "Go the Distance," Hercules develops into a true hero, winning battles against the multi-multi-multiheaded Hydra (modeled after the computer animated version in *Hercules and the Amazon Women*) and the rumbling mountainlike Titans, who represent natural disasters. His final triumph, before his colorfully animated apotheosis, requires him to swim through the River of Death, a rather magnificent variation on the original Greek labors, in which Hercules conquers death, but another concept that is probably beyond the grasp of the film's primary audience.

The ancient Greeks had other mythological heroes besides Achilles, Ulysses, Hercules, Jason, and Perseus. Athens was the greatest city-state in Greece, and her favorite son was Theseus, who sailed to the island of Crete to kill the monstrous, semibovine progeny of King Minos. *The Minotaur* (1960, also entitled *Theseus Against the Minotaur* and *The Wild Beast of Crete*) stars two-time Olympic decathlon champion Bob Mathias. As you might expect, the film includes a sequence in which Theseus sportingly competes with a friend in the javelin, discus, and pole vault. All the characters from the Athenian/Cretan myth are in the film—Minos and his wife Pasiphaë, their daughters Ariadne and Phaedra, Theseus's father, Aegeus, and the Minotaur—as is the famous labyrinth in which the Minotaur is housed. But none of the characters has any complexity, and the myth has had major surgery: Aegeus does not commit suicide, Phaedra does not marry Theseus, and Theseus does not abandon Ariadne. Yet the use of the appropriate Minoan snake-goddess dresses, the reproduction of actual Minoan frescoes, and the atmospheric, turquoise Aegean hue that pervades most of the film improve at least the visual quality of the film and lend it at least a tincture of authenticity.

The labyrinth scene is the most praiseworthy of *The Minotaur*. The famed maze opens onto the king's court, where a mouth-shaped portal (à la *Cabiria*) takes seven maidens and seven lads to a horrible sacrificial death each year. Theseus enters the dark and cavernous labyrinth with torch and sword in hand, and in the echoing hollows he hears the threatening growling of the half-man, half-beast. Ariadne follows Theseus, cleverly tying a thread from her shawl to the portal so that she will be able to find her way back. Such well-known details from the ancient myth make an otherwise bland film palatable.

But fidelity to the myth alone cannot make a bad film good. Another Italian export, *My Son, the Hero (Arrivano i Titani,* 1963, also released as *The Titans),* contains a curious mixture of extensive mythological motifs and inane acrobatic antics. In the Underworld we see Sisyphus rolling his eternally burdensome rock, Tantalus reaching for inaccessible food, and Tityus offering his liver to hungry vultures. The Titans are chained to the rocky walls of Hades; Krios, their leader, sees the three Fates measuring, spinning, and cutting Destiny's thread. Medusa's famous beheading is here, too, as is a cyclops and Hades' cap of invisibility. Perhaps the most interesting of these mythological details is the scene from the Knossian bull-jumping fresco from Crete—not a painting, but the ritual itself. None of the mythological scenes is intelligently developed, though, and the characters are even sketchier. Equal proportions of muscle, acrobatics, humor, and mythological accuracy do not make *My Son, the Hero* any more than a harmless and mindless panorama of Greek mythology.

In contrast, a handful of films treat the images of Greek myth more symbolically. *Fellini Satyricon,* for instance, uses the image of escaping the labyrinth to illustrate a rite of passage from ridiculed youth to experienced adulthood. George Lucas's first film, *THX-1138,* a futuristic film about a totalitarian world, contains a climactic sequence in which the state prison turns out to be a labyrinth so pure and white that it needs no walls.

Both these films, like almost all the other symbolic treatments of Greek myths, belong to the post-*Cleopatra* (1963) era. But two seminal films by French directors, Jean Cocteau's *Orphée* (1949) and Marcel Camus's Brazilian *Black Orpheus* (1959), were the first to explore some of the profound meanings inherent in Greek myths. Not coincidentally, both treat the myth of the title character's heroic journey to Hades and conquest of death, but these passages of Orpheus look very different from the similar scenarios in Disney's *Hercules* and *My Son, the Hero.* Most obviously, rather than strictly re-creating a costume version of the well-known myth of love, death, tragedy, and triumph, Cocteau and Camus adapt the story of Orpheus and Eurydice into modern milieus to create films with a broader intellectual and temporal impact.

Cocteau cynically announced that *Orphée* set out to be "nothing but the para-phrase of a classical Greek myth," and he repeatedly tried to discourage deep interpreta-tions of the film.[3] In the film itself, Orpheus, a young French poet, is told, "You try too hard to understand what it all means, my dear sir. This is a great defect." But Cocteau is playing with us. He uses visual symbols, obscure phrases, and subtle touches of artistry to elevate the film from the "paraphrase of a classical Greek myth" to cinematic poetry. When we hear a sentence like "L'oiseau chante avec ses doigts" (The bird sings with its talons) broadcast over the radio of an imposingly dark Rolls-Royce, how can we do anything but try to figure out what it means? Yet Cocteau later disclosed that the sentence was nothing more than a favorite line sent to him by his fellow poet Guillaume Apollinaire in 1917.

Visual symbols at first confuse those who would analyze all of the film's eccen-tricities. "Hades" is entered by passing through mirrors. But Cocteau illuminates the puz-zling choice of a gateway to the Underworld: "Mirrors are the doors through which Death comes and goes. . . . Watch yourself in a mirror as you age and you will see death at work." Using the ruined military school of St. Cyr for Hades, Cocteau creates a stark and cold at-mosphere for his Land of the Dead. He mattes slow-motion and normal-speed shots in the same scenes to enhance photographically this strange atmosphere. Similarly, by using a large tub of viscous mercury, Cocteau makes a mirror "dissolve" as the gloved hand of Orpheus disappears into the nether region.

Death is the pervading theme of *Orphée,* but it goes hand in glove with love. Eury-dice wants death by suicide because Orpheus (Jean Marais) does not return her love; Orpheus does love her, yet he also loves and is loved by personified Death (Maria Casares); Orpheus goes back and forth between death and life, between a living love and a dead one. Both he and Eurydice wish for death, but they both come back from death after achieving it. Mixed with the themes of love and death are explorations of free will (especially in Heur-tebise's arguments with Death) and poetical inspiration (the radio obscures Orpheus's). The sum of all these themes suggests that a poet must love and die a number of times before he can reach perfection, and that in reaching death by putting one's gloved hands through a mirror, the poet does indeed "sing with his talons." But it would be foolhardy to reduce *Orphée* to this single meaning.

Cocteau refuses to restrict himself to a toga-clad, lyre-playing poet whose one purpose in life is to bring his Eurydice back from death. Instead, he transforms a gracefully aging Greek myth about a poet and death into a modern statement on poetry and death. In doing so, he makes a mythic contribution to the cinema. Much in the tradition of Vergil and Monteverdi, he has revived an age-old story in a brilliant piece of contempo-rary art. He continued to explore the themes of poetry, immortality, fame, and death in the delayed sequel, *The Testament of Orpheus* (1959).

Though less profound than Cocteau's masterwork, *Black Orpheus* (*Orfeu Negro,* 1960) was no less poetic and won an impressive share of awards in 1959–1960, including the Palme d'Or at Cannes and the Academy Award for best foreign-language film. Produced and shot in Brazil, it remains one of the few Brazilian films to become popular in the United States. During Carnival, white-dressed Eurydice (Marpessa Dawn, Camus's wife) comes to Rio de Janeiro to visit her cousin. The handsome streetcar conductor Orpheus (Breno Mello) sees the innocent newcomer, and gradually they fall into a gentle love, flavored by the lovely music that Orpheus sings and plays on his guitar. Also present are the mythological dog Cerberus who guards a metaphoric Hades and the elderly streetcar conductor named Hermes (in the myth, Psychopompos, "leader of souls"). In the tragic denouement, Eurydice is accidentally electrocuted; Orpheus takes her from the morgue as if to revive her, but he is struck in the head by a stone thrown by a jealous ex-girlfriend. He falls to his death with Eurydice in his arms. In Greek myth, when Orpheus is stoned to death by frenzied Bacchantes, his music carries on. In *Black Orpheus,* when Orpheus dies, three children pick up his guitar and sing, play, and dance to his song.

As in *Orphée,* the sequence in Hades is one of the most poetic. Instead of embarking on the traditional *katabasis* down into the Land of the Dead, this Orpheus travels up in an elevator to the twelfth floor of a modest skyscraper. It is the middle of the night, so the only person he finds there is the custodian, who, like Charon punting his ferry along the River Styx, has his hands grasped around a handle—of a broom. With that broom he pushes papers, countless pieces of small paper, each of which, he tells Orpheus, represents a person in the Lost and Found department. Camus is telling us that in the modern world we "lost souls" are bits of bureaucratic data, and then the final irony is that we learn that this Charon cannot even read! At the end of the scene we see scores of lost souls—pieces of paper—floating down the middle of a lengthy spiral staircase. The image suggests Dante's Hell, circle after circle inhabited by souls whom Dante and his guide Vergil compare to falling dead leaves. In case there is any doubt about Camus's symbolic purpose, at the bottom of the staircase Orpheus encounters a (one-headed) dog named Cerberus.

The plot of *Black Orpheus* is straightforward, but it is enlivened by its setting during Carnival. With scores of shots of smiling dancers and bouncing musicians, the colorful spectacle of the city between mountains and sea is a delight for the viewer. The splendid array of bright shades and all the colors of the spectrum scattered through the rhythmically active masquerading celebrants create an overwhelming environment of cheerfulness; in such cheerfulness the tragic death of Eurydice and Orpheus's desperate attempt to find her become all the more pitiable. An entire city's wild celebration dissolves suspensefully into Orpheus's solitary despair. The contrast between the peak of social revelry and the depths of personal tragedy make *Black Orpheus* an extraordinarily moving film. Elemental joy yields to elemental pathos, and Orpheus and Eurydice are crushed by inevitable forces of evil. Like *Orphée,* Camus's film borrows its plot from the Greek myth, then completely revitalizes it with a new setting and different approach.

Italy exported a few other mythological films in the early 1960s, most of them focused either on ancient history or on Hercules. In *Atlas Against the Cyclops (Maciste in the*

Land of the Cyclops, 1961), Capys, the daughter of Circe, presents Penelope and Ulysses' son and presents him to the vengeful Cyclops; in *Colossus and the Amazons* (1960), the Greeks return victoriously from Troy only to be imprisoned by the warrior women; and for Jordi Grau's Spanish film *Acteon* (1964), based on the story of Diana and Acteon, Ovid actually receives screenwriting credit. In the horror genre, Christopher Lee and Peter Cushing starred in Hammer Productions' *The Gorgon* (1964), in which the Gorgon Megaera inflicts terror and calcification on a German village; and Roger Corman and Charles Griffith, just months after releasing the camp classic-to-be *Little Shop of Horrors* (1960), offered their own Italianate film called *Atlas* (1960), an even worse film than the Italian sequels to the sequels.

Hercules, the Golden Fleece, and Hades are subjects of Greek mythology still recognizable to most people today, but fewer people associate the lost continent of Atlantis with ancient Greek myth. But long before the many books that have been published in the past three decades about the "real" Atlantis, the search for the famed lost world had originated in the dialogues of Plato in the fourth century B.C. Plato tells us Atlantis was a huge island in the ocean beyond the "Pillars of Hercules" (Gibraltar). Its inhabitants amassed a huge military force and invaded Greece and the Mediterranean world. The Atlanteans were defeated in battle, and soon afterward Atlantis suffered violent earthquakes, which sank the entire island to the ocean's depths.

George Pal's production of *Atlantis, the Lost Continent* (1961) followed this basic Platonic outline. Using modernistic technology worthy of his earlier production of *Destination Moon,* director-producer Pal equipped the ancient mythological kingdom of Atlantis with a gigantic solar-powered ray gun and a fleet of submarines. The combination of ancient world and modern scientific technology evokes memories of a serial in the 1930s, and indeed the twelve-part *Sharad of Atlantis* (1936) probably influenced Pal, but his film is far more polished. While Demetrius, an ancient Greek fisherman, and Antillia, the princess of Atlantis, row their little boat out in the "Atlantic Ocean," a submarine slowly and subtly appears in the background. It seems almost as if Pal expected everyone in the theater to rub their eyes in disbelief at the anachronism until the sub actually surfaces next to Demetrius's boat. The sequence is a memorable introduction to Atlantean technology.

The earthquake that levels Atlantis, a product of A. Arnold Gillespie's special effects, brings the mythological fantasy to a magnificently destructive conclusion. Gillespie borrowed scenes from MGM's earlier fiery holocaust in *Quo Vadis?* in rendering the flames, upheaval, and panic that culminate in the explosion of the powerful solar ray-gun. The towering white (model) buildings of Atlantis are voraciously swallowed by the voracious sea. The Atlantis that survives thus becomes mythology and speculation.

Atlantis appeared in several other films, none particularly notable. *The Siren of Atlantis* (1949) placed lost Atlantis under "a sea of sand"—in the Sahara Desert. Ruled by an evil but voluptuous queen, Atlantis lures unsuspecting French Foreign Legionnaires to their disgraceful deaths. The film features some interesting Tuareg music and choreography, but its pace is sluggish, and few would mind if *Siren* were lost with the legendary continent it deenergizes with a testudinariously slow cinematic pace. Atlantis appeared twice in muscleman epics, first in the previously mentioned *Hercules and the Captive Women (Ercole alla conquista di Atlantide),* whose palace is entered via Mycenae's Lion Gate, and then in *Kingdom in the Sand* (1963), where Atlantis is patrolled by an army of robot-powered zombies. The Hercules film does have one of the muscleman genre's most amusing moments: Androcles, ruler of Thebes and friend of Hercules (Reg Park), decides to invade Atlantis, but he fears that someone "will sit on my throne during my absence." Hercules assures him that he need not worry, picks up the stone throne, raises it above his head, and throws it to the floor, where it breaks into a hundred pieces. Androcles sullenly bemoans the whole affair: "What a waste of a good throne."

Roman mythology, like almost all Roman culture, is essentially the same as the Greeks'. Rome did produce some marvelous myths about her early history, though. The *Aeneid,* Vergil's epic poem about Rome's early mythological history, was the basis of *The Last Glory of Troy* (1962, also known as *The Legend of Aeneas*), a muscleman vehicle for Steve Reeves. The warrior Aeneas takes shiploads of his fellow Trojans from their city when, thanks to Ulysses and his wooden horse, it is destroyed. He leads the refugees to Italy, where they in turn become the invaders. After many battles with the local citizens, Aeneas finally wins and founds a new city. This city would in a few generations be relocated and renamed Rome. The film makes certain to include Nisus and Euryalus from Vergil's poem, as well as Pallas, Lavinia, and Turnus, though the gods are omitted.

The story about the mythological founding of Rome by Romulus, the famous twin brother of Remus, is elaborately told in the *Duel of the Titans* (*Romolo e Remo,* 1961). Written by Sergio Leone, the film starred two of the more talented musclemen of the era, Steve Reeves as Romulus and Gordon Scott as Remus, and costars included such genuine Italian actors as Massimo Girotti (Tatius) and Virna Lisi (Julia). *Duel of the Titans* traces the lives of the twins from their abandonment in the woods of Italy and their rescue by a she-wolf that nurtures the orphaned children with her milk. The boys grow up not knowing that their real mother, Rhea, was impregnated by a god, Mars. But when they find out, Remus is overcome by lust for power while Romulus desires peace, brotherhood, and civilized life in their newly founded city. At the climax of the film, Romulus performs the ceremonial investiture of a king, plowing the first furrow of the city with two white oxen. But Remus rides in to fight it out with his brother once and for all. In an impressive yet quick struggle full of energy and strength, Romulus kills Remus.

Duel of the Titans, a fairly faithful borrowing from Plutarch's *Life of Romulus* and Livy's *History of Rome,* takes care not to leave out Amulius, king of Alba Longa, and Titus Tatius, king of the Sabines. It also shows Romulus receiving his famous vulture omen. True, a bridge defender is obviously based on Horatius Cocles, a much later historical figure, but the film's chronology is not much more fanciful than Livy's. The look of the film

80   Steve Reeves, right, and Gordon Scott as the mytho-historical Romulus and Remus in *Duel of the Titans* (1961). One of the better muscleman epics, this film re-creates the primitive atmosphere surrounding the founders of Rome.

is enhanced by expansive crane shots of the beautiful, wooded Sabine hillsides not far from where the events of the ancient stories were supposed to have taken place in 753 B.C. Rapidly ascending and descending scales in the musical score by Piero Piccioni reflect the massive human migration that takes place as the humble proto-Roman caravan clatters with wood, rope, animals, and peasants. The costumes are fittingly simple and ragged for the relatively small crowds of villagers that would someday be described as the "illustrious" ancestors of mighty Rome. This primitive atmosphere elevates the film above most other sword-and-sandal movies of its day, making it worthy of bronze mythological and cinematic laurels. One other version of this classic ancient story has been filmed: *Romulus and the Sabines* (*Rape of the Sabines,* 1961), starring Roger Moore. Nor should we forget the "Sobbin' Women" sequence from Fox's early CinemaScope musical *Seven Brides for Seven Brothers* (1954), which is so dependent on the *Life of Romulus* that the lyric proclaims, "That's what Plutarch says."

A younger contemporary of Vergil's, Ovid wrote a number of Latin poems which helped make the entire corpus of Greco-Roman myths an artistic database for the next two millennia. Although the pre-animé Japanese compendium *Winds of Change* (1978) is the only film to concentrate solely on myths of Ovid's *Metamorphoses,* Julie Taymor's *Titus* (1999) re-creates several shocking moments from Ovid's gruesome tale of Philomela (*Met.* 6.424–676), who concocts a human stew to feed as punishment to the tyrant who raped her and ripped her tongue out; her prime ingredient was the tyrant's son.

Other films that are not centered in ancient myth contain several fine mythological sequences. Terry Gilliam created a vivid birth of Venus (Uma Thurman) sequence in *The Adventures of Baron Munchausen* (1989), and Mary Lambert used the symbolic iconography of Hades as the key introduction to *Siesta* (1987). Perhaps best of all is the "metahistorical" first half of Pasolini's *Medea* (1970), to be discussed in Chapter 7. But of all the categories of films produced about the ancient world, the mythological is probably the most difficult to film and therefore the most poorly represented to date. Far more than films about ancient history, mythological films need convincing special effects, or thought-provoking concepts, or an exotic ambience, or all three. The world of myth is by nature an unreal world, one in which action and events are either larger than life or more profound than the mundane events that normally take place in our world. Film by nature reveals an unreal world, but it too easily creates the illusion that its unreal word is real. Ray Harryhausen's SuperDynamation work—whether in his outer space films of the 1950s, his Sinbad films of the 1970s, or the specifically Greek *Jason and the Argonauts* and *Clash of the Titans*—has the look of myth because his images belong to another world that looks different from ours. Monsters, magic, and metamorphoses abound, and the two Greek films in particular take place both in Olympian heaven and on earth. But as magical as they are and as mythological as they seem, neither *Jason and the Argonauts* nor *Clash of the Titans* is intellectually profound. By contrast, Cocteau's *Orphée* and Camus's *Black Orpheus* are profound in their treatment of life, death, poetry, and song, but because they are placed in contemporary settings, they forfeit some mythic ambience. Mario Camerini's *Ulysses* has some fine effects and some of Homer's profundity, but its production values are clumsy. All of these films set good standards, yet a truly superb film of ancient Greek myth still waits to be made.

And David arose and went, he and his men, and slew of the Philistines two hundred men; and David brought their foreskins, and they gave them in full number to the king, that he might be the king's son-in-law. And Saul gave him Michal his daughter to wife.

—I SAMUEL 18:27–28

I wish my accusers would read their Bible more closely, for in those pages are more violence and sex than I could ever portray on the screen.

—CECIL B. DEMILLE

Film producers have made it standard operating procedure to seek much of their material from the literary world. From *Gone with the Wind* to *The English Patient,* some of the most highly regarded films have been based on extremely popular books. Because no book has ever come close to the Bible in popularity—more than two billion copies sold!—it naturally offers itself to cinematic treatment. Perhaps even more than Greco-Roman history or mythology, the Bible offers the film director an opportunity to work with a preestablished plot that an audience will know before entering the theater; the audience will then focus on the director's skill in adapting the Bible to a visual medium, not on the director's (and the screenwriter's) ability to contrive a good plot. On the other hand, the director must face the fact that each of his viewers has a lifelong visual preconception of biblical stories and characters, and that many of them have religious interpretations of the Bible that will not tolerate any wayward digressions. Cocteau had no problem adapting and rearranging the Orpheus myth in *Orphée* for an audience that had limited knowledge of Orpheus and no theological stake in his story. But similarly rearranging stories from the Bible entails serious risks; the source is known too well and means too much to too many people. Even in *The Green Pastures* (1936), for example, in which the Old Testament has been liberally adapted, the spirit behind the adaptation remains reverent.

But reverence is not the ultimate criterion for a biblical film either, for reverence can lead all too easily to boredom, vapidness, and even unintended comedy. For instance, *Sodom and Gomorrah* (1963) attempts to present Lot as a powerful, muscular, and tormented Hebrew leader who in his intense spirituality despises the human slavery practiced by the Sodomites. The approach is reverent, but when this powerful, physical Hebrew is portrayed by the well-mannered, thin-framed, Oxfordian Stewart Granger, the effect is likelier to inspire laughter than awe. *Sodom and Gomorrah* would have been better off with less superficial reverence and more pervasive cinematic reality.

Filming the Old Testament and filming the New Testament demand two very different approaches. The Old Testament (1) consists of many heroes and patriarchs in all lands from Syria to Dan to Beersheba and from Egypt to Mesopotamia; (2) comprises stories that range from childish and delightful to complex and absorbing to primitive and gruesome; (3) offers miracles and spectacular passages that often demand the disruption of the entire planet; and (4) avows a religious message that revolves around the celestial, invisible deity generally known as Jehovah. The New Testament (1) concentrates ultimately on one figure, Jesus; (2) comprises four sophisticated, stylized narratives; (3) presents generally less earthshaking miracles, involving only the tiny land of Palestine; and (4) introduces a religious message that revolves around the earthly, anthropomorphic Christ.

In filming the Old Testament, the director must (1) select which of the numerous characters and tales he will include, (2) select which biblical narrative style he will employ for his story, (3) be prepared to execute some spectacular effects, and (4) select a forceful and convincing method for presenting the invisible but omnipotent Jehovah.

In the Beginning . . .

In 1961 Dino De Laurentiis decided to film the entire book of Genesis, from the creation to Joseph's sojourn in Egypt. He was prepared to spend $90 million (of other people's money) on this twelve-hour, multidirector film. The directors he sought were Orson Welles for the Abraham and Isaac episode, Luchino Visconti for the Joseph episode, John Huston for the creation, and Fellini for the flood. Maria Callas was to play Sarah, Igor Stravinsky was to compose the score, and God was to be Olivier. Such dreams, we might imagine, often frequented the minds of movie producers in the early 1960s. The reality that emerged from this fantasy was Huston's *The Bible . . . In the Beginning* (1966), which episodically covered the first twenty-two chapters of Genesis, from the creation to the abortive sacrifice of Isaac.

Huston characteristically joked that "I've always wanted to create the heavens and the earth," and he went about his task with unmatched originality. He wisely decided not to attempt a uniform presentation of all the stories. The Old Testament itself does not have a consistent narrative approach, and the same cinematic treatment cannot possibly serve both the majestic, physical creation of the earth by an unseen yet mighty God and the very human and heart-warming pregnancy of the nonagenarian Sarah. *The Bible* therefore eschews the qualities that typical films demand—continuity, climax, and coherence. In this sense the film is not ultimately satisfying, and it tends to relinquish its hold on the viewer after the first two of its three hours. But despite the lack of overall dramatic tension, each episode has its individual charm or excellence, and is this not what one should realistically expect from a film of Genesis?

The Bible omits the usual opening credits (which would have been terribly untimely and premature before a film subtitled *In the Beginning*) and begins with Huston's rich and articulate narration of the opening chapters of *Genesis*. The screen is covered with an abstract red blur that grows whitish when God says, "Let there be light." As days two through five gradually unfold, the obscured screen begrudgingly reveals Ernst Haas's artistic shots of surging ocean waters, smoking, fiery lava, crashing waterfalls, primeval mossy trees, a majestic sunrise over the ocean and an equally captivating full moon, then dolphins, seals, slippery whales, and gulls playing in and above the seas, and cattle, horses, and scaly lizards on the dank, fresh earth. Finally our attention is focused on a clump of dirt in vaguely human form. Urged on by the climactic choral music of Toshiro Mayuzumi and high violins, Adam finally raises himself from the earth and walks over his new domain.

The scenes of Adam and Eve in Eden are delicate and simple. Although both prototype humans are stark naked, the film teasingly shies away from revealing angles. Filmed through a camera lens thinly coated with Vaseline, the mildly hazy effect of the Eden scenes is enhanced further by a gold filter and by gold-painted leaves and shrubbery. Adam (Michael Parks) and Eve (Ulla Bergryd) hardly match the titanic stature that many interpreters might attribute to the first man and woman; they instead appear plausibly as two innocents, fresh and naive and all but anonymous, who belong in this lush, fertile primordial morning. In a most charming moment, God (in Huston's voice) tells our two ancestors to "be fruitful and multiply." The camera looks down at the two from twenty-five feet above, as if the picture were capturing the subjective god's-eye view of Eden. In response to God's rather suggestive command, Adam and Eve merely hug; explicit sex is not needed, and in the novelty and innocence of the earth's early moments, a tender, tentative hug is the perfect cinematic touch.

The uniqueness of Huston's interpretation next visits itself upon the serpent in the Tree of Knowledge. Huston originally sought the lithe Rudolph Nureyev for the part, then tried a thirteen-foot, 102-pound python that just refused to hiss on cue, so he ended up hiding the human face of the serpent behind the thick foliage of the educational Tree. When God punishes the reptilian fiend, the human face is seen slithering down the Tree to dissolve obscurely into a more familiar type of ophidian.

Following Cain's barbaric fratricide, *The Bible* eases into its fourth and most individual episode—Noah and the flood. Some critics in 1966 complained that it was poor planning for Huston to play Noah, narrate *Genesis,* and sound the voice of God all in this same episode. But Huston's multiple roles cannot confuse anyone who knows the story (everyone), and it accents the individuality of Huston's interpretation. What really separates this scene from all others based on episodes from the Old Testament is Huston's folkish humor. As God's voice calls upon Noah, the sheepish man runs and hides. He timidly

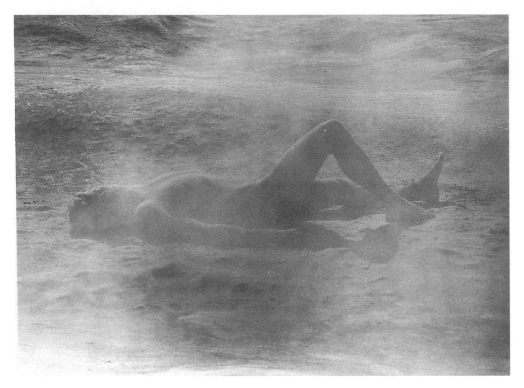

81   "Then the Lord God formed man of the dust of the ground," says Genesis 1:7, and here John
Huston's *The Bible . . . In the Beginning* (1966) captures an appropriately dusty Adam (Michael
Parks) in man's first living seconds. Huston smeared his camera lens with Vaseline to create a hazy
effect for the Eden scenes. The nudity of Adam and Eve is teasingly but tastefully elusive.

looks up and hears God's most explicit instructions: three hundred cubits by fifty cubits by
thirty cubits. Noah walks away puzzled but obedient, comically gesturing and sizing up
the strange dimensions with his hands. One night Noah works on the ark by himself; he
accidentally catches his foot in the bucket of pitch and slides down the sloped deck on his
six hundred–year–old derrière. The bucket thumps into the head of his lazy son Japheth,
but Japheth just continues sleeping. Huston has taken a bold step by adding light visual
comedy to biblical narrative. His inimitable ability to develop such drollery into a folkish
atmosphere makes the risk pay off. The visual drollery continues as we see the shaved
heads and bone jewelry of Noah's sinful critics, or the tree trunks that constitute the ark's
scaffolding. Such images also set the primitive tone and natural atmosphere for the real
essence of the episode: the animals.

     After collecting 270 animals from various European zoos and a German circus,
Huston penned them all in at De Laurentiis's studios outside Rome. He spent weeks training the pairs of beasts to file into the ark calmly and without incident. Unfortunately, pairs

82   John Huston leads pairs of zebras, elephants, camels, giraffes, and llamas into one of the five arks
he constructed (full-scale and miniature) for *The Bible . . . In the Beginning*. In this Noah sequence,
Huston narrates Genesis, speaks the voice of God, and plays the part of Noah. The folksy humor and
primitive setting give this sequence its unique charm. The three unadorned tree trunks, the hull's
webbing of tree branches, and the tree stumps scattered about show whence the ark came.

of male and female animals penned in at close quarters tend to become threesomes and litters. Several animals became ill, and one rambunctious water buffalo ran up the gangplank
to the ark, crashed through its walls, and galloped onward toward Rome as no four-legged
beast had done since Hannibal's elephants. After five months of such unpredictable disturbances, Huston decided to film the more ferocious beasts from behind glass. The film
seems to show all the animals filing into the ark, but they actually filed into the doorway
and right out the other side of a flat set; a different set was used for the interior scenes.
Huston used five different arks — miniatures, full-scale, interior, and exterior.

The resulting ark scenes are marvelous. Bears cautiously sniff the doorway to the
ark before entering, pelicans peck the rumps of the preceding chimpanzees, pairs of tigers,
deer, elephants, giraffes, zebras, cassowaries, dromedaries, toucans, yaks, gnus, burros,

swans, and cranes all parade into the hull beneath the impressive superstructure. As Noah feels the first few drops of rain on his outstretched palms, he picks up two lethargic turtles and carries them quickly into the ark. Inside is a veritable menagerie. A dark wooden atmosphere is pierced by the overwhelming roars, chirps, cries, growls, and screeches of our animal kingdom's prototypes. Noah and his wife humorously feed all the beasts; Noah pours a pail of milk into the hippo's gaping bidentate mouth; he feeds the giraffe from a pouch in his robes; he offers milk to the lions ("They're only great cats, wife"); and he toys with the huge elephant. As the zoological specimens amble out onto the steamy terrain of Mt. Ararat after the flood has receded, Noah has to fight back the tears. All the lightness and humor of the episode have come to their touching conclusion. *The Green Pastures* (1936) may have provided inspiration for the drollery of Huston's ark sequence into a unique biblical vision.

After the Tower of Babel disperses its babbling multitudes of multilingual laborers, *The Bible* concentrates on the stories of Lot, Abraham, Sarah, Hagar, and Isaac. The scenes bog down with Christopher Fry's neo–King Jamesian dialogue, which has its poetic qualities but tends to be impersonal and mundane. But Abraham (George C. Scott) is played in chillingly prophetic proportions, and his night raid on the region of Dan to rescue Lot—Huston borrowed the torches tied to rams' tails from Samson in *Judges* 15:4 —is spirited. The scenes of *Sodom and Gomorrah* almost resemble an adult film. It is left to Peter O'Toole, as all three of the story's angels, to maintain the appropriate biblical tone. A bestial menagerie that Noah wouldn't have allowed on his boat noisily slither their slimy, gaudily jeweled, caressed and caressing bodies to Lot's door and demand to "know" the Angel, only superficially conveying the idea of a twentieth-century B.C. city. But perhaps Huston purposely left the ancient temporality of Sodom in question, for the "rain upon Sodom and upon Gomorrah brimstone and fire from the Lord out of heaven" (*Genesis* 19:24) is portrayed as a nuclear blast and its all-too familiar mushroom cloud.

Huston gave *The Bible* a novel cinematic interpretation, based on a fresh, intelligent vision unlike any of his predecessors'. He avoided the mistake of the 1921 version of *The Bible* that merely presented the Old Testament as a stage play. His Eden sequence, thanks to the blond wig of Ulla Bergryd, with its long, dangling strands pasted to her breasts, avoided the cheap sexuality of Albert Gout's *Adán y Eva* (Mexican, 1956), which starred Christiana Mattel, Miss Universe 1953. Dino De Laurentiis had produced a low-budget *Adamo ed Eva* in the 1950s, and Disney Productions had released a corny but clever semianimated musical version of the Noah episode in 1959. Their 1999 version in *Fantasia/2000* is much better, with Donald Duck playing Noah's assistant and working in time with the music of Edward Elgar's "Pomp and Circumstance," just as Mickey Mouse had played the Sorcerer's apprentice in the 1940 original version. An artistic amateur production of *Lot in Sodom* (1933) exploited double or kaleidoscopic exposures, heavy chiaroscuro effect, bizarre focusing, and symbolism to become known as a classic of nonmainstream cinema. Then, of course, there was *The Green Pastures* (1936), which we shall examine in Chapter 8.

Of a vastly different nature was Fox's *Sodom and Gomorrah* (1963, also called *Last Days of Sodom and Gomorrah*). Starting with the biblical outline that Lot had two daughters, lived in Sodom, and saw his wife turned into a pillar of salt, the film ladles on blood and cheap spectacle without consideration for the Bible's narrative, and the special effects are practically an insult to Jehovah. Unfortunate miscasting gives us Stanley Baker as the lascivious lover of the Sodomite Queen Bera (Anouk Aimee; *King* Bera, by the way, is mentioned in Genesis 14:2), while Miklos Rozsa's moving music has little real drama to accompany. The entire affair attests to its Italian cloak-and-sandal production. The film overemphasizes salt-mining and "the one unforgivable sin" of Sodom—slavery. To be sure, Queen Bera walks into her bedroom with her pet leopard to illustrate the maxim "When in Sodom, do as the Sodomites," but bestial sodomy offended the smarmily self-righteous Lot less than slavery. Lot proudly announces to the heathen Sodomites that Jews do not tolerate slavery. Would Hagar have agreed? This is a classic example of the perils of moral anachronism. Modern thought should not be imposed upon a second-millennium B.C. Hebrew.

In 1928 Daryl Zanuck had just joined Warner Brothers, and he promised "the greatest picture ever made." He hired a *novus homo* in the American film world, the young director Michael Curtiz, who had recently emigrated from Hungary. The result one year later was *Noah's Ark*. Like most films about the ancient world that were produced in the 1920s—including *Sodom und Gomorrah* (1922), directed by Curtiz while in Austria—the story included both ancient and modern settings. The modern setting of *Noah's Ark* concerned criminals and First World War espionage, the highlight of which was a spectacular rainy night's wrecking of the Orient Express on a bridge spanning a deep river channel. The ancient setting combines the biblical story of Noah and his pious family with a hodgepodge of Babylonian sin and paganism. Of particular interest is the opening scene, which reveals a Tower of Babel modeled after the famous painting by Brueghel, as well as ark and flood scenes.

The ark itself looks enough like Huston's craft to have been the later director's iconographical source, and Curtiz's animal procession includes the now familiar profiles of elephants, horses, camels, lions, cows, zebras, bears, oxen, llamas, goats, deer, pigs, and monkeys. With a tighter budget than Huston's, Curtiz could not rent his animals, so he sent his photographer Hans Koenekamp to different zoos to film the various creatures. When all the beasts had been shot, Koenekamp then matted as many as eighteen shots onto one frame of the final version to make it seem as if the animals were all boarding the ark at the same time.

For the great flood a huge tank holding six hundred thousand gallons of water was built adjacent to the set. From the tank large spillways ran across the tops of the columns of the Babylonian temple. The plan was to dump all this water onto the Babylonian set while the extras and stuntmen were standing there. Photographer Hal Mohr quit when he heard of this dangerous plan, but the plans proceeded unchanged. With

83   "Queen" Bera (Anouk Aimee) is about to take her lover (the spotted one) into her chambers to prove that she really is the royal Sodomite in *Sodom and Gomorrah* (1963). The Bera of Genesis 14:2 was a King.

three hundred extras on the set and another 105 men to create wind, lightning, rain, and flooding, fifteen cameras were set up, and prebroken joints in the buildings were set with dynamite and detonation wires. This $40,000 dollar special-effects extravaganza was executed in a matter of seconds, and despite some unconvincing model work, the results are spectacular even today. But Mohr was right to be cautious: several men were seriously injured; one lost his leg. But as good came from the evil of the biblical flood, so did some good come from the outrage caused by the carelessness in putting this sequence on film. Soon afterward, safety regulations were established in Hollywood, and thereafter special effects were rarely as hazardous to actors and extras.

The greatest difference between the flood sequences of *Noah's Ark* and *The Bible* is one of perspective. Huston concentrated internally on the safety and relative security of Noah and the animal passengers, while Curtiz focused externally on the violent and indiscriminate destruction that surrounded those wooden walls. He featured shots of frightened Mesopotamians clinging to the high walls of the ark in the driving rain and fighting the surge of the waves. As the survivors sail away, we see a mass of humanity drowning behind them, as the evil Babylon suffers a tortured (and unbiblical) destruc-

84   This still from Michael Curtiz's silent version of *Noah's Ark* (1929) reveals the wood chips and shavings remaining from Noah's prudent construction project. Noah (Paul McAllister) and family pray piously and seriously, quite a different touch from Huston's folksy humor. Like most "ancient" films of the 1920s, *Noah's Ark* contains both ancient and modern sequences.

tion. Despite the studio's much publicized effects, the film was a box-office failure. Nonetheless, it was reissued in 1958—two years after *The Ten Commandments*—with a complete soundtrack.

A number of biographies of Old Testament figures were filmed in the twentieth century. Henri Andréani produced a number of French silents—*Caïn et Abel* (1911) and *Esther, La Mort de Saül, Rebecca,* and *La Reine de Saba* (all in 1913). Two versions of the Joseph story appeared in 1914—Eugene Moore's first film, *Joseph in the Land of Egypt,* and Louis N. Parker's filmed play *Joseph and His Coat of Many Colors* (1914)—followed by Carl Froelich's German *Joseph und seine Brüder* (*Joseph and His Brethren,* 1922). Of all the patriarchs, Joseph, with his mistreatment at the hands of his brothers, his imprisonment, visionary skill, and ultimate triumph in Egypt, is the most dramatic and cinema-photogenic. A new batch of Joseph films appeared in the sound era: Maurice Elvey's *Her Strange Desire* (1930), based on Edgar Middleton's play *Potiphar's Wife; Joseph and His Brethren* (1930), by Adolph Gartner, whose biblical credits also included *The Sacrifice of Isaac* (1932); and George Roland's Yiddish version of *Joseph in the Land of Egypt* (1932).

In 1960 Columbia shot some thirty-seven thousand feet of an epic version of the never released and barely extant *Joseph and His Brethren* starring Rita Hayworth, and the Italian revival of the ancient-film genre in the early sixties produced a few more films based on Genesis, including *Giacobbe ed Esau* (*Jacob and Esau,* 1964); *I Patriarchi della Bibbia* (*The Patriarchs of the Bible,* 1963), which ranged from Adam to Joseph and added a prediction of the Messiah; and another *Joseph and His Brethren* (1962). *Joseph* resembles *Sodom and Gomorrah* in that it combines well-known American or British actors (Robert Morley as Potiphar, Finlay Currie as Jacob, and Belinda Lee as Henet, Potiphar's wife) with Italian extras, and inflicts one-dimensional characterizations and a preposterous script— Joseph and Potiphar go on a hunt for lions and (stuffed) elephants "in the jungles of Egypt" —on everyone. The sets are transparently phony; Joseph is thrown into the pit and sold to Midianite merchants on a barely disguised soundstage with crudely painted palm trees and wheelbarrowed sand. Perhaps the one saving aspect of *Joseph and His Brethren* is that it attends to many of the details of the story told in Genesis. But biblical narrative is confused with screenwriter's fantasy, and overall effect is about as believable as Methusalah's nine hundred and first birthday. Bosley Crowther called it "the clumsiest, the silliest, the worst of the quasi-Biblical pictures to come along since the wide-screen was born."[1]

Decades later television offered a medium for a new group of films based on Genesis, one of the first of which was *The Story of Jacob and Joseph* (1974). Directed by Michael Cacoyannis, this film helped establish the style for made-for-television films, which enjoy an expanse of time at the expense of dramatic tension and form. Two decades later Turner Broadcasting produced *Abraham* (1994), *Jacob* (1994), *Joseph* (1995), and *David* (1997). Of all the films in this series, *Joseph* is perhaps the most engaging, with such marquee stars as Ben Kingsley playing a sincere Potiphar, Lesley Ann Warren playing his emotionally fragile wife, and Martin Landau playing the aging patriarch Jacob. *Joseph* also enjoys a thoughtful script that exploits the contrasts between monotheistic and polytheistic religious systems, varies the complex dynamics among Jacob's many sons, and at least toys with blurring biblical distinctions between good and evil. Several sequences in the film are also enhanced by Ennio Morricone's music.

Ten Commandments Times Two

Turning the gilt-edged pages to Exodus, movie directors have filmed the story of Moses eight times. The first three were admirable silent versions by Pathé (*Moses,* 1907), Henri Andréani (*Moïse sauvé des eaux,* 1911), and Vitagraph (*The Life of Moses,* 1909–1910), and these were followed by Michael Curtiz's Austrian *Moon of Israel* (*Die Sklavenkönigin,* 1924), which starred the fabulous María Corda. But as the power of Pharaoh yielded to that of Moses and his god, so does any praise for these silent versions yield to that bestowed upon Cecil B. DeMille's 1923 version of *The Ten Commandments.* In creating his first great ancient spectacle, DeMille characteristically looked at hundreds of ancient works of art and European paintings to find the most appropriate and/or attractive costuming. He insisted that the sets be designed after Egyptian originals. He also sent his assistant Florence Meehan on a twenty thousand–mile trip to Egypt, Palestine, Syria, India, Persia, Burma, Kashmir, China, Siam, and Japan to collect oriental jewelry, costumes, tapestries, silks, swords, and other props. He commissioned the construction of three hundred chariots—an order that could have put ancient chariot makers back in business after a lapse of two millennia—bought two black, Kansas thoroughbreds for $5,000, and hired 225 Orthodox Jews to "look like their ancestors." He sent copies of the Bible to everyone on his payroll and planned to shoot the Exodus scenes in Egypt. Paramount's Adolph Zukor, remembering the recent commercial failure of *Intolerance,* rejected this last idea, and he was skeptical about the entire project: "Old men wearing tablecloths and beards! Cecil, a picture like this would ruin us."[2] But DeMille traded upon his previous successes and assured Zukor that there would be "plenty of box office–worthy sinning" in addition to the religious message, so the studio boss let him proceed with the project.

In keeping with this promise, DeMille centered his approach to the story around the Golden Calf revelry; this scene could tie the ancient story into a parallel modern orgy, and its one hundred thinly clad women would certainly give it huge mass appeal. DeMille had his writer Jeanie MacPherson prepare an ancient account of Exodus that could dissolve into a modern parallel after the Golden Calf episode. The result was a modern story about a man who disrespects the Bible and even calls the Ten Commandments, which his mother has just read to him at the dissolve, "a lot of bunk." He goes through life sinning and cheating everyone but ultimately encounters justice and suffers guilt when the church he has lucratively built from cheap cement cracks and topples onto his devout mother.

The ancient story of *The Ten Commandments* is very much abbreviated. The first sequences show the Israelites suffering under Pharaoh. The titles read from Exodus 1:13: "And the Egyptians made the children of Israel to serve with rigour," so the hapless slaves tug at huge ropes before the gates of Pharaoh's (here unspecified) city. Dathan, the Hebrew, shakes his fist at Pharaoh Rameses, and all the slaves are lashed with the whip. Rameses announces, "If a man clog the wheels of Pharaoh, he shall be ground to dust." And to be sure, a Hebrew man is soon crushed to a pulp by a huge granite wheel. The scene quickly changes to Pharaoh's court. Moses and Aaron have already set nine plagues upon Egypt. Moses now warns Pharaoh, who sits between two live lions chained to double columns, about the coming death of Egyptian firstborn, but Pharaoh's young son is unafraid and whips Moses. The next scene shows Pharaoh mourning over his dead son; at last, he consents to let Moses' people go. Because the titles for these ancient scenes are derived from passages of Exodus, the action appears to be little more than a pantomime of the Bible story.

To shoot the ensuing Exodus scene DeMille had taken his cast of 3,500 people and 6,000 animals to Guadelupe, in Santa Barbara County—about two hundred miles

85   The skeleton of a colossal entrance pylon rises in the rear of this photo from DeMille's silent *The Ten Commandments* (1923), while plaster sphinxes lie by their future pedestals. DeMille shot the Exodus scene from the top of the pylon. After shooting was completed, this Orange County site was not dismantled but simply backfilled; in the 1980s archaeologists excavated the set, then backfilled it again for future generations to rediscover.

from Los Angeles. There he set up a camp with its own cows, government, hospital, and restaurants (including a Kosher restaurant for the 225 Orthodox Jews). A private police unit enforced the strict orders to all cast members that there was to be absolutely no "un-biblical" behavior at the camp. DeMille's reasons for these orders were twofold: first, that there should be no scandal that might cause adverse publicity for the picture, and second, that all would act their parts better if they lived in the spirit of their biblical roles for a few weeks. For DeMille, not only lead actors but all the extras had to live their parts; he believed that an authentic atmosphere would create the most realistic film.

The resulting scene became one of the more impressive of the silent era. Leaving the Egyptian city through a huge pylon 750 feet wide by 109 feet high—one of the largest exterior sets built to date—and an avenue of twenty-four sphinxes, the excitedly disenthralled Israelite mob is burdened with camels, goats, sheep, chickens, donkeys, and baggage, as wagons share the road with masses of disorderly pedestrians. (This extraordinary movie set was itself the object of an archaeological excavation some seventy-five years after it was buried in the California desert.) In the midst of this crowd, DeMille focuses his camera on several tender familial scenes, a girl with her doll, a woman with her goat, and a family feasting together. The contrast between the intimate personal scenes and the massive crowd scenes produces a well-rounded impression of the joy of the occasion. And all the while DeMille had the "authentic" Orthodox Jews singing Hebrew chants.

When Pharoah's heart hardens one last time, and he sends three hundred chariots swiftly across the sands (of the Mojave), the aerial shot shows each chariot casting its dramatically long, late-afternoon shadow, bringing home the cause for panic amid the Israelite caravan. At one point, some of the chariots crash into each other. According to some reports in 1923, DeMille had purposely and privately sawed through some chariot axles to cause the spectacular crash. At any rate, it looked stupendous, so it remained in the final print of the film; in fact, DeMille used parts of the scene again in his 1934 *Cleopatra.*

The chase sequence culminates with the marvel of marvels—the parting of the Red Sea. After a double-exposed pillar of fire holds off the Egyptians, the waters roll spectacularly back, giving the Israelites dry passage. When the Egyptians follow, they are drowned as the sea reclaims its bed. To create this effect, Roy Pomeroy covered a table top with gelatin molded around gas jets. He ignited the powerful jets, and the gelatin melted in a bubbling swirl. The film was then run in reverse to create the effect of the waters crashing together over the pursuing charioteers.

The ancient sequences of *The Ten Commandments* come to a close after Moses receives the tablets on Mount Sinai and returns to find wild, lascivious revelry among his people. Worst of all, the crowd is worshiping a huge Golden Calf (with an Egyptian Hathor crown and sun-disk), which is caressed with particular perversity by one paganizing Israelitess. Moses hurls the tablets, which splinter against the rocks. The sinner begs Moses for forgiveness and purification, but a sudden bolt of lightning smashes the calf and sends all into a panic. Here the story dissolves into the modern parallel.

The Ten Commandments, in addition to dramatizing Exodus, provides a convincing cinematic account of the events and lessons to be learned from this pivotal section of the Old Testament. The design of DeMille's huge moral and historical show becomes clear in the first title, with its easily digestible message: "The 10 Commandments are not laws—they are the LAW." Such parallels of biblical and modern morality may seem old-fashioned, but this version of *The Ten Commandments* was a smashing success in 1923, and it ensured the continuance of "ancient" films throughout the twenties. Michael Curtiz's *Moon of Israel* had equally successful special effects and impressive crowd scenes, but it lacked the modern parallel story that gave *The Ten Commandments* its powerful claim to moral profundity. Yet DeMille typically spices the morality entrée with generous sprinklings of sex, dance, action, spectacle, and historical realism.

In 1943 an Italian film entitled *The Ten Commandments* was produced, starring Valentina Cortese and Rossano Brazzi, but its ten vignettes about the Mosaic laws were set only in modern times. The film was released in the United States only after the success of DeMille's second version of the story.

When DeMille began work on his sound and full-color VistaVision production of *The Ten Commandments* (1956), he was seventy years old. His seventy films had reportedly grossed more than $575 million, so he essentially had carte blanche in preparing his new film. Taking advantage of a huge budget, DeMille was able to fulfill his unsatisfied desire from the first version—to shoot the Egyptian and Sinai scenes on location in Egypt and on Mount Sinai. He increased the number of extras from 3,500 to almost 20,000 (many drawn from the Egyptian army) and upped his expenses from the $1.5 million of the first version to more than $13.5 million; critics jested that "he spent over $1 million per commandment."[3] But the money and four years spent allowed DeMille to expand this new *The Ten Commandments* into the biggest, grandest, and most awe-inspiring film of its kind.

DeMille had once remarked, "I use a big canvas," and the painterly metaphor is apt.[4] To him the parting of the Red Sea, the exodus of thousands of Hebrew slaves, the massive chase of six hundred Egyptian chariots, forty years of wandering through wilderness, and Jehovah's presentation of the tablets of law to Moses could not be sufficiently portrayed on a small scale. Bigness was an innate part of the film's design. The result was the colossal magnitude of *The Ten Commandments*. To portray the building of Sethi's desert city, DeMille combined full-scale sets, miniatures, and mattes for a panorama filled with laboring slaves, half-built sphinxes, high-rising pylons, and a tall stone obelisk. As Moses, the master architect, gives the signal, men with mallets smash the thick chain fastenings to release rough, six-inch-thick ropes. They unroll around a whirring windlass, and the scene is dominated by the thundering and hissing of wood, rock, and rope; the one hundred–foot obelisk begins to rise over the heads of the sun-browned slaves as several taut cables snap with a cracking sound. The few thousand slaves pull with all their might, urged on by Egyptian whips, but the wood support underneath the multiton granite breaks in half, and several slaves meet their death. The close-up camera now yields to a long-distance shot (of a miniature), and the mighty obelisk gradually rises the rest of its precalculated path and at last slides efficiently into its position between the pylons. Moses proudly explains to Pharaoh Sethi that sand now supports the obelisk, and nonchalantly adds that "a thousand slaves will remove that later." The scene is expanded by several more shots of other half-built stone monuments, all of them blending well with the tawny sand and granite colors that overwhelm the scene.

This scene does not occur in the text of Exodus. For that matter, the Bible does not mention Sethi by name, nor does it mention Moses as master architect (let alone prince) of Egypt. But DeMille's research staff (Henry Noerdlinger) and special consultants (including faculty and staff at the Department of Antiquities at Luxor, the Metropolitan Museum of Art, and the Oriental Institute in Chicago) informed him of Rameses' build-

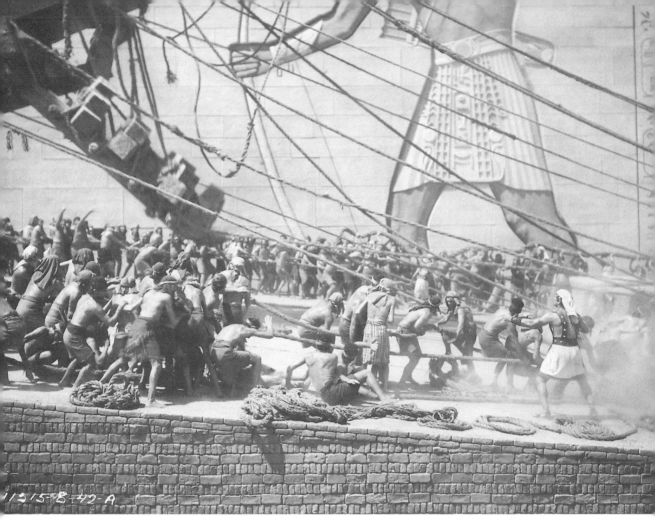

86   DeMille's miniatures, mattes, and full-scale models are edited together to create the illusion of the colossal. This is a full-scale shot of Hebrew slaves raising Sethi's obelisk into place in *The Ten Commandments* (1956). The huge ropes snap, windlasses whirl, and the supporting wood beam breaks under the weight of the huge granite block (upper left). Several slaves will appear to fall over the foreground wall to their death. The scene is so absorbing that one hardly notices when the mattes and miniatures replace the full-scale. Such skill won the Oscar for special effects in 1956.

ing programs in the thirteenth century B.C. at Luxor and Karnak. Combining this information with Exodus 1:11—"And they built for Pharaoh store-cities, Pithom and Raamses" —and assuming that this pharaoh was Rameses II, DeMille decided to show this massive, one-sentence, biblical building program at one of its most exciting moments. He had his art directors Hal Pereira and Walter Tyler re-create actual Egyptian buildings, pylons, sphinxes, and an obelisk, and all the biblical and archaeological research was then molded into the story line of the film. The biblical setting essentially belongs to Exodus 1:11, and the Egyptian buildings authentically derive from those of Rameses and Queen Hatshepsut, but the noise, color, spectacle, and gigantic scale are DeMille's. His purpose: to show something more than whipped and tortured Hebrew slaves, to show the grandeur and might of Egypt—the same might Moses and his Israelites would have to defeat in the months to come. After this scene, the viewer can truly appreciate the power of Nineteenth Dynasty Egypt so that the eventually victorious power of Jehovah will seem all that much greater.

Few matched DeMille in re-creating realistic and authentic historical spectacle; none matched him in fitting historicity into his plots. During this same building sequence Moses and Rameses—the two aspirants to Sethi's throne—accuse each other of incompetence. Sethi has been marveling at Moses' architectural project, but the envious Rameses

87   The obelisk-raising scene from DeMille's *The Ten Commandments* (1956). This multimatted shot of full-scale and miniature stems from one sentence in Genesis, four years of academic research, and a lifetime of DeMillean imagination. The terrace is a reconstruction of Queen Hatshepsut's temple (1480 B.C.), called Sethi's in the film, and the obelisk and pylons are reconstructions of various ancient monuments. Although the scope of the scene is overwhelming, DeMille subtly employs the spectacle to further his narrative.

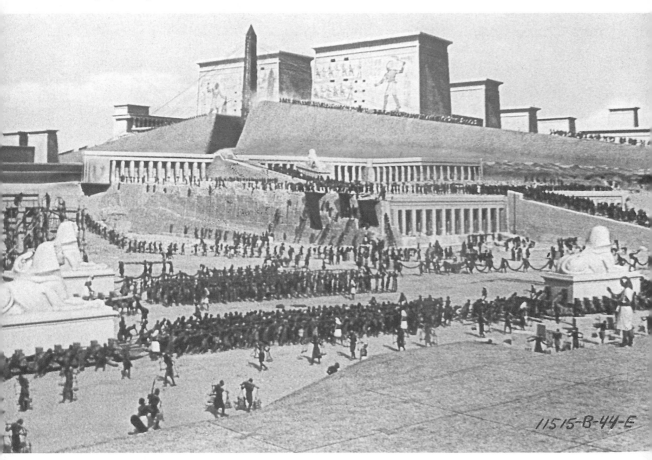

88 Queen Hatshepsut's temple as it appears today in the Valley of the Kings. Frustrated by his inability to shoot his 1923 version of *The Ten Commandments* in Egypt, DeMille exploited all the authentic sources he could in 1956.

89 The entrance pylon of the temple of Horus at Edfu, Egypt. DeMille had his art directors reduplicate the shape, size, and painted exteriors of several pylons. The large standing figure and double row of sitting figures on the temple were adapted for Sethi's monument in *The Ten Commandments* (1956).

now informs Sethi that Moses has illicitly opened the priestly granaries; he puts a small weight on the nearby balance. Then he informs Sethi that Moses has been supplying this "divine grain" to the Hebrew slaves; he puts a second weight onto the scales. Finally he informs Sethi that Moses has given the slaves one day of rest each week; he puts a third weight onto the balance, which finally sinks all the way to the bottom. In his defense before the now suspicious pharaoh, Moses replies that the strong, well-fed slave builds better bricks; he puts a huge brick on the balance which now plunges to the bottom on Moses' side. Mathematical calculation and architectural exactitude had been the underlying theme of the spectacular obelisk-raising sequence until Rameses' dispute with Moses. But now, because of DeMille's astute appreciation for historical realism, architectural exactitude and its mathematical balance have become the underlying strength of Moses' verbal argument.[5] At the same time, DeMille gives us a personal reason—ambition and jealousy—for Rameses' desperate hatred of Moses. In his fury Rameses swears the vengeance that will prevail throughout the rest of the film: "The city that he builds shall bear my name; the woman that he loves shall bear my child; so shall it be written, so shall it be done!"

And so the entire basis for the Egyptian plot that culminates in the spectacular parting of the Red Sea is established in this quarrel—the very quarrel that arose directly from a spectacular effects sequence, and that was developed via an authentic ancient balance. DeMille juxtaposed spectacle and authentic detail with human emotions and plot development. This ensures that his characters do not stand isolated before historical backgrounds or in historical costumes; they move realistically within a seemingly authentic atmosphere; they use both spectacular events and minor properties like true ancients. DeMille does more than re-create a real obelisk, sphinx, or architectural balance; he absorbs them into his historical vision.

One other scene emphasizes the magnificence of the Egypt that Moses must one day force into submission. Because biblical information about Moses is sparse between the time of his discovery amid the bulrushes and his slaughter of an Egyptian taskmaster, DeMille decided to establish Moses as a prince, the adoptive nephew of Pharaoh Sethi and cousin of Rameses. When Moses returns from a victorious campaign against Saba (Sheba) in the south, he enters a brightly sunlit throne room strewn with rose petals. He is dressed in shining Egyptian armor, and Sethi receives him dressed in full pharaonic splendor—a long white robe, the flail and scepter, and the *pschent,* the double crown of Lower and Upper Egypt. Moses presents for him a colorful spectacle: the king of Ethiopia (Woody Strode), whose powerful drummers set the rhythm for Ethiopia's tribute. Huge, rainbow-colored feather gowns, piles of glowing semiprecious stones, rich furs, dark logs of ebony, and branches of myrrh are laid onto the pharoah's gold floor. Such bright color and pageantry are typical of the scenes portraying the Egyptian royals—including, of course, the pre–burning bush Moses.

In stark contrast are the drab, depressing scenes of the Hebrews in bondage. After he discovers that he is a Hebrew, Moses descends from the golden sunlit splendor of the previous scenes to the quagmire of his compatriots' existence in the brick factory's mud pits. Nefretiri (Anne Baxter), once his beloved Egyptian princess, summons Moses to her chambers. He wears a ragged loincloth, a scraggly beard, and a coating of caked mud. Nefretiri wears a bright green gown and carries a green fan made of soft ostrich plumes. The deep-voiced Nefretiri (not to be confused with the better known Eighteenth Dynasty queen, Nefertiti) teases the lowly Moses: "First friend of Pharaoh, keeper of the Royal Seal, Prince of Ammon, Prince of Memphis, Prince of Thebes, Beloved of the Nile God, Conqueror of Ethiopia, General of Generals, Commander of the Eastern Host, a Man of Mud!" She finishes with an alto laugh.

A man of subtleties as well as hokey showmanship, DeMille creates a powerful change of mood by using different atmospheric colors to film Egypt's plagues. The darkened sky from which the ominously silent hail begins to fall, the deep red blood that swims out from Aaron's staff into the divinely contaminated sacred waters of the Nile, and the sickly, pervasive, lethal green smoke of the Angel of Death change a wealthy kingdom into a dying land. The atmosphere and colors change again as the film shows the miraculous pillar of fire, the parting of the Red Sea (never called "Red" in the film because of the water's obvious lack of red coloring), and Moses on a crimson-toned Mount Sinai. The biblical pillar of fire came "between the camp of Egypt and the camp of Israel; and there was the cloud and the darkness here, yet gave it light by night there" (Exodus 14:20); the Academy Award–winning special-effects expert John P. Fulton created this chiaroscuro effect on the screen.

Even more brilliant, technically and imaginatively, was the parting of the Red Sea. DeMille had a 360,000-gallon water tank built, and the visual effect was created by pouring water from the tank and reversing the film. Smoky and threatening clouds swirl over the churning waters, and each cloud reflects the biblical darkness of storm and brightness of morning. When the frothing waters part, their imposing walls rise to dominate the whole assemblage of up to thirteen matted shots with a metallic sea-green hue. In the foreground before this impressive barrage of variegated tints, Moses' bright, God-inspired eyes and gray-streaked hair set off his red cloak. The environment in which the parting of the waters takes place differs so much from the light and colors seen elsewhere in the film that the special effects become even more marvelous and miraculous. Such brilliant use of color and special effects helped to make this scene one of the most recognizable, iconic, and inimitable sequences in the history of filmdom.

This grand assemblage of atmospheres and colors could not carry *The Ten Commandments* on its own. The special effects that make the plagues and the exodus so vivid are especially powerful because they are presented in service of fine acting and epic screenwriting. Perhaps no one ever played Oriental despots and kings like Yul Brynner (Rameses), and Anne Baxter is dagger-sharp yet kittenish as his wife Nefretiri. Rameses' father, Pharaoh Sethi, is played by Sir Cedric Hardwicke, who conveys the aging, kindly, but regal personality of "the old crocodile." Charlton Heston, fresh from DeMille's similarly

90   This interior scene from *The Ten Commandments* (1956) demonstrates DeMille's insistence on archaeological detail. Pharaoh Rameses II (Yul Brynner) wears the unstriped pharaonic *nemes* and sits beside a column with lotus designs (bottom) and cobra reliefs alternating with cartouches. The cartouche just to the left above Brynner's head is the authentic hieroglyphic insignia for the historical Rameses II. At right is the famed "seated scribe." Rameses' child (Eugene Mazzola) wears an authentic Egyptian hairdo, and his general Pentaur (Henry Wilcoxon), left, wears an authentic layered military headdress. The votive ax, far left, is also authentic.

spectacular and convincing *The Greatest Show on Earth* (1952), carved out a unique niche in the history of the cinema by avoiding the commonplace, overstudied, pseudoprophetic approach to biblical figures. Instead, he played Moses with vitality and energy. The cinematic Moses does not mimic the Moses in Exodus—the Moses that stutters and bungles until he hears from Jehovah at the burning bush. But Heston adapts well to the young, princely Moses, the slaving, mud-caked Moses, the demanding, plague-bearing Moses, and the grizzled, lawgiving Moses. The part of Moses presented great challenges and difficulties, and Heston met them brilliantly. In Heston's own words, "It was an enormous role—like Christ—unplayable. It was beyond my capacities then, and it would be beyond my capacities now. I dare say it would be beyond Olivier's capacities."[6]

91/94   Ancient sources for DeMille's portrayal of the pharaoh's court: a seated scribe, who did his work sometime between 2563 and 2423 B.C., in the Fifth Dynasty; a carved relief from the Twentieth Dynasty temple of Rameses III showing the military headdress of shipboard warriors; a Twentieth Dynasty painting illustrating the hairdo of Pharaoh's son; and an Eighteenth Dynasty ax with a curved wooden haft, leather binding, and a curved, figured blade inlaid with precious stones.

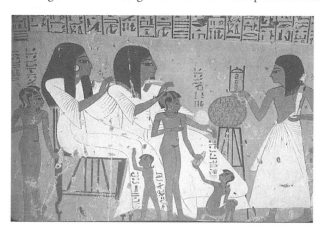

95   Moses (Charlton Heston) has Aaron (John Carradine) change the sacred waters of the Nile
to blood in *The Ten Commandments* (1956) as Pharaoh Rameses (Yul Brynner) and his general
(Henry Wilcoxon) find their own blood boiling. The idol to the right is Amon, who is authentically
half-ram, half-human. Rameses wears a *nemes* with a cobra-tipped *uraeus* (diadem), the priests are
authentically bald, and the columns are authentically designed to represent bundles of papyrus.
The priest at far left wears the *ankh* around his neck.

DeMille also assembled an accomplished supporting cast. Edward G. Robinson
enlivened the part of the perfidious Dathan, and who could better portray the slimy, villainous Baka than Vincent Price? The script by Æneas MacKenzie and Jesse Lasky Jr. provides literate, amusing, and expressive lines for a variety of well-known actors and actresses. Memnet (Judith Anderson) tells Sethi's sister and Moses' adoptive mother, Bithiah
(Nina Foch), that she is going to inform Moses of his Hebrew birth. Bithiah lashes back:
"That tongue will dig your grave." A fine stichomythic exchange between Prince Rameses
and the stool pigeon Dathan culminates with convincingly Egyptian phraseology. Rameses wants Dathan to find the rumored "Hebrew deliverer." Slipping a gold ring onto his
spear point, Rameses offers the bribe to Dathan and calls him "a rat's ear and a ferret's
nose." Dathan responds: "To use in your service, son of Pharaoh." When Moses sees the
Hebrew slave Yochabel (whom he will later discover to be his real mother) about to be

96/97 The funerary mask of Pharaoh Tutankhamen, "King Tut." The blue and gold stripes and cobra visor are re-created in *The Ten Commandments* (1956), but Yul Brynner does not wear the ceremonial beard-wig, which adorned all Egyptian heads of state, even queens. The Eighteenth Dynasty (c. 1400–1360 B.C.) temple of Amon in Luxor features papyrus-bundle columns.

crushed by a huge block of granite, he argues with the Egyptian taskmaster that "blood makes poor mortar." He saves the woman, and she praises Jehovah: "The Lord has lightened my burdens." Moses, still a doubting Egyptian prince, advises with irony, "He would have done better to *remove* them." The film also includes a fair amount of narration that is partly biblical and partly in biblical style. DeMille himself narrates these lengthy transitional passages with fervor. The voice of Jehovah, contrary to reports, was not DeMille's; it was provided by Heston and part-time actor Donald Hayne.[7]

Also important to the flowing script were several oft-repeated ancient idioms. Most memorable was the byword of Rameses: "So shall it be written, so shall it be done." Another conveyed a hint of humor to several scenes: when Sethi hears the court crier announce his seemingly endless titles with the greatest pomp — much like the previously quoted titles with which Nefretiri mocked Moses — Sethi impatiently calls him "the old windbag." Then, on Sethi's death bed, he once again hears the bombastic crier praying to the Gods of the Dead. He whispers poignantly in weeping Nefretiri's ear: "The old windbag."

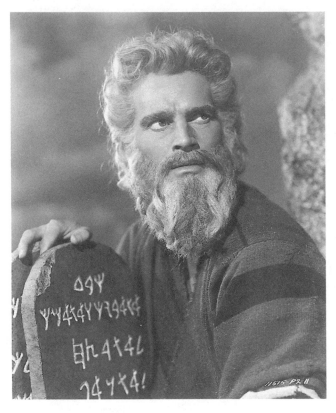

98/99   One of the reasons DeMille chose Charlton Heston to play the part of Moses in his VistaVision version of *The Ten Commandments* was that he *looked* like Moses. DeMille released this publicity shot, which bears a striking resemblance to Michelangelo's *Moses*. Directors of "ancient" films often rely on paintings and sculptures by the European Masters, as well as archaeological remains from antiquity. Michelangelo's was the most widely recognized depiction of Moses—until DeMille made his 1956 film.

Other touches of humanizing humor appear in *The Ten Commandments*. When the excited Hebrews are leaving Pharaoh's city in the great exodus, an ass balks in the middle of "the glorious chaos." His owner comically laments, "Four hundred years of bondage, and *today* he won't move!" But DeMille presumably was not laughing when he got a foretaste of his own earthly exodus. Climbing up the 107-foot entrance pylon (essentially unchanged in design from the one used in his 1923 version) to observe the Hebrews' exit, DeMille suffered a mild heart attack. In an impressive show of inspiration and determination, he continued up the rickety ladder, checked his camera angles and perspective, then descended the ladder unaided. Two days later he was on the set again, and he completed the last three weeks of location shooting in Egypt. So it was written, and so it was done.

Thirty-three years after his groundbreaking silent version of the film, DeMille's new *The Ten Commandments* expanded still further the possibilities of the epic film. Combining knowledge of cinema with a passionate yet intelligent love for the Old Testament, DeMille saw his life's ambition blossom into a colossal reality. His magnificent vision and command of the Exodus material more than compensate for the heroic exaggeration and the occasional narrative lapses that by nature accompany any epic—cinematic, operatic, or literary. In using more than nine hundred sources (and saying so in the credits), he filled the gaps in the biblical text with fictitious yet plausible conjectures—Moses' upbringing in the Egyptian court, his love for Nefretiri, his personal enmity with Rameses, the presence of a (late–Bronze Age) Trojan embassy at the (late–Bronze Age) Pharaoh's court. He also expanded some inconsequential parts of the actual biblical text into full-blown cinematic realities: the biblical Dathan appears only in Numbers, not in Exodus; the cinematic Joshua (John Derek) is a key to the motivation of the Egyptian Moses, yet the biblical Joshua is of no importance until after the exodus; and the biblical, personal grief of Pharaoh (Rameses) at the death of his first born is much expanded. Moreover, DeMille's unparalleled skill at directing huge crowds was evidenced in his control over ten thousand extras for the exodus scene alone, not to mention two hundred camels controlled by electronically charged wires. He also rented airplanes, had them flown to the south of Cairo, and had the wind from their propellers blow on the Israelites crossing the desert, then added the parted Red Sea later. DeMille's bold use of location shooting was enhanced when this old crocodile personally climbed Sinai to approve some of the film's final scenes, with their eerie red tint and murky lighting. All this skill and manipulation elevated an already effective script into the realm of filmic masterpiece.

The crowning touch for *The Ten Commandments* was Elmer Bernstein's dynamic score. He composed several different themes that served as leitmotifs throughout the film. The basses and trombones sound the low, triumphant Ten Commandments theme during the overture, while the obelisk is being raised for Sethi's city, and when the Hebrews pass through the aquatic walls of the Red Sea. Bernstein also works the theme into such scenes as the burning bush and Mount Sinai sequences, but here it is sounded by soft violins amid angelic harmonies. The theme is heard so frequently and in so many different arrangements and instrumentations throughout the three and two-thirds hours of the film that it becomes a welcome and satisfying part of the whole experience. Like "So shall it be written, so shall it be done," it gives us something familiar to grasp onto at significant parts of the overwhelming narrative. The adaptability of Bernstein's artistry is evident in the Egyptian court scenes, with the orientalizing triangle, Nilotic flutes and harps; in the Israeli dance of Jethro's daughters; and in the marching exodus of the Hebrews.

When the film opened on November 8, 1956, it immediately impressed a number of people, except, of course, "the big city critics" with whom DeMille had had a two-generation-long feud. He was received by Pope Pius XII, West German President Theodor Heuss, Winston Churchill, and Queen Elizabeth. His four years of work and Paramount's

$13.5 million investment brought to a magnificent close the directing career of Cecil B. DeMille. *The Ten Commandments* was to be the magnificent triumph of one of Hollywood's founders and most memorable directors. In terms of scope, inspiration, color, and biblically (divinely?) inspired special effects, the film has still not met its equal.

In fact, no one dared again to touch the subject of Moses until Avco Embassy's 1975 *Moses, the Lawgiver,* starring Burt Lancaster. First released episodically for television, the film was later cut and released to theaters. Director Gianfranco De Bosio sensibly realized that he could not possibly reach DeMillean heights of spectacle and showmanship, so he tried to play down these crowd-pleasing elements. He did just that; the film has no spectacle, no dramatic substance, and is as a result quite verbose and static. One interesting

100   The crowded, joyous exodus scene from DeMille's 1956 version of *The Ten Commandments.* Rameses II's entrance pylon, complete with painted reliefs of plumed and caparisoned horses, pharaonic cartouches, soaring Nekhebet, and bow-shooting Pharaoh, is authentic, as is the avenue of sphinxes. The four seated statues next to the pylon are reproduced from Rameses II's rock-cut temple at Abu-Simbel.

101/103   Exodus sources: the entrance pylon and the avenue of criosphinxes (ram-headed sphinxes) at Rameses II's temple of Amon at Karnak; a painted wooden box on which Pharaoh Tutankhamen is shown riding his chariot against the ringlet-bearded Assyrians while Nekhebet, the protective deity in vulture form, soars above two cartouches (pharaonic name-seals); and the rock-cut temple at Abu-Simbel. Built by Pharaoh Rameses II, the temple was moved piece by piece and reconstructed elsewhere when the Aswan Dam was built.

aspect—academically, not cinematically—is De Bosio's Red Sea sequence. By 1975 biblical scholars had suggested that a historical Moses would have led his people across the marshy Sea of Reeds in northern Egypt rather than through the deep-watered Red Sea, and so *Moses, the Lawgiver* shows about 150 cloth-draped extras ho-humming their way across shallow waters. Once again we see that historical authenticity and cinematic vitality are not always compatible.

Perhaps appropriately, *Moses, the Lawgiver* revived enough interest in Moses to inspire a slow-witted spoof, *Wholly Moses* (1980). A much better comedy based on the Pentateuch is *The Green Pastures* (1936), which included the story of Moses and Rameses; here, however, it was a Moses in checkered shirt and trousers marveling at the bush "dat ain't burnt up," and "His Honor Old King Pharaoh." These films will be discussed in more detail in Chapter 8. More germane here is DreamWorks' *The Prince of Egypt* (1998), which in a revival of accomplished animated features and computer-generated special effects offers architectural splendors, crowd scenes, and deity-generated special effects of a scope that surpasses even DeMille's. The scene in which Moses threatens Pharaoh with his staff-turned-serpent grows into a magnificent and tuneful display by the Egyptian priests (singing "You're Playing with the Big Boys Now"); the Red Sea parts in a physically plausible hydraulic explosion; and young Rameses and Moses race their chariots along precariously high catwalks stretching from one colossal monument to the next. Perhaps the most creative scene is the dream sequence. The purpose of the clever expository episode is to inform the previously naive Moses that his Hebrew family gave him away to the house of Pharaoh. To deliver the message, the dream brings Egyptian wall paintings to life, animated with parading soldiers and refugee hordes of helpless commoners, making the great Ramesid monument of Medinet Habu quite static by comparison.

The producer, Jeffrey Katzenberg, who had been in charge of a number of successful Disney animated features before leaving to form DreamWorks with David Geffen and Steven Spielberg, aimed beyond the juvenile audience. He boasts of consulting with more than seven hundred scholars, clergymen, and assorted authorities—shades of De-Mille, but two hundred sources shy—and he toned down the humor and eliminated the talking animals that characterized *The Lion King* and his other successes. The result is a reasonably intelligent film that forces the viewer to confront the incongruity of animated characters and sets and the sobriety of the theological message.

Judges

Far removed from the Pentateuch's revolutionary plague-inflicting, lawgiving Moses, Judges' revolutionary Samson fought his people's tyrannical overlords with hirsute brawn, a clever wit, and a few breaths from Jehovah's nostrils. Also unlike Moses, Samson had a moral weakness that led him more than once into romantic disaster. Moral weakness? Romance? Disaster? Sounds like a good idea for a movie. And so it was, first in Pathé's

104   Authenticity does not necessarily a movie make. Here the Israelites cross not the biblical Red
Sea, but the authentic Sea of Reeds—a marsh to the north of Egypt. Modern disbelief in miracles
and insistence on scientific rationale are incompatible with the parting of the waters of Exodus
(and DeMille), but cinematic illusion and dramatic effect are incompatible with 150 drab extras
ho-humming their way through unmiraculous miracles in this early made-for-television film, *Moses,
the Lawgiver* (1976).

1903 *Samson and Delilah,* then in Theo Frenkel's 1911 version, then in Universal's 1914 production (which cost a mighty $100,000), and then in Alexander Korda's 1922 Austrian ver-
sion. Korda's film starred Maria Corda, Alfredo Galoar, and the Hungarian Paul Lukas (born
Pál Lukács). Like DeMille's first version of *The Ten Commandments,* Korda's film followed the
post-*Intolerance* tendency to combine ancient and modern sequences. The film was apparently a financial failure, but it at least gave Korda his first lesson in assembling huge, international costume epics. Korda's assistant producer was young Mihály Kertész (Michael Curtiz);
Curtiz went on that year to make his modern/ancient version of *Sodom und Gomorrah.*

　　DeMille first conceived an idea for a film about Samson in 1935. He ultimately
chose the book *Judge and Fool* by Vladimir Jaborinsky and then set to work adapting
novel and Bible for his 1949 film *Samson and Delilah,* starring Victor Mature. Because the

story of the adult Samson consumes only three chapters in the Old Testament, DeMille had to flesh out the story—in more ways than one. Taking the clue from Judges 15:2 that Samson's first wife had a younger sister, he expanded the role of Semedar (Angela Lansbury) as the sister of Delilah (Hedy Lamarr). This created the opportunity for much romancing and sibling jealousy, in addition to the semibiblical burning of Semedar, her father, and their house. The other episodes from the Bible appear as well—the riddle of the lion and honey and the thirty-garment bet, the three lies to Delilah about the source of Samson's strength, the blinding of the hero, the gristmill drudgery, and the collapse of the temple of Dagon onto a few thousand sporting Philistines.

The screenplay by Jesse Lasky Jr. and Frederic Frank milks every possible metaphor and irony out of this robust tale of love and deceit. After Samson confesses to Delilah that the answer to his riddle is "honey in a lion's belly" (Judges 15:18), the two kiss. Samson flatters her, "You're sweeter than honey," and Delilah responds in kind, "Oh, stronger than a lion." One unforgettable Samsonian line is preserved verbatim from the Bible: when Semedar tells the answer of Samson's riddle to the Philistines and they in turn inform Samson that they know the correct answer, Samson protests, "If ye had not plowed with my heifer, Ye had not found out my riddle" (Judges 15:18). Following Sophocles' lead in *Oedipus Rex,* the screenwriters emphasize the irony of Samson's blinding and the haircut that made him vulnerable: "When my eyes could see, I was blind to your deceit, Delilah," he says, and "If I haven't the strength to fight you Philistines, I need no eyes to see you." Of course, the usual run-of-DeMille apothegms and ancientish hokum appear as well: the Philistines devising treachery are warned, "The trouble you brew today you will drink tomorrow!" And when Delilah rushes to Samson's arms after he has slayed the lion barehanded, he jocularly protests, "Hey! One cat at a time!"

Samson and Delilah was quite spectacular compared to its contemporaries; the audiences of 1949 and 1950 apparently thought so, buying $11 million worth of tickets. If the color and spectacle in *Samson and Delilah* pale in comparison with DeMille's subsequent *The Ten Commandments,* the difference was due in part to a limited budget and less exotic setting: rocky, sparse Palestine lacks the richness and color of Nilotic Egypt. But the underlying reason was that the colorful biblical spectacle simply didn't exist as a film genre in 1949. *Samson and Delilah,* in fact, created the genre and served as the prototype that was to culminate in DeMille's hands seven years later.

The story of Samson offers opportunities to the special-effects man. For some reason DeMille and technician Gordon Jennings decided to omit the scene in which Samson burns down the Philistine cornfields and vineyards by tying torches to the intertwined tails of 150 pairs of jackals (Judges 15:4; Huston later used the scene out of place in *The Bible*). But we do see Samson receive the gusting inspiration of God in a windy mountain pass, burst the thick ropes that have been wound tightly around his shoulders and arms, pick up the spectral jawbone of an ass, and crush vast numbers of helmeted skulls in the name of Jehovah.

105   The enchanting, beguiling Philistine beauty, Delilah, as captivatingly portrayed by Hedy Lamarr in DeMilles's *Samson and Delilah* (1949).

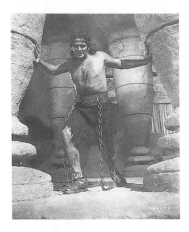

106   Samson (Victor Mature) begins his well-situated destruction of the temple of Dagon in *Samson and Delilah*. Scholars know that Delilah's Philistines were actually a seafaring people who might have come to Philistia from Minoan Crete, so DeMille used the inverted Minoan for these Philistine columns.

107   DeMille orientalized his putatively Minoan Philistines by painting scenes from the Standard of Ur on the interior walls of his temple of Dagon in *Samson and Delilah*. The Standard is Sumerian (Mesopotamian) in origin and dates from circa 2700 B.C.

    As DeMille was to make the architectural balance an unobtrusive yet vital prop in that early scene in *The Ten Commandments,* so he subtly introduces the equine jawbone long before Samson's miraculous victory. A Philistine dwarf earlier had taunted Samson with the mandible, little suspecting how many human skulls that lifeless jawbone could still consume. One anecdote about this jawbone is full of insight into DeMille's approach to historical films. DeMille looked at numerous paintings by the European masters to find the most appropriate depiction of this jawbone scene in Judges 15:15. He saw that all the paintings showed Samson smiting the Philistines with half the jawbone. DeMille immediately ordered his properties man to find the jawbone of an ass. Before long he had one in his un-Samsonesque hand and was repeatedly and forcefully swinging the bone, creating piles and piles of imaginary Philistine corpses in his Hollywood office. By actually trying out the fabled technique, DeMille instantly realized that the full jawbone made a more forceful weapon than did the half, so he used the full jawbone in the film. But before Samson could get his hands on the jawbone, DeMille had the dwarf practice ventriloquism with its moving parts.

Paramount spent more than $3 million on the film itself and another million on advertising. Advertising expenses ranged from lecture tours by the noted historian Arnold Toynbee to Kellogg's gimmicky "Samson-sized Cornflakes." For the lead roles DeMille sponsored talent contests, but Mr. America of 1947 yielded to an overweight Mature, and numerous aspiring Hollywood queens fell before the glamour of the Viennese Lamarr. Mature lost thirty pounds, but he apparently suffered from several phobias, including an understandable lack of enthusiasm for filming the lion-killing sequence with a genuine lion. The resulting combination of shots—Mature vs. stuffed lion, stuntman vs. real lion—disappoints the DeMille aficionado. This was an important role for Mature, who went on to play in five additional "ancient" roles, and he so identified with this role that years later, long after his retirement, he returned to make a cameo as Samson's father in the 1984 made-for-television version. (This was the first of two made-for-television versions; the second, directed by Nicholas Roeg in 1996, starred Eric Thal and Elizabeth Hurley.) Hedy Lamarr played her part with the proper wiliness and alluring poses, aided during one sequence by a gown made of almost two thousand peacock feathers. George Sanders perfected the villainy of the Saran of Gaza, with his pointy beard, vengeful sneers, and insidious conniving.

The Italian revival in the early 1960s had to have its own *Samson* (1961), of course, but this is a horrible film. Even worse were most of the sequels that it spawned or the predecessors that it followed: *Samson and the Sea Beasts* (1963), with Kirk Morris fighting post-Renaissance pirates in the West Indies; *Samson in King Solomon's Mines* (1964), with Reg Park in ancient Africa; *Samson and the Treasure of the Incas* (1964), much like *Hercules Against the Sons of the Sun* but with Alan Steel; *Son of Samson* (1960), which is actually a Maciste film *(Maciste nella Valle del Re); Samson and the Seven Miracles of the World* (1961), with Gordon Scott battling thirteenth-century Tartars; and *Samson and the Slave Queen* (1963), also called *Zorro vs. Maciste,* in which Alan Steel (credited as Sergio Ciani) lives now in the era of Philip II, King of Navarre. Several of these and other "Samson" films have titles translated from the original Italian "Maciste" titles; American distributors knew that American audiences would associate Samson or Goliath or Son of Hercules with heroic strength much more readily than Maciste. Similarly, a Mexican film character known as Santo became known in the United States as Samson, but films like *Samson vs. the Vampire Women* (1961) and *Samson in the Wax Museum* (1961) have nothing to do with long hair, biceps, Palestine, or antiquity.

Much better than these is *Samson and Gideon* (*I Grandi Condottieri,* 1965), which is sufficiently biblical to include Samson's angelically announced birth and his stealing the gates of Gaza. The jawbone and temple of Dagon sequences are modeled after DeMille's, but the remake's temple and its destruction suffer from a Styrofoam toyishness. Samson is muscular but not muscle-bound, and he even displays some Semitic chest hair for once. His left-handedness is disturbing—the ancients were very partial to righties—though not as disturbing as his water-soaked Nylon shag wig. The first half of the film features the story of Gideon from earlier in the book of Judges (6–8). It shows a folksy, mildly humorous approach similar to *The Bible*'s Noah sequence, though less sophisticated; the film's finest moment is Gideon's humorous reduction of his cowardly army to a faithful and dependable three hundred.

The stories of Saul, David, Goliath, and Bathsheba from the two books of Samuel have appeared in nearly a dozen films, from Kalem's *David and Goliath* (1908) and Vitagraph's *Saul and David* (1909), through the Italian *David, King of Israel* (1912) and J. Gordon Edwards's *The Shepherd King* (1923), to the colorful *David and Bathsheba* (1951) and three modern Italian versions, to a recent made-for-television film. *David, King of Israel* offers a primitive dramatization of the young David, who slays Goliath with his sling, cuts off his head, and parades the severed head, which has been fixed onto a spear shaft. The film also includes a brief portrayal of the Absalom episode—even the tree branch that abruptly halts his flight. Otherwise, unconvincing mattes of Jerusalem's walls and Palestinian palm trees stand behind over-robed actors with ringlet beards, and the scenarios are too quick and characterless. Edwards's *The Shepherd King* boasts some hand-colored sequences and a huge crowd of fifteen thousand extras hired from the army of Emir Abdullah of Transjordania.

Twentieth-Century Fox's *David and Bathsheba* took the two-chapter episode of romance and sin from 2 Samuel 11–12 and made it the central event of the life of David. Needless to say, a 1950s Hollywood screenwriter (in this case, Philip Dunne) had ample opportunity for drama and sex when given as a starting point this suggestive yet unembellished biblical passage: "And it came to pass at eventide, that David arose from off his bed, and walked upon the roof of the king's house; and from the roof he saw a woman bathing; and the woman was very beautiful to look upon. And David sent and inquired after the woman. And one said 'Is not this Bath-Sheba, the daughter of Elam, the wife of Uriah the Hittite?' And David sent messengers, and took her; and she came in unto him, and he lay with her; for she was purified from her uncleanliness; and she returned unto her house. And the woman conceived; and she sent and told David, and said: 'I am with child'" (2 Samuel 11:2–5).

The film supplied a reason for David (Gregory Peck) to go to his rooftop: a quarrel with Saul's daughter, Michal, one of the wives in David's harem. Some teasing shots of Bathsheba (Susan Hayward) bathing were bound to be worth a few million in box-office receipts. Bathsheba's meeting with David is so confidential that Bathsheba can tell David that she had *wanted* him to see her bathing. And the scene in which Bathsheba tells the monarch that she is with child involves a whole new set of complicated bickering.

But after David confesses his sin before Nathan the prophet (Raymond Massey) and then asks Jehovah for forgiveness, the last half of the film gathers momentum as a direct result of the slow-paced romancing of the first half. Peck is convincing as a once-heroic monarch who now must face an angry constituency and atone for his sins. Nathan and David raise some interesting questions about justice and injustice in their quarrel, and the king compares the strengths of his merciful and merciless God. Although the film never becomes theologically profound—nor was it meant to be—it does reach a unique climax: the drama's protagonist faces religious and philosophical torment instead of the more hackneyed military or physical crisis.

The essence of the religious drama of *David and Bathsheba* is revealed when David admits his horrendous sin to himself and walks to the tent of the Ark of the Covenant (1 Chronicles 16:4 ff.) to meditate. Jehovah's raining and thundering sky intensifies David's guilt, and the king makes a lengthy speech about mercy and forgiveness to his God. He concludes with, "Look not on this sinner, but on the boy he was," and places his hands on the sacred Ark. The lightning and thunder introduce flashbacks of David as a boy. He is chosen from all of Jesse's sons to succeed Saul as king of Israel and is then anointed by Samuel; he polishes Saul's shield and volunteers to meet the gigantic Goliath of Gath in combat; he whirls his sling and implants a smooth pebble into the huge Philistine's forehead, and this long-forgotten moment of boyhood triumph returns to the penitent, adult David on his knees before the Ark of the Covenant. Instead of emphasizing the Goliath episode as a pleasant introduction to a glorious military career, Dunne and director Henry King selected to begin the tale in medias res and save the Goliath episode for the climax of the film. The episode is used to epitomize the guilt-ridden agony that the older David experiences; he started as such a wondrous and God-loved boy, and now, in contrast, he has fallen so far.

The narrative about David in the Old Testament consumes so many pages and years and involves so many different aspects of the king's life that no film could include them all and expect to maintain its dramatic tension. Many episodes are sensibly omitted in *David and Bathsheba*—David's quarrel with Saul, his early days with Michal, the problems of succession after his reign, the final entry of the Ark into Jerusalem, just to name a few. But the many omissions leave the film with inadequate action before the final scenes. In the only early scene even suggesting action, David imagines hearing the noises from the battle at Gilboa, where he has sent Uriah to his death. Moreover, because David's romance with Bathsheba emphasizes their conversational ability more than any romantic fervor, monotony prevails throughout much of the film, until its religious climax.

David and Bathsheba oscillates between the ends of the authenticity scale. The bath of Bathsheba fails to convey the biblical mood because the censors insisted that this naked wife of Uriah the Hittite be obscured by a screen. At first the filmmakers tried a translucent screen, which preserved the sensual, flesh-toned curves of the naked adulteress-to-be. But fearing the censors, they opted for an opaque, wooden screen that might have been expected to make the whole scene as inticing to David as Goliath's sweaty boots. Speaking of the giant from Gath, the wrestler Walter "The Polish Giant" Talun heaved his 6-foot-8½-inch, 320-pound frame across the screen with impressively mammoth strides.

Also commendable is the inclusion of the scene in which Uzza tries to save the falling Ark of the Covenant from hitting the ground but is cruelly struck dead by an ungrateful

108   The prophet Nathan (Raymond Massey) and King David (Gregory Peck) examine the newly arrived and authentic-looking Ark of the Covenant in a scene from *David and Bathsheba* (1951). Exodus 25:10–22 describes the ark as made of wood, overlaid with gold, equipped with four rings to accommodate staves by which the ark could be carried; above it sat two cherubim. Such detailed authenticity in "ancient" films is often combined with inauthenticity. The ancient Jewish star was five-pointed, for example, but the film audience expects the modern six-pointed symbol, and authenticity in this regard might seem inauthentic.

Jehovah (2 Samuel 6:6–7). Even Jehovah becomes a more convincing cinematic "character" when portrayed with human imperfections.

As Fox's answer to Paramount's multimillion-dollar *Samson and Delilah*, *David and Bathsheba* controlled its share of the "ancient" market until the arrival a few months later of MGM's *Quo Vadis?* The Fox film became one of the top-grossing pictures of 1951 ($7,100,000) and therefore inevitably spawned Italian imitators. *A Story of David* (1960) leads Jeff Chandler through a number of biblical and nonbiblical adventures, and the Italian-Spanish production of *Saul and David* (1964) put its $750,000 budget to efficient use, clinging carefully, if romantically, to the biblical narrative. *David and Goliath*

109   The young David (Leo B. Pessin) slays Goliath during the flashback episode in *David and Bathsheba.* Goliath is played by Walter "The Polish Giant" Talun, a professional wrestler, whose size is considerable but believable. The shot is framed to maximize the scope of the Philistine army in the background.

(1961) starred Orson Welles as Saul and Ivo Payer as David. The shallow and clumsily King Jamesian script falls short of Welles's histrionic abilities, yet his portrayal of the brooding, vengeful Saul does give the film what little dramatic energy it has. A number of other "Goliath" films were made in Italy in the early 1960s, all falling into the post-Hercules muscleman genre. The best known of these are *Goliath at the Conquest of Baby-lon* (also called *Hercules and the Tyrants of Babylon,* 1964); *Goliath and the Barbarians* (1959), with Steve Reeves in Northern Italy, A.D. 568; and *Goliath Against the Giants* (1962), with Brad Harris and Fernando Rey. Like "Samson" films, two of these "Goliath" titles are translations for the original Italian "Maciste."

Of surprising quality was *The Story of David,* a 1976 made-for-television movie, part of which was shot on location in Israel. The four-hour film consists of two parts; in the first Timothy Bottoms plays the young David in his struggles against Saul (Anthony

Quayle), and in the second Keith Mitchell plays David as the adult and then aging patriarch. The film suffers from the monotony and lack of artistry endemic to made-for-
television films and miniseries, but the script, the acting, the biblical authenticity, and the
intrinsic quality of the biblical David episodes make this a worthy film. The biblical text
is followed to the letter: Saul rends Samuel's robe (1 Samuel 15:27); the populace chants
the verse "Saul hath slain his thousands, / And David his ten thousands" (1 Samuel 18:7);
and there is even the dowry of foreskins (1 Samuel 18:25–28), as well as the appropriate
Goliath, Saul, and Jonathan episodes. The teleplay also surpasses the normal television fare
in that it deals with material not ordinarily seen in the family hour. When Saul asks David
to acquire the Philistine foreskins, for example, David comments, "I fear men without
foreskins, but never foreskins without men." When Bathsheba has some important news
to announce to David, she tells him, "I am four weeks late; for ten years I am with the
moon always." One other somewhat corporeal line was delivered as a joke around an
evening campfire: "The lion of Judah roars. Why? Because you eat beans for supper and
your bellies grow full of wind." (The film postdates *Blazing Saddles* by two years.)

Guided by Professor David Noel Freedman of the University of Michigan, the
filmmakers paid careful attention to historical authenticity. For David's singing, the in-
strumentation was limited for the most part to harp and tambourine; the vocal part called
for the appropriate microtonal mordents in David's delivery. One particular literary and
biblical triumph was a subtle remark by David to his court scribes that the book they are
writing—the nascent Bible, that is—"should not overlook the faults" of the early Hebrew
leaders. Adding to the authenticity, Goliath and the Sea-Peoples actually speak in a different tongue from that of the Hebrews, military discussions focus on exotic peoples as the
Hittites and Hurrians, and such archaic curiosities as primogeniture quarrels, harem bickering, and charlatan prophets inject a unique feeling for ancient patriarchal life. At the
same time, such elements as monarchs who are publicly pious but privately pragmatic lend
an element of timelessness to the tale. Effectively shot in the dry, dusty areas of Israel and
often on the ancient citadel of Jerusalem itself, *The Story of David* is one of the very few
"ancient" movies in which historical authenticity and intelligent biblical interpretation
outweigh lack of spectacle and monotonous delivery—two drawbacks that become particularly hazardous when viewed not in CinemaScope but on a television screen, with
commercial interruptions.

The Story of David was certainly superior in many ways to Paramount's 1985 release *King David* starring Richard Gere, whose performance garnered him a Razzie Award
in the "Worst Actor" category. Also of interest insofar as it attempts to humanize otherwise
legendary figures and events is another made-for-television film, Turner's *David* (1997) starring Nathaniel Parker as David, Jonathan Pryce as Saul, and Leonard Nimoy as Samuel.

From the first book of Kings, Hollywood somehow derived *Solomon and Sheba*
(1959), a film that reveals both the advantages and disadvantages of production in that
California hamlet during the late 1950s. The upside of the film's Hollywood origins in-

cludes competent special effects in the Jehovah-bred destruction of Solomon's temple and in the battles against the Egyptians. In one of those battles (shot in Valdespartera, Spain) we are treated to Solomon's brilliant tactic of using his Israelite army's burnished, sun-reflecting shields to blind the Egyptian attackers. The wisdom of Solomon is further evidenced, of course, by the king's judgment upon the two women who claim the same child. The sets of *Solomon and Sheba* are colorful, especially those of the Sheban encampment, the Egyptian court, and the Jerusalem temple. The temple displays the biblical "molten sea" in its forecourt and cherubim in the interior, but it also has some inappropriate reliefs from Persian Persepolis and is inaccurately towered like an eight-story ziggurat. But such objections could be considered pedantic.

More serious disadvantages of the film's late-1950s Hollywood origins are its irreverent and irrelevant digressions from the biblical text and its inevitable concentration on a vapid romantic plot. The three screenwriters and director King Vidor understandably conflated the Queen of Sheba's biblical visit to Solomon (1 *Kings* 10:1–13) with Solomon's biblical yearning for foreign women and strange gods (1 *Kings* 11:1–8). Thus Solomon (Yul Brynner) falls in love with the Queen (Gina Lollobrigida) and begins to worship her god Ragon. This romance and pagan worship then lead to civil strife when Solomon's exiled brother Adonijah (George Sanders) leads the Egyptians against the Hebrew army. Ultimately, of course, the Hebrews win a miraculous and smashing defeat, and Sheba returns to her kingdom a devout believer in Jehovah, the biblical narrative by this time completely crushed under Hollywood's chariot wheels.

This mishing and mashing of biblical history did not approach the romantic heights that the filmmakers hoped for. The title characters act stiffly as royal lovers, and the "orgy" of Ragon should be classed as one of the more anticlimactic climaxes in the history of the cinema. Lollobrigida's foreign accent ("Geeve heem to mee"), her nude bath amid improbably adhesive suds, and her wardrobe of what one critic described as "Oriental Undies" are all alluring, but they do not create any of the romantic sophistication that we might associate with Old Testament royalty.[8] Brynner had the difficult task of replacing Tyrone Power, who died halfway through the filming. He is fabulously kingly, as if by nature, and he does his best to play the degenerating Hebrew monarch who had seven hundred wives, three hundred concubines, and a fascination for foreign gods. Even so, he fails to find the character of Solomon completely, for the screenwriters gave him little to work with. Biblically inexplicable are the substitution of Ragon for Sheba's authentic and much better known female deity, Ishtar (Attar), the unpatriotic characterization of Adonijah, and the conversion of Sheba to Judaism. Unfortunately, the proverbial wisdom of Solomon was conspicuously lacking behind the camera.

Vitagraph's *The Judgment of Solomon* (1909) contained only a brief vignette, but the West Arabian queen has been depicted variously in other films. The first was Fox's *Queen of Sheba* (1921), directed by J. Gordon Edwards and starring Betty Blythe (Sheba) and Fritz Lieber; its climax was, mirabile dictu, a chariot race between Queen Vashti (of

110   The Egyptians foolishly tempt the strength of Solomonian wisdom in this scene from *Solomon and Sheba* (1959). The Hebrews have spent the night polishing their shields, so the reflected sun blinds their assailants and sends them into a conveniently situated chasm. The chariot is the Egyptian type, which held a driver and one warrior; Hittite chariots held a shield bearer as well. But one wonders just what this soldier intends on doing with his sword; it will not reach beyond the equine rumps.

111   A ninth-century B.C. stone-relief depicts an Assyrian chariot entering the fray, complete with driver, spoked wheels, and spear box. This Assyrian knows how to fight from a chariot—with bow and arrow.

Esther provenance) and the Queen of Sheba! Curiously, the film is too embarrassed to mention that Solomon had seven hundred wives, yet it displays scores of thinly clad women, unidentified but vaguely royal. The second depiction of this legendary Semite was an Italian *Queen of Sheba* (1953), which rises above the dullness and ventriloquized dubbing of the contemporary Italian films *Fabiola* and *Messalina,* but its story is absurd. Rehaboam (Gino Leurini), the son of Solomon (Gino Cervi), leaves Jerusalem to spy on Balkis, the Queen of Sheba (Leonora Ruffo). He naturally falls in love with her, and a few complications and battles precede an avalanche that brings the pompous, dry romance to its unfortunate close. *Queen of Sheba* does boast some effective camera angles—particularly a shot of a battering ram pounding its insistent weight directly toward the camera lens. The costuming is a garish blend of authentic Assyrian garb and the wildest contemporary Roman fantasy, with a touch of Minoan (thanks to *Samson and Delilah*). Director Pietro Francisci *(Hercules)* had not yet found his unique recipe for comic, light, tongue-in-cheek heroism and romance. Four decades later came two made-for-television versions, one in Italy, RAI's *Solomon* (1997), starring Ben Cross as Solomon and Max von Sydow as David. An American *Solomon and Sheba* two years earlier featured an African American, Halle Berry, as the Queen of Sheba, thus becoming the first film version to acknowledge that the historical queen was dark-skinned.

In 1953 Lippert produced a fourth film based on the first book of Kings, *Sins of Jezebel*. This bland production starred Paulette Goddard as the Baal-worshiping queen who clashes spiritually and physically with the prophet Elijah. One of the many books about the twelve prophets suggested one film—*Jonah and the Whale,* but the project was hardly launched before financial difficulties swallowed it completely. *The Story of Ruth* (1960), however, found enough material in its four-and-one-half-page biblical source to show 131 minutes of fairly successful drama and biblical narrative. The book of Ruth tells us nothing about Ruth's childhood as a Moabite, so writer Norman Corwin and director Henry Koster hypothesize that she was a priestess of the (authentic) Moabite god Chemosh. The sacrifices of children to Chemosh, to which the cinematic Ruth objects and which, not surprisingly, are shown with great relish, are more or less historically sound and add colorful spectacle to the film. Unfortunately, the crudely enacted sacrifices are not very competent cinematically.

The Bible tells us that "Mahlon and Chilion died both of them" (Ruth 1:5), being no more specific than this. *The Story of Ruth* goes on to invent a dramatically plausible slave pit for Mahlon (Tom Tryon), who is the husband of Ruth. With this plausible metabiblical material established, Ruth joins her mother-in-law Naomi and sojourns to Judah. The touching biblical narrative about Ruth's gradual acceptance by her kinsman Boaz is expanded into a lengthy tale of anti-Moabite feelings and intrafamilial trickery. The biblical council of Elders (Ruth 4:2) becomes a jury to decide whether or not Ruth is a Moabite, and the "nameless kinsman" of the Old Testament becomes a rather messy and distasteful Tob (Jeff Morrow). The biblical scene on the threshing floor is preserved, but with an insidious twist. All these minor variations on the Old Testament's text make *The Story of Ruth* a less charming but more involved story. Clever and harmless tricks played by Boaz and Naomi on Ruth give the narrative several intricate turns, and the ultimate manipulation of the Leverite law—spending the night on the threshing floor with kinsman Boaz—brings the trickery motif to its satisfactory culmination. All in all, *The Story of Ruth* treats the Old Testament with respect but not stultifying reverence.

Several other films have been based on the later books of the Old Testament. From Esther comes *Esther and the King* (1960); from Daniel come *Belshazzar's Feast* (1905, 1913), *Slaves of Babylon* (1953), and, in part, *Intolerance* (1916); and from the story of Judith in the Apocrypha come four different films. But because these films concern life in Persia and Mesopotamia as much as they do biblical life, they will be discussed more appropriately in Chapter 6.

Two other films, both made in Italy, are based on apocryphal sources, *I Maccabei* (1910) and *Il Vecchio Testamento* (*The Old Testament,* 1962). Both narrate the story of the second-century B.C. Maccabee family in its heroic struggle against the Hellenistic King Antiochus IV of the Seleucid Empire. *Il Vecchio Testamento* is full of the muscularized feats and shallow romance characteristic of its Italian genre. *I Maccabei,* directed by Enrico Guazzoni (*Quo Vadis?* [1912], *Marcantonio e Cleopatra* and *Julius Caesar* [both 1914]), is a travesty of historical authenticity. The Antiochids wear Egyptian garb, and the entire plot revolves around Antiochus's wife Astarte (historically Laodice; Astarte is another name for the goddess Ishtar) and her unrequited love for Judas Maccabeus. As we have seen, a film that so unmercifully rearranges a biblical plot is apt to fail, for it has lost its claim to biblical stature and sophistication and must stand on its own, costumed, romantic merits.

Of the approximately fifty films based on the Old Testament, a handful are truly fine films. The films that fail seem to suffer from similar imbalances—too much romance and dialogue, too little action and excitement *(The Story of Ruth);* or too much excitement and action with too little romance or thought *(Sodom and Gomorrah);* or too much reverence for the biblical narrative with too little concern for dramatic considerations *(Moses, the Lawgiver);* or too free an adaptation of the biblical narrative *(Solomon and Sheba),* sometimes with an additional lack of dramatic tension *(Joseph and His Brethren).* Part of the difficulty stems from the general public's knowledge of the Bible and its marvelous stories; if filmmakers digress too far from the biblical narrative, they inevitably produce a plot that seems inauthentic and far-fetched. On the other hand, if the filmmakers restrict themselves completely to the Old Testament narrative, they will almost inevitably produce a dry and undramatic enactment. The made-for-television films of the past three decades have taken the middle path and are as a group fairly good. But true cinematic directorial giants are needed to find an artistic balance, and in this Old Testament branch of the genre DeMille and Huston stand taller than the rest.

In addition, depicting prophets, patriarchs, miracles, and Jehovah's presence poses another problem for all filmmakers. Movie audiences, conditioned by a century-long association between the ancient world and the epic cinema—expect such characters as Adam, Abraham, Moses, Solomon, and Sheba, and events such as the slaying of Goliath or the crossing of the Red Sea, to be larger than life and portrayed with the titanic qualities that only a few thousand years of maturation can develop. A historically conscious adult David described this maturation process. In *David and Bathsheba* he acknowledges, "I must admit that Goliath seems to grow a little bigger every year." To be sure, a Goliath or Hebrew king or any biblical character or event that fails to possess the demanded cinematic stature is doomed to failure. For all their contrivance, DeMille's parting of the Red Sea in 1956 and his Samsonian destruction of the temple of Dagon, Huston's folksy Noah, and George C. Scott's chillingly prophetic Abraham will be remembered as the most representative and iconographical Old Testament depictions of the twentieth century.

I tell you there are strange forces at work here. For instance, there's this

"Messiah," King of the Jews, who will lead them all into some sort of anti-

Roman paradise. Then there's a wild man in the desert named John, who

drowns people in water. There's a carpenter's son who goes around doing

magic tricks, "miracles" they call them. This man is different: he teaches that

god is near—in every man. . . . It's actually quite profound, some of it.

—TRIBUNE SEXTUS, *BEN HUR* (1959)

With the debatable exception of the debatable creation of Adam and Eve, no single event that took place in the ancient world has had as great an impact on the subsequent history of the Mediterranean and the Western world as a Roman provincial governor's reluctant execution of a local Jew known generally as Jesus of Nazareth, called by some the Christ. Within two generations his name and teachings spread from the tiny province of Judea through the great cities of the Roman Empire—Ephesus, Philippi, Corinth, Athens, and Rome herself—thousands of Jews and Gentiles practiced his teachings and died for their beliefs, and eventually the entire Roman state succumbed to the overwhelming appeal of the Christian movement and its indomitable momentum. The spiritual roots of the next two millennia of European history are buried deep in the Levantine soil upon which this Nazarene had trod. From Giotto's lovely Scrovegni Chapel in Padua to Bach's impressive *Passions,* for centuries the iconography of Jesus' life gave the Western arts their most inspirational material.

The art of film has been no exception. Beginning with the first filming of the famed decennial Passion Play at Oberammergau in 1897 and Luigi Topi's ten tableaux of 1900, the passion of Christ and related narratives have appeared in more than forty major films. These films include one of the American film industry's first epics *(Intolerance),* two of the medium's most successful epics (the 1925 and 1959 productions of *Ben-Hur*), the first CinemaScope film *(The Robe),* one of the most expensive films ever shot in America *(The Greatest Story Ever Told),* one of the most elaborate made-for-television movies ever made *(Jesus of Nazareth),* and two of the most controversial films of the second half of the twentieth century *(The Last Temptation of Christ* and *Life of Brian).* Cinematic versions of the tale of the Christ have attracted such noted directors as Cecil B. DeMille, Mervyn LeRoy, William Wyler, D.W. Griffith, Sidney Olcott, Pier Paolo Pasolini, Franco Zeffirelli, and Martin Scorsese.

Directors and actors who attempt to portray the life of Christ or the era of early Christianity inevitably tread on perhaps the thinnest ice in filmdom—a border between the sublime and the ridiculous, between reverence and boredom. Clothing a serene, emotionless actor in white robes and crucifying him amid the gentle tears of women may yield some of the devotion desired from the scene at Golgotha, but without the banter of the dice-throwing Roman soldiery and the skeptical Jewish leaders and elders, without the stormy heavens and the trembling earth, without the anguish of the disrobed, derided, beaten body of the Messiah and the triumph of his unswervingly divine purpose, the scene will not work. Too much bland reverence yields a dramatic void. The transfiguration of Christ into a glowing god on earth has spiritually satisfied millions of humans for centuries, but it will leave a cinematic audience flat. What is more, such a portrayal is false to the complex character of Jesus as portrayed in the Bible. After all, it was in large part the glorious combination of Christ the transfigured son of God, Christ the prophet, Christ the healer, Christ the rebel, Christ the man, and Christ the suffering, crucified mortal that made the first four books of the New Testament the compelling theological foundation of Christianity.

Christ is the most difficult cinematic figure to portray—even more difficult than an Old Testament patriarch like Moses. He must be a believable human, yet he must reveal his divine spirit; he must stand above humans and never sway from his purpose, yet he must fall victim to human misunderstanding and have his brief moments of emotional doubt and physical pain. He must be able to soothe and heal the meek and suffering, yet he must be capable of terrifying an entire religious establishment and of single-handedly overturning the market inside the Jerusalem temple. He must boldly walk across water, yet meekly be whipped and spat on by his adversaries. He must know that he is the Son of Man, yet he must be able to plead, "My God, why hast thou forsaken me?" And if all that weren't challenging enough, each viewer has a preconception of what Jesus looked like. It is almost easier for a camel to pass through a needle's eye than for an actor to portray Christ with both reverence and dramatic conviction.

The Gospel According to Hollywood

One of the most severe difficulties the earliest cinematic attempts at a portrayal of Christ faced was simply the silence to which they were necessarily bound. A complex characterization of Christ was hardly possible, for film was still a visual medium, not a verbal one. Consequently, films such as *The Star of Bethlehem* (1908), *Jerusalem in the Time of Christ* (1908), *The Crimson Cross* (1913), *From the Manger to the Cross* (1912), *The Life of Our*

Savior (1914), *Christus* (1915), and *Intolerance* (1916) all present what seems to modern viewers a monotonous series of picture-postcard tableaus—the Nativity, the Magi, the raising of Lazarus, the Last Supper, the Transfiguration, the Crucifixion. Kalem's *From the Manger to the Cross* (also known as *Jesus of Nazareth*) shies away from showing the violent moments in Christ's life. When Jesus chases the money changers and dove sellers from the temple, he merely waves a cloth at the transgressors; the entire treatment of the Jerusalem arrest, trial, and execution is curtailed, while the majority of footage shows Christ gesturing to crowds and putting his gentle hand onto the heads of the unfortunate. By no means a bold film, *From the Manger to the Cross* does have its precious, innocent moments. When the titles (from the Gospels) tell us that John the Baptist is "a voice crying in the wilderness" (Matthew 3:3), for example, we see a shaggily clothed man cupping his hands around his mouth. The film charmingly includes the rarely filmed episode from Luke 2:41–50, in which the young Christ is separated from his parents in Jerusalem. The film is also interesting for its primitive use of special effects: unable to shoot at night, the filmmakers show the "midnight arrest" in the Garden at Gethsemane in broad daylight; the fury of the sky above Golgotha is depicted on a moving roll of scenic backdrop; and Christ ascends to heaven on a hoisted rope.

In 1915 the Italian studio Cines followed Kalem's *From the Manger to the Cross* and Pathé's *The Life of Our Savior* with *Christus*. This film resembled *From the Manger to the Cross* in its location shots in Egypt (the flight to Egypt) and Palestine (most recognizably the Via Dolorosa) and in its heavy reliance on New Testament quotations for titles. *Christus* had little chance for success in its 1917 American release, for by then D. W. Griffith's spectacular *Intolerance* (1916) had shaken the film world.

Griffith's revolutionary format—running four simultaneous stories of human intolerance—left much of the Passion footage on the cutting room floor. Because the purpose of *Intolerance* was to "show how hatred and intolerance, through all the ages, have battled against love and charity," Griffith concentrated on the struggle that Christ led against the hypocritical and unjust leadership of the Pharisees. He shows the mobs of Hebrew laborers halting their work perforce while the "reverent" Pharisees walk past in prayer. During the wedding feast at Cana (John 2:1–11) Christ, in a long white robe and shoulder-length brown hair, changes the water into wine. Semibiblically (the Bible has similar scenes in different contexts) Griffith lets the scornful Pharisees into the party, and they protest against the merrymaking. In a typical Griffith touch, a footnote beneath the titles assures the viewers that drinking wine was perfectly acceptable in ancient Palestine.

Griffith's footnotes in *Intolerance* are unique in cinematic history, but this particular note tells us something about the dynamics or morality and drama of New Testament films. It is clear in the Gospels that Christ and his disciples drank wine, both at Cana and at the Last Supper, whence the celebration of the all-important eucharistic ritual. When modern caution and American puritanical ethics demand that a filmmaker go out of his

112   The Resurrection was one of the sequences technicians hand-colored for DeMille's *The King of Kings* (1927). The long shadows, gleaming and streaming light, subtly reflecting armor, and deep-shadowed foreground of this scene exemplify the technically brilliant lighting effects throughout the film. The rock-covered entrance to the Tomb of Jesus is as authentic as can be expected, given that scholars do not know exactly where and how Jesus was buried.

113   Coffins were not used in first-century A.D. Palestine, and many tombs had a rolling rock door. This one in Jerusalem, known as Herod's Tomb, was re-created in *The King of Kings* (1927), *King of Kings* (1961), *Barabbas* (1962), and several other films.

way to justify behavior that might more sensibly be taken for granted, Christ loses some of the character drawn by the evangelists. Wine drinking is scarcely the most important aspect of Christ's earthly existence, but unless the filmmaker includes such mundane elements, we are apt to be left with a cinematic Christ sanctified beyond all human interest. Such unhistorical, inauthentic, unbiblical, and unnecessary purification of Christ turns complex biography and profound religious drama into simplified devotional whitewash. If Christ was divinely pure, he nonetheless lived as a man among men.

Christ appears only briefly in the rest of *Intolerance*. He stops the hypocrites from stoning the prostitute, he carries his cross to Golgotha, and he is crucified in the film's fast-moving climax. But the real meat of *Intolerance* came from two of its other three stories.

Griffith's influence on the Hollywood film industry was immense, and he had no more successful pupil than Cecil B. DeMille. Not surprisingly, DeMille's second "ancient" epic expanded *Intolerance*'s glimpses of the life of the Messiah. *The King of Kings* (1927) was actually DeMille's second choice. He had wanted to do a film called *The Deluge*, but Warner Brothers rained on his parade with *Noah's Ark*. So DeMille turned to his twelve research specialists and had them dig up as many New Testament facts and authenticities as possible. Typically, when set designer Paul Tribe showed the cinemogul his drab, plain, but authentic Palestinian set designs, DeMille rejected them and demanded something more elaborate. Tribe insisted that these were authentic, but DeMille then revealed the other side of the authenticity argument, as well as his feel for the workings of the silver screen: no one *really* knew *exactly* what first-century B.C. Palestinian buildings looked like anyway, he said, and he wanted something that would make an impression on the screen. Tribe was fired, and Mary Magdalene was given an ornate atrium complete with pond, swans, and lily pads. It may not have been authentic, but it certainly sold tickets. After taking on two clergymen as special consultants, DeMille subjected them to his innate know-how as well. They once argued over the authenticity of set designs, whereupon DeMille told one of them to "go to hell!" The clergyman replied, "I can't; I already have a reservation elsewhere."[1]

If DeMille was quick to fudge historical authenticity if it got in the way of cinematic impact, he was inflexible in his insistence on biblical morality amid the cast and crew. As he had when filming *The Ten Commandments* (1923), he distributed copies of the Bible to the company of *The King of Kings*. He had an organ installed in the studio to play inspirational hymns for the actors. He insisted that H. B. Warner (Christ) eat and sleep in solitude, that he ride in a curtained limousine, and that he wear a veil over his head while walking to and from the studio. DeMille's moral dicta had little effect. Warner's solitude reportedly revived an old drinking problem, and the Virgin Mary (Dorothy Cummings) was in the process of suing her real-life husband for divorce.

While exercising moral conservatism, DeMille was spending liberally. When the bills reached $2.5 million, his backers began to insist that he merge his company with Pathé. But the ultimate result of DeMille's demands, artistic, moral, and monetary, was one of the most popular films of all time. The amount of money earned by *The King of Kings* is not relevant, for DeMille gave away all his profits to charities, and many church groups bought prints of the film to lend free to congregations, missionaries, and private organizations. But *The King of Kings* was probably viewed more often than any other film ever made before the 1975 revolution.

Among other strengths, the film is distinguished by powerful and variegated lighting. Cameraman Peverall Marley looked at three hundred biblical paintings by the European masters and attempted to duplicate as many of them as possible on the screen. To achieve these painterly effects he used seventy-five different lenses, seven different kinds of film, and the relatively new Technicolor process. Marley's boldness and technical wizardry breathed life and religious awe into the massive sets of the Jerusalem temple, its Nicanor Gate and Holy of Holies, the streets of Nazareth and Jerusalem, and the Mount of Olives.

Before the film's initial glimpse of Jesus, a little blind girl comes to him on the Sabbath and asks to be cured of her malady (see John 9:1–41). Even though the Pharisees insist that there is to be no healing on the Sabbath, Jesus declares, "Whosoever shall believeth in me shall not abide in darkness." Taking the line literally and subjectively, DeMille blackens the screen and gradually crosses it with a dim ray of light. The dim light begins to turn ever so slowly into a hazy grayness, which expands to cover the entire screen. Very slowly the haze begins to become focused, and we see for the first time the first thing that the little blind girl sees—her healer and savior.

The most impressive scene in *The King of Kings* is the crucifixion. The camera focuses on the foot of the heavy wood cross while it is slowly dragged along the dusty ground. The painful hammering of the nails is not shown; DeMille considered such details as unnecessary and distasteful gore. Instead we see a huge mass of weeping humanity, with the three Golgothan crosses in the distance. The two thieves ask Christ to save them (Luke 23:39–43), and Christ says his last seven words and dies. Instantly the wind begins to howl, and the dust from the ground begins to swirl in the air; the very foundations of Calvary begin to quake, and flickering lightning rips the veil of the temple in half (Luke 23:45). The scene is awesome, and its awesomeness demanded numerous expensive technical preparations by Marley and DeMille. To re-create the dramatic chiaroscuro of paintings by Rubens and Gustave Doré, Marley had to employ twenty-seven thousand amperes of lighting. Yet he had to be careful that this strong lighting did not cause streaks on the swirling dust; the scene had to have a cloudy, torrential look while neither revealing light streaks nor being too dark to film. Finally, the entire scene had to be shot before the whirling clouds of a $70,000 cyclorama. The ultimate result of the sophisticated special effects: the height of human gloom and divine anger, of earthly storm and heavenly torrent. Incidentally, while DeMille was filming this scene, D. W. Griffith walked into the studio. DeMille was honored and asked the pioneer to direct a brief sequence. Griffith did so, though without distinction.

Although DeMille used every conceivable shade and expression of white, black, and gray in his film, he knew that certain scenes had to appear even more visually complex and powerful than the rest. So he had his staff hand-paint the resurrection scene in a dramatic orange hue. Then they gilded the sequence in which Lazarus is raised. The cost of preparing such scenes was huge and the amount of exposed film was vast—reportedly 1.5 million feet—but by visually highlighting the episodes, DeMille was able to avoid a narrative digression that might have ruined his cinematic Gospel. DeMille, like countless readers of the Scriptures, was not completely convinced that Judas betrayed Jesus only for the thirty pieces of silver. Though John (12:6) explains that Judas was Jesus' treasurer and embezzled some of the Messiah's funds, DeMille imagined an affair between Mary Magdalene (Jacqueline Logan, though Gloria Swanson was originally offered the part) and Judas (Rudolph Schildkraut, whose son Joseph played Caiaphas). Fortunately for cinematic history this part of the narrative was edited out before the film's final release—for considerations of length, not accuracy or taste.

The Hollywood premiere of *The King of Kings* was also the opening of Grauman's Chinese Theater (its sidewalk not yet dented with celebrity paw prints), on May 19, 1927. The film became so well established that no other major cinematic portrayal of the life of Christ was attempted in America until 1954. In the meantime, however, Julien Duvivier directed *Golgotha* (also called *Ecce Homo,* 1932) in France. Unlike his predecessors, he treated only the last week of Christ's life and the resurrection. And unlike DeMille, he overzealously emphasized the innate piety in the story of Christ; consequently, he created a lengthy, plodding, monotonous film. Still, Duvivier's failure was not from lack of ambition and spectacle. Magnificent mattes of Jerusalem and panning subjective shots of its Passover crowd (of "hundreds of thousands," which may have been a little too ambitious) start *Golgotha* off impressively. Jacques Ibert's full but themeless music is an unfortunately apt accompaniment to this sincere but colorless narrative.

Golgotha does not suffer from lack of fidelity to the sources, either. The film includes the tribute to Caesar, Judas's cupidity, the Last Supper on an "upper balcony" (Mark 14:15), Peter's triple denial of Christ (and the subsequent cock's crow), the dream of Pilate's wife (Matthew 27:19), and Jesus' instructions to Simon Peter—"Feed my sheep" (John 21:17). But typical of *Golgotha*'s pious and unsubtle approach to the Gospels, this last statement by Christ is followed, preposterously, by a shot of a flock of sheep. Duvivier thought that the same literary symbols that elevate the style of the Bible could elevate his film. He was wrong, but at least he did not juxtapose shots of Peter and a rock.

Many privately produced films of the life of Christ had appeared over the years. Not counting the short-lived *The Great Commandment* (1942), one modest production ($600,000) surfaced in 1954. *Day of Triumph,* the Rev. James K. Friedrich's fifty-third film, starred Robert Wilson as Christ and Lee J. Cobb as Zadok. Zadok was a high priest mentioned in the Old Testament, but this fictitious Zadok rebels against Roman tyranny. We see Jesus through Zadok's eyes, and Judas betrays Jesus to further the goals of the revolutionary group, to which the Iscariot also belongs. This plot is not quite so far-fetched as DeMille's affair between Judas and Mary Magdalene; there was indeed an insurrection against Roman provincial rule in Judea in the thirties A.D., though its biblical proponent was Barabbas (Mark 15:7), not Judas Iscariot.

The post-*Ben-Hur* splurge of "ancient" films in the early 1960s gave birth to a handful of new films about the life of Jesus. The first of these Scripturamas was a full-bodied, wide-screen, colorful *King of Kings* (1961). The film had an impressive list of production credits—produced by Samuel Bronston, narration written by Ray Bradbury and delivered by Orson Welles, and music by Miklos Rozsa. It was shot in Spain and used much of its $8 million budget to photograph its three hundred-plus sets and twenty thousand extras (the numbers according to MGM propaganda).

The film does have impressive and authentic moments. During the Sermon on the Mount, Christ (Jeffrey Hunter, whence the film's nickname "I Was a Teenage Jesus") realistically seems to hold his crowd spellbound. Some members of the crowd ask their teacher questions, and the mobile camera keeps interest alive during the lengthy theological and moral exegeses. Siobhan McKenna's Virgin Mary is also commendable, surpassed only by Frank Thring's ringlet-bearded, sleazy-smiled, intelligent but evil Herod Antipas. The film strives for authenticity in matters large and small. The historian Josephus wrote that the newly arrived Pontius Pilate angered his subjects by displaying medallions bearing the image of Emperor Tiberius. These medallions and the ensuing arguments are depicted in *King of Kings.* The traditional Passover feast includes the eating of "the bitter herbs," and these symbolic indelicacies are included in the film's Last Supper sequence. And Palestinian tombs were opened and closed by stones rolled across the door, just as Christ is temporarily entombed in the film.

King of Kings also contains many unacceptable moments—unacceptable both historically and dramatically. Jesus' visit to John the Baptist's prison cell is unbiblical, and his representation by a Roman advocate before Pilate undermines much of the meaning and purpose behind the Passion. Perhaps more disturbing is the heavy emphasis on the insurrection led by Barabbas (Harry Guardino). To portray Barabbas as an anti-Roman insurrectionist is authentic, as we have seen, but to displace the spiritual message of Jesus with political and physical street fighting is inappropriate. Several traditional biblical eccentricities were underplayed as well—John the Baptist's wildness and Salome's sexuality, for example. Robert Ryan as John the Baptist seems more like a pious preacher from Ohio than "a voice crying in the wilderness," and Brigid Bazlen's "dance of the seven veils" omits the unbiblical but artistically traditional unveiling. Lastly, director Nicholas Ray avoided the "da Vinci syndrome" in staging the Last Supper, but if Leonardo's positioning all the apostles on one side of the table was implausible, Ray's Y-shaped table was no more historical. In reality, if Jesus' party followed the Greco-Roman custom of their rulers, they would have been at three couches arranged in a U-shape.

Any artist who tries to film a cinematic portrait of Christ must face an initial problem in deciding which of the Gospels to use, or, if using more than one, how to com-

114   The kiss of Judas (Otello Sestili) from *The Gospel According to Saint Matthew* (1964). Harsh and ultrarealistic, Pasolini's cinematic gospel avoids the clichés of Christmas-card Scripturamas. Unshaven and testy, Pasolini's Christ (Enrique Irazoqui) can wither a fig tree; he embodies Christ's power, not his tenderness.

bine them and bring them into concord. The makers of *King of Kings* chose the route taken by all of its predecessors—to combine the four Gospels. During the crucifixion sequence Jeffrey Hunter recites Luke 23:34: "Father, forgive them for they know not what they do." Then he tells another condemned man, "Today you will be with me in Paradise" (Luke 23:43). Ignoring Christ's pain and suffering, and making it seem as if he had nothing better to do than recite memorable apothegms from his cross, *King of Kings* now turns to John 19:26 and has Christ say, "Woman, there is your son." Not content with a single set of dying words, the script demands that Jesus proclaim both John's "It is finished" (19:30) and Luke's "Father, into Thy hands I commend my soul" (23:46). The conciseness and unity of Christ's last remarks from the cross in each of the four Gospels give the literary works some of their most poignant and succinct moments. To bunch five of these statements together in the one moment of film overburdens this poignancy.

When Pier Paolo Pasolini began his version of the life of Jesus, he took into consideration the different approaches of each of the four evangelists. Choosing not to blend them all into one account, he based his film on Matthew alone. The resulting *The Gospel According to Saint Matthew* (*Il Vangelo secondo Matteo*, 1964) thus became the first film about the life of Jesus that had a revolutionary, albeit ancient, unifying principle. Pasolini followed Matthew in offering a stark, unembellished portrait of the Messiah, and, unlike his predecessors, Pasolini included the unpleasant and controversial episodes in Jesus' life. One gaunt Galilean whom Jesus heals has a grotesque tumor on his nose and forehead; Jesus stares coldly at his mother and says, "Who is mother to me?" (Matthew 12:48); Jesus is unwelcome and rejected in his native Nazareth (13:54–58); he wills a fruitless fig tree to wither (20:19); he suffers a draining moment of despair at Gethsemane (26:37–39); and he screams "with a loud voice" just before he dies on the cross (27:50).

Pasolini's production is perfectly suited to the spare tone of Matthew. The film adopts a rough, grainy texture: Christ wears a scraggly ten-day beard; Caiaphas and his

Pharisee mob wear tall, suggestively papal miters; the miracles are executed without hoopla; and the bleak, hillside landscapes (of Calabria) decorate the entire setting with an effectively primitive aura. The dreary music of Prokofiev's *Alexander Nevsky* and the lonesome strings of Bach and Mozart add to the stark realism, as do Pasolini's cast of unknowns. Jesus is played by a young Spanish economics student (Enrique Irazoqui), Judas by a Roman truck driver (Otello Sestili), and the Virgin Mary by Pasolini's mother. Pasolini used these amateur actors and a physical crudeness to create a mundane, human climate, unlike the artificially shimmering sanctity of all previous and most subsequent films about the life of Christ. He shoots them with repeated long close-ups of unassuming, unmade-up faces, and he frequently uses the zoom lens to create intentional disturbances in the narrative. Pasolini's interpretation of Matthew is accurate, believable, and theologically powerful. If only he had smeared a bit of honey on the lip of this cup of bitter absinthe, he might have created one of the most widely acclaimed films of its era. But the Marxist director, whose original Italian title, *Il Vangelo secondo Matteo,* intentionally avoided use of the word *saint,* chose instead to present a powerful, intellectually frightening curiosity, a cinematic voice crying in the wilderness.

At about the time *King of Kings* was released in 1961, the producer, director, and writer George Stevens, who had been planning a film based on the life of the Messiah, was flying to Israel and Lebanon to examine horizons for location shooting. He decided that the Holy Land looked too eroded and unimpressive, so he shot his version of the life of Christ, *The Greatest Story Ever Told,* amid the mesas of Utah, which, he insisted, "looked more authentic."[2] His words sound twisted, but his point is a familiar one, and a sound one: historical authenticity cannot be allowed to interfere with dramatic necessity or with the traditional understanding of certain biblical events. In short, give unto history what is history's; give unto art what is art's. If Giotto could paint imaginative and inauthentic scenery for his scenes of Christ's life in the Scrovegni Chapel in Padua, then why should Stevens not shoot the magnificently imposing mesas of Utah for the cinematic Palestine? Of all the critics who panned *The Greatest Story Ever Told* in 1965, not one denied the merits of the splendid scenery or the film's beautiful cinematography. The miraculous feeling surrounding the raising of Lazarus is enhanced by the setting, along the foreboding side of a steep, rocky mesa. The evocative environment and the exultation of the Hallelujah Chorus from (appropriately enough) Handel's *Messiah* help make this one of the most sensuous moments in any film version of the New Testament.

115/116   John the Baptist (Charlton Heston) is about to baptize "Him by Whom he should be baptized" (Max von Sydow, left foreground, facing page, top) in *The Greatest Story Ever Told* (1965). Director George Stevens thought that this Utah location "looked more authentic" than Palestine. A Renaissance depiction of the baptism of Christ (Joachim Patinir, c. 1500) is set in a similarly rocky, unworldly setting. Any artist, whether Renaissance painter or twentieth-century film director, has the option of rejecting historical authenticity in favor of artistic expression.

Unfortunately, the massive topography of *The Greatest Story Ever Told* is reflected in the elephantine pace of the film. The visual impressions are marvelous, the dramaturgy downright ponderous. Stevens had promised "vigorous ideas" for his film, but his version of the "greatest story" lacks the profundity reasonably expected from such a bold multi-million-dollar enterprise.[3] Christ (Max von Sydow) acts with full Messianic devotion, but his interminable succession of parables and quotations pouring forth from his oral mal-occlusion lack the vitality that revolutionized the spiritual basis and undermined the entire Olympian substructure of the ancient world. Von Sydow delivers his lines as effectively as possible, but New Testament parables and quotations, which work so well in print, cannot really develop a dramatically viable figure on film. Moreover, Christ is portrayed only as an inspirational figure. Perhaps Stevens intended a one-dimensional portrayal to convey Christ's divinity; if it does so, it does so by default, for no other aspect of Jesus' character is effectively presented.

Individual sequences of the film reveal considerable artistry. Claude Rains's Herod the Great interviews the three Wise Men in the dark, bare atmosphere of an ancient stone palace. Another creepily naturalistic evocation of the ancient world is the slaughter of the innocents, executed without a word. Some thirty years later, the turmoil and despair aroused by the mechanically patrolling Roman troops suggest a political climate perfectly ripe for the wild prophet in camel's hair. The crucifixion sequence gathers its compelling momentum visually from brilliantly severe editing, and aurally from the thunderous shouting of the huge crowd around Golgotha, which is effectively drowned out by alternating moments of spiritual silence and rich music.

One of the most severely criticized aspects of *The Greatest Story Ever Told*'s 222 minutes was the inclusion of scores of Hollywood stars and starlets—some in decidedly minor roles. Charlton Heston (John the Baptist), Roddy McDowall (Matthew), Sidney Poitier (Simon of Cyrene), Carroll Baker (Veronica), Shelley Winters, Ed Wynn, Pat Boone, John Wayne, Angela Lansbury, Victor Buono, Joseph Schildkraut, and Sal Mineo never really find the opportunity to display their talents or to enhance the quality of the narrative; in fact, "star-hunting" distracts the viewer from the film's supposed biblical essence. In one sense, this misuse of such a wealth of thespian talent parallels the film's misuse of the awe-inspiring mesas of Utah: the setting and the leading cast members were unquestionably well chosen by Stevens, but his script (based on Fulton Oursler's novel) and direction failed to mold this raw material into the titanic work of art it originally purported to become. *The Greatest Story Ever Told* rises majestically above many of the other films about the ancient world, yet it lacks the unifying dramatic vision and spiritual uplift that should have shaped it into a true masterpiece. It is as if the film were a magnificent and gigantic block of flawless marble that was skillfully chiseled but never given the final, essential sculptural embodiment of unity and life.

The countercultural revolution of the sixties made possible the portrayal of a "hipper" Christ, and in 1973 two musical adaptations of Jesus' life, *Jesus Christ Superstar* and

117   Judas's ghost (Carl Anderson) fronts the dazzling Motown sequence from *Jesus Christ Superstar* (1973), one of two musical versions of the Passion. Two decades later the animated feature *Hercules* (1997) revived the Motown style for its opening number by the Muses.

Godspell, moved from stage to film. Norman Jewison's uneven *Jesus Christ Superstar* had some successful moments. Judas (Carl Anderson) in a bright Da-Glo orange jumpsuit sings atop some staggering Israeli scenery, and Herod (Joshua Mostel) hilariously wiggles and jiggles his rubber-tire gut beside his plastic swimming pool—which he tauntingly invites Jesus to walk across. Although the work sprang from a "pop" sensibility, the theological and political problems posed by Judas—who praises Christ for beginning with an inspiring idea, but accuses him of overreaching—are sophisticated and believable. Judas's guilt after the betrayal is adapted well to harrowing guitar rhythms; Jesus' crucifixion is presented with cyc-opening silhouette photography; and the glaring lights behind the Motown dance of Judas's ghost succeed in carrying both spiritual message and show-biz pizzazz.

    Jesus Christ Superstar also has some severe flaws. The Andrew Lloyd Webber–André Previn rock-operatic score makes Jesus (Ted Neeley) sing too frequently in the outer limits of falsetto, and the "heavy" symbols—tanks rolling across the Israeli desert and Phantom jets soaring above—are trite attempts at contemporary political relevance. The often sensitive lyrics (Tim Rice) occasionally cross the line between the sublime and the ridiculous:

118   The Crucifixion, as presented in *Jesus Christ Superstar.* Roman helmets become hard-hats; cuirass and cloak become T-shirt and jeans; and machine guns supplement spears. Such weak attempts at contemporary political relevance marred the film.

119   The Crucifixion, as presented in *Godspell* (1973). Anachronisms, childish and amateurish humor, a dated peace-and-love philosophy, and Jesus crucified on a Manhattan Cyclone fence modernize the Passion but leave it devoid of meaning and stature.

God, Thy will is hard,
But you hold every card.

Even with its flaws, *Superstar* is a positively divine effort compared with *Godspell*. From the opening scenes, in which a female "apostle" is called from her heathenish Xerox machine to be baptized in a sanctified Manhattan fountain, to the closing scene, in which Judas blows his Cracker Jack–box whistle and crucifies Christ (in his Superman T-shirt) on a Cyclone fence, *Godspell* tries hard to be clever and contemporary. But guided by the powers of a cinematic Beelzebub, it fails miserably. Tony and Maria made more believably sanctified figures dancing along their *West Side Story* Cyclone fences. Incessant mediocre imitations of the Three Stooges, John Wayne, Howard Cosell, and Chester Conklin signal only the film's adoration of its own adorableness. These flower children could never have withered a fig-tree, and somehow the Last Supper loses some of its prototypical symbolism when the wine is drunk from Dixie cups. To be sure, *Godspell* offers some artistic

120   The Crucifixion, as presented in *The Greatest Story Ever Told* (1965). The sharp, unified marching of these Roman troops characterizes the stern, legal climate under which Christ was executed. The soldiers carry pikes and sledges in their right hands, *scuta* (rectangular, curved shields) in their left; they wear the *lorica segmentata* (segmented chest armor). A few extras are smiling.

musical numbers on skyscraper rooftops twelve hundred feet above Manhattan bedrock, but the film is otherwise childish and tasteless. A curiosity of the short-lived peace-love era, *Godspell* lacks the grace and breadth of understanding necessary for a successful cinematic rendering of the New Testament.

Franco Zeffirelli's *Jesus of Nazareth* reused several motifs employed in the earlier versions of the life of Christ. In assembling this 1977 made-for-television movie, which at $18 million was by far the most expensive television movie produced to date, Zeffirelli included a conversation between the three Wise Men (à la *Ben-Hur* [1959]), a rocky canyon in which John could do his baptizing (à la *The Greatest Story Ever Told*), a Simon Peter who could raise the roof with his boisterous behavior (à la *The Big Fisherman*), and an extraordinary emphasis on the anti-Roman political climate of first-century A.D. Palestine (à la *King of Kings* and *Barabbas*). Another borrowing from *The Greatest Story Ever Told,* a cast full of luminaries of the cinema, inevitably leads to "star-hunting." While we should be concentrating on the art and the story line, we find ourselves forced to recognize Anne Bancroft (Mary Magdalene), Peter Ustinov (Herod the Great), James Earl Jones (Balthazar), Laurence Olivier (Nicodemus), Ralph Richardson (Simeon), James Mason (Joseph of Arimathea), Olivia Hussey (Mary), Anthony Quinn (Caiaphas), Ernest Borgnine, Donald Pleasance, James Farentino, and others. The problem is not so much the crowd of famous actors but rather that the New Testament does not give those actors enough to do. The script is necessarily sparse, the characterizations are necessarily underdeveloped, and even a great actor can look holy or blasphemous in only so many ways.

Before the film was first screened, a great controversy arose when Zeffirelli told an interviewer that "Jesus will be portrayed as an ordinary man." Letters by the thousands poured in to protest the heresy, and General Motors, which had originally agreed to sponsor the film, was forced to reverse gears and back out of the project. Obscuring the corporation's real concern that thousands of offended Christians would turn to Ford or AMC, GM released this announcement: "General Motors found the program so sensitive and beautiful that they think it would be wrong for a commercial company to take advantage of it."[4]

For all the uproar, this Jesus hardly turned out to be an ordinary man; Zeffirelli used the same stereotypical blue-eyed, soft-spoken Jesus moviegoers had come to expect. But *Jesus of Nazareth* has other problems. When Jesus threatens the entire destruction of the world (Matthew 10:34), he sits calmly, munches on a pomegranate (an ancient symbol of fertility), and mumbles in an undistinguished monotone, "Do not suppose that I have come to bring peace on the earth. I have not come to bring peace, but a sword." Such a line was much better suited for Pasolini's angry Jesus. Zeffirelli employed consultants from Catholic, Jewish, and Islamic quarters to enhance the picture's historical authenticity, but for some reason he omitted numerous New Testament set pieces, like Jesus' summoning of Peter to be a "fisher of men," instead adding several excruciatingly dull scenes.

In one, Judas and Zerah, his fictional go-between with the Sanhedrin, plot Jesus' capture. In another, Jesus tells the parable of the prodigal son, unbiblically at tax collector Matthew's house. Zeffirelli should have learned from his predecessors that politics and parables do not work in a screen version of the life of Jesus.

Zeffirelli's *Jesus of Nazareth* does succeed in creating a marvelous cultural and atmospheric background in which the life of Jesus takes place. He opens the floodgates of history when he has Joseph and Mary arrange their marriage contract amid white stucco buildings separated by dusty Palestinian alleys, intense sunlight, and sharply falling shadows. His film borders on neorealism as Joseph suspects his immaculately pregnant wife of infidelity and as Mary's labor pains force her to scream out in harrowing cries. Here Zeffirelli's Jesus is indeed an ordinary man, or an ordinary baby, anyway. And when we see his bar mitzvah, we have a genuine feeling that the young Jesus belongs to this world; his divine mission has not yet begun. Later, when an extraordinary Jesus delivers a young boy possessed by an extraordinary demon, the boy growls, gasps, grovels, foams, and shrieks with compellingly primeval terror. (Might Zeffirelli have included such a scene in the pre-*Exorcist* days?) Each of these scenes plays its part in establishing a tangible, historical, human background to Jesus' life.

Other atmospheric touches make watching the film a remarkable visual encounter with history. The traditional cow and ass in the stable, the stream of sunlight performing the annunciation to Mary, and the tableau of Mary and Elizabeth standing before two well-framed arches reveal Zeffirelli's admiration for Renaissance iconography. The smoky air inside the Jerusalem temple, its obscured walls echoing forth muffled Hebrew prayers along with the bleating of marketable sheep, creates the perfect arena for Jesus' disruption of business. Best of all is the sequence in which Jesus bears his cross up the Via Dolorosa. The Christ suffers the pain of bearing the heavy cross (here a historically authentic crossbeam and not the whole cross), and yet his tolerance is admirable. The entire journey toward Golgotha, maddening in its haste, confusing in its intent, pitiable in its execution, captures more successfully than any other film about the Passion the essential pace and desperation of that angry and agonizing passage. Everything happens so fast that Jesus himself and his followers can hardly believe that they are helpless to do anything about it. When this sequence culminates with Jesus being roped and nailed to the crossbeam, raised to the vertical beam, and crucified, the rain-drenched deposition and the palpable grief of Mary provide an ironically calm counterpoint to those hectic hours that just elapsed.

But wonderful as many scenes are in *Jesus of Nazareth*, Zeffirelli's work is undone by an equal number of hideously inappropriate episodes: the endless talk at Matthew's house, the incessant and ridiculous yelling by John the Baptist, the gathering of zealots at the Baptist's grave, and the contrived political duping of Judas Iscariot. The smoke-filled temple, the Renaissance tableaux, the haunting dogs barking in realistic ancient Palestinian streets, and the frantic struggle up the Via Dolorosa—all these Zeffirelli films with great subtlety and genius—but as soon as the film steps out of its first-century A.D. Judeo-Roman ambiance into an unhistorical and unfilmable world of ideas, theology, and verbose arguments and parables, it loses its relevance, its continuity, and its artistry. The director would be well advised to go and cinematically sin no more.

Perhaps it was Zeffirelli's production that inspired the Monty Python comedy troupe to satirize the whole affair in their *Life of Brian* (1979), a film to be discussed in Chapter 8. But another interesting and controversial variation on all the film versions of the life of Christ came in the form of Martin Scorsese's *The Last Temptation of Christ* (1988), a film adaptation of Nikos Kazantzakis's novel. Warned by a prefatory disclaimer that the film is about the "incessant, merciless battle between the spirit and the flesh," we are presented with a shockingly human portrait of Christ, played by Willem Dafoe.

Before his mission becomes clear to him, Jesus serves the Romans as the carpenter who prepares crosses for crucifixions, but the anti-Roman zealot Judas (Harvey Keitel) helps him realize the error of his ways. But even as Christ begins his mission, he does not understand his relationship with God. Confusing Judas and the other disciples he has picked up along the way, this ever-evolving, "fragmented, almost schizophrenic" Christ first plans to save the world with love, then determines to fight with the sword, then finally realizes, much to his horror, that he must face crucifixion.[5] His physical torment—during his audience with Pilate, when he is beaten and crowned with thorns, as he carries his cross in slow motion and is painfully nailed and raised into place—leads logically to the extraordinary climax of the film. On the cross he experiences visions of his young guardian angel, surveys the beautiful earth as the celestial visitor remarks that "sometimes we angels envy you," and then has visions of his own, lovely earthly life as it might have been. He envisions his wedding to Mary Magdalene (whom he has always desired), fathering a child, growing old, and, above all, escaping the horrors of crucifixion. As an old man he hears Paul preaching about Jesus, who died on the cross. When Jesus interrupts Paul to show that he is still alive, Paul tells Jesus that he can crucify and resurrect him if he needs to: "My Jesus is much more important!" Finally Jesus envisions his old friend Judas, who accuses him of cowardice and reveals that this lovely "guardian angel" is in fact Satan, offering another, final, glorious temptation. Judas tells Jesus that his crucifixion is the key to universal salvation. So Christ submits spiritually to his necessary martyrdom and utters the ultimate biblical phrase, "It is accomplished."

Scorsese's vivid portrayal of Christ's reverie of the normal human familial existence caught the attention of a number of Christian groups long before Universal released the film, and when it became clear that the film contained a scene in which Christ not only desires Mary Magdalene but even has sex with her, they mobilized. They boycotted businesses owned by the MCA corporation, and five thousand people picketed Universal Studios as early as one month before release. When Kazantzakis's book was published in

1955, it caused public disturbances in Greece, but protest of the film assumed a global scale. On the Left Bank of Paris an arsonist torched a theater that was showing the film, and Zeffirelli himself withdrew his *The Young Toscanini* from the Venice Film Festival because it had listed Scorsese's "completely deranged" film on its program. Never mind the disclaimer that tells the viewer at the outset that the film is fiction, and never mind that Christ's corporeal family life is a mere vision that is revealed as part of Satan's plan to undermine the crucifixion and frustrate human salvation, Scorsese's film was condemned from the outset.

But controversy bred box-office interest, and *The Last Temptation of Christ* broke box-office records in Los Angeles during its first weekend of release. Amid all the controversy, the film itself was rarely subjected to rational critique. But Roger Ebert of the *Chicago Sun-Times* and the widely watched *Siskel and Ebert* television program devoted his entire review of the film to defending the Christian legitimacy of the concept. And more than a decade removed from the publicity glare of its release, it is much easier for the viewer to appreciate how Scorsese rejected the customary genteel pageantry of previous film versions of the life of Christ. Dafoe as Christ is a disturbed genius, and he walks in a world where animal blood sacrifices persistently hint of the essence of crucifixion. The words he speaks are not scriptural or King Jamesian but modern English from the pen of Paul Schrader, who also wrote Scorsese's *Taxi Driver* and *Raging Bull,* other films about tormented souls, and he is surrounded by a cast who speak in unabashed New York accents. Although the Jerusalem temple scenes are visually impressive, crowd scenes are noticeably absent; in fact, one of the most interesting aspects of the temple sequence is a practical explanation of why money has to be changed there—to collect temple tax monies in non-Roman, thus "pagan," coins. Helping to establish the wide spectrum of atmospheres and moods, Peter Gabriel's orientalizing music ranges from mournful to dionysiac and earthly to visionary.

Supporting Characters

A universally acceptable film based on the New Testament is probably an impossibility. Christ in the Gospels looms above all as a keen, energetic, forceful, dramatic, intriguing, humanized divinity. Portrayed on the screen by a mere mortal, he necessarily *becomes* a mere mortal, whether Scorsese's struggling visionary or Pasolini's vengeful crusader or George Stevens's greeting-card good shepherd. It is not that these films are not good films; it is just that they fall understandably short of otherworldly expectations. Realizing the unfathomable scope the figure of Jesus demands of the cinema, a number of filmmakers have turned instead to stories that include Christ or the Baptist or the Apostles—for example, Rossellini's *Atta degli Apostoli* (*Acts of the Apostles,* 1969)—but concentrate instead on a non-Gospel narrative. Such stories do not try to re-create the New Testament on film. *Day of Triumph* (1954), the modernized *The Last Supper* (1914), and *Anna und Elisabeth*

121   Willem Dafoe heals and comforts poor children in Martin Scorsese's *The Last Temptation of Christ* (1988). Similar to Pasolini's *The Gospel According to St. Matthew,* Scorsese's film focuses on a human Christ who interacts with other humans. The film's release caused a tremendous theological controversy, and the film is still rarely shown on cable more than a decade later.

(1933) made meek attempts at such an approach, as did the silent versions of *Salome* (1908 and 1913). Later, Theda Bara's *Salome* (1918) was based loosely on the ancient account recorded by Josephus; in this it followed Richard Strauss's and Oscar Wilde's versions. Alla Nazimova's financially disastrous *Salome* (1922) also found its basis in Wilde's play; in fact, the costumes and sets designed by Natasha Rambova (Rudolph Valentino's second wife) try to re-create the drawings Aubrey Beardsley executed for the Wilde drama. The resulting cotton-ball pearl wigs, thick makeup, and bird-cage jail made the two lone sets of *Salome* into a linear visual feast, albeit limited without Richard Strauss's full score and Oscar Wilde's dialogue.

Columbia gave the Judean princess still another cinematic chance to dance for the Baptist's head in *Salome* (1953). But Jesse L. Lasky's story and Harry Kleiner's screenplay take more than considerable liberties with the New Testament and Josephus. They have Salome (Rita Hayworth) dance to *save* John the Baptist from the destruction that Queen Herodias (Judith Anderson) demands. While Rita whirls and spins skillfully before the previously jaded but now excited King Herod (Charles Laughton), the Roman Claudius (Stewart Granger) tries to help John out of his prison cell. Salome's plan fails, and the

122   Salome (Alla Nazimova) and Jokanaan (John the Baptist, played by Nigel De Brulier) stand
before the memorable linear designs and bird-cage prison of *Salome* (1922). The costumes and sets
are based on the drawings executed by Aubrey Beardsley for Oscar Wilde's *Salome*.

revolting silver platter is soon carried in. Claudius and Salome leave the palace and are next
seen listening to a well-known, white-robed, Judean prophet addressing a mountainside
crowd in familiarly parallel phrases, "Blessed are they . . . "

       To make matters worse, this pro-Baptist stance by Salome comes as a sudden re-
versal at the end of the film. Previously she had been a bitter enemy of Claudius, the Romans, and their anti-Herodian politics. This hatred for Rome and Romans had begun
when the Emperor Tiberius banished the whoring princess from the capital. The liberties
and inconsistencies go on and on. Only Salome's dance deserves commendation, and no
doubt this dance was the tasty core around which the rest of the rotting apple was originally designed.

       The story of Salome has always been a popular cinematic source. Theo Frenkel's
Herod (1908) was one of the first biblical films ever made, and then there were Spanish
versions in 1940 and 1970 and an Italian version in 1972. Another Italian film, *Erode il
Grande* (*Herod the Great,* 1958), starred Sylva Koscina and Edmund Purdom, and Ken

Russell's British *Salome's Last Dance* (1988) featured Glenda Jackson as Herodias. Other Italian films of the sword-and-sandal era set in the early days of Christianity include *Pontius Pilate* (1964), with Jeanne Crain, Basil Rathbone, and John Drew Barrymore, and *Sword and the Cross* (*La Spada e la Croce*, 1958), which outdid DeMille's foiled plot for *King of Kings* by having Barabbas kidnap Mary Magdalene.

One other major film focuses on a specific New Testament personage. *The Big Fisherman* (1959), based on Lloyd C. Douglas's last novel, tells a tale about Peter but offers little authenticity and little entertainment. The Arabian Princess Fara (Susan Kohner) swears to kill King Herod and rides to Judea to do so. There she becomes a good friend of John the Baptist, then of Simon the fisherman. She and the piscatorial Simon quickly and unconvincingly become converts to Jesus' preaching, and her murderous resolve weakens as Jesus' "Thou shalt not kill" echoes in her mind. Meanwhile, Simon (Howard Keel) has repented of his earlier atheism and become a "fisher of men."

123   Rita Hayworth performs the traditional dance of the seven veils in the perplexing *Salome* (1953). At far left foreground is a salivating Herod (Charles Laughton), and to the right is the anti-Baptist Herodias (Judith Anderson). In this film, Salome dances to *save* the Baptist's head!

124   Simon (Howard Keel), soon to be called Peter, leaves a career in traditional piscatology to become a fisher of men in *The Big Fisherman* (1959). Christ is not shown in this scene, and elsewhere the camera glimpses him only from behind. Several films tried to depict Christ in an elusive style; William Wyler's *Ben-Hur* (1959) succeeded best.

The film's 180 minutes are hardly filled with taut drama. The plot never decides whether it should emphasize piety, adventure, or romance. The architect of the sets apparently never learned that in antiquity (as well as in modern times) columns were usually built to hold something up, not to stand alone as superfluous and expensive rows of landfill. The distastefully painted red-marble interior columns also detract from the film's visual value. Director Frank Borzage chose not to depict Jesus' face, so he had to portray the Christ with voice alone; unfortunately, the chosen voice sounded more like a narrator for *The Bell Telephone Hour* than anyone God would send as his representative on earth. And how much research would it have taken to establish that when the knowledgeable Princess Fara reads Greek scrolls, she should read from left to right, not Semitically right to left?

None of this appeared to bother Howard Keel or Herbert Lom. Lom seems genuinely to enjoy his role as the evil Oriental despot Herod Antipas, and Keel playfully bangs heads together, yells angrily, gestures wildly, and even prays with the same robust and hearty spirit that he injected into all his work. Before his conversion, he boasts: "God can send all the storms he wants, just so long as I can catch all of His fish that I want." Biblical authenticities appear sporadically—Jesus renames Simon as Peter, establishing him as the "rock" upon which he will build his church, and he heals Peter's mother-in-law (Matthew 8:14), though in the film she is said to be Peter's nurse because the cinematic Peter is unwed. For archaeological authenticity, or near authenticity, Herod's palace includes several panels from Augustus's Ara Pacis.

The most popular films about Jesus have depended less on the accounts of the evangelists or the invention of screenwriters than on the material of best-selling novels, all but one of which blend the story of Christ with the glory of Rome. From five historical novels the screen was enriched by nearly a dozen successful films—*Barabbas, The Last Days of Pompeii, Ben-Hur, The Robe,* and *Quo Vadis?*—making Rome and Christ a screen pairing to rival cowboys and Indians. The screen adaptations of Bulwer-Lytton's *The Last Days of Pompeii* have already been discussed in connection with Roman history; only the 1935 RKO version and the 1960 Italian version adapt the novel to include the story of the Christ, dramatically (and unhistorically) connecting his crucifixion with the most famous eruption of Vesuvius.

In 1962 Dino De Laurentiis (*Ulysses, The Bible . . . In the Beginning*) produced *Barabbas* (1962). The screenplay by Christopher Fry (*The Bible . . . In the Beginning*) was based on Pär Lagerkvist's 1951 Nobel Prize–winning novel, which had already in 1952 been turned into an unheralded Swedish film by Alf Sjöberg. The cast includes Anthony Quinn, Silvana Mangano, Arthur Kennedy, Katy Jurado, Harry Andrews, Vittorio Gassman, Jack Palance, Ernest Borgnine, and Valentina Cortese. Even the nonspeaking Christ has a familiar name—Roy Mangano, Silvana's brother and Dino de Laurentiis's brother-in-law.

Because Lagerkvist's novel probes thoroughly the relationship between Barabbas and Jesus, director Richard Fleischer is careful to draw close parallels between the two. He has every historical right to do so: the paleo-Christian author Origen tells us that Barabbas's first name was Jesus, *bar Abbas* means "son of the father" in Aramaic, and early Christian mythology generally conceived of Barabbas as "the dark side of Jesus." Fleischer initiates this Jesus-Barabbas connection in the opening scenes. While the Roman soldiers scourge Jesus in the same dark dungeon in which Barabbas has been imprisoned, Barabbas (Anthony Quinn) hears the Romans' laughter. Soon after his release from the lightless cell, his eyes temporarily useless, Barabbas's groping hand accidentally finds the warm blood recently shed by the Christ. Then the pure darkness of the dungeon that has been effectively covering the screen abruptly flashes into bright sunlight; the wooden outer doors of the dungeon open with a thundering but dull thud. The bright glare of the sun makes Barabbas rub his shocked eyes; he cannot see anything because of the sudden brightness, but what he cannot see is Pontius Pilate washing his hands of Jesus' blood. Shading his pained eyes, the freed Barabbas then washes his own hands in a public fountain. Has the blood of Christ come off *his* hands?

Back at Barabbas's favorite inn, the whores and drunkards declare that he is a more appropriate King of the Jews than Jesus, and they mockingly perform an investiture, just as the Romans did with Christ, here with basket crown and broomstick scepter. Just then Christ wends his struggling, cross-bearing way past Barabbas, and thereafter the curious but uncomprehending Barabbas witnesses the unnatural darkness around Golgotha (the eclipse is authentic, filmed at Nice), the entombment of Christ, and the resurrection.

The freed Barabbas resumes his degenerate criminal life—thieving, drinking, and murdering—but he begins to wonder why he was saved instead of Christ. He thinks he understands when Pontius Pilate explains to him that a prisoner freed on a holiday cannot be put to death; Barabbas sees a distorted relationship between himself and Jesus— that Jesus died to save him, and that he, like Jesus, cannot really die. Through the sulfur mines of Sicily and the gladiatorial arenas of Rome, Barabbas survives overwhelming odds. After many years he finally finds sympathy for Christianity; he hears that the Christians are burning Rome, so he grabs a torch but is caught by Roman soldiers. Ironically, Barabbas now hears that this Neronian conflagration was not at all planned by the Christians. Disappointed, he finds that he still cannot understand Christ's purpose, the Christian plan, or his own purpose. Ultimately he is crucified as a Christian martyr and entrusts his soul to Christ; as the "son of the father" he has almost become a second Christ. Barabbas has died for Christ, the debt is paid, and the question is answered: Christ died for Barabbas so that Barabbas could die for Christ.

Barabbas is an Italian-produced "ancient" film of the early 1960s that is raised above the rest by the captivating mystery surrounding Barabbas's purpose in the early Christian movement. Uncertain whether his own apparent immortality is a blessing or a curse, Barabbas finds himself gifted with an unnatural luck. Years of hard labor and fighting mature the one-time thief and murderer, but they cannot clarify the Christian doctrines for him. Anthony Quinn plays this role with the spirit of his Zorba and the grotesquerie of his Quasimodo, and somewhere underneath the vulgarity lies a probing intelligence. It was a cruel, filthy, laborious life for an ancient criminal, and Quinn accentuates the earthiness of his plight as well as the uniqueness of his divine relationship.

Visually, *Barabbas* is not a remarkable work of art worth its $10 million budget, except for one sequence set in the Sicilian sulfur mines. For minutes we are plunged into an inhumane, troglodytic darkness in the bowels of a mountain. From a wizened veteran of Roman cruelty Barabbas learns to wear a kerchief over his eyes to prevent blindness. For years he labors in murky, cramped, tomblike trenches, and regularly he is "promoted" to the next lower level, each time reaching closer and closer to Hades. Finally an earthquake shakes the entire sulfur mountain, and the interior that had been dark for so many years now explodes into deadly sulfuric fires. Helpless, nameless slaves struggle to free themselves, but all that is left at the end is a massive tableau of strewn limbs and mud-spotted, broken bodies.

Faith, Hope, and Chariots

Of all the novels written about Rome and Christ, none has been so successfully adapted to the cinema as *Ben-Hur.* Born in the mind of an Indiana lawyer, nurtured in the New Mexico territory, and finished under late-night lamps that offered up his creator as an easy target for the vengeance of Billy the Kid, Judah Ben-Hur from his very conception met every challenge with conviction and rode his chariot triumphantly out of middle America, through fifty years of best-seller lists, onto the treadmills of the Broadway stage, across the standard and wide screens of Hollywood, and ultimately into the bulging coffers of thousands of businessmen. Not quite "the best business venture since General Motors," *Ben-Hur* nonetheless ranks as one of the most successful literary, theatrical, and cinematic productions of all times.[6]

Why? Rome, Christ, and Humanity: the indomitable might of an ancient civilization, the sudden rise of the son of God and of spiritual fervor in the Judean hotbed of rebellion, and a believable hero who finds himself inextricably involved in and challenged by the power of both clashing forces. This overwhelming political and religious battle between Rome and God creates or smashes friendships or bitter enmities, makes or breaks families, and inaugurates the ultimate triumph of the good over evil. This awe-inspiring combination separates *Ben-Hur* from other novels about the ancient world; it is a theological-philosophical-romantic adventure story of universal proportions. There were imitators by the dozens, but *Ben-Hur* remained the essentially inimitable tale of the Christ and the most dependable theatrical war horse of the century.

It all began when General Lew Wallace—son of a West Pointer, Indiana state senator, general, both hero and goat in the Civil War, and governor of the Territory of New Mexico in 1878 during the rampages of Billy the Kid (whom he had personally antagonized)—published the novel *Ben-Hur* in 1880. It sold poorly for the first year, then blossomed into popularity. Eventually it sold more than two million copies, ranking second to the Bible on all-time best-seller lists for fifty years—until *Gone With the Wind.* Wallace himself became so well known that an admiring President Garfield sent him to Turkey in 1881—ostensibly to be minister of the United States, but actually to give him the opportunity of experiencing the Mediterranean area firsthand: despite the detailed descriptions in *Ben-Hur,* Wallace had never seen Rome or the Holy Land.

In 1899 the Broadway producers Marc Klaw and Abraham Erlanger put this fascinating man's more fascinating book onto the stage. After observing the three-and-one-half-hour dress rehearsal (with William S. Hart as Messala), the impresario Charles Frohman warned the producers that they would lose their shirts. "The American people will never stand for Christ and a horse race in the same show." This turned out to be probably the worst prediction in the history of terrible theatrical predictions. The play ran for twenty-one years and earned some $10 million. The chariot race was normally run on a 12,000-foot treadmill, and when the aging Wallace himself saw a stage performance of the race, he said, "My God, did I set all this in motion?"[7]

125   The aftermath of the sulfur-mine explosion in *Barabbas* (1962). This is one of the better visual sequences in the $10 million film. Viscous mud, strewn limbs, and splintered rafters cover the well-composed screen.

In 1907 Sidney Olcott directed the first film version of *Ben-Hur.* It consisted of one dozen scenes of extremely limited scope. Twenty soldiers and spectators view the three-lap chariot race, Governor Gratus is wounded by a tile that falls four feet, and the boyhood friendship between Judah Ben-Hur and Messala is omitted. Nonetheless, Harper Publishing and the Wallace estate sued Kalem for filming the book without their permission. There had never been such a test of copyright violation before, and this particular case set the precedent for novel-based films: Kalem had to deliver $25,000 dollars to the plaintiff, and as a direct result books became a regular part of filmdom's source material—for a fee.

By 1924 *Ben-Hur* had earned its reputation as "the greatest play on the stage," as William Jennings Bryan dubbed it. Following the success of DeMille's silent version of *The Ten Commandments,* executives of the recently formed MGM corporation decided to film *Ben-Hur.* When the studio had trouble negotiating a purchase price, they offered to pay the owners of the copyright 50 percent of the film's gross. This business venture turned into financial misery for MGM, for the film eventually earned more than $7 million but cost $4 million to produce; MGM lost money, but Harper Publishing did not—

not at more than fifteen dollars per word. The film earned its huge profits even though it was banned in Italy (where it had been shot); Mussolini objected to the film's triumph of Jew over Roman.

This version of *Ben-Hur*, released on Christmas Day 1925, starred Ramon Novarro as Judah Ben-Hur and Francis X. Bushman as Messala. Two years in the making and running more than twelve thousand feet, the film established once and for all the credibility and viability of the Hollywood epic. The sophistication of the film's spectacular effects stands up even to today's standards. The opening crowds outside the towering walls and Joppa Gate of Jerusalem, the shining star over the desert and the revolutionary three-strip Technicolored Nativity sequence, the fiery naval battle, and the chariot race are still impressive.

Building the huge Joppa Gate ramparts and the chariot circus consumed much of the production's expense and time. The $300,000 Antioch circus was designed by Cedric Gibbons—who shortly thereafter designed the "Oscar" statuette—and it covered five acres and held more than three thousand extras. When the race was filmed, forty-two cameras were used, and each cameraman was allotted more than one thousand feet of film. This was *spectacle*. The results may fall short of the 1959 version's chariot race, but that is like saying that emeralds are not as precious as diamonds. To create a realistic race, director Fred Niblo offered a prize to the stuntman who finished first; the crowd of extras even began betting on certain favorites. But all of this excitement caused a rather dramatic crash during the shooting of the race. This time, DeMille could not be blamed for sawing the axles.

The naval battle was filmed off Livorno, and it developed into such a consuming process that one of the triremes caught fire from the smoking smudge pots, forcing scores of armored Italian extras to save themselves by leaping overboard. That evening the equipment manager found three suits of armor missing and three extra sets of street clothes. Wishing to avoid adverse publicity, he secretly sank the three extra sets of street clothes in the ocean. One version of the story ends here and blames MGM for three deaths. Another version claims that the three men returned the next day, explained that they had been rescued by a fishing trawler, and demanded their clothes back. MGM gladly bought the men brand new suits. In any event, Louis B. Mayer and Irving Thalberg brought the production back to California to finish what at first appeared to be a looming disaster.

This version of *Ben-Hur* follows the novel, particularly the final third of the book, much more closely than either the 1907 Olcott silent version or the 1959 sound and color version. Toward the end of the film Judah leads a Christian army of rebellion as a crusader for the Messiah, but the ill-conceived army falls to its knees in prayer upon hearing that Christ ordered them to "forgive their enemies." Several sequences from the New Testament are included, and this version also presents the near fistfight that Judah and Messala have before the chariot race. Both MGM versions, however, eventually edited out the romantic triangle of Messala, his concubine Iras, and Judah; the moral and narrative complications of an involved novel cannot all be accommodated in a two-, or even three-and-one-half-hour film.

Lacking a soundtrack, the 1925 version delights its viewers instead with pictorial charm, whether in the light, romantic play after Judah recaptures Esther's pet dove in the marketplace, or in Messala's attitude toward Judah upon returning to Jerusalem as a Roman commander — first cold in front of his assembled troops, then tender once out of public view. Although the sound version embellished this scene, the emotion is conveyed perfectly by Novarro and Bushman. Vivid emotion of a different sort can be seen in the galley scene, when one desperate slave begins to bite his chains. When words are necessary, the titles of the silent version are succinct and periodic. Judah, after his adoption by Quintus Arrius the elder, tells Sheikh Ilderim that he will race against the now-hated Messala in the chariot race "not as Arrius, the Roman, for glory, but as the unknown, for revenge." When Messala and Judah are about to quarrel, Judah grasps Messala's arm and says, "It is good to have a Roman who understands the Jews." Messala replies, "The Jews must learn to understand the Romans."

The 1925 *Ben-Hur* was rereleased in 1931 with a partial soundtrack. The pounding of horses' hooves, the crack of whips, and the shouts of crowds gave the film part of the dimension it was lacking in the new sound era. But the film, for all its merits, fell into relative obscurity in the onrush of color and sound. Then, just as *Intolerance*'s Griffith had appeared in DeMille's studio to help him direct a piece of *The King of Kings,* so did some ironic historical continuity occur in the productions of *Ben-Hur:* one of Metro's junior staff members assigned to assist in crowd control for the shooting of the chariot race in 1924 was a fledgling Hollywoodian director named William Wyler.

Thirty-four years later, the same William Wyler sat high above a new reconstruction of the Antioch circus. This one covered eighteen acres, cost an even million dollars to build, and would be filmed in Technicolor, stereo, and wide-screen Camera 65. Just before shooting was to begin, Wyler turned to his assistants who were about to return to their duties of crowd control and mused, "I wonder which of you is going to be the director of the *next Ben-Hur.*"[8]

Wyler's 1959 version of *Ben-Hur* establishes from the beginning the vital threads around which the rest of the plot will be woven — Rome, Christ, and the complicated friendship between the Jewish Ben-Hur and the Roman Messala. Following delicately handled scenes of Joseph and Mary entering Jerusalem, the Wise Men in the desert beneath the starry sky, and the humble Nativity, a shofar blast celebrating the birth of the Redeemer dissolves into a trumpet blast from a Roman legionnaire. Brightly and impressively clad Roman spearmen and archers file past a carpenter's shop in the little village of Nazareth. As they file through the town, the camera glimpses the scrubby field in which the young Jesus contemplates his mission. Rome and Christ.

The quarrel between Ben-Hur and Messala is written with smooth, powerful phrases and shot in the dank stone corridors of Jerusalem's Roman garrison. When Judah (Charlton Heston) and Messala (Stephen Boyd, with black contact lenses darkening his blue eyes) first see each other, they embrace warmly and instantly pick up their childhood friendship. "Down Eros, up Mars!" they shout laughingly after they have sportively hurled javelins into the arsenal's wooden cross-beams; little does Judah know how other wooden cross-beams will change his life, and little do they both know that their friendship has only hours to live. Judah tries to remain cheerful and warm toward the loving but insanely ambitious Messala, but the news that two more Roman legions are on their way to Jerusalem digs deep at his Hebrew roots. (Decades later Gore Vidal, who wrote most of the first half of the script, reported that Boyd was told to play the part as if they had been homosexual lovers in their youth.) Judah warns the swaggering Roman, "Rome is an affront to God!" But Messala understands the Realpolitik of the period: Caesar "is God, the *only* God, he is power, real power on earth, not—" Here he roughly gestures upward to the sky and Judah's invisible god. Messala then ironically echoes the words of the New Testament when he delivers his ultimatum, "Judah, either you help me or oppose me; there is no other choice. You are either for me or against me." "If that is the choice, then I am against you," decides an angered Judah, and the two part in an enmity that now looms far larger than their lifelong love for each other. Friendship and politics.

Growing from this bitter quarrel is Messala's triumph and the destruction of the aristocratic House of Hur. Wyler depicts these events not with dialogue but through skillful direction. Wyler understood the demands presented to him by the epic scope of the project, pacing the film regally but not ploddingly. From the rooftop of their house Judah and his sister, Tirzah, watch the martially impressive entry of the Roman Governor Gratus through the streets below. The magnificence of the scene is equally due to Miklos Rozsa's compelling march music and to the visual spectacle, but when Tirzah accidentally knocks a tile loose from the roof, it gathers momentum as it slides and bounces toward earth, unluckily causing Gratus's horse to rear and smash the governor's head against a brick wall. Messala's soldiers burst into the Hur courtyard and arrest everyone. Judah pleads with the silent Messala succinctly: "It was an accident." With all the Heston teeth and their glorious enunciation, Judah repeats, "It was an accident." Messala remains silent. "At least let the women go," pleads Judah, realizing that Messala will not believe him. Messala says coldly to his troops, "Let the *servants* go." Judah, Tirzah, and their mother are dragged off to years of torture and misery. After a dissolve Messala alone walks up to the roof to examine the tiles. Without saying a word, he looks around and then touches several tiles lightly; to be sure, one slides down and plunges to the street below, causing a different horse to neigh. No human words are necessary; it was an accident. Fate and, ultimately, revenge.

Judah next encounters two strangely parallel characters who propel him toward his destiny. The first is Christ, who is a minor character in the film—a character whom Judah sees but does not know. When Judah is being led in chains across the desert to the sea (shot on location in Israel), Christ's gentle hands offer him a drink and stroke his hair. Then, toward the end of the film Judah sees Christ bearing his cross along the Via Dolorosa. "I know this man," realizes Judah, knowing him only for his human kindness, not for his divine origins. Unlike in most New Testament films, Christ is not the protagonist; his crucifixion is merely a contemporary political event. Yet Judah feels a strong bond with this Christ and tries to repay the gift of water while he bears the cross. Wyler, with the help of Rozsa's music, is careful to draw a parallel between the two water sequences.

The other key figure in Judah's story is Quintus Arrius, played by Jack Hawkins. (Wyler chose British actors to portray his Romans, Americans to portray the Hebrews.) Arrius is the Roman consul whose life Judah saves and who in turn gives Judah his freedom. Before the attack by the Illyrian pirates, Arrius orders that "number forty-one" (a less sonorous number sixty in the novel) be unchained. As Judah recalls that "another man saved me once," we hear Rozsa's Christ theme, and we understand that Arrius serves as a Roman parallel for Christ. Critics in 1959 were disappointed that most of the naval battle was enacted with models in an MGM tank in Hollywood (beneath a fifteen thousand–foot cyclorama). But the real emphasis of the battle is not on the outcome of the military and political struggle but on the outcome of the human struggle above and below the deck of Arrius's flagship. Never mind the model ships, any shortcomings in the exterior scenes are far outweighed by Rozsa's insistently accelerating music, the famous "battle speed . . . ramming speed" of the pounding *hortator,* the frenzy of the slaves as they tug at their chains until their ankles bleed, desperately attempting to free themselves before the pirate ship rams their galley, and finally, Judah's heroic rescue of Arrius, echoing the consul's words: "We keep you alive to serve this ship."

In the novel and the 1925 film version, Judah becomes an ardent follower of Christ long before the Crucifixion. Wyler's Judah, though, becomes a believer only when the stormy hour of Christ's death heals his long-lost mother and sister of leprosy. The timing of Judah's conversion makes its climax more poignant: Christ died to save others, and Judah is one of the first benefactors of Christ's death. Judah believes, his family is restored, his vengeance satisfied, and his odyssey at an end.

Immediately after MGM's success with *Quo Vadis?* in 1951, *Ben-Hur* was conceived specifically as the studio's next "spectacle." At the time *Ben-Hur*'s $15 million budget made it the costliest film ever produced. The shooting script called for three hundred sets, one hundred thousand costumes, and ten thousand extras, not to mention the numbers of goats, sheep, asses, and camels. Jerusalem was reconstructed at Anzio (where much of *Cleopatra* was shot three years later), Nazareth was reconstructed at Foggia, and the massive *Quo Vadis?* sets from 1951 were reconstructed, too. The book rights cost nothing, of course; MGM had already paid dearly for them in 1925. Seventy-eight trained thoroughbreds were bought in Yugoslavia, and they were fitted to eighteen 900-pound chariots. Cowboys and stuntmen were hired to drive them. The million-dollar Antioch circus was then constructed, and forty thousand tons of sand and crushed lava was supplied for its racing surface. On top of all this expense, two cameras were knocked over during a racing mishap.

And indeed it is the spectacle of *Ben-Hur,* not the carefully planned connection between Christ and Judah, that is most memorable. As if the Broadway treadmills had run continuously for sixty years, the chariot race and *Ben-Hur* had become synonymous. In fact, when MGM producer Sam Zimbalist approached Wyler with an offer to direct the new film, Wyler's first wish was to direct only the chariot race. In the event, the majority of the work on that scene was executed by second-unit directors Andrew Marton and Yakima Canutt. Heston was excited about the chariot race, too. The day after he arrived in Rome he began taking three-hour lessons in driving a *quadriga* (followed by one-hour instructions on javelin throwing), but most of Judah's charioteering was performed by a stuntman. For the racing scenes in which he did appear, Heston was fitted with a pair of contact lenses to prevent flying sand from injuring his eyes.

General Lew Wallace had planned his book so that Judah's bitterness should peak just before the great race. Every step Judah took through the Israeli desert, every agonizing stroke of the galley's oar, every heart-rending thought of his imprisoned mother and sister had been mental and physical preparation for this moment of vengeance. And for Messala it was life or death—defeat his worst enemy or die. Wyler skillfully emphasizes the climactic importance of the race with the evil stares that the contestants give each other before the start, with the heavy betting before the race (four to one odds for Messala: "The difference between a Roman and a Jew," snaps Messala to Sheikh Ilderim), and with the last-minute terror—the unveiling of Messala's sharply picked chariot wheels.

The nine contestants stand abreast, and from a crane high above we see them parade their handsome chariots around the evenly lined sands of the arena surface. The Antioch crowd, eight thousand strong, roars with anticipation, and a Tyrian-purpled Pontius Pilate pompously strolls to his magnificent box. The central *spina* is jammed with people and statues, and above it rest the seven gold-plated fish that will mark off the successive laps. Numerous camera angles capture the grandiose parade and magnificent setting beneath the Syrian mountains (matte), but everyone from ancient Antioch to the modern movie audience is nervously waiting to see how Judah is going to avoid those frightening blades.

The names of the contestants are read; they hail from the corners of the Roman Empire—Alexandria, Messina, Carthage, Cyprus, Rome, Corinth, Athens, Phrygia, and Judea. Pilate (Frank Thring) raises the white handkerchief, and all crouch for the start. A false start triples the tension. One last hateful look between black-robed Messala and Judah, and then Pilate drops the flag.

Immediately Messala rushes into the lead. In the opening fury one chariot takes the turn too close and hits the granite spina. Messala then sidles over to the Cypriot's chariot and drills through his spokes with his whirring, razor-sharp scythes. The first fish goes down; lap one. Rozsa's driving music from the naval battle and his heavenly Christ theme are conspicuously absent. Instead, our ears are overwhelmed by the thunder of twelve dozen hooves, the clanging of metal, and the sharp crack of whips, sounds that helped earn an Academy Award. Our concentration is focused on the rhythmic gallop of hand-

126/127 One of the great strengths of Wyler's
Ben-Hur was its treatment of Christ's Passion as a
political event of contemporary significance to
Judah and his family. Here Judah (Charlton
Heston), his leprous sister (Cathy O'Donnell) and
mother (Martha Scott), and Esther (Haya
Harareet) watch Jesus along the Via Dolorosa.
Throughout the film Christ's face is kept from our
view, but other players see it and react strongly to
make him seem all the more compelling. Similar
Passion iconography can be found in Hieronymus
Bosch's *Procession to Calvary*, c. 1488. The Roman
soldiers wear conventionally contemporary armor.
Such representations have popularized the
misconception that Christ carried the entire cross
to Calvary; he probably carried only the cross-
beam. But historical accuracy and artistic
necessity belong to different families. Notice that
the T-shape of Bosch's cross is duplicated in the
Ben-Hur shot, but not in most other cinematic
crucifixes, which are T-shaped.

128/130   The circus from the most spectacular action sequence from all the "ancient" films—
the chariot race from *Ben-Hur* (1959). The columned edifice in the rear houses the *carceres* (cells)
where the contestants first lined up their chariots. The mountains and the upper-deck crowds are
painted mattes. The awning to the right covers Roman Governor Pontius Pilate's box. The *spina*
(center strip) contains three columnar *metae* (goals) at each end. On the spina are the metallic
dolphins that mark off the laps. This circus cost $1 million to build, and the chariot race took
three months to film. An authentic chariot race from a second-century A.D. Roman mosaic found
in Lyons, France, shows similar details: the spina, dolphins, metae, whips, *quadrigae* (four-horse
chariots), and carceres. In antiquity up to twenty-four seven-lap races were run in a single day.
In another cinematic chariot circus, this one from Guazzoni's silent *Messalina* (facing page, 1922),
eggs just behind the metae mark off laps. This spina also includes a central obelisk. The imperial
box, right, is quite elaborate.

somely trim horses. We marvel at their dark manes and forelocks flying behind and above their speeding, glistening, sinewy necks, and at the natural symmetry of their four-abreast muscular bodies. The wreckage and driverless horses of the Cypriot are just cleared away when Messala rams his deadly blades into the Corinthian's spokes. The frail wood splinters with a grinding, grating buzz (the special-effects technicians used dynamite charges to splinter the spokes and wheel hubs), and the doomed Greek is suddenly dragged along the rough sand at thirty miles an hour. He frees himself and with an agile leap narrowly escapes the furious onrush of the next team of horses. But he has just leapt in front of a second team. In a flawlessly edited cut, the Corinthian is trampled under sixteen relentlessly pounding hooves. The scurrying slaves bear his body in on the stretcher but must rush out again from the spina after the next lap to carry off the Phrygian, forced into the wall by Messala. There is no law in the arena; many die.

The third fish has been marked off above the spina. The camera closes in on Ben-Hur and Messala, then provides a subjective shot from Ben-Hur's view as he maneuvers his handsome Arabians (actually Andalusians) between two other teams. We just begin to appreciate the broad backs and sinewy grace of the charging steeds when the Athenian and Carthaginian run afoul of each other and smash into the wall. Another subjective shot closes in on the slaves clearing up this wreckage. We have Ben-Hur's vantage point, and he cannot avoid the crippled chariot chassis. His own chariot flies into the air, and Ben-Hur is left with a deep gash on his face. (Contrary to rumors, it was not Heston's gash, but that of stuntman Yakima Canutt's son, Joe.)

131   The end of the chariot race —Judah's victory and Messala's bloody destruction—in *Ben-Hur* (1959). Messala, thrown from the chariot, was dragged down the stretch by his horses; to avoid such injury, ancient Roman charioteers carried knives to cut the reins. The silent 1925 version of *Ben-Hur* was banned in Mussolini's Italy because Jew triumphs over Roman.

The sixth fish. Messala finally closes in on Judah. His blades start to drill into the Judean's spokes, but Judah pulls away. Messala closes in again and demolishes the outer rail of Judah's chariot. Judah again pulls away in the nick of time. Messala furiously turns his whip on Judah as the seventh and final fish is marked off. Crack after crack of the Roman's whip lands around Judah's head, but the determined Hebrew takes the stinging leather with his strong forearm. Messala is closing in for the kill when his wheel locks with Judah's. The wheel rides up Judah's sturdy axle, flies off, and flips Messala out of his chariot. Messala has wrapped the reins around his wrists, so his body is dragged down the stretch for an excruciating length of time. He courageously frees himself but is immediately trampled by the Alexandrian's team. In desperation he grabs onto the yoke and is dragged by the panicked team. Victorious, Judah finishes the race and rides slowly past the horribly mangled Messala lying in the sand.

After Judah is crowned by Pilate, the next scene takes us to the opposite extreme. No crowd, no colorful pageantry, no handsome rushing horses, no thundering noise. Messala, bloodily black and blue, his body crushed, lies in a dim room. The doctors must amputate immediately if the tribune is to live, but Messala insists on seeing Judah. Messala has not lost after all, for he cruelly informs Judah that his mother and sister are lepers. Messala falls into convulsions and his hand, despite the spasms, grabs Judah's arm. His blood-garbled voice, wretched in intent and grotesque in its very sound, taunts Judah, "Look for them . . . in the Valley . . . of the Lepers . . . if you can recognize them. . . . It goes on, Judah, the race."

The entire galley of humanity beneath the deck of the political, military, and religious struggles of first-century A.D. Judea gives *Ben-Hur* its unique quality. An eccentric Arab sheikh (Hugh Griffith) kisses his horses goodnight, chastises a careless charioteer by saying, "You treat my horses like animals," and later remarks to the monogamous Judah, "One god I can understand, but one wife? That is uncivilized!" The character adds an Oriental mystique to the film and is a supportive friend to Judah. Similarly, Simonides (Sam Jaffe) and Esther (Haya Harareet) help to make Ben-Hur into a believable person rather than an impenetrable superman. And enmeshed in this humanity, spectacle, and political furor is the tempering Passion of Christ. This, General Wallace, you did indeed set into motion.

Ben-Hur was a huge critical and financial success. Nominated for twelve Academy Awards, it won eleven of them, a number unmatched until *Titanic,* nearly four decades later. The only nomination that failed to produce an Oscar, Best Screenplay, was the victim of a union quarrel over crediting Christopher Fry along with Karl Tunberg, S. N. Behrman, and Gore Vidal. Two years of planning and nine months of shooting, three months for the race alone, which included one hundred miles of practice laps, paid off in the end. Until 1975 *Ben-Hur* ranked ninth on the all-time money-making list (just behind *The Ten Commandments*), the book inspired an animated version in 1980, and a CD set of Rozsa's marvelously sweeping and full-bodied soundtrack is in print more than forty years later. During 1959 and 1960 $20 million worth of Ben-Hur merchandise was sold: toy swords, helmets, armor, model chariots, armor, candy, umbrellas, barrettes, towels ("Ben-His" and "Ben-Hers"), and hardcover and paperback editions of the novel. As always, Ben-Hur meant Rome, Christ, art, and money.

Bigger Than Biblical

For reasons of size, dependability, expense, and familiarity, "ancient" films seemed to appear whenever the industry underwent a dramatic technical or economic change—at the dawn of the epic film (*The Last Days of Pompeii,* 1908), when the first large budgets were allotted (*Intolerance,* 1916), when black-and-white or color effects were improved (*The King of Kings,* 1927), when the made-for-television movie became popular (*The Story of Jacob and Joseph,* 1974), or when cameras and lenses were perfected. In the early 1950s

132   The insane Roman Emperor Caligula (Jay Robinson) tests Christ's "magical" robe in
Demetrius and the Gladiators (1954), the sequel to *The Robe*. He kills a prisoner, then holds the robe
and orders the corpse to rise—a Roman's misconception of Christ's message. The robe is an
abayeh—a long woolen garment seamed only at the shoulders. Caligula wears a sleeved,
embroidered *tunica* and a felt *palla* (cloak).

Hollywood faced a viewership crisis: television was stealing audiences from the movie theater. Some industry leaders thought that the ultimate solution to the problem was a bigger, bolder picture than viewers could get in their homes. So Twentieth-Century Fox developed an anamorphic lens that would broaden the actual size of a movie's visual
appearance and allow it to encompass more "scope"; it would thus lure away the unsatis-
fied viewer back from the limited nineteen-inch box. The commercially practical wide
screen was born in 1953, and a novel set in ancient Judea and Rome was called upon to
make or break the revolutionary CinemaScope process. Lloyd C. Douglass's best-selling
The Robe did the job masterfully. Audiences raved about the panoramic views of Golgotha,
of Roman troops, of Galilee, of Rome, and even of Victor Mature's nose.

Billed as the super-colossal film of the day, *The Robe* actually lacks the battles
and special effects that characterize so many "ancient" films. Instead, Richard Burton
(Marcellus Gallio) and Jean Simmons (Diana) enact a rather convincing love affair that

is complicated by two obstacles. The first is the jealousy of crazed Emperor Caligula (Jay Robinson), and the second is the strange insanity that has overcome Tribune Gallio since his Judean service, during which he dutifully participated in the crucifixion of Christ. His slave Demetrius (Victor Mature) becomes a believer in Christ and hides the Savior's "magic" robe from his master. Ultimately the weakened Marcellus sees so much good in Christianity that he chooses to die a Christian with Diana rather than live a pagan under Caligula.

One secret of *The Robe*'s success (some $20 million worth) was the novelty of the wide screen. But the passion of Christ is handled tastefully (his face is never shown, as in *Ben-Hur*), the action moves quickly, and the conversion of Marcellus is believable. The admiration that the viewer develops for the lovely Diana and young Marcellus changes to sincere pity when they are sent to their deaths. As one might expect, Alfred Newman's angelic score gives *The Robe* one foot in heaven already, and Michael Rennie (Peter) and Dean Jagger (Justus) help make the Christians of the film decent people rather than snippety zealots. Richard Boone is a more convincing Pontius Pilate than one might expect of a type-cast bad guy, while Jay Robinson as Caligula raises his eyebrows, his voice, and his capacity for self-proclaimed divinity with humorously insane hamming. What *The Robe* lacks in profundity, this campy Caligula adds in entertainment.

The printers had barely completed their work on *The Robe* before Fox sent them the unprocessed reels of *Demetrius and the Gladiators* (1954). Part of this sequel was shot concurrently with *The Robe*. Mature, Rennie, and Robinson repeat their roles, and Susan Hayward, Debra Paget, Anne Bancroft, and William Marshall joined the cast. Even Franz Waxman used much of Alfred Newman's score from *The Robe*. Who knew that from this one piece of red homespun so much film could be fashioned?

Caligula is now searching for the magical robe; trying to hide it, Demetrius is arrested and sentenced to the gladiatorial arena, where he becomes chummy with a likable Nubian ex-king named Glycon (William Marshall), a pagan who is curious about Christianity. But when Demetrius tells him that Christ declared that "slave and king were all the same in His eyes," the dethroned but still proud Nubian monarch replies, "No wonder they crucified him." Glycon soon converts, but soon Demetrius finds himself in the clutches of sharper claws than those he faced in the arena — the claws of Messalina (Susan Hayward), the lecherous wife of Claudius. After Peter and Glycon make the newly debauched Demetrius see the error of his ways, he repents and spearheads a revolt that results in the death of the loony Caligula and the accession of his uncle Claudius. As in the unfinished *I, Claudius,* the intelligent monarch is played with a distinguished air. Barry Jones delivers Claudius's restrained but characteristically witty lines to the Praetorians: "You have made me Caesar and I will act the part. I am not a god, nor am I likely to become one." *Demetrius and the Gladiators* is even less profound than *The Robe,* yet its action carries it well enough. Demetrius says it best when he remarks to Messalina, "To be a Christian is anything but dull these days."

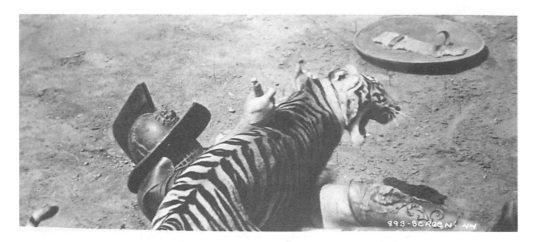

133/134   No film about early Christianity can ignore the beast-filled arena. Here Demetrius (a stand-in for Victor Mature, who had had enough trouble strangling the lion in *Samson and Delilah*) does his best against a half-nelsoning tiger in *Demetrius and the Gladiators*. Directors complained that carnivorous cats sometimes stubbornly refused to attack the Christian extras. The beasts seem hungrier in an ancient terra-cotta relief, which shows gladiators battling two lions and a bear in an ancient Roman arena. Gladiators who fought against animals were known as *bestiarii*.

Whither Goest Thou?

In 1905 the Polish novelist Henryk Sienkiewicz won the Nobel Prize for literature with his positivist novel *Quo Vadis?* set in Neronian Rome. By 1912 an ex-interior decorator named Enrico Guazzoni had put the story onto celluloid for Cines. Guazzoni later directed *Julius Caesar* (1914), *Fabiola* (1916), and *Messalina* (1922), and each of these four films reveals his philosophy: "To employ spectacular architectural masses on various planes, each filled with a wealth of detail, to express the supreme majesty of space."[9] The lovely painted-marble, three-dimensional interiors and handsome costuming in his *Quo Vadis?* make the film visually complex, and the occasional location exteriors (some along the Appian Way) expand the visual space. The fire with which Nero levels "old Rome" so that he can build his "new Rome" is somewhat disappointing, but five camera angles and many shots of the panicking populace compensate for the mediocre special effects.

Besides the architecture and decor, the film succeeds in its engaging characterizations and its unprecedented epic length. Chilon, the ragged go-between, and the corpulent Nero, who likes to look through his colored eyeglass, help dispel the ennui embedded in the cumbersome plot. Guazzoni might have done better, as did Wyler with *Ben-Hur,* to simplify the novel's story, for four hundred literary pages just do not fit well into two silent pictorial hours. But Guazzoni was pioneering the epic film, and he must be excused. There is a surplus of Romans saluting other Romans, but the film is still worth viewing. It was extremely successful in Italy, throughout Europe, and in America in 1912 and 1913. Beyond the film's own merits, it contributed to the cinematic idiom a strong man, Ursus, and an impish quidnunc, Chilon, who influenced Maciste and "the Monkey" in Pastrone's *Cabiria* the following year.

Ambrosio's 1924 *Quo Vadis?* repeated the one major mistake that Guazzoni's had made. In trying so hard to include all of the narrative intricacies of the novel, the film unfolds very slowly. Moreover, without a soundtrack, the book's Christian philosophy and Peter's impressive sermon in the Roman catacombs are ineffective. In their place we see mere drawings of the Christian fish symbol in the sand and the pious looks of the martyrs before their deaths in the arena.

In 1951 MGM shot *Quo Vadis?* (printed as QVO VADIS on the film's title screen) in Italy and made it into their first ancient spectacle since the silent *Ben-Hur.* Produced by *Ben-Hur's* Sam Zimbalist, this Technicolor production outsizes the silent versions of Sienkiewicz's novel in many ways. Where they had been mere romantic melodramas set in ancient Rome, this version is a spectacular cinematic vision of Rome in which a melodrama unfolds. The gilded splendor of the interiors in Nero's palace, the crowd filling the huge, bluish courtyard beneath it in the dim light of dusk, the pomp, excitement, and massive crowds in the Forum, Marcus Vinicius's entry along a refurbished two-mile stretch of the Appian Way, and the huge, sixty thousand–seat arena could exist only in a multi-million-dollar Technicolor film of the 1950s. Yet the sets, sumptuous and rich, are rarely gaudy. Visually, MGM's *Quo Vadis?* is magnificent, and if the film has one chief hero, it is ancient Rome.

The authenticity of the sets, characters, minor properties, and dialogue derive from the Oxfordian education of Hugh Gray (*Ulysses, Helen of Troy*). Thanks to him Nero plays a lyrelike cithara instead of a fiddle, the triumphal Vinicius hears the traditional "Remember, thou art mortal," and the imprisoned Christians sing authentic Yemenite hymns from the centuries surrounding the birth of Christ. Most of Gray's fact-filled notebooks went unread, for MGM had a film to shoot, not a lecture to give. Nonetheless, the Roman

135   Many iconographical scenes from the European Masters have been re-created for the screen versions of the Passion, but none so closely or so strikingly as this Last Supper rendition à la da Vinci in *Quo Vadis?* (1951).

authors Petronius, Seneca, and Lucan all find their way into the romances, and Tacitus's statement (*Annals* 16:19) that the dying Petronius left a nasty note for Nero is realized. The authenticities were neither overplayed nor underplayed; they fit suitably into the sweeping pageantry of the film.

The screenplay of *Quo Vadis?* is a welcome improvement over its silent pre-decessors. Peter's (Finlay Currie) sermon in the catacombs allows the Roman commander Marcus Vinicius to overhear the recitation of numerous biblical passages, most important "Upon this rock I will build my church." The sermon adds an important dimension to the way Marcus Vinicius understands (or fails to understand) Christianity. The episode also includes flashbacks to the raising of Lazarus, the Last Supper (staged exactly like da Vinci's), and the crucifixion. Currie's kindly interpretation of the apostle brings to life the gentle words, derived from another of Jesus' dictums, that Peter speaks to a young boy: "We'll go to Greece and fish for men there; and maybe we'll have time to fish for fish, too." Currie also enlivens the scene described in the Acts of Peter in which Peter sees Jesus going toward Rome. "Quo Vadis, Domine?" he asks—"Whither dost thou go, Lord?"

Marcus Vinicius (Robert Taylor) has some interesting reactions to Christian doctrine. When he hears about "the dead carpenter, a rabbi who was crucified," he abruptly replies, "I'm just a heavy-skulled soldier; what in the name of Jupiter is a 'rabbi'?" A condescending Marcus is amazed that Lygia (Deborah Kerr) believes in Christ: "That beggar-faced philosophy shouldn't be stuffing your luscious face full of nonsense." And Marcus's offer to worship Christ if it will win Lygia's love has a distinctly Roman tenor: "I'll accept your god if you want. I'll have a large statue of Christ carved from marble. There's an army of gods these days; we can always find room for another."

The screenplay by John Lee Mahin, S. N. Behrman (Ben-Hur), and Sonya Levien also gives a marvelous characterization of the articulate and reluctantly flattering Petronius, the author of the *Satyricon*. He commits suicide when he falls out of favor with Nero, and when he does so he muses that "It will be interesting to see if the Christian afterlife does indeed exist." Then he dictates the Tacitean letter to Nero:

> To Nero, Emperor of Rome, Ruler of the World, Divine Pontiff:
>   I know that my death will be a disappointment to you since you wished to render me this "service" yourself. To be born in your reign is a miscalculation, but to die in it is a joy. I can forgive you for murdering your wife and mother, for burning our beloved Rome, for befouling our fair country with the stench of your crimes. But one thing I cannot forgive: the burden of having to listen to your songs.

Peter Ustinov's Nero is one of the most magnificent pieces of hamming in the history of film. Raging with power, bursting with horrible music and poetry, full of insecurity, and suspicious of all, he burns Rome to enhance his own experience of his poem about the burning of Troy. He sighs and complains of his divinity and responsibilities, and he occasionally becomes comically pretentious. His last words, "Could this be the end of Nero?" seem to parallel the similar words of another cinematic Caesar (with the *praenomen* Rico) in the twentieth century—the director Mervyn LeRoy's own *Little Caesar* (1931). Like Jay Robinson's Caligula in *The Robe* and *Demetrius and the Gladiators*,

Ustinov's campy exaggeration provides an important comic touch, even as it reflects the darker side of humanity. His adviser Tigellinus (Ralph Truman) represents totally committed evil; when the soon-to-be martyred Christians sing devotional hymns in the arena, Tigellinus calmly comments, "The lions will sing louder, I think." And Nero's wife, Poppaea (Patricia Laffan), is a real lizard.

Just as Wyler had worked on the production of the 1925 version of *Ben-Hur* before directing the 1959 production, Mervyn LeRoy earned his "ancient" bona fides as an Israelite extra in DeMille's 1923 *The Ten Commandments*. In fact, LeRoy—like Wyler a Jewish-born director of a "Christian" film—developed his epic techniques from those he saw DeMille use in 1923. Besides his experiences with "the Master," LeRoy drew on his own childhood memories of the 1905 San Francisco earthquake in filming the sequence in which Rome burns; the same sequence was reused ten years later in MGM's *Atlantis, the Lost Continent*. LeRoy wrote in his autobiography that he had always wanted to do an epic, and the energy he injected into *Quo Vadis?* evidences this desire. Well aware that a failure could ruin MGM, LeRoy used every penny of the $12 million budget to create a top-notch piece of epic entertainment.

The ten months of shooting went smoothly, but a few incidents did make headlines. Robert Taylor had an avidly publicized separation from his wife, Barbara Stanwyck (presaging the *Cleopatra* scandal). Then the fifty-plus lions LeRoy had brought from circuses all over Europe refused to attack the Christians. The tamers told LeRoy to feed the lions less food, so he tried to shoot the martyrdom sequence after two weeks of virtually starving the lions. Still nothing. He finally had to settle for some fake close-ups, which mar the film. DeMille had the same problem in filming the arena sequence from *The Sign of the Cross* (1932); some people swear that in the soundtrack of the lion sequence of that film DeMille can be heard shouting in the distance, "God dammit! Get going!" LeRoy mused over historical fact: "I still don't know how the ancient Romans staged their bloody circuses."[10] (Answer: When in Rome, do as the Romans; catch them live from Africa instead of renting them from German zoos and circuses, and your Christians will be eaten.)

Two other incidents that occurred during the shooting of *Quo Vadis?* are well established legends of Hollywood. One day during the filming of the arena sequence, LeRoy received a phone call from Elizabeth Taylor, who was on vacation in Rome. She had just had a fight with husband Nicky Hilton and wanted some place for refuge. What better way to hide than to dress up in a toga and join an already togaed crowd of $\overline{\mathrm{LIX}}$DCCCCXCIX (59,999) in a reconstructed Roman arena? And one hired member of the Triumph sequence's crowd of cheering Italian extras was reportedly the aspiring actress Sophia Loren.

With his score for *Quo Vadis?* Miklos Rozsa became the master of the "ancient" film score. Inspired by the research of Hugh Gray, he used what few fragments of ancient Greco-Roman music have survived and adapted them for his score. In addition to the Christian's Yemenite hymns, most notable was Nero's song about the burning of Troy/

Rome, the lyric of which was originally inscribed on a tombstone nearly a century after Nero's reign. Rozsa later scored *Julius Caesar, Ben-Hur, King of Kings,* and *Sodom and Gomorrah.*

Quo Vadis? appeared again in an Italian 1985 made-for-television version, but Nero's persecution of the Christians had long been a popular forum for films. Besides Arrigo Frusta's *Nerone* (1909), which has some superb mattes, Guazzoni's *Agrippina* (1910), Caserini's *Nerone e Agrippina* (1913), J. Gordon Edwards's *Nero* (1922), a half-dozen schlocko attempts were made in Italy during the early 1960s revival, including *Ten Gladiators* (1963), *Challenge of the Gladiator* (1964), *Le Calde Notti di Poppea* (1969), and *Fire Over Rome* (1963). DeMille's *The Sign of the Cross* (1932) has also had its part in lionizing Nero. Following two silent versions of the Wilson Barrett play (1904 and 1914), DeMille as always found satisfaction in the unique combination of fantasy and sober historical authenticity. The street scenes of Rome—with their little shops, fountains, bakeries, inns, fountains, and peddlers' carts—create a feeling for the life of the average Roman. DeMille uses these humble settings well. Marcus (Fredric March) wants to know "which fountain Mercia [Elissa Landi] goes to," reminding us that water in antiquity did not normally come from private sinks; two Christians draw "the sign of the cross" in the dust by the curb of a crowded street; and a Latin advertisement for gladiatorial contests is posted on the wall. This poster morphs into English for the benefit of the film audience, a device also used in DeMille's *The King of Kings* to translate *INRI.*

Staying within Paramount's budget of $650,000, DeMille could not create the lavish Neronian Rome that he might have liked. Nero's (Charles Laughton) court consists merely of a throne, a marble ledge, and a stairway, which DeMille carefully keeps within the camera frame; the crowd scenes are doubled with a prismatic lens. DeMille did find time and money to include gladiators, dwarfs, amazons, lions, tigers, an elephant, and a bull in the arena sequence, and Poppaea's bath of asses' milk became one of the best-known symbols of DeMillean antiquity. But only DeMille would cut from a naked Poppaea (Claudette Colbert) amid the foaming lactic suds, to another woman disrobing and climbing into the bath to entertain the empress, then to two kittens leaning over the edge of the pool and lapping up the milk. The DeMillean touches are there, but the story lacks power. Nonetheless, the film was successful enough to be rereleased in 1944 with a Second World War anti-Roman—Mussolini's Rome, that is—prologue.

Besides Columbia's *Salome* and Fox's *The Robe* and *Demetrius and the Gladiators,* two other films based on the New Testament and early Christianity were produced in the wake of *Quo Vadis?*—MGM's *The Prodigal* (1955) and Warner Brothers' *The Silver Chalice* (1954). *The Prodigal* is loosely based on the parable of the prodigal son in Luke 15: 11–32; the story had been filmed previously by Raoul Walsh as *The Wanderer* (1925). Edmund Purdom plays Micah, the titular son who takes his prematurely inherited bag of silver to Damascus; there he "squandered what he had in reckless living"—says Luke—by

136   A chaste external scene from DeMille's controversial milk-bath sequence in *The Sign of the Cross* (1932). The asses' milk poured into the huge bucket at the top of this bucket brigade of lactic lackeys leads into Poppaea's palace bath via a small spout.

trying to buy his way into the fleshy arms of sexy Samarra (Lana Turner), high priestess of Astarte—says Hollywood. The buildings in Damascus are more or less appropriately covered with frieze decorations and double-horse columns from Persepolis, but "the gifts from Bagdad" that Samarra receives are a little premature for the ancient world; Bagdad was not built until the Middle Ages. The "tinted wall" of Damascus, however, where one can purchase his venereal pleasures, is based on Herodotus's description of the prostitute market in ancient Babylon. Ultimately, despite the talents of Purdom, who here plays the same type of dissolute, resolute role he played in *The Egyptian,* and Louis Calhern (the high priest), *The Prodigal* looks rich but plays absurd. Bosley Crowther's assessment—"pompous, ostentatious, vulgar, and ridiculous"—was unkind, but not unfair.[11]

   The Silver Chalice was based on a best-selling novel. But unlike the films adapted from the literary *Ben-Hur, The Robe, Quo Vadis?* and *The Last Days of Pompeii,* this film fails to bring either profundity or entertainment to the screen. Howard Bristof's theatrical set decorations are eye-catching and original, and Jack Palance does his best to portray the evil magician Simon, but this story of the Holy Grail just does not hold water, let alone divine liquids. How Virginia Mayo's eyebrows were rotated to a vertical plane must remain a mystery. Perhaps Paul Newman evaluated *The Silver Chalice* best. The young actor had been "introduced" in the film, and when this debut was about to be shown on television in Los Angeles for the first time, Newman took out advertising space in the local papers and apologized for his performance. Describing his feelings when he looked at the embarrassing film, Newman said, "I was horrified."[12]

Mention should be made of several films in which mobs of early Christians face mobs of Roman soldiers or mobs of ravenous lions. *The Sword and the Cross* (1960, not to be confused with the 1958 film of the same title) martyrs Christians in 120 A.D. Cilicia; *A Sword for the Empire* (1965) martyrs them under Commodus, *Gladiator of Rome* (1962) under Caracalla, and *Fabiola* under preconversion Constantine. *A.D., Androcles and the Lion,* and *Constantine and the Cross* have been discussed in Chapter 2. And lastly, one of the founding fathers of Christendom, *Augustine of Hippo* (1972), had his lone screen appearance in an artistic Roberto Rossellini film. But here we have abandoned our ancient chariot for a medieval cart.

And here let those

Who boast in mortal things, and wondering tell,

Of Babel, and the works of Memphian kings,

. . . when Egypt with Assyria strove

In wealth and luxury.

—MILTON, *PARADISE LOST, I.692–722*

The age-encrusted names of such mysteriously elusive Eastern kings as Tiglathpileser of Assyria, Gilgamesh of Uruk, Naram-Sin of Akkad, and Suppululiumas the Hittite of Hattusas will never garnish Hollywood marquees with the same frequency as Cleopatra. But a considerable number of films have honored the exploits of the best-known ancient Oriental personalities: Nebuchadnezzar, Semiramis, and Daniel of Babylon; Cyrus, Xerxes, and Esther of Persia; Hannibal and Hamilcar of Carthage; and Pharaohs Cheops, Ikhnaton, and Rameses of Egypt; not to mention Goliath of Gath and even David of Jerusalem and the Nazarene King of Kings. Hollywood and Cinecittà have built cinematic replicas of the great non-Western cities of antiquity — Jerusalem, Memphis, Karnak, Babylon, Nineveh, Damascus, Susa, and Carthage. And the great gods Chemosh, Moloch, Baal, Serapis, Isis, Osiris, Tanit, and Ishtar have all been idolized in twentieth-century A.D. celluloid.

This filmic expansion beyond the temporal and spatial barriers of the Roman Empire has brought both blessings and curses to the reputation of films portraying the ancient world. *Intolerance* (1916) was for years considered to be outrageously expensive and incomprehensible, yet *The Ten Commandments* (1956) was a smashing success. *Land of the Pharaohs* (1955) has been called one of Howard Hawks's most disappointing films, yet *The Mummy* (1932) played its part in vaulting Boris Karloff and Karl Freund into cinematic immortality. The splendiferous realms of the ancient Orient attracted the lire-hungry producers and directors of the recent Italian spear-

and-chariot revival, yet they also attracted American directorial giants, not only Griffith, DeMille, and Hawks but Raoul Walsh, John Huston, William Wyler, and Michael Curtiz, among others.

Although the sources of this subgenre overlap with Greco-Roman history and mythology, as well as with the Bible, these films set in ancient Carthage, Persia, (non-Hebrew) Palestine, Mesopotamia, Arabia, and Egypt deserve separate treatment. As far as the Colosseum is from the Nile or the Euphrates, so different is filming ancient Rome from filming the ancient Orient. One reason for this difference is that scholars cannot give film directors as much information about Babylon or Carthage as they can about Rome. They do not have nearly as much extant literature, and they know less about specific personages and everyday life and customs. Even the cities themselves have generally eroded into near oblivion. Unlike Rome or Athens, Babylon, "the wonder of all tongues" (as Milton called it), the city that remained the cultural capital of the ancient world for well over one thousand years, is now little more than a crumbling protrusion of an eroded clay civilization on an arid plain in Iraq. Of Carthage there remains practically nothing other than a quaint harbor jutting out from the coast of Tunisia. Furthermore, the ancient Orient generally has little meaning for today's general public; the name of the great Babylonian lawgiver Hammurabi does not conjure up the same sort of imagery as the Caesar or Alexander. Finally, to speak plainly in terms of Western civilization, the Romans won; almost all of the other civilizations of antiquity either perished at the hands of the Roman Empire or were absorbed into it. Our modern Western culture has many more visible roots in Athens and Rome than it does in Babylon or Egyptian Memphis. If Rome and Athens are our parents and Jerusalem and Eden our grandparents, Memphis and Babylon are our great uncles—related, but distant.

In spite of this relative lack of cultural affinity, filmmakers have occasionally visited their cameras upon ancient Babylon. The very name and its implications have an allure for twentieth-century moviegoers—Hollywood itself, after all, has been nicknamed Babylon. And the relative lack of information about ancient Mesopotamia allows filmmakers to interpret Babylon as if it were an ancient Hollywood, full of wealth, irreverence, and degeneracy, or to use the vaguely ancient and "Oriental" setting as an excuse for camel-filled bazaars, thinly clad harem girls, and quivering belly dancers. Yet in light of this great temptation to exploit Babylon and her Eastern sisters, the several films that do follow a sincere and sober path through Babylon's Ishtar Gate into the subtle realities of the ancient Orient have been blessed by the Muse of History. This is historical justice, and Hammurabi would have judged it so.

Babylon itself has appeared in a number of films, some of them biblical. John Huston's *The Bible* offered a brief view from atop Babylon's ziggurat, a multistoried temple now commonly known as the Tower of Babel. The matted location scenery reveals the marvels of special effects, for the bottom of the tower was shot in Rome, the top in Egypt. Stephen Boyd (Nimrod), in eye makeup worthy of Cleopatra, embodies Eastern luxury and decadence. But Huston's Babylon, an interpretation of the city from the book of Genesis, does not really attempt to portray the magnificent Mesopotamian metropolis at its zenith. Michael Curtiz's *Noah's Ark* (1929) characterized Babylon as the virtual successor to Sodom; Curtiz adapted Noah's flood and the destruction of that first sinful batch of humanity such that Jehovah's great deluge obliterated sinful Babylon. Ignoring this biblical confusion, we expect some sobriety and authenticity from Curtiz and Warner Brothers, and, as expected, there are costumes that look very much like Hammurabi's, a model of the antediluvian city of Babylon that is based on the prototype at the Oriental Institute of the University of Chicago, and a glass-painted imitation of Pieter Brueghel's *Tower of Babel*.

Probably the most financially successful silent film about Babylon was Raoul Walsh's decadent and moralistic *The Wanderer* (1925), based on the New Testament tale of the prodigal son and a twentieth-century play. Unlike the 1955 MGM version, which sent the spendthrift lad to Lana Turner's tantalizing temple in Damascus, *The Wanderer* packs off its hero Jether (William Collier Jr.) to Babylon, where he attends the feast of Ishtar (the chief goddess of Babylon) and loses all of his money thanks to the loaded dice of Tola (Ernest Torrence). Again, a matte of the famed ziggurat can be seen, as well as the human-headed, winged-bull deities that archaeologists dug up in Khorsabad (Iraq). After the great orgy, the destruction of the city brings the film to its climax. An unintentional high point occurs when Pharis (Noah Beery) goes to bed slipping under the soft embroidered silk covers while still dressed in his full suit of armor! Authenticity is one thing, common sense another.

The axiom that the better "ancient" films are based on Scriptures or well-known novels generally holds for Babylon and the ancient East. Yet William Castle's *Slaves of Babylon* (1953), based on the Old Testament's intriguing story of Daniel's Babylonian sojourn during the kingship of Nebuchadnezzar, is an unfortunate exception. Very lacking in apocalyptic character, *Slaves of Babylon* falls into the common post–*Quo Vadis?* trap of inserting an absurd love theme where some action, thought, or real passion would have been much more welcome. Cyrus in this film invades Babylon not to satisfy territorial ambition but to avenge the theft of his concubine by Belshazzar (Michael Ansara). Daniel (Maurice Schwartz) is thrown into the lions' den not by Darius the Mede, as Daniel 5:31–6:16 has it, but by wicked Belshazzar. The hideous special effects exacerbate the inaccuracies, and when the three Hebrews—Shadrach, Meshach, and Abednego—walk out of the furnace, they seem rather bored by the whole process. When Daniel is being led through the streets, which are filled with an angry mob, he is struck on the cheek by a stone; he should at least flinch, but he seems not even to feel the prop—er, rock. A biblical prophet should exhibit piety and strength, but not at the cost of involuntary muscular reaction.

Nil desperandum. This Bible-based romance released by Columbia does have its worthy moments. Some scenic mattes of Babylon's famous Hanging Gardens, the construction of a temple to Bel-Marduk in the city, and the double-exposed handwriting of

137/138   Although strongly influenced by Art Nouveau, this interior of the temple of Hadrashar from Michael Curtiz's *Noah's Ark* (1929) reveals some authentic costuming on the male priests. Their tiered hats and skirts re-create the dress of the Babylonian lawgiver Hammurabi, as seen in a stele from early in the second millennium B.C., now in the Louvre.

the Hebrew *Mene Mene Tekel Upharsin* on the wall (featured earlier in Pathé's 1905 *Belshazzar's Feast*) are attractive effects. The quick shot of Nebuchadnezzar eating grass (Daniel 5:21) as well as Cyrus's worship of the Persian god Mithra (if not Ahura Mazda) add to the authenticities of *Slaves of Babylon*. Another rather clever sequence combines a Greek myth with the Persian myths surrounding the birth of Cyrus. The Greek historian Herodotus details the Persian part of the story: Astyages, King of the Medes, had a dream that his daughter urinated all over Asia; fearing the consequences of such a divine omen, Astyages ordered his daughter's child to be exposed on a hillside (like Oedipus). But a shepherd saved the child and reared him. The film adds this touch based on the lesser-known Greek myth of Philomela and Procne: Cyrus as a young man did not know of his kingly origins, and the tongue of the shepherd's wife had been torn out so that she could not reveal the truth. Denied her voice, she depicted the story in a tapestry, and in this way Cyrus learned of his royal birth.

Another biblical work about Babylon under Nebuchadnezzar retold on the silver screen is the Apocrypha's Judith. When Nebuchadnezzar took control of Palestine, he established Holophernes as an overlord. Eventually, just outside the town of Bethulia, Judith enticed the Babylonian captain into drunkenness so that she could murder him. But she found Holophernes not completely unattractive. She struggled with herself while she tried to decide the proper course of action—love or murder—but then she resolutely decapitated the Babylonian, took his head back to her fellow townsmen, and was rewarded for her "piety."

Judith has had four screen portrayals, the first in *Giudetta ed Oloferne,* a Cines film of 1906. The story moves quickly, and the sets are confining, but this primitive biblical reenactment does have its charm. Who could object to a 1906 film that gives an angel cardboard wings? Still, the film is predictable and curiously dispassionate throughout its series of stereotypical gestures. That *Quo Vadis?* should present so much more sophistication only six years later is a true attestation to the later film's importance in the history of the cinema.

While this same *Quo Vadis?* was pulling in Broadway's first large movie crowds in 1913, D. W. Griffith sat in a New York hotel room thumbing through his copy of the Scriptures. He decided to make a film about Judith, basing his film on a poetic and dramatic adaptation by Thomas Bailey Aldrich. He shot *Judith of Bethulia* in less than two weeks, even though the exterior scenes were filmed in California and the interiors in New York. The result was one of the first full-length films, and one of the most ambitious films in America to date. Following *Judith*'s success, Griffith planned to film Flaubert's *Salammbô* and Sardou's *Cleopatra,* but these never materialized.

Judith of Bethulia shows already the complex action, photographic wizardry, and comprehensive effort that in three years bloomed in *Intolerance*. The large, drunken Holophernes (Henry Walthall, actually quite a small man, who was photographed from angles and vantage points that made him loom large) in his tent, and the confused Judith

141   The "Tower of Babel" known from Genesis and then re-created in Brueghel's painting as well as in Curtiz's *Noah's Ark* and John Huston's *The Bible,* was actually the Ziggurat of Babylon. A ziggurat was a quasi-pyramid construction used for worship in ancient Mesopotamia. The ruins of the Ziggurat of Uruk show that the reconstructions by Brueghel, Curtiz, and Huston are inauthentic, but few members of a movie audience would know what a ziggurat actually looked like.

(Blanche Sweet), who is torn between love and hate, between mercy and murder, between *corpus dilecti* and *corpus delicti,* complement each other perfectly. The action scenes are not up to the standards Griffith later established, but the multiple camera angles for the Babylonian ambush at the Bethulian well make the best of a tight budget. As in *Quo Vadis?* the interior scenes bulge with waving arms, smoking altars, tall urns, elaborate carpets, flowing draperies, and ocular-tailed peacocks. Authentic Assyrian winged-bull gods can be glimpsed in the rear of several scenes, and the soldiers wear ringlet beards that match archaeological evidence. A few Greek helmets with crests can be seen, but these may be Greek mercenaries. At any rate it does not really matter whether they are authentic or not; in 1913 archaeology and the cinema were both young sciences, and the cinematic combination of Greek armor and Babylonian or Assyrian armor neither offended nor enlightened the visually thrilled audience.

Following a lesser-known Italian version in 1928, the indefatigable Italian film industry returned in 1960 to Bethulia with *Head of a Tyrant.* The gruesome title of its American

139/140   The Tower of Babel as depicted in Michael Curtiz's *Noah's Ark* (facing page, top). The tower is painted on glass. Its spiraled, tiered construction, its incomplete state, and its partial cloud-cover originate in Pieter Brueghel's sixteenth-century rendition of the *Tower of Babel.* Before Brueghel, all representations of the tower were designed according to contemporary architecture. Brueghel modeled his tower after the Colosseum in Rome, thus the tiered construction and repetitious arches.

142   One of the most elaborate historical sets of the silent cinema—the courtyard of Babylon
from D. W. Griffith's *Intolerance* (1916). Built in Hollywood, the set includes authentic Mesopotamian eagle-headed, pinecone-bearing divinities, lower left and right corners and top center; human-
headed winged-bull deities, on the landing of the large flight of steps; and a statue of Gilgamesh,
just above the human-bull divinities, as well as Persian tribute bearers, along the inside of the large
steps. The elephantid columns are not Mesopotamian; Griffith borrowed them directly from *Cabiria*.
The entire scene was captured by a camera mounted on an innovative moving platform.

release (the original was simply *Giudetta e Oloferne*) can be misleading. It cannot match
Griffith's semiclassic *Judith,* but convincing acting by Massimo Girotti (Holophernes)
—a welcome regular in many "ancient" films shot in Italy in that era—raises this film's
Holophernean head a foot or two above the shoulders of the other sword-and-sandal
bombs of the period.

   Intolerance (1916) presented another literature-based film about Babylon. This
D. W. Griffith masterpiece memorialized the sixth-century B.C. reign of Nebuchadnezzar
(Nabukudurri-usur) and its end at the hands of Cyrus the Persian. *Intolerance* broke more
ground in the American cinema than did Cyrus in Babylonia. In fact, had it not been for
Griffith's film there might never have been a *Ben-Hur* or a *Ten Commandments* or any

143/144 *Intolerance* sources:
the eagle-headed, pine-cone
bearing divinity of Assyria,
carved in relief on the walls of
Assurnasirpal II's Palace at
Nimrud, c. 875 B.C., and
inscribed in cuneiform; and a
propylaeum set from the Italian
Cabiria (1914). Griffith never
acknowledged the influence of
Cabiria, whose director,
Giovanni Pastrone, took the idea
from ancient Indian art,
specifically the North Torana of
Stupa I at Sanchi. The wall
paintings in the rear of the
Cabiria set are stylized blowups
of ancient Assyrian reliefs.

other historic epic after the Italian Golden Age. In any case, *Intolerance* set a standard for scope and detail that helped shape the genre. It was a massive, four-part epic that ran an unheard-of thirteen reels and cost a whopping two million 1916 dollars. For the first time in America, huge replicas of authentic sets like the walls and interior of Babylon were erected (on Griffith's lot) in Hollywood, and costumed extras by the hundreds—not to mention the elephants—ran up the cost to $12,000 per day. And this was for just one of the film's four parts.

The plot of *Intolerance* twists and turns like the labyrinth in which Theseus met the Minotaur—a path can be found, but not a direct one and not on the first try. It consists of four stories—a modern melodrama, the crucifixion of Christ, the St. Bartholomew's Day massacre, and the siege of Babylon by Cyrus—and, to quote one of Griffith's titles, "each story shows how hatred and intolerance, through all the ages, have battled against love and charity." The four stories run concurrently and intermittently, all culminating in an exciting climax in which Babylon falls, Christ is crucified, and an unjust modern hanging is halted in the nick of time. Unfortunately, the simultaneity of the narrative does not quite work in the final cut because two of the stories, the Passion and the massacre, are

145/146   This exterior shot from *Intolerance* (facing page) shows the rhapsode (Elmer Clifton) sitting in the rear, left, and the mountain girl (Constance Talmadge) seated in the foreground. Although Griffith had a story to tell and a profound point to make, he did not ignore historical authenticity—a particularly admirable trait in 1916, when archaeology was still a relatively young science. The wall relief is a reconstruction of a work showing the Assyrian King Assurnasirpal II on a lion hunt in the ninth century B.C.

hardly developed at all. But Griffith's scope took in all of human history, and even to have attempted this on the screen, let alone to have almost succeeded, helped to make Griffith one of early filmdom's most widely respected titans.

As DeMille did after him, Griffith first had his set decorator (Frank Wortman) look into several scholarly books. Most inspirational was James Henry Breasted's recently published history of the world entitled *Ancient Times*. Also influential were several paintings, including Georges Rochegrosse's *Fall of Babylon* (1891), John Martin's *Belshazzar's Feast* (1821), and Edwin Long's *Babylonian Marriage Market* (1875). Griffith may well have seen Long's painting in Louis Martin's popular New York restaurant, which featured a Babylonian decor. Then Wortman and Griffith found authentic Mesopotamian archaeological remains that could be easily copied. At great expense they reconstructed copies of the walls of Babylon (at the corner of Sunset and Hollywood) and covered them with plaster reliefs based on Assyrian and Persian originals. As in most films about the ancient Orient, general authenticity is all that can be expected, and so Griffith combined Persian, Assyrian, Sumerian, and Babylonian ingredients into one Irano/Mesopotamian stew. Thanks to Wortman's research the majestic and often photographed setting in which the wild orgy of Belshazzar takes place reveals the famed elephantids (borrowed both from *Cabiria* and from ancient India), the Persian staircase from Persepolis, complete with its tribute bearers and attendants, the Assyrian human-headed, winged-bull deities from

Khorsabad (and Persepolis), the eagle-headed, pinecone-bearing divinity of Assyria, and the Assyrian depiction of the Tree of Life. Not one to be bound by research, however, Griffith filled this reasonably authentic Chaldean scene with hundreds of orgiastic men and women; then he shot all this from a magnificent moving platform, the famous tracking shot closing in gradually on the dynamic details. The scene, with its authentic archaeological detail, its massive setting, its kinetic humanity, and its technical innovation, exemplifies why *Intolerance* is one of the first great wonders of the cinematic world, a landmark of the cinema. Griffith himself was so pleased with the result that he demoted the Passion and massacre sequences to allow for more footage of Babylon.

Griffith employed literary research in a similar fashion as archaeological research: he absorbed the research, then shot the movie around it. He tells us in his titles that he uses Herodotus and the newly discovered Nabu-naid tablets. The tablets reveal that King Nabu-naid of Babylon (known in the film by his Hellenized name, Nabonidus) was too tolerant of deities other than the chief Babylonian god, Marduk; his polytheistic indulgence agitated the intolerant monotheistic priests of Marduk. Further undermined by lax rule, bureaucratic graft, and oppression of the peasantry, the reign of Nabonidus (Carl Stockdale) and his son Belshazzar (Alfred Page) was doomed to collapse, as Isaiah 45–48 was wont to threaten. The overthrow of Babylon was finally effected by Cyrus (George Siegmann) the Persian. So far, history and cinema agree.

Much to his dismay, Griffith found that the historical Cyrus never besieged Babylon. But the film needed spectacle, so a massive assault was written into the film. Now, should the gigantic fifty-foot-high and ten-foot-thick walls of Babylon be breached during the film's assault? History (Herodotus again) tells us that the Persians found a gap in the walls of Babylon where they meet the Euphrates River and sneaked into the city without breaching the walls. Griffith adapted this Herodotean information: his jealous and intolerant priests of Marduk are the traitors who lead the Persian invaders to the gap. Babylon's great walls, then, are never quite breached; history, spectacle, and the theme of the film are all satisfied.

Griffith forced himself into a peculiar corner by following the Nabu-naid tablets, for they contradicted the Daniel narrative; Griffith feared that his audiences would be shocked to see him tampering with the biblical plot. Any audience that had read Daniel carefully might insist that Nebuchadnezzar, not Nabonidus, was the father of Belshazzar; that Belshazzar was king, not crown prince, of Babylon; and that Darius the Mede, not Cyrus the Persian, conquered Babylon. But the Nabu-naid tablets had recently proved the biblical narrative to be historically confused, and Griffith felt that he had to employ the tablets. But not wanting to alienate his audience, he explained his deviation from Daniel in a note. The same is true for his Herodotean citations; audiences might not believe the huge size of the Babylonian walls without literary "proof." The footnote for Christ's wine-drinking also reflects Griffith's dual aims of authenticity and accommodation.

147/148   The slave market from *Intolerance*. The top of the photo reveals the feet of a Persian royal archers tile series like the glazed-brick originals from the Persian palace at Susa, c. 375 B.C. At right are Babylonian or Persian floral tile designs. The man at upper left holds cuneiform tablets; above his left hand, Assyrian trees of life are painted on the walls. The Assyrian men wear reasonably authentic ringlet beards and hairstyles.

149/150   Another revolutionary
scene from *Intolerance*—the siege of
Babylon with its crowded, crenellated
ramparts, huge siege engines, and
smoky destruction. Siege warfare was
the most sophisticated and techno-
logically advanced aspect of ancient
military science, and at left are gigantic
siege engines on rollers. At extreme
right is a tall Persian archer of glazed
brick, and the base of the Babylonian
walls reveal four, human-headed,
winged-bull deities. One bull's head is
turned sideways; another style has a
frontal head.

Besides the magnificent orgy scene (Daniel 5:1–4), *Intolerance*'s Babylonian sequences are most memorable for the great siege of the city. The reconstructed Chaldean walls—the originals built by Nebuchadnezzar, these by Griffith—hold hundreds of ringlet-bearded, armored Babylonian warriors who cast huge stones and pour boiling oil down onto the vulnerable heads of the besieging Persians. The Persians valiantly try to bring up a battering ram against the great gate, Imgur-Bel, but their attempts earn nothing other than defeat and death. Huge elephants push hundred-foot-high rolling towers toward the crenellated tops of Nebuchadnezzar's walls. As the siege engines reach the walls, ramps are lowered from their tops, and bold Persians run into the staunch spears of the defending Babylonians. One tower is toppled to the earth directly toward the camera. The siege continues even at night; Griffith lit flares that he had implanted into the walls of the set and realized three minutes of fantastic effects. The smoke eddying to the dark sky and the dogged efforts of deeply shadowed besiegers and besieged create an unforgettable nocturnal tableau. That the rickety surfaces of the plywood walls put the California extras into constant fear that the whole set would at any moment topple and cause them serious injury is irrelevant to the audience. These are the walls of ancient Babylon; this is solid brick and clay; this is the horrifying realism that made ancient siege warfare as cataclysmic to the minds of the ancients as nuclear warfare is to our own minds.

Ironically, an equally cataclysmic and unforeseeable modern historical event stood between *Intolerance* and popular success. The film was released just as the United States was entering the First World War, and it was hardly time for an expensive, lengthy sermon on tolerance, understanding, and peace. But even before modern politics became a determining factor, the moviegoing public seemed to sense that the film was brilliant but not enjoyable. They were distanced by the frequent interruptions to the four narratives, and their interest quickly waned. Griffith lost a fortune—all the profits he had made from *Birth of a Nation*. The film faded, and Griffith's marvelous walls began to crumble in situ like their authentic Mesopotamian prototype. In 1919, as Griffith recut the negative and rereleased the Babylonian portions alone as *The Fall of Babylon* (the title of one of the paintings that initially inspired Griffith), a movement to make Griffith's sets a national monument was as doomed as Belshazzar's kingdom, and the insensitive armies of time and progress soon cleared them away. A second Babylon, *Intolerance* had to wait years before the more sober judgments, learned opinions, and gentle hands of film archaeologists established its greatness. But the film is now recognized as a classic, so much so that the Taviani brothers wrote their feature *Good Morning, Babylon* (1987) about two of the artists who helped construct Griffith's famous sets.

The Hero of Babylon (1963) also covers the reign of Belshazzar and its overthrow by Cyrus in 538 B.C. But here a rather muscular "Prince Nippur" (Gordon Scott) controls the flimsy reins of Babylon when all the fighting is finished, and this Nippur turns out to be none other than the son of Hercules (whence the cacophonous alternate title *The Beast of Babylon vs. the Son of Hercules*). Accompanying this most improbable

151   *The Prodigal, The Big Fisherman, Ben-Hur* and *Solomon and Sheba* gave us glimpses into ancient Arabia. This shot from *Ben-Hur* (1959) is set in the tent of Sheikh Ilderim (Hugh Griffith) and provides a refreshing contrast to the Roman and exterior desert sequences. At left sits Judah Ben-Hur (Charlton Heston) and at right Balthazar of Nativity fame, played by Finlay Currie, who also appeared as Peter in *Quo Vadis?* (1951), David in *Solomon and Sheba* (1959), Jacob in *Joseph and His Brethren* (1960), Titus in *Cleopatra* (1963), and a Roman senator in *The Fall of the Roman Empire* (1964).

appearance by Hercules' progeny is a certain Hammurabi, but rest assured that he is not the famed second-millennium B.C. Babylonian lawgiver, who by this time would be just about 1,260 years old.

Eight other Italian films were set in ancient Babylon, including two innocent attempts at love and luxury by Ambrosio called *La Vergine di Babilonia* (1910) and *The Queen of Nineveh* (1911). In the early 1960s, love and luxury met war and treachery to produce *Hercules and the Tyrants of Babylon* (1964), which has nothing to do with received history or myth; *Goliath and the Sins of Babylon* (1963), also called *The Sins of Babylon,* which has nothing to do with anything; *I, Semiramis* (1962), which reenacts the famed queen's loves and heartbreaks in Babylon and Nineveh with a script so slow-moving that it might have been written in cuneiform; and *The Seventh Thunderbolt* (1962), also released as *Syria Against Babylon, War Gods of Babylon,* and *La sette folgori di Assur,* in which the semilegendary Sardanapalus (Herodotus 2.150) finds his home city of Nineveh wrecked by a flood of the Tigris. Of some interest in this otherwise genre-bound film is the appearance of Zoroaster, the "messenger" of the Persian deity Ahura-Mazda, and the human-headed winged-bull statues that *Judith of Bethulia* and *Intolerance* had made a necessary detail of any film about Babylon. Sardanapalus had also appeared in De Liguoro's *Sardanapalo, Re dell'Assiria* (1910).

Ricardo Montalban and Rhonda Fleming starred in one other Babylonian romance, *Queen of Babylon* (1956), set during the occupation of the city by the Assyrian "Assur" (Assurbanipal?). This Fox production has a higher visual standard than many other mid-1950s "ancient" films; occasional Sumerian dress and relief statues of Gilgamesh strangling a lion create an attractive, authentic background for the romance between Amal (Montalban, with dubbed voice) and Semiramis (Fleming). The crocodile torture pit seems a little out of place both historically and narratively, but there is some light fun to be had in this and-they-lived-happily-ever-after film.

Ancient Arabia is a civilization about which historians and archaeologists know very little, so the cinema has always assumed, perhaps correctly, that Arabs lived essentially the same way before the rise of Islam as they did after the rise of Islam around A.D. 600. And so the full-length robes, *galabiehs* or *haiks,* camels, desert, scantily clad belly dancers, bejeweled princes, and veiled women of the harem pop up in several sequences of *The Prodigal, The Big Fisherman,* and *Ben-Hur* (1959). *Ben-Hur,* of course, gloried in its Arabian scenes, for Sheikh Ilderim (Hugh Griffith's Oscar-winning performance) humorously and tantalizingly lures Judah into racing his horses against Messala at the Antioch circus. Lastly, because Arabs, Babylonians, and Assyrians are all Semites, the Semitic *Queen of Sheba* (1953) and the feminine half of *Solomon and Sheba* (1959) and the other films featuring the Queen of Sheba should also be mentioned here as belonging to the world of ancient Arabia.

One other important group of Semitic people has found its heritage in filmdom, the natives of ancient Carthage. Besides *Cabiria* (which was inspired in part when director Giovanni Pastrone saw an impressive exhibition of Carthaginian art and artifacts in Paris in 1912), *Hannibal,* and *Carthage in Flames,* three other films have concentrated on this North African metropolis and its inhabitants. After an unheralded attempt by Ambrosio called *Lo Schiavo di Cartagine* (1910), *Salambo* (1914), one of the first films to have a score written specifically for its musical accompaniment, offered the first film version of Gustave Flaubert's wartime romance *Salammbô.* This cinematic version of *Salambo* takes advantage of its North African locale by dressing up several cast members in leopard skins and long-plumed headdresses. Some influence from *Cabiria* can be seen in the stone elephants that appear at the base of Carthage's walls. Historically, Carthaginians used elephants for warfare and for crushing convicted criminals to death.

The action in this film moves quite briskly, and the subplots do not interfere with the momentum. The plot is derived from Polybius 1.65–88: Matho leads the mercenaries who fought on Carthage's side during the First Punic War with Rome. They have not been paid for their services, so they attack Carthage. But Matho happens to be in love with Salambo, the daughter of the Carthaginian leader, Hamilcar. Matho and Hamilcar try to work out a payment, but the evil Narr Havas (Narauas—in leopard skin and plumed headdress) replaces the chests full of gold with chests full of rocks. In the ensuing imbroglio Hamilcar emerges as victor, Narr Havas is executed, and Matho and Salambo live happily ever after. (Just for the record, this Hamilcar was the father of Hannibal, and Salambo is actually a Babylonian name.) The same plot was used in *The Loves of Salammbô* (1959), an Italian-American version starring Jeanne Valerie, Jacques Sernas (Matho), and Edmund Purdom (Narr Havas). May the great Carthaginian god Tanit never see this film.

Crossing the desert sands of Tunisia and Libya, we arrive at the banks of the Nile and look deep into its ageless waters for a great number of films about ancient Egypt. Many of them have already been discussed elsewhere—the reigns of Sethi and Rameses in *The Ten Commandments* and other films, the governorship of Joseph in *Joseph and His Brethren, Joseph,* and others, the unspecified Pharaoh with whom Adonijah allied in *Solomon and Sheba,* and, of course, the most gossiped-about Ptolemaic ruler of Egypt, Cleopatra, in numerous *Cleopatra*s, *Caesar and Cleopatra,* and other films. Egyptian films tend to have several details in common: a Pharaoh with his flail and crook, a half-naked, seated scribe, male characters wearing the *nemes* (squared-off head cloth), lotus-ornamented or papyrus-bundle columns, pharaonic cartouches and pictogrammic hieroglyphs carved or painted on the walls, an *ankh* or two, and a matte of the pyramids and/or the Great Sphinx. Put these recognizable touches into a scene, and presto, ancient Egypt.

On the other hand, the records and documents from ancient Egypt are much better preserved than those of most ancient non-Western civilizations, and so a few filmmakers have striven particularly hard to re-create an authentically detailed ancient Egyptian atmosphere. Other than the archaeological transformations in *The Ten Commandments,* which have already been discussed, DeMille manipulated the literary information (1) that Rameses II had an older brother (2) from whom he usurped the throne of Sethi (3) and whose name he struck from all the records and monuments, and (4) that he married Nefretiri. DeMille (1) makes Moses this older "brother" (actually, an adopted cousin), (2) from whom Rameses usurps the throne, after which (3) Sethi announces that Moses' name shall be stricken from all the records. Finally, (4) Rameses marries Nefretiri, who previously had been in love with Moses. DeMille was the master at combining history with fiction; it was almost as if the proof of his own narrative was the historically stricken name of this brother. For DeMille the lack of historical proof that Moses was not this brother equaled the historical possibility that he was, and that possibility justified the portrayal. Highly improbable but authentically possible—that was enough for the Master.

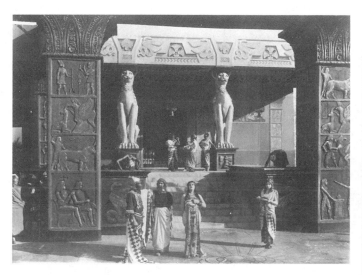

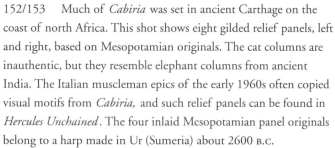

152/153   Much of *Cabiria* was set in ancient Carthage on the coast of north Africa. This shot shows eight gilded relief panels, left and right, based on Mesopotamian originals. The cat columns are inauthentic, but they resemble elephant columns from ancient India. The Italian muscleman epics of the early 1960s often copied visual motifs from *Cabiria,* and such relief panels can be found in *Hercules Unchained*. The four inlaid Mesopotamian panel originals belong to a harp made in Ur (Sumeria) about 2600 B.C.

Rameses appears again as Ramsisu in *The Pharaoh's Woman,* a 1960 Universal release bought from Italy. In this film Sabaku (John Drew Barrymore) fights with Ramsisu (Armando Francioli) over both the twentieth-century B.C. throne of Egypt and a Nilotic beauty Akis (Linda Cristal). Historically there was a general Sebek-khu who lived in the nineteenth century B.C., and Rameses I lived in the fourteenth century, but five hundred years is a mere speck in the Egyptian desert as far as an Italian sword-and-pyramid film is concerned. Vague struggles between Upper and Lower Egypt and between Egypt and Assyria are mentioned and unconvincingly fought in the film, but not even the authentically shaved head, skull cap, and cobalt-blue *khepresh* (warrior's helmet) can save this childish Nilodrama. Rameses had also appeared much earlier in Cines's *Ramesses, King of Egypt* (1912).

Michael Curtiz scaled greater heights of both historical realism and dramatic force in *The Egyptian* (1954). Like so many historical films, *The Egyptian* began as a best-selling novel, by Mika Waltari. Twentieth-Century Fox nearly outspent the Pharaohs with the production, spending some $5 million on more than sixty sets and five thousand—plus extras. The pharaoh's throne room alone, with its lotus columns and wall paintings, cost $85,000. The research department deserves special commendation, for the film displays exquisitely detailed reproductions of Nefertiti's famous straight-sided headpiece, Akhnaton's gilded and carved throne, and the fascinating sun-ray symbolism so often employed by Akhnaton in the Amarna reliefs and paintings. But more important to the average film viewer, who would not notice these specific reproductions, are the atmospheric sets that bring to life a culture that thrived thirty-three centuries ago. The street scenes on the waterfront of Thebes hum with the sound of stonecutters and the sights of carpenters using string saws, porters hustling to and fro, and slaves bearing the wealthy on litters. The scenes create a unique window through which the modern viewer can briefly glimpse ancient Egypt.

154   The $85,000 throne room from *The Egyptian* (1954). Sinuhe (Edmund Purdom) and Horemheb (Victor Mature) wear sandals with heel-caps. To the right of Horemheb is Queen Nefertiti (Anitra Stevens), with an authentic headpiece. Pharaoh Ikhnaton (Michael Wilding) wears the *pschent*—the double crown of Lower and Upper Egypt. He sits on a reproduction of an authentic ancient Egyptian throne. At right are Ikhnaton's mother Tiy (Judith Evalyn, called Taia in the film) and Baketamon (Gene Tierney), wearing authentic wigs. A Nubian slave stands behind Tiy, and an authentic lotus column can be seen at upper left.

155/158   Sources for *The Egyptian*'s throne room scene: a black granite statue showing Pharaoh Rameses II of the Nineteenth Dynasty in Egypt wearing the *khepresh* (blue war-helmet) with *uraeus* (cobra-headed band) and holding the royal crook; a Twelfth Dynasty wig made of wood with gold ornament; a bust of Nefertiti (Nofretete), wife of Ikhnaton, from the fourteenth century B.C.; and an Eighteenth Dynasty folding chair.

These and other realistic scenes are not given undue emphasis; they serve simply as a historical backdrop for the romantic drama that develops in the film. The discomforting scenes in which Sinuhe (Edmund Purdom) performs brain surgery, and the desolate, depressing scenes at the tawny cemetery of the Valley of the Kings and at the fume-filled embalming factory, which bursts with bandages, huge vats, and canopic jars, remind us that the ancient Egyptians were as obsessed by life after death as they were by life itself.

The taut romance of Waltari's novel naturally loses some of its captivating quality in the translation into film, yet Curtiz's direction and the competent acting carry the slowly unfolding narrative to a satisfactory climax. The opening scenes in which Sinuhe—who was a character of ancient Egyptian folklore and literature—persistently seeks the unobtainable love of the Babylonian Nefer (Bella Darvi) are slow, yet they accomplish a specific purpose: Sinuhe goes to such extremes to buy Nefer's love that he gives away his

159   Sinuhe (Edmund Purdom), an authentic hero of ancient Egyptian folklore and protagonist of *The Egyptian,* finds himself in exile. Sinuhe and his monocular servant Kaptah (Peter Ustinov) visit Minoan Crete. The bull-jumping fresco on the rear wall is authentically Minoan, a ritual reenacted in *My Son, the Hero*.

copper medical instruments and his foster parents' right to a decent burial (and life after death). From these amorous extremes grows Sinuhe's total disillusionment with life. The disillusionment peaks when Sinuhe is betrayed by his old friend Horemheb (Victor Mature). Sinuhe takes his amusing, one-eyed assistant, Kaptah (Peter Ustinov), and sails to the ends of the ancient earth—to China, Minoan Crete, and a Hittite encampment in Syria. There, after performing brain surgery on the Hittite chieftain, Sinuhe asks as payment a sample of the Hittites' strange "black metal"—iron, the historical invention of the Hittites (which, incidentally, they passed on to the Philistines and thereby made them a difficult match for Saul's Israelites). Sinuhe swallows his pride and takes the metal back to his native land and the new commander of Akhnaton's Egyptian army, who is now his friend turned bitter enemy Horemheb.

　　The historicity of Horemheb (Harmhab) and Pharaoh Akhnaton is well attested. But beyond the mere mention of their names, *The Egyptian* characterizes these two men precisely as history describes them. Horemheb is the ruthless, hard-nosed warrior who

160   Sinuhe (Edmund Purdom) holds in his right hand the secret weapon of the Hittites—an iron sword—in *The Egyptian*. He is about to prove its strength to his friend-turned-enemy Horemheb (Victor Mature), captain of Pharaoh Ikhnaton's army. The power of this cinematic moment can be appreciated best by those who appreciate the importance of the historical moment—the dawn of the Iron Age.

covets and captures the pharaonic crown (historically succeeding Tutankhamen, cinematically succeeding Akhnaton), and Akhnaton is the monotheistic dreamer who preceded even Moses in his worship of one god—the Sun god Aton. History (in fact, Akhnaton's own library) tells us of his fanaticism, his lined, drawn face, his inability to cope with the military disruption of the Egyptian empire, and his alienation of both the military and the priestly classes, and all these characteristics are captured on film. Michael Wilding gives a convincing interpretation of the pensive, gentle pharaoh, even if Britishness flows a little too thickly in his blue Theban blood. Victor Mature plays probably his best and best-suited role of his "ancient" repertoire (including *The Robe, Demetrius and the Gladiators, Androcles and the Lion, Samson and Delilah,* and *Hannibal*). He is vulgar, brash, demanding, childish, insolent, power hungry, and unlikable.

By combining authenticity, an intimate presentation of both the humble, common life and the splendid court life of ancient Egypt, a glimpse into the religious dreams and the military realities of the Eighteenth Dynasty, and an engaging love story, *The Egyptian* succeeds as well as any other nonepic "ancient" film. The charming presence of Merit (Jean Simmons) and the antics of the one-eyed Kaptah (Ustinov, hired after his similarly amusing role in *Quo Vadis?*) help to tighten and then release the intensity of the drama. Little Egyptianisms flavor the screenplay of Philip Dunne (*The Robe*); after all, an

161/162   Pharaoh Ikhnaton (or Akhnaton) believed in one god—Aton (or Aten), the Sun God, known later as Amen-Ra. His monuments often contain the sun disk with its life-giving rays. Such a sun-disk is re-created in this scene from *The Egyptian*. The angling, passionate wave of human arms stretching toward the sun-disk creates a massive feeling of physical emotion, an excellent use of epic tools. A relief sculpture from Ikhnaton's reign depicts him, his wife Nefertiti in the familiar headpiece, and their three daughters. Between Ikhnaton and Nefertiti is the sun-disk.

163/165   The discovery of Pharaoh Khufu's full-sized solar boat in Egypt in 1954 inspired three "Egyptian" films within two years. This scene from *Land of the Pharaohs* (1955) employs a reproduction of a solar boat. Above it marches the funeral procession of Pharaoh Khufu (Cheops), including an authentic-looking wood coffin, bald-headed priests, and his Cypriot Queen (Joan Collins). The scene is set inside the Great Pyramid of Giza. A painting executed for the tomb of Meye (Thebes) at the end of the Eighteenth Dynasty shows the authenticity of the re-created solar boat. Note the oblique oars, V-shaped designs, reed construction, and tapered, bound ends. A slab-stele of Princess Nofretiabet provides evidence, from Khufu's own Fourth Dynasty, for the priests' leopard-skin attire. Leopard skins were worn only on somber occasions.

Egyptian film needs the occasional line like "I'm so hungry I could eat a hippopotamus!" And whole paragraphs can scarcely equal the antique feeling in four words of Sinuhe's humble, trembling naïveté when confronted by an inhuman-looking grave-robber (John Carradine) in the Valley of the Kings: "Are you a god?"

In the late spring of 1954 an Egyptian official clearing a tourist road by the famed pyramids of Giza accidentally unearthed a full-sized solar boat that had been buried almost five thousand years before. The boat belonged to Pharaoh Khufu and it was left to carry the deceased pharaonic sun-god across the heavens during his afterlife. This unearthing caused quite a worldwide stir, and part of the stir was *The Egyptian,* which became one of the top-grossing pictures of 1954. Not far behind it were *Valley of the Kings* (1954) and *Land of the Pharaohs* (1955). The former concerns a modern archaeologist (Robert Taylor) who travels through sandstorms, scorpions, Tuaregs, murder, intrigue, romance, and the marvelously photographed ruins of Karnak, Luxor, and Philae to find definite proof that the biblical Joseph had a decisive influence on this same Eighteenth Dynasty monotheistic Pharaoh Akhnaton, here referred to as (or confused with) Ra-Hotep. The film successfully integrates Egyptian antiquities into the action, climaxing in a fistfight to the death high atop one of the statues of Rameses II at his temple at Abu Simbel.

Land of the Pharaohs also capitalizes on the fresh interest in archaeology. Jack Hawkins plays Khufu (here called Cheops), the Fourth Dynasty pharaoh who built the Great Pyramid at Giza circa 2500 B.C. Much of this Howard Hawks film, shot on location in an impressive WideScreen format, is staggeringly impressive. Thousands of modern Egyptian extras play their ancestors pulling huge, multiton blocks of limestone in 120-degree heat, hoisting the blocks onto rafts, floating them down the Nile to the pyramid itself, then dragging them up stubborn ramps to their final resting places. These *fellahin* had a particularly difficult time reenacting this truly great architectural triumph of early civilization: the film was shot during the Islamic Holy Month of Ramadan, during which no Moslem is allowed to eat or drink during daylight hours. Adhering to their faith despite the extreme discomfort, many of the Egyptian extras passed out from heat exhaustion and then refused to be revived by a sip of water. Although the shooting of *Land of the Pharaohs* occurred five thousand years after Khufu, Hawks and Warner Brothers were shown a modern reflection of the fierce, irrational determination that drove one hundred thousand ancient Egyptian men to spend twenty years building a stone tomb for one pharaoh. The marvelous scenes of loin-clothed brown humanity, measuring with plumb lines and swinging crude mallets to the rhythm of their devotional a cappella singing, culminate in one last magnificent shot of the deep entrance ravine that leads into an actual tomb (possibly belonging to Khufu's son).

Then the granite and limestone turn to sand. With a script by William Faulkner, Harry Kurnitz, and Harold Jack Bloom, the film should have soared even higher than the pyramidical monument it was physically reconstructing. But Faulkner confessed to Hawks that he was out of his element. "I don't know how a Pharaoh talks. Is it all right if I write him like a Kentucky colonel?" Kurnitz demurred, "I can't do it like a Kentucky colonel, but I'm a student of Shakespeare. I think I could do it as though it were *King Lear.*"[1] The result of this inexperience with antiquity is a tasteful but inappropriate and nonperiodic script. Because of the emphasis on the commonplace romance between Khufu and the greedy princess of Cyprus (Joan Collins), the pyramid itself retreats into the background, and every time the scenes switch from the pyramid construction to the scandalous throne room or bedroom the film loses its impact. *Land of the Pharaohs*—with its monarch who grew up in Kentucky and reigned on an Elizabethan stage—never delves into the fascinating peculiarities or archaic profundities of Egyptian eschatology.

The end of the film returns from the bedroom melodrama to the spectacular machinery that finally lowers the huge sealing blocks and sand into the corridors of the completed pyramid. As the sand weighs down the rope pulleys, sending wooden beams and limestone blocks into their eternal resting places to close off the pyramid forever, the loyal, bald-headed priests who subtly file past a replica of the solar boat meet the glorious entombed death that to ancient Egyptians was the ultimate reward of life.

Just as the discovery of the long-lost Egyptian solar boat sparked the productions of *The Egyptian, Land of the Pharaohs,* and *Valley of the Kings,* the discovery in 1922 of the tomb of King Tutankhamen—better known as King Tut—had resulted in one of the best-known films about ancient Egypt, Universal's *The Mummy* (1932). Only one flashback scene actually takes place in antiquity, when Imhotep (Boris Karloff) breaks sacred law by reading aloud the Scroll of Thoth to his beloved dead princess Ankh-es-en-Amon. But *The Mummy* effectively projects the cold, mysterious atmosphere surrounding the Egyptian belief in life after death. The thick, graying gauze that the walking mummy drags determinedly across many an eerily scraped modern floor sent chills up and down the spines of movie audiences in the 1930s. Much of the credit for this realism belongs to two creative geniuses who probably never heard of Akhnaton or Horemheb, director Karl Freund and makeup artist Jack Pierce. Freund's well-placed shadows and angular camera shots and Pierce's patient eight-hour preparation of Karloff (with beauty clay and paint) in their own way rival the spectacular construction scenes in *Land of the Pharaohs.* The films approach their tasks differently, but both create a memorable cinematic impression of ancient Egypt.

Although the success of *The Mummy* spawned no Italian cloak-and-gauze films in the 1960s—there has *not* been a *Mummy vs. the Son of Hercules*—it did awaken additional horrors in *The Mummy's Hand* (1940), *The Mummy's Tomb* (1942), *The Mummy's Curse* (1944), and *The Mummy's Ghost* (1944). All these are Universal films, so they freely reused scenes from the Karloff original, though Lon Chaney Jr. had by now assumed the moldy linens as Kharis, the lovelorn, chokeholding mummy gone amok in the modern world. These films inspired such comedies as The Three Stooges' *Mummy's Dummies* (1948) and Universal's *Abbott and Costello Meet the Mummy* (1955). Then Hammer Films produced in sequence *The Mummy* (1959), which contains a colorful Egyptian funerary

166   Ancient Egyptian civilization did not die out in the first millennium B.C., as witnessed here by
Peter Cushing in Hammer's *The Mummy* (1959). Cinematic archaeologists who dared to break the
sacred seals on Memphian tombs often found a Boris Karloff, Lon Chaney Jr., or, as here,
Christopher Lee, to whom apologies would not be enough.

parade complete with an elongated bed modeled after that of King Tut, *The Curse of the
Mummy's Tomb* (1964), and *The Mummy's Shroud* (1966). *The Mummy's Shroud* is notable
for its use of the ancient Egyptian spoken language, which was also used in the ancient
scenes of Universal's intentionally campy action-adventure horror version of *The Mummy*
(1999) starring Brendon Fraser. In this later version, a detailed but familiar computer-
generated mummy ultimately grows into a monstrous phantom rising hundreds of feet
above the Egyptian desert covering the mythical city of Hammunaptra. Still other films—
Sphinx (1981), for example, and *The Awakening* (1980), starring Charlton Heston and
based on a Bram Stoker book—feature ancient Egyptian curses.

 One other "mummy" film, *The Curse of the Faceless Man* (1958), deserves mention, but only because it abandons Egypt and brings to life a plaster-cast mummy (!) from
the Pompeian section of the Naples museum. Quintillus, a long-deceased Roman gladia-

tor, destructively roams the modern streets of Italy looking for a reincarnation of his ancient paramour while an unbelieving Neapolitan police inspector understandably insists, "I believe this killer is a great deal younger than two thousand years."

Still more films have been set in ancient Egypt. Ernst Lubitsch's *The Loves of Pharaoh* (*Das Weib des Pharao,* 1922) concerns a slave girl Theonis who is loved both by an Egyptian slave boy Ramphis (Henry Liedtke) and by Pharaoh Amenes (Emil Jannings). The magnificent scale of this film established Lubitsch's reputation in America, and he first arrived in the United States with a print of this film under his arm. *Faraon* (1966) is a lavish Polish film set during the reign of Rameses XIII. If the plot of *The Loves of Pharaoh* sounds familiar, it is because it is the sexual opposite of Verdi's *Aida;* here the male Rhadames is loved by two women, one royal and the other a slave. Edison first put *Aida* on film in 1908, and in a 1954 version Sophia Loren mouths the libretto's words sung by an unseen Renata Tebaldi. This *Aida* was an Italian film, and it was soon followed by a few cheap productions. *Queen of the Nile* (1961) saw Edmund Purdom, Vincent Price, and Jeanne Crain amid an Italian crew and cast trying to marry off aristocratic Nefertiti, the daughter of a priest, to a measly sculptor in 2000 B.C. *Cleopatra's Daughter* pitted the titular Ptolemaic Egyptian (Debra Paget) against the armies of Syria, and *The Son of Cleopatra* (1965) places her sibling, a Caesarion who somehow survived, in the midst of a plastic-sword imbroglio between Romans and Egyptian Bedouins. Lastly, *Maciste in the Valley of the Kings* (also called *Son of Samson,* 1960) combines some very fishy-looking Romans, Egyptians, and Persians in one very briny bouillabaisse of ancient warfare.

Speaking of Persians, *Esther and the King* (1960) gives us a filmic glimpse into their court life at Susa (Shushan) under Xerxes (Ahasuerus). The biblical Book of Esther provided the plot for this semi-Italian, semi–Raoul Walsh miscarriage. Once again Fox scores pluses in the authenticity of its properties. The reliefs from Persepolis, the human-headed winged-bull statues, the double-capital columns, the palmette ornaments, and the bald-headed eunuch all lend some credibility to the setting of the film, but all are painted garishly. The biblical plot is maintained to a respectable extent, but the biblical disagreements between Haman and Mordecai (Dennis O'Dea) too easily fall prey to the typical Italianate palace-intrigue clichés of the time. Joan Collins is unable to do much with the part of Esther except look sincere and beautifully innocent, and Bosley Crowther declared, unfairly perhaps, that "Richard Egan [Ahasuerus] looks about as Persian as an offensive back on the Baltimore Colts."[2] Egan at least does a better job than Alan Ameche might have. Although it raises expectations of great vision and subtlety, *Esther and the King* is a mediocre costume drama and nothing more

A more triumphant cinematic presentation of Xerxes and his Persians is *The 300 Spartans,* and Robert Rossen's *Alexander the Great* impressively shows us the fall of Darius III and the rise of Macedonian Alexander the Great as the new king of Persia. The Italians jumped into the last days of Persian supremacy with *Goliath and the Rebel Slave Girl* (1963), which is set in Sardis (Asia Minor) just before its conquest by Alexander. This

Sardis was the capital of the rich and luxuriant kingdom of Lydia, whose King Croesus to this day symbolizes wealth and gilded splendor. Croesus himself appears in one film, a Hollywood romantic-fantasy entitled *Night in Paradise* (1946).

Lastly, Alexander the Great's latter-day "son" Sikander reappeared in the film version of the Rudyard Kipling story *The Man Who Would Be King* (1976). Here Sikander appears in the guise of Sean Connery amid the same Afghani mountain tribes that had once worshiped the original Alexander. As *The Mummy* (1932) captured the mystery of ancient Egyptian ritual and eschatology, *The Man Who Would Be King*, despite its nineteenth-century A.D. setting, captures the unparalleled frenzy and zealous loyalty felt by the real Alexander's Asian subjects. And the natural Oriental beauty of the modern Roxanne (Shakira Caine) convinces us of the captivating beauty of her ancient predecessor. In this sense, Rudyard Kipling's and John Huston's *The Man Who Would Be King* equates the modern Alexander with the ancient; both Alexanders entered the uncivilized reaches beyond the Hindu Kush and found themselves worshiped as a god by wild, unpredictable tribes. Eastern Central Asia becomes a time warp in which nothing really changes in two thousand two hundred years—except the man called Alexander/ Sikander. In such an instance, antiquity becomes a matter of spirit rather than a matter of time.

Besides ancient Babylon, Assyria, Egypt, Carthage, Arabia, and Persia, still other Oriental lands have served as backdrops for films. *Herod the Great* (1958) presents a gloomy atmosphere in which the Judean King Herod (Edmund Purdom) struggles with politics and familial treachery just before the birth of Christ, and the various versions of *Salome* put Herod's dancing granddaughter in the Judean center stage. Opposite two of the most famous Hebrews who have adorned the silver screen are the non-Semitic Philistines Delilah and Goliath. The Hittites appear in their iron splendor in *The Egyptian,* an ambassador from King Priam of Troy meets Moses in *The Ten Commandments* (1956), and various ambassadors, kings, and commoners of the Kushites, Elamites, Moabites, Amorites, Sodomites, and numerous other ancient -ites pop up elsewhere in a usually indistinguishable abundance. *The Fall of the Roman Empire* depicts second-century A.D. Armenia, as does *The Warrior and the Slave Girl* (1959). Farther North, *Jason*

167/169   Richard Egan as King Ahasuerus (Xerxes) welcomes the Hebrew Esther (Joan Collins) into his throne room in Raoul Walsh's *Esther and the King* (1960, facing page, top). The double-horse columns in the rear, the human-headed winged bulls by the throne, and the glazed-brick lion at extreme right are reasonably authentic. Standing at far right is the royal eunuch. Persian double-horse columns now housed in the Louvre originally held the roof over the palace of Xerxes at Persepolis. A glazed-brick lion from the throne room of Nebuchadnezzar's palace in Babylon, c. 600 B.C. The floral motif was imitated in the slave market set for *Intolerance*.

170/171   Another cinematic Xerxes, this one played by David Farrar in *The 300 Spartans* (1962), is dumbfounded as he watches his troops inexplicably beaten by the small Greek army. The Persian aide to his right is Hydarnes (Donald Houston), and the Greek to his left is Damaratus (Ivan Triesault, who also played the emperor in *Barabbas*). Persians wore pants, Greeks did not. An Attic red-figure amphora from the fifth century B.C. offers a similar contrast between Greek and Persian costume. The Persian on the right wears pants, long sleeves, and a helmet with long flaps falling over his shoulders. The Greek wears hoplite dress.

172   Shakira Caine as Roxanne, the Asian wife of the new Alexander the Great in *The Man Who Would Be King* (1976). Antiquity can be a matter of spirit and atmosphere rather than a matter of years and historicity. The original Alexander's Roxanne could not have looked too different from this filmization of Rudyard Kipling's Roxanne.

and the Argonauts and *The Giants of Thessaly* venture into ancient Colchis in the south of Russia, and to the West *The Viking Queen* (1966), *The Giants of Rome* (1963), *The Slave of Rome* (1960), and *Gold For the Caesars* (1963) explore the Western barbarians who battle against Roman legions from Britannia and Gallia to Hispania. Returning to the relative Westernization and comfort of ancient Rome, our journey into the cinematic world of the ancient Orient has come to an end.

Every tragedy must have these six parts: plot, characters,

poetry, thought, spectacle, and music.

—ARISTOTLE, *POETICS*, 1450ᴬ7–10

The vast majority of films about the ancient world have been based on ancient literature. Besides the scores of films based on the Old and New Testaments, Plutarch's *Lives* provided the literary sources for *Spartacus, Alexander the Great, Julius Caesar* (via Shakespeare), and *Cleopatra;* Homer's *Iliad* and *Odyssey* provided the literary source for *L'Odissea, Helen of Troy, Ulysses,* and *The Odyssey;* Vergil's *Aeneid* provided the literary source for *Last Glory of Troy;* and Plato's *Euthyphro, Crito, Phaedo,* and *Apology* supplied Rossellini with his *Socrates. Quo Vadis?* re-created Tacitus; *Androcles and the Lion* re-created Aulus Gellius; *Cabiria* re-created Livy; *The 300 Spartans* and *Intolerance* Herodotus; *Salambo* Polybius; and still other Greek and Roman authors wrote down the histories and myths that were eventually re-created on celluloid two millennia later, give or take a few centuries. Aesop's *Fables* found their way into numerous children's shorts and cartoons produced between 1921 and 1967, and Plutarch's *Life of Romulus* even developed through Stephen Vincent Benet's *Sobbin' Women* into the MGM musical *Seven Brides for Seven Brothers* (1954). But history and mythology are far behind us, and ancient comedy will find its proper place in the next chapter. For now the spotlight falls on Greek tragedy.

There were hundreds of tragedies produced in Athens in the fifth century B.C., but only thirty-three survive reasonably intact. Of these thirty-three extant Greek tragedies, seven have been turned into feature films: Sophocles' *Antigone* and *Oedipus Rex,* and Euripides' *Bacchae, Electra, Medea, The Trojan Women,* and *Iphigenia at Aulis.* In spite of the high attrition rate, it is no small achievement for a play to be "running" on the silver screen some two thousand four hundred years after its Athenian debut at the Dionysian Festival.

Sophoclean Tragedy

Oedipus Rex, the Sophoclean drama about the king who has unknowingly killed his father and married his mother, has been made into five different films, from Giuseppe de Liguoro's *Edipo Re* (1910) to Philip Saville's *Oedipus the King* (1967). Tyrone Guthrie's 1957 *Oedipus Rex* was performed by the Stratford Shakespearean Festival Players of Canada (the troupe to which the young William Shatner belonged). Guthrie's production, in which the players wear masks and recite their Sophoclean lines from William Butler Yeats's free translation, is not suited to film. There is only one set; there is no action; there are no quick or graceful movements; and there is no photographic enhancement. To shoot a close-up of a man in a mask is only to shoot a close-up of the mask; the facial expressions do not change, and so the effect of the shot is static. The masks themselves are fetching—brazen images of haggard cheeks and troubled brows—but they alone cannot carry the effect of the drama.

Still, *Oedipus Rex* features the fantastic intricacies and twists of Sophocles' plot that have earned his play a reputation as one of the greatest ever written. The hidden ironies and cruelties of the Theban king's fate remain compelling: when Oedipus thinks he is free of his fate because his "father," Polybus, has died of natural causes; or when Jocasta tries to relieve her father-murdering husband (and son) by telling him that a "brigand" slew her first husband Laius "at the crossroads"; or when Oedipus begins to realize that he himself might be the murderer; or when the blind seer, Teiresias, warns Oedipus that "he sees but does not see," anticipating the moment when Oedipus, having "seen," blinds himself. No film can ruin the story, its Sophoclean ironies, and its powerful impact. But a film must be film and and not merely a play on celluloid. *Oedipus Rex* fails in that respect.

Two very different film versions of Sophocles' play appeared in 1967. The first was *Edipo Re,* which director Pier Paolo Pasolini called a voyage into metahistory. The modern prologue and epilogue delve into Pasolini's own Freudian interpretation of the Oedipus complex; he emphasizes the father's resentment toward the son much more than the son's textbook resentment toward the father. Although the Sophoclean drama is stretched irretrievably, many critics, including Pasolini himself, have considered the modern prologue one of his best sequences.

The "ancient" part of the drama is based on Pasolini's own translation of both *Oedipus Rex* and *Oedipus at Colonus.* Shot in Morocco and set to Romanian and Japanese music, these "ancient" sequences reenact only selected Sophoclean scenes, embellished by such mythologically oriented scenes as Oedipus's visit to the oracle of Delphi and his brief verbal battle with the Sphinx; Cocteau's *The Testament of Orpheus* (1959) included a somewhat different sequence with Oedipus and the Sphinx. Like *The Gospel According to Saint*

Matthew, for example, *Edipo Re* does create a metahistorical atmosphere, set in no recognizable time or place in the past (or future or present). But Pasolini's genius in treating Greek tragedy did not really blossom until *Medea,* three years later.

The same year, Victor Saville directed a version of *Oedipus the King* that was as distinguished by intensity and fine acting as his *The Silver Chalice* had been undistinguished. *Oedipus* boasts an arrogant, strong-willed title character (Christopher Plummer), a matronly, lovely Jocasta (Lilli Palmer), a capable, kingly Creon (Richard Johnson), and a weighty, profound, and imposingly prophetic Teiresias (Orson Welles). The film was shot along the angular, chipped limestone *cavea* of the ancient Greek theater at Dodona, and the ruins reflect Oedipus's crumbling claims to legitimacy. Welles's Teiresias looms large over Oedipus and the Theban elders with his divine admonitions and human anger, like lofty Mount Pelion over the spreading Aegean Sea. The tensions and twisted ironies of Sophocles' poetry are ever present, and even the relatively unpoetic speeches of the shepherd and messenger breathe with life and absorbing narrative. Saville shows the horrors of Jocasta's hanging and Oedipus's blinding with just enough realism; the scenes convey the catastophe to which Oedipus's stubborn search for his origins have inevitably led, yet the blood is not excessive. And the film's shots of the scrubby northern Greek scenery, of the curvilinear patterns of the Dodona theater, and of the flashbacks in Oedipus's mind—that day at the crossroads where he "killed a man"—create a depth and scope to which no stage production could aspire.

For all its merits, Saville's *Oedipus the King* would never have won first prize at an ancient Athenian contest. It would have pleased the judges (and Aristotle) with its plot, its characters, poetry, and philosophy, but it lacks the spectacle and music that changed, at some stubbornly obscure point in Athenian history, mere poetic dialogue into full-blown theater. In essence, the problem is the same one film directors meet in portraying a cinematic Christ: too much cinematically uncreative reverence produces boredom, whether this reverence is directed toward the Christ or toward the Greek dramatic chorus. Modern film directors generally treat the Greek chorus with too much respect, but this type of unwarranted stiffness and inauthentic purity destroys the original effect of that device. *Oedipus the King* presents the chorus as a group of robed and bearded elders; fine. They interpret, digest, and react to the drama unfolding around them; fine. But they merely recite their lyrics in unison, individually, or in sequence, and they never dance a step. Thus the film lacks its authentic music and spectacle. Ancient Athenian tragedy, for all its psychological and theological profundity, for all its macabre plots and immortal poetry, appeared on the ancient stage with a full battery of ancient music and "special effects." To omit the musical spectacle is the same as if someone were to find the script for *Top Hat* two thousand years from now, refilm the script while omitting the dances, and merely recite the lyrics to "The Piccolino" and "I'm Putting on My Top Hat." A chorus, by nature and definition, whether it be an ancient Greek chorus or a Busby Berkeley chorus, sings and dances. Without song and dance, be it ever so archaic or limited in its production, a Greek tragedy can be only a skeleton of its real self.

173   Oedipus (Christopher Plummer) explains to King Creon (Richard Johnson) that he blinded himself because his eyes "saw but did not see" in *Oedipus the King* (1967), just one of the many film versions of Sophocles' tragedy. The film was shot at the theater of Dodona in northern Greece. On the rear wall, a blowup of a vase painting (Hercules and Cerberus) can barely be seen.

Several European television productions of one or all the plays of the Sophoclean Oedipus cycle have been produced, most notably the 1984 BBC trilogy directed by Don Taylor and featuring John Gielgud as Teiresias, as well as German versions of *Antigone,* the second play in the sequence, produced in 1973 and 1992. There is also the simplistically reduced cribbing of the climax of *Oedipus at Colonus* in *Hercules Unchained.* Unfortunately, the sole major theatrical film of Sophocles' *Antigone* is an early Greek attempt by George Tzavellas in 1961. Despite a noble attempt by Irene Papas in the title role, Tzavellas's interpretation of this ancient drama based on the conflict between human and divine law lacks vigor. His direction and the acting are for the most part as monolithic and austere as the setting, and so when Creon weeps, realizing that his insistence on human law and order has resulted in the deaths of his wife and son, it means little emotionally to the viewer. This film about Oedipus's daughter also suffers from lack of respect for the film medium. Only one exterior shot is used very effectively: the deeply shadowed cave in which Antigone and Haemon die is viewed from the inside out; this subjective shot contrasts strongly with the gloom in which the deaths must occur and the Hellenic brightness outside. Otherwise, the visual elements in this production are as disappointing as the dramatic elements.

174   Michael Cacoyannis's adaptation of Euripides' *Electra* (1962) was shot at the ruins of Agamemnon's palace at Mycenae in southern Greece. Here Agamemnon (Theodore Demetriou) passes through the lion gate as he arrives home from the war at Troy. The scene is a visualization of the Euripidean prologue.

Euripidean Tragedy

Electra (1962) was the first of three Euripidean tragedies produced and directed by Michael Cacoyannis. To prepare the modern audience for this powerhouse of vengeance and action, Cacoyannis includes an initial scene in which the victorious Agamemnon comes home from Troy only to be murdered in the bath by his wife and her lover. This scene establishes for the modern viewer the need of Agamemnon's children Electra and Orestes for matricidal vengeance. The film also departs from Euripides' text in omitting the ex machina appearance of the Dioscuri Castor and Polydeuces. To execute their divine appearance convincingly would, of course, have rent the film's fabric of realism.

The desolate surroundings of *Electra* distinguish it from many other films about the ancient world. Cacoyannis places his actors amid the wilds of southern Greece, which effectively lose their Mediterranean sheen when filmed in black and white. Similarly, the Homeric wealth and gold of ancient Mycenae are exchanged for the lifeless ruins of Mycenae as they stand today. Electra's house is a mere hut in the barren farmlands of the Peloponnese, and the women of the austere chorus are the convincingly sympathetic local wives with whom any ancient (or contemporary) Mediterranean woman would naturally have spent the majority of her time.

Amid these bleak, pitiable, humble, ideally Euripidean surroundings, Irene Papas (Electra) bears in her dark brow and expressive eyes the desire for vengeance at any cost—even the cost of killing her mother. The resolve with which Electra goes about finding a method of punishing the assassins, the cold barrenness of the rocky, gray Greek countryside, and the geometrically arranged postures of the chorus within it take the film out of the definable ancient mold and into a less tangible world of psychological motivations, timeless characters, and primordial murders.

Electra, which earned an Academy Award nomination for best foreign film, is in this sense a successful film adaptation of an ancient Greek play. Not overburdened with costumes or weighted by orally demanding poetry, *Electra* thrives on its profound plot, its unthinkable consequences, and its austere setting. Cacoyannis does not attempt to elicit the theatrical experience of an ancient Athenian audience, instead using a spare idiom to present Greek drama to a modern film audience. For some inexplicable reason, once all the authentic color and costumes are added to a Greek play on film, the psychological horror behind the murders and the matricide tend to lose some of their primordial impact.

This counterintuitive principle becomes clear in Cacoyannis's next, more successful cinematic adaptation of Greek tragedy, *The Trojan Women* (1971), which reached an international audience. The all-star cast includes Irene Papas (Helen), Katharine Hepburn (Hecuba), Vanessa Redgrave (Andromache), Geneviève Bujold (Cassandra), and Patrick Magee (Menelaus), and all play their parts with the proper Euripidean intensity. Hepburn physically reveals little of a fiery, undefeated, and vengeful face beneath her tattered embroidery and torn mantle, but her limitless anger and hatred for the "fair-haired Helen" fills the screen. Papas's exotic accent and dark figure create for modern viewers a vivid impression of the haughtily beautiful Helen. Such a haunting appearance and beguiling spirit could conceivably have caused a war.

The Trojan Women, written as the denouement to a cycle of three plays, is not by any means Euripides' best play, but it nonetheless has a number of highly effective scenes. When Andromache finds out that her little boy, Astyanax, the only son of the mighty Hector, must die, and again when she receives his tiny battered body, Redgrave's torment and agony are harrowing—even to the Greek guard who bears the evil tidings. The chorus of Trojan Women convey their implacable hatred toward Helen with inhuman screams whenever they view the Spartan queen locked inside a crude wooden cage, but Helen's beauty soon softens Menelaus's bitterness; the camera's one glimpse of the long-separated husband and his enticing wife on shipboard assures the audience that Helen's inimitable charms have rekindled Menelaus's love for her, as some ancient sources attest.

The fine acting, smooth-flowing verse (translated by Edith Hamilton), and deep-seated passions of the film are complemented with pure cinematic ornament: Euripides did not portray Helen's smile on the boat or the smoking remnants of the Trojan citadel in the background of the action. Cassandra's fit of madness is followed closely by the camera as she rants, raves, sings, gasps, and shouts her Apollonian prophecies that none except

175   Helen (Irene Papas) attempts suicide, but her estranged husband Menelaus (Patrick Magee) frustrates her death wish. Hecuba (Katharine Hepburn), once queen of Troy but now a Greek slave, pleads for Helen's death in this scene from Cacoyannis's *The Trojan Women* (1971).

the audience quite comprehend. When Astyanax is thrown off the top of the walls of Troy, the camera spins and whirls for a moment as if to deprive us of our senses in empathy. The filmic touches enhance the play instead of merely documenting it. The choral laments are still not lavish or authentic; no film seemed able to capture the true essence and color of the Greek chorus until Woody Allen's ironic *Mighty Aphrodite* (1995). But at least the weeping Asian women move convincingly, and the setting beneath the smoldering ruins of Troy, though far from the stylized stage that Euripides might have prescribed, creates the atmosphere of defiant fatalism that must have pervaded the ancient city in its last hours. Cacoyannis's *The Trojan Women* thrives in its realistic portrayal of the cruelty of war and the slavery, pillaging, and executions that inevitably followed.

Cacoyannis's third Euripidean adaptation was *Iphigenia* (1977), which earned him another Academy Award nomination for best foreign film. This version of *Iphigenia at Aulis* is a powerful film dependent on stark contrasts. At the outset a god-sent calm stills the winds and prevents the Greek army from launching its punitive expedition against Troy, but when Agamemnon hears from Calchas that all that is needed is a sacrifice to the

176/177   The stark contrasts of Cacoyannis's third Euripidean adaptation, *Iphigenia* (1977), appear even in the countenances of the lead characters, a gritty, angry, armored Agamemnon (Kostas Kazakos) and the fair, innocent, soon-to-be-filleted virgin Iphigenia (Tatiana Papamoskou).

gods, the celebration is deafening. The broad exteriors along the shoreline and in the hills suddenly shift to the dark interior of Agamemnon's hut as he learns that the sacrifice must be of his daughter Iphigenia. Agamemnon's anger becomes explosive, even frightening, and this in turn contrasts sharply with the lovely domestic scenes of his home in Mycenae. There Clytemnestra and Iphigenia receive a note beckoning Iphigenia to Aulis to marry handsome young Achilles, "the pride of Greece." Their delight turns to horror when they learn the true purpose of Agamemnon's ruse.

Although unknown to audiences outside of Greece, the actors who play the principal parts convey these contrasts brilliantly. Kostas Kazakos (Agamemnon) portrays both a father giving his daughter the loving tenderness she requires and a dutiful general who insists on leading the Greek expedition to Troy while struggling with the personal horror of the divine command he has received. The young Tatiana Papamoskou (Iphigenia) looks at her father with an innocent trust that breaks the viewer's heart, and as she learns her fate and becomes resolved to it, she takes on the fine stature of nobility. Irene Papas (Clytemnestra) displays power while insisting on attending the "wedding," despite Agamemnon's repeated attempts to send her away.

The colorful sets are appropriately archaic, if not authentic for the period, but as the tension builds throughout the film, we pay less attention to them and focus instead on the looming murder of an innocent. The dramatic pace of the film allows the mood to develop slowly. Each emotional confrontation is given ample attention; Euripides would have been pleased to see his human tragedy properly performed, readily distinct from a Sophoclean divine tragedy. When Iphigenia is ultimately sacrificed and the wind blows at long last, the ships sail away to Troy, leaving behind Clytemnestra and a viewing audience painfully ennobled.

178   Greek tragedy can be filmed in costumed antiquity or in modern dress and setting. Here a
New England Agamemnon (here named Ezra Mannon, played by Raymond Massey) points an
accusatory finger at his wife (Clytemnestra is named Christine here, and played by Katina Paxinou),
while his faithful daughter (Electra /Lavinia, Rosalind Russell) plans vengeance in this film
adaptation of Eugene O'Neill's *Mourning Becomes Electra* (1947), itself a modern theatrical
adaptation of Aeschylus's *Oresteia*.

Timeless Tragedy

There is no one best method for presenting Greek tragedy on the screen. Because the themes
are universal, a variety of approaches can work effectively. One successful method is to remove
the Greekness of the play—that is, to place the players and action in a more modern setting.
This Dudley Nichols did with Eugene O'Neill's *Mourning Becomes Electra* (1947), based on
Aeschylus's treatment of the Electra myth in the *Oresteia*. Instead of King Agamemnon returning from Troy to Mycenae, General Ezra Mannon (Raymond Massey) returns from the
Civil War to a New England seaport. Instead of Clytemnestra slaying Agamemnon by the
sword, Christine Mannon (Katina Paxinou) slays her husband by withholding from him his
vital heart medicine. The Mannon mansion takes the place of a Greek palace or temple, and
the wise Mannon groundskeeper, Seth (Henry Hull), stands in for the Greek chorus.

The film version of *Mourning Becomes Electra* runs just under three hours and yet is still only half as long as O'Neill's original 1931 stage trilogy. O'Neill approved the film and insisted that Nichols, an old friend, be the producer, adapter, and director. As long as the film is, its tale of revenge and the horror of intrafamilial hatred and bloodshed never leaves room for even one breath of relief. The film reveals an ever-broadening threshold of horror. Because hatred and perfidy are the keys to understanding the self-destructive Mannon family, the gruesome drama can be horrifying without explicit violence, gory without blood. Savage hearts and stinging tongues turn the heavy costuming into shrouds and the bare interior of the Mannon mansion into a mausoleum. Cold and cruel, Lavinia Mannon (Rosalind Russell) is the lone survivor at the end of the deaths, and she realizes that "death will always come between" her and the rest of the world. She feels bound to her Mannon dead and, hounded by New England Furies, she decides to remain entombed inside her mansion for the rest of her guilt-ridden days.

The primordial passions of this well-known Greek myth resonate equally in the barren Peloponnese or in humid New England, and Pier Paolo Pasolini searched for them in Africa. *Notes for an African Orestes* (*Appunti per un'Orestiade Africana,* 1970) consists of series of shots of black Africans who might play Agamemnon, Orestes, or Pylades, a classroom full of students discussing the essence of the *Oresteia,* native rituals, and contemporary warfare, all narrated as if these were indeed filmic "notes." Pasolini searched in Africa because he felt that there he could find primitive divinities, extant spirituality, and "the residue of an ancient spirit." He often used nonactors in his films, but here in particular he hoped to give his *Oresteia* a folk quality to make it clearly "a tragedy of the people." In contrast, the modern urban university is associated with Athena in Pasolini's understanding of the final play of the cycle, *The Eumenides:* there the goddess establishes "a human court of democracy and reason." *Notes for an African Orestes* is not a satisfying feature film, but with a seasoning of pro-Chinese Marxism and avant-garde jazz provided by Gato Barbieri, it is an instructive glimpse into how one of the most creative filmmakers of the 1960s and 1970s formulated his ideas about Greek tragedy and the myths underlying them.

Jules Dassin created a modern Hellenic adaptation of a Greek tragedy in his lively *Phaedra* (1962). In a way this film is the flip side of Dassin's earlier *Never on Sunday.* Both *Never on Sunday* and *Phaedra* are set in modern Greece, but in the earlier film Dassin's hero tries to capture "the Greek spirit" in its most classical and innocent form; in *Phaedra* Dassin captures ancient Greek myth in its most primitive and barbaric form.

Phaedra is based on Euripides' *Hippolytus,* a play, first filmed in 1910, in which Phaedra, second wife to King Theseus, desires the love of her chaste stepson Hippolytus. Like Potiphar's wife, she is rebuffed and becomes vengeful. She hangs herself, but only after leaving a note for Theseus in which she blames her suicide on Hippolytus, who, she says, raped her. Theseus calls a curse upon his son, who, banished from the palace, rides his chariot toward the sea. There Poseidon summons up a monstrous bull, which frightens

Hippolytus's horses; the chariot crashes and Hippolytus dies. Only afterward does Theseus learn of Hippolytus's innocence.

Dassin's film makes its Theseus a modern Greek shipping magnate (Raf Vallone); Hippolytus is a young, car-loving student named Alexis (Anthony Perkins). Phaedra, whose name is unchanged, is played by Melina Mercouri. The huntsman's chariot becomes a sleek Aston Martin, and the monstrous bull is a speeding truck that causes Alexis to swerve off a seaside road and plunge to his Hippolytean death by the appropriate Hellenic waters. But amid all this modernization are several visual references to the ancient world, particularly when Alexis visits the Parthenon sculptures in the British Museum. The greatest divergence from the Euripidean original is that Alexis accepts Phaedra's advances and falls in love with her. The film thus works Oedipal hatred into the Phaedra myth. While such mythological confusion is legitimate in a modernized adaptation of a Greek myth, the actual romance between Alexis and Phaedra lacks the dramatic credibility that it needs. Melina Mercouri and a young Anthony Perkins seem improbable lovers; she looks more apt to devour him in one bite. Nonetheless, Perkins brings to his awkward role the bizarre intellectual and psychological introspection characteristic of many of his early roles.

Perkins played a Hippolytus figure in another cinematic adaptation of the same myth, Delbert Mann's *Desire Under the Elms* (1957). Based on another Eugene O'Neill play with a New England setting, this film casts Sophia Loren and Burl Ives in the roles of Phaedra and Theseus. As in *Phaedra,* this film has Phaedra and Hippolytus (Anna and Eben Cabot) realize their love, and this time they have a baby. A driving quest for old Ephraim Cabot's inheritance causes the two lovers to quarrel, but Anna strangely tries to prove her love for Eben by killing the baby; to her way of thinking, Eben alone would now inherit the farm, not her and her baby. Meanwhile, old Ephraim, suspecting that the baby is his own, has his wife and son carted off to jail under a murder charge.

Not quite as absorbing as *Mourning Becomes Electra, Desire Under the Elms* still bears the unmistakable mark of neo-Hellenic, O'Neillean, intrafamilial barbarity. Burl Ives brings a cold dominance to the film, his massive farmer's back crisscrossed by the suspenders of power, and the savage results of the insidious plottings by Sophia Loren and Anthony Perkins enliven the story. But the crude sound-stage setting undercuts the film's Heliconian ambition, as does its monotonous plane of strangeness. This persistent "inherent fear of joy" gives *Desire Under the Elms* its tragic ambience, but a true Aristotelian tragedy moves up and down a steeper curve of emotion.[1]

The Hippolytus tragedy has inspired three other films. The first was a silent Pineschi film of 1919 entitled *Fedra* (the title of Seneca's Latin adaptation of Euripides' play), the second is Manuel Mur Oti's Spanish-language *Fedra* of 1956, and the third is the French *Phèdre* (1968). Pierre Jourdan, brother of the actor Louis Jourdan, directed this adaptation of Racine's 1677 drama. The story of *Phèdre* differs from the other versions of the myth, in that Hippolytus loves a girl named Aricie, and thus Phèdre's (Marie Bell) suicide is motivated more by jealousy than by Hippolytus's chastity. When she finds out about her rival, she decides to take poison, and the film ends as she walks slowly and determinedly out of the picture to swallow the fatal draft.

The film displays all the color, costuming, grace, and grandeur of French Classical tragedy, but as a result, it looks like a filmed performance of a stage play. Nonetheless, the setting is splendid: rich reds and oranges fill the lavish halls, and nothing is cluttered or excessively ornate. Hippolytus (Claude Giraud), his muscles sharply defined under smooth skin, seems chiseled from marble. Unfortunately, the acting is statuesque as well, a style that may have worked three centuries earlier under the Sun King Louis XIV but is manifestly unsuited to a twentieth-century film.

Three other adaptations of Greek tragedies are set in historical periods other than the modern era. *The Bacchantes* (1961) purports to reconstitute Euripides' *Bacchae,* but it does so in an ancient Greek setting typical of the sword-and-sandal era in which it was made. This French-Italian production is set in drought-beset Thebes, under the rule of King Pentheus, who does not believe in the blond-haired, white-booted Dionysus ("who conquered his hoards of frenzied barbarians with inebriating wine"). The script concentrates on a palace intrigue spearheaded by Agave and a priest of Demeter, at the same time telling a romantic tale about Teiresias's daughter Manto and her lover, who are lucky enough to be the first Greeks to sample Dionysus's marvelous liquid. Director Giorgio Ferroni's film, the first of his six sword-and-sandal unextravaganzas, is a mess, and Euripides is not served well, though bits of the *Bacchae* pop up periodically, and the film does contain a silly sort of charm as the Dionysiac worshipers celebrate the climactic victory of their new god.

In chronological contrast, *Year of the Cannibals* (1971) adapts Sophocles' *Antigone* to a futuristic setting. This sci-fi allegory describes a future civilization so lawless and dehumanized that political enemies are killed on the streets and left unburied. The futuristic Antigone buries her dead brother and then appropriately faces the consequences for revolting against the society in which she lives.

Certainly one of the most extraordinary adaptations of Euripidean tragedy is Pasolini's *Medea* (1970). Like Cacoyannis's *Electra,* this film includes a prologue that explains the mythological background to the drama. In this case, Pasolini reconstructs the voyage of the Argo, with its heroes Jason, Orpheus, Castor, and Pollux (Polydeuces), from Greece to the eastern land of Colchis. Pasolini concentrates not on the heroic voyage itself—here made on a large raft, without incident—but on life in Colchis. Euripides describes Colchis as a barbaric, uncivilized land at the end of the Greek world. Pasolini reconstructs anthropological and spiritual rituals, particular vegetation rituals, that make such a metahistorical world so innocently savage. These vegetation rituals involve *sparagmos:* the tearing apart of sacrificial victims, scattering their limbs among the crops, and wetting the fields with their blood. The theme of this ritual is resurrection: the dead sacrificial victim is expected to rise again with healthy crops in the following harvest to bring prosperity to the community and communion with the gods.

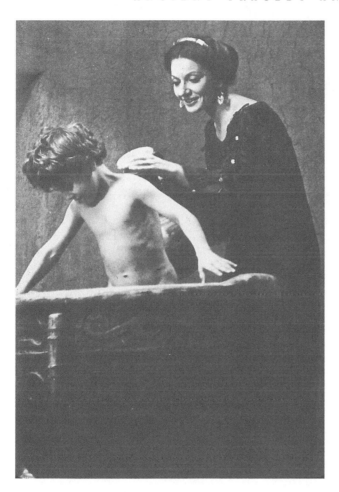

179 Maria Callas plays the title role in Pier Paolo Pasolini's *Medea* (1970). Her absorbing countenance dominates much of the film. Here she bathes one of her two sons, knowing full well that she will cut their throats in just a few minutes. There have been few characters like Medea in the cinema, and Pasolini paradoxically updates the myth by giving it a neolithic substratum of human sacrifice.

The reenactment of the bloody ritual, with the visual detail and starkness so often associated with Pasolini, reveals the essence of the "barbaric" culture of which Medea herself is a vital part. Not only is she a priestess, she is the granddaughter of the sun god. Pasolini makes it clear that this ritual is as real and important to Medea as is the sophisticated culture of Greece to Jason (and Euripides). Medea can be understood only in terms of her culture. Death, blood, and sacrifice are her life, hope, and salvation. Early in the film, when Jason coldly steals the Golden Fleece from her native Colchis, he is in a sense robbing Medea of this ritualistic lifeline. She submits herself to Jason and his Hellenic culture. But when Jason (the Olympic high-jumper Giuseppe Gentili) leaves her for the Corinthian princess Glauce, Medea returns to her ritualistic origins, praying to her divine solar grandfather. The camera gazes at the hazy ball of fire rising over the still, ashen, morning sea; and prepared by the geophysical and animistic setting in the early sequences of the film, we accept this sun as a god and Medea's grandfather. Pasolini has reached beyond the historic barriers of Greek mythology and to the primeval rites that sustained the

180   Maya (Melina Mercouri), an actress playing the part of Medea, visits the prison cell of Brenda (Ellen Burstyn), an American Medea, in *A Dream of Passion* (1978). Mercouri is trying to understand the visceral passion that compelled Burstyn to kill her innocent children.

earliest cultures. Medea's calculated slaughter of her babes is a manifestation of her cultural imperatives.

To enhance the visual presentation of this prehistoric animism, Pasolini shot the Colchis sequences in the valley of Göreme in central Turkey. Here majestic rock cones jut seventy-five feet into the sky, some of them hollowed out into chalky Byzantine chapels that provide the sacred housing for the Golden Fleece and its priests. Once removed from Colchis, the Fleece itself does not glitter or change color as in Ray Harryhausen's *Jason and the Argonauts;* instead, its bland, unremarkable yellow implies that marvelous rumors from distant eastern islands may not be founded in fact. The magic of the Fleece, deriving only from its primitive ritualistic importance in Colchis, is lost on civilized Jason.

The vegetation ritual that opens the film graphically depicts the sacrificial death of a young male victim. Piero Tosi's costumes, furs, bells, and strangely bulky jewelry enhance the visual oddity of the sequence. Persian santur music and close-harmonied Balkan choral singing contribute an aura of plaintive provocation. In contrast, Pasolini portrays a more civilized Greek Corinth, representative of modern, Western society. The palace of King Creon (Massimo Girotti) becomes the cathedral and famed baptistery of Pisa; its white marble and verdant malls alone remind us that the rocky moonscape of Göreme and Colchis belong to a different civilization. A man of subtlety and symbolism, Pasolini shows several boys eating juicy red watermelons on the palace steps—an ironic visual parallel with the bloody red human victim in Colchis.

The death of Glauce provides a further cultural contrast. Medea, as in Euripides' play, sends her two boys to the princess with a wedding gift; she wants Glauce to know, she says, that there need not be hard feelings between the two women in Jason's life. When Glauce puts on Medea's magical raiment, she bursts into flames and flees, finally leaping from the walls of the palace to her death. Such action was not shown on the Athenian stage; it was, as usual, described in the speech of a messenger. But Pasolini shows the sequence

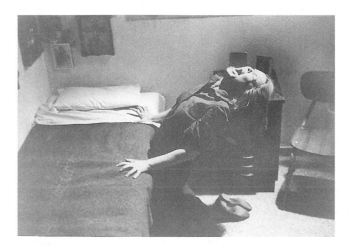

181   Brenda (Ellen Burstyn) displays the intense emotion that haunts a woman who murdered her children, in *A Dream of Passion*.

twice, once as dreamed by Medea, and once as it actually happens. Medea's dream is introduced by the haunting traces of Colchis: a double-exposed shot of Göreme's cones and the sound of the santur music. The two death sequences have their differences, however—the differences between reality and mental conception. In addition, Pasolini shoots the interior of the palace of Corinth in Pisa but the exterior walls (from which Glauce leaps) at the ramparts of the castle above Aleppo, Syria.

To effect the frightening barbarity and savage vengeance in the story, Pasolini needed a Medea who could dominate the screen and seem perfectly natural in this role. She had to be an actress of priestly, royal, aristocratic manner, capable of loving a man and two children, yet also capable of killing the children to spite him. The operatic soprano Maria Callas is perfect. Without singing a note, other than humming a lullaby to one son just before his death, Callas dominates the screen whenever she appears. Her strong cheeks and proud nose peer from under a black mantle; she is serene during the vegetation rites and just as serene during the execution of her sons, and yet her agony is somehow apparent. In a truly mythological performance, Maria Callas displays the grandeur, sorcery, evil, and power that have always been associated with Medea, yet with the slightest touch of mortal, womanly emotion. Mother, lover, daughter, and sister, by the film's end Medea has destroyed all the males in her life and she knows it.

Pasolini's greatest achievement in *Medea* is to account for the title character's ability to kill her children by establishing the killings as distant echoes of a ritualistic child sacrifice. Indeed, even the chorus in Euripides' play asks how could she murder her children, and that same question plagues Melina Mercouri in Jules Dassin's *A Dream of Passion* (1978). This fascinating film, which was nominated for a Golden Globe Award as best foreign film, serves as a filmic monument in preserving Mercouri's final film appearance.

It was also the last film written by Dassin, and as ever he filled his script with an examination of the parallels between ancient and modern Greece. Mercouri portrays

Maya, a beloved but aging film and theatrical star who is playing the lead role in a major Greek production of Euripides' *Medea*. We see a number of powerful rehearsal scenes played without interruption until the insightful director (Andreas Voutsinas) criticizes her "women's lib"–inspired interpretation: "Medea is all about love and passion and witchcraft. Medea is in another universe—a universe of love potions and poisons and mysteries and magic. Medea's goddess is Hecate, Medea is night and fiends and demons and revenge . . . not current events!"

After an initially defensive reaction, Maya determines to understand Medea's passion by interviewing Brenda Collins (Ellen Burstyn), an American expatriate serving a life sentence in a Glyphada prison for murdering her three children. Burstyn's character is devoutly religious, and she believes that her children had to be protected from the shame of their father's adultery. The volatile confrontations between the actress-Medea and the real-life Medea—and the inward struggles of each, which fuel their fury—bring to the screen the raw emotional power of *Medea,* the great tragedy about divorce, a parallel easily recognizable from the rehearsal sequences of the play.

Mercouri comes to comprehend Burstyn's pain, and the conclusion of the film shows us her brilliant performance at the ancient theater of Delphi. The focus is on the murder scene, but Dassin conflates all the elements of the film by intercutting sequences of the Greek chorus responding to the sounds of murder from the ancient house, Mercouri's visions of Burstyn's murders, and the struggle outside Burstyn's modern house as she hunts down her children with horrifying, god-inspired determination.

Other-Ancient-Worldly

The ancient world produced relatively few novels, a form of prose literature not to be popularized for nearly two millennia. But two ancient novels have inspired films. The gently erotic *Young Aphrodites* (1963) was based loosely on Longus's Greek novel *Daphnis and Chloe* and the poetry of Theocritus. This limited production (five actors, a herd of goats, and a few birds) imitates the unsophisticated pastoral tone of the Greek texts. It parallels the nearly wordless sexual encounters of an adult couple and two naive teenagers, and though the sexuality and the film as a whole are intentionally unsophisticated, the tragedy that brings the film to its understated close is not easily dismissed. Although the sexuality of *Young Aphrodites* is somewhat dated, the film's director, Nikos Koundouros, won the best director award at the Berlin Film Festival in 1966.

A far more ambitious treatment of an ancient novel is *Fellini Satyricon* (1969). Federico Fellini's colorful treatment of Petronius's Roman novel *Satyricon* offered viewers one of the cinema's most provocatively individual approaches to the ancient world. Fellini was the perfect filmmaker to meet the challenge of filming this herky-jerky ancient narrative. Typical of most ancient novels, Petronius's work features sharp breaks, sudden interruptions, lengthy and irrelevant digressions, and strange, unbelievable coincidences or accidents that happen to young, nondescript, romantic adventurers. Making matters

182   Hired mourners accompany the Widow of Ephesus to the burial of her husband in *Fellini Satyricon* (1969). Typical of Fellini's approach to antiquity, the story comes from Petronius's Latin novel, and hired mourners are referred to elsewhere in ancient literature, but the white grave markers protruding from the earth are total fantasy. The film has many authentic touches, yet Fellini's interpretation is ultimately subjective.

worse, the *Satyricon* that has survived is incomplete; only books 14, 15, and 16 of perhaps twenty books are extant, meaning that the novel has no beginning or end. But the fragment seemed perfectly comprehensible to Fellini, whose own narrative patterns had become quite idiosyncratic since the early 1960s.

Fellini was always keenly aware of modern Italy's ancient heritage (hence his *Nights of Cabiria*), but as soon as he began this project he turned to numerous books about ancient life, especially Jerome Carcopino's *Daily Life in Ancient Rome*. He acquired a particular fascination with Roman frescoes, wandering through the ruins of Pompeii and Herculaneum and reconstructing in his own vision the Rome of two millennia past. The

183   A gigantic whore (Maria De Sisti) from the Suburra sequence in *Fellini Satyricon*.
Fellini constantly bombards his audience with strange faces, bodies, gestures, colors, sounds, and
atmospheres to create "personalities who breathed another air, ate other foods." He creates another
world, then sets this world in antiquity.

film begins and ends with ancient Roman frescoes coming to life and returning to their ruined state.

Fellini Satyricon presents plentiful filmic evidence of Fellini's research: the theater in which Vernacchio performs a mime; the *insula* (multistoried apartment house) in the Suburra (the degenerate section of ancient Rome); the art museum, which includes numerous Pompeian-style frescoes; Greek readings from Homer, Lucretius's descending-syllable line (*eliciuntur [et] eripitur persona manet res* [3.58]), and Hadrian's *animula vagula blandula;* the Petronian story of the Widow of Ephesus, during which authentic hired mourners beat their breasts rhythmically; the presentation of Trimalchio's first beard in a box; the reading of the estate accounts at Trimalchio's feast; Giton's subdued song constructed only of Pythagorean fifths and fourths; the sacrifice of the calf at the shipboard wedding; the ancestor masks in the dead patricians' deserted house; and the Carthaginian infanticides (from the last extant paragraph of Petronius's *Satyricon*).

Fellini rarely reproduces these or other authenticities without some personal comment or rearrangement. Romans during the Empire were fond of building colossal statues, so Fellini shows a stylized twelve-foot marble head being dragged through the crowded streets at night; the concept is realistic, the execution surrealistic. The whorehouse in the Suburra is architecturally not the normal Roman *insula* that Fellini saw at Pompeii or Herculaneum but a layered *pueblo,* and the fat whores, tongue-wagging pimps, and salivating customers within the *insula felix* resemble those of the barren-walled, cubicled red-light districts of modern Tunis, only with one step more into unreality. Although the song sung by Giton (Max Born) is authentically antique in style, the lyre he plays is a complete fabrication by Danilo Donati *(The Gospel According to Saint Matthew).* The authentic baths in the opening scene have modernized abstract designs on the walls. And in the art museum, Eumolpus talks of famous Greek artists like Apelles and Lysippus while standing before authentic Pompeian frescoes (and a Mesopotamian cuneiform inscription), yet behind him a double-decker trolley filled with Roman commuters passes the large window in the wall.

The language and music of *Fellini Satyricon* also convey the director's eccentric appreciation for antiquity, especially for the scope of the Roman Empire under Nero (during whose reign Petronius lived, as his appearance in *Quo Vadis?* testifies). While the Greek of Homer is being recited at Trimalchio's banquet, an alto female voice is translating it in the background—not into Latin, or Italian, or English, but into Turkish. Later, when Enculpius (Martin Potter) and Ascyltus (Hiram Keller) find a light-brown-skinned slave girl in the otherwise deserted villa of the suicidal Roman patricians, she speaks an Oriental language that may have come from an obscure earthly tribe or Fellini's fertile imagination. Whichever it is, it and the Turkish rendering of Homer remind us that of the millions of people living within the confines of the Roman Empire, relatively few spoke Latin as a first language.

Some of the music of the film is composed by Nino Rota, whose blurping, grinding music is executed on synthesizer, much superior to an attempt at synthesizer effects in *Hercules* (1957). The rest of the music is contemporary ethnic music: Balinese Gamelan, Ramayana chants, and the central African *niegpadouda* dance. The frail melodies of the *sansa* (thumb piano) also add to Fellini's nonurban, non-Greco-Roman characterization of the fringe or fantasy lands of the Roman Empire.

The humor of *Fellini Satyricon* is vulgar. Critics in 1969 were disgusted with Fellini's trashy presentation of Neronian Rome. But the vast majority of Fellini's profanities are word-for-word Petronian: Trimalchio, for instance, "goes to the pot" in Petronius (27), and two giggly, drunken women at the feast kiss each other repeatedly (Petronius 67). A freedman tells Ascyltus, "You're nor worth your own piss!" (Petronius 57). Many other one-liners are lifted from Petronius: Eumolpus "will give his inheritance to whoever will eat his corpse" (141). Trimalchio decides that he does not want his wife's statue in his tomb, "so at least when I'm dead I won't have any more fights with her" (74). And at the feast, when someone begins a story, "A rich man and a poor man were enemies," the wealthy Trimalchio interrupts, "What's a poor man?" (48).

Many critics did not understand that Fellini drew a line between authenticity and personal creation, however fuzzy and irregular this line might be. Gilbert Highet, for instance, a brilliant classicist and an early promulgator of the classical tradition, was appalled by all the sex, disturbed by the "improbable sets," and bothered by the absence of "Petronius' decadent chatter at Trimalchio's banquet." Highet wondered whether "Fellini really believes that just before a dinner party in Rome all the guests bathed naked in a swimming pool lit by scores of candles."[2] As a creative artist Fellini reconstructed and reinterpreted the literary work of art upon which his own cinematic work of art was based. Petronius has no such bath, but Fellini does; it is that simple. Fellini stretched, reinterpreted, and reinvented some aspects of antiquity and the Petronian book, but that does not mean that his *Satyricon* is wholly inauthentic. It is a mistake to expect Fellini's art to be slavishly imitative; Fellini's art is creatively imitative.

The feast at the house of corpse-faced Trimalchio (played by Mario Romagnoli, "Il Moro," a restaurateur in contemporary Rome, though Fellini first asked the aging Boris Karloff to play the part) provides the most insightful glimpse into Fellini's artistic method and into his penchants for both historical authenticity and personal creativity. The scene in Petronius bursts with outrageously decorated dishes and such typical gourmet Roman foods as thrush tongues in purplish sweet-and-sour sauce, and roasted chicken stuffed with pheasant brains, sow's udder, and field mice. Fellini takes this culinary authenticity and then invents a dining room with an upper-deck balcony for the guests of lesser importance and improbably long straws through which the important guests can drink cool water from a central mass of melting ice. To be sure, these touches are inauthentic, but the reclining position of the important guests and the sitting position of the others, the U-shaped arrangement of the three couches, the lechery and vul-

184/185   Fellini re-creates Petronius's *Satyricon* on the screen, adds numerous authentic historical and archaeological elements, and then filters the whole process through his own visual creativity. Ancient Romans reclined while eating, wore wreaths, used couches arranged in a U shape, could choose the food to be cooked while it was still alive, and ate in incense-filled rooms, but Fellini gives all these details his own twist. Trimalchio (Mario Romagnoli) sits on the left, accompanied by his wife Fortunata (Magali Noël). Fortunata's hairstyle was quite the fashion in first-century A.D. Rome, as can be seen from a bust in the Capitoline Museum in Rome showing the emperor Titus's daughter, Julia, with the same croquignole curls.

garity of the guests and host, the incense-laden, steamy, smoky atmosphere, the hang-ing, fleshy bellies of the half-dressed slaves and cooks, the tall, ringlet, croquignole curls of the ladies' coiffeurs, the recitation of Greek, the trick of the ungutted yet already stuffed and cooked pig, and, above all, the murky brown and inky purple blend of the pheasant brains and Lucanian sausages—these details go beyond scholarly authenticity into visual genius. There is no need to detail the banter of Petronius when Fellini has transformed literature into its visual counterpart; this is cinema. Some pieces of the film may belong in a classroom, some pieces may belong in an asylum, and some may belong in the bathroom, but the entire creation ultimately results in a revitalized cinematic im-pression of the spirit of the ancient novel.

During and after the shooting of the film Fellini amused himself by stretching the philosophy and meaning of *Satyricon.* He described his work to interviewers as "a pre-Christian film for the post-Christian era." Critics gobbled up this little thrush's tongue with relish and peered into *Satyricon* in search of deep political and theologi-cal comment. But Fellini's additional comments went further in clarifying the film's oddities. He was, he said, trying "to evoke an unknown world of two thousand years ago, a world that is no more. To work as an archaeologist does, when he assembles a few potsherds or pieces of masonry and reconstructs not an amphora or a temple but an artifact in which the object is implied. . . . These characters were personalities which seem to have breathed another air, eaten other foods. They behave differently because they *are* different."[3] Only with this preface can Fellini's more famous statement be un-derstood: "It is a science-fiction film projected into the past."[4] Pasolini would call this metahistory.

How does one re-create a culture in which people breathed different air and ate different foods? Fellini does it by virtually eliminating the commonplace cinematic im-pressions that we all have about antiquity—the columns, togas, chariots, gladiators, lions in the arena, Christians, the mob, and the splendor and grandeur—all the things and people that Hollywood, Cinecittà, and others have successfully (and unsuccessfully) reconstructed and re-created over nearly a century. Instead, Fellini establishes numerous lesser known and less tangible authenticities, and to these he adds his own creations (and Danilo Donati's), which are ancient but modern, Roman but Italian, fragmentary and mysterious. The red-lipped, white-caked and cracked cheeks of the powdered whores, the expressive and perfectly timed farts of Vernacchio, the imposingly anachro-nistic steel-clad ship of Lichas, the delicate but odd hand-gestures of Giton, and the unfamiliar and almost unhuman sounds emitted by Oenothea's chanting attendant ("oooph, oooph"), the gravel-voiced theatrical slave with the wooden hand-clappers ("ah-ah-ah-ah-ah-ah-ah"), and the two rough men in the whorehouse playing "patty cake" with bricks, all these belong not to our modern world. They are not necessarily Roman either. They belong to the Fellinian interpretation of the ancient novel's artis-tic fantasy world. The dubbing of German Max Born, British Martin Potter, and American Hiram Keller into Italian is intentionally off-track to help create the otherworldly, disconcertingly different atmosphere; and the brash, vulgar, bizarre, and colorful bombardment that persists throughout the film knocks our senses out of today and into the film's own time and world.

Because of Fellini's unique view of ancient Roman life and manners, his unparalleled acumen in finding bizarre faces and bodies, and his unique creativity in inventing facial, vocal, and hand gestures, no one seems to have breathed, let alone visualized, the different air of ancient Rome quite as deeply as Federico Fellini.

Although they produced their best work three decades ago, Fellini and Pasolini both had an indirect but profound influence on several subsequent American film directors. Much of this lies beyond the scope of this book, but Julie Taymor called on the services of *Medea*'s production designer Dante Ferretti for *Titus* (1999), her film adaptation of Shakespeare's *Titus Andronicus*. Not surprisingly, the sets, costumes, and makeup are metahistorical. Saturninus campaigns for the throne wearing a tuxedo and driving in a limousine, the Gothic Queen Tamora is covered in tattoos, and Roman soldiers caked in mud wear modernized ancient-looking armor.

LYCUS: Here's a good bottle of wine.

PSEUDOLUS: Was 1 a good year?

— *A FUNNY THING HAPPENED ON*

THE WAY TO THE FORUM (1966)

Perhaps we sometimes take the ancient world too seriously. The clashing battles, complex politics, passionate romances, profound theologies, and majestic locales were only one side of ancient life. The other and less known side was laughter. Even Socrates was known for his irony, as was Cicero for his wit. Aristophanes, Menander, Plautus, and Terence wrote raucous comedies, Juvenal and Lucian wrote satires, and some lesser known sources offer pages of jokes, riddles, and ribald tales.

The ancients delivered their humor in forms similar to our own: slapstick, trickery, anecdotes, graffiti and pasquinade, one-liners, impersonations, plays, musicals, satires, and farces. But if the forms of ancient comedy are familiar to us, the content is not. Ancient comedy, like the comedy of any culture, thrived only within its own time and place. Just as a Chris Rock joke about race relations or a breathless riff of Dennis Miller's commentary would have left an ancient Roman audience completely stone-faced, so do Cicero's puns or Aristophanes' jokes about fifth-century B.C. Athenian political figures fail to amuse modern audiences. We simply do not "get" most of their jokes. The references are obscure, the vernacular confusing. What verbal jokes we do understand are often so hard to grasp at first reading that, like all jokes that "have to be explained," they fall flat.

The ancient world had a number of famous comedians, both performers and writers. But with the effectiveness of their humor lost to all except a handful of knowledgeable classical scholars, only the comic playwrights can boast of any wide following in the modern era. And the two best known of these, Aristophanes and Plautus, will have noticed from the marquee of the Elysian Theater in Hades that a few of their plays have been made into films.

Aristophanes' sharp political wit has been studiously neglected by the Judeo-Christian world, in part because of his obscure, fifth-century B.C. political references but mostly because of his explicit, X-rated vulgarity. But Aristophanes and his audience laughed loudly and unabashedly about Greek politicians who were homosexuals, about foreigners who had circumcised penises, and about all the human body's excretions that occurred as insistently then as now. The only one of Aristophanes' eleven extant plays that has been made into a movie is his immortal antiwar sex comedy, *Lysistrata*. (*The Acharnians* was filmed in 1976, but it simply records that summer's performance at the ancient theater of Epidaurus.) The action of *Lysistrata* centers on a pact among the women of Greece, who, weary of the continuing Peloponnesian wars between Athens and Sparta, refuse to have sex with their husbands until the fighting is halted. Lysistrata is the leader of this Pan-Hellenic sex strike. Not only are the men exasperated by the pact, but the women, too, find their self-imposed abstinence agonizingly oppressive. And so the comedy has many directions in which to travel. One relentless female feigns pregnancy by stuffing a helmet underneath her tunic. Another begins to yield to temptation and agrees to make love with her husband on the Athenian acropolis—but frustrates him by leaving intermittently to get a set of box-springs, then a mattress, then a blanket and a pillow, then some ointment.

Lysistrata has been filmed six times in various countries. The first, an Austrian version in 1948, suffers from tedious acting and some damaging censor cuts, though Judith Helzmeister (Lysistrata) performs her role as ringleader well. A 1954 French *Lysistrata* has a quicker pace but becomes a little too wacky for Hellenic taste. In addition to a 1962 Spanish adaptation *(Escuela de Seductoras)* and a 1968 Swedish modernization featuring Bibi Anderson *(Flickorna),* Universal produced a version called *The Second Greatest Sex* (1955).

In *The Second Greatest Sex,* Lysistrata has migrated to Osawkie, Kansas, 1880. There an ongoing feud between the men of Osawkie and Mandaroon/Jones City about the location of the county seat is stopped by Liza McClure (Jeanne Crain) and her sexually continent cohort. The film includes a number of gymnastic boot-slapping dances and spirited songs, which like the Western setting of the film itself are inspired by Fox's successful CinemaScope *Seven Brides for Seven Brothers* (itself indirectly derived from Plutarch's *Life of Romulus*), which had appeared a year earlier. In fact, not only does the balletic Tommy Rall dance in both films, but both films include musical numbers based on their ancient sources, "That's What Plutarch Says" in the earlier film, Sherrell and Moody's "Lysistrata" in this one. The inclusion of songs and dances is authentic in that Aristophanes' original also included choral songs and dances, though in quite a different style.

Of course, *The Second Greatest Sex* lacks the biting satire and sexual explicitness of real Aristophanic comedy, but any attempt at filming *Lysistrata* is apt to fall short of the ideal. Aristophanes treated sexual politics with flagrant matter-of-factness, and films of the 1940s, 1950s, and 1960s could hardly be expected to match the open-mindedness of fifth-century B.C. Greece. The permissiveness of current Hollywood R-rated and NC-17 films seems to invite a filmmaker to don the protruding phallus and reenact an authentic *Lysistrata*. But in fact, such a film was produced in Greece in 1972, under the oppressive atmosphere of the junta, a clumsy but daring *Lysistrata* directed by Giorgos Zervoulakos and starring Jenny Kareze.

The Roman comic playwright Plautus has fared much better on the silver screen. In 1935 the German Universum company released its musical production of Plautus's *Amphitryon,* subtitled *Aus den Wolken kommt das Glück (Happiness Comes from the Clouds).* The film tells the story of the conception of Hercules: Jupiter appears on earth in the guise of Amphitryon, the mortal husband of Alcmene, and impregnates her. The god Mercury, meanwhile, disguises himself as an earthly servant, Sosias. The real Amphitryon and Sosias come home from war while all this Olympian hanky-panky is going on, and the pretense, trickery, and changes of disguise that follow bring the comedy quickly to its close.

The cinematic *Amphitryon* stands somewhere between operetta and Broadway musical; the dialogue is recited lyrically in concordance with the rhythm of the background music—a little shy of recitative—and a few songs are sung. This fresh method of delivering the dialogue (used as well in Hollywood at the time, in Wheeler and Woolsey's *Diplomaniacs* [1933], for instance) gives the film its very light yet sophisticatedly funny air. The comedy is enhanced by Juno (Adele Sandrock), who hauls her Wagnerian girth around cloudy Olympus, practicing her incessantly thundering scales. Jupiter (Willy Fritsch), who has had enough of this solfeggio, calls for Mercury, "the God of Swiftness." Mercury (Paul Kemp) swiftly roller-skates across the marble floors of Olympus while holding an umbrella (in lieu of wings) above his head, and the two gods float to earth. Jupiter sniffs around earth, looking for a "schöne Frau." Seeing a statue of Jupiter, he snorts, "It's a bad likeness of me."

Jupiter drinks a magic potion to change from his bald, aged self into the dashing young warrior Amphitryon. Mercury tries the same thing, but he turns into an ugly imp. From this point the mistaken identities and complicated romantic interplay dominate the film, highlighted by the now-mortal Jupiter's catching a cold and getting quite drunk. The farce comes to a close after Juno swoops down from Olympian Valhalla as gracefully as a large, crippled, mechanical swan and takes her beloved "Jupi" out of mischief and back to his rightful appearance and position. Although the mistaken-identity sequences pale in comparison to the opening third of the film, *Amphitryon* maintains its elevated yet hilarious style to the very end. Plautus would have enjoyed this production.

Plautus would also have enjoyed *A Funny Thing Happened on the Way to the Forum* (1966), the screen adaptation of the Broadway musical that in turn was based on Plautus's *Pseudolus, Poenulus, Mostellaria,* and *Miles Gloriosus.* The film looks convincingly Roman, and just as original Plautine comedy contained musical *cantica, A Funny Thing*

186   Two lovely couples: the pimp Lycus (Phil Silvers) with the glum Erronius (Buster Keaton),
"whose children have been stolen in infancy by pirates," and Hysterium (Jack Gilford) with the wily
Pseudolus (Zero Mostel) in *A Funny Thing Happened on the Way to the Forum* (1966). Such
characters made Plautus's comedies popular twenty-two centuries ago, and they make Plautus's
comedies popular now.

Happened on the Way to the Forum offers some extremely clever songs. "Comedy Tonight,"
sung by Pseudolus (Zero Mostel), serves as the Plautine prologue and introduces the characters of the film, and several songs, especially "Everybody Ought to Have a Maid," glory
in Stephen Sondheim's devilishly suggestive lyrics ("sweeping out, sleeping in"). Ken
Thorne omitted a few numbers from the original Broadway show, which was revived in
1996, but he well deserved the Academy Award for best adapted score in 1967.

The plot of *A Funny Thing Happened on the Way to the Forum* is no more complicated than any of Plautus's plays—about as simple, in other words, as building a tower
in Babylon. His plays involve pimps and slaves who are busy procuring maidens or whores
for young aristocratic boys while either the boy's father or girl's proper owner is away on
business; or a father who discovers that his son or daughter whom he lost in infancy has
been returned to him; or other complications that require the return of someone's borrowed money or the illicit "borrowing" of someone's house. All of this Plautine merriment
makes its way into *A Funny Thing Happened on the Way to the Forum*.

Buster Keaton (Erronius) plays the glum father "whose children have been stolen in infancy by pirates," and his understated appearances top this Plautine macédoine with a spoonful of cinematic nostalgia. Pseudolus, "with a face the size of Brazil," has the capacity for so much mugging that the slightest twitch, not to mention a gigantic pout or smile, can carry an entire scene.[1] Lycus the pimp (Phil Silvers) and Hysterium (Jack Gilford) end up in drag, a hoary gimmick that works when two true masters of low comedy don the wigs and dresses. The rest of the cast stands out for its character acting and for its descriptive names—the braggart soldier Miles Gloriosus ("braggart soldier"), and the hyperactive, shimmying, luscious, and jingling courtesans Gymnasia, Vibrata, Panacea, and Tintinabula.

Director Richard Lester, who had just recently perfected his cinematic comedy style in the first two Beatles films, embellishes the original stage musical with his characteristic camera antics and a generous dose of sight gags. The huge (prism) mirror in the whorehouse typifies his frequently amusing anachronisms. But at times the restless camera, the merciless editing, and the occasional tasteless humor detract from the whole for the sake of the part. The chariot race at the end of the film overstays its welcome, but Lester's problem is never a lack of ideas, but rather the inability to pick and choose among his gags. When the chariots get caught in the long spokes of the millstone, when Pseudolus's chariot breaks apart, and when Pseudolus is then left to "water-ski" on the chariot platform, Lester and second-unit director Bob Simmons display comic inventiveness—even if Lew Wallace would never believe that he set *that* into motion.

Equal credit belongs to Melvin Frank and Michael Pertivee for their screenplay. Pseudolus looks at a jazzy, corporeal display by a leopard-skinned African courtesan named Vibrata and sighs, "I was hoping to live past my wedding night." At the gladiatorial arena, after a line of slaves is amusingly felled one by one beneath the efficient mace of a gladiator who is merely practicing for the next day, Pseudolus mortally wounds the gladiatorial instructor (Roy Kinnear, a Lester regular). The instructor, the pedagogue of form until the end, breathes his dying words of stylistic advice: "You're (gasp) still jerking the wrist." And finally, at the end of the film, when Erronius thinks his long-lost daughter is Hysterium (Jack Gilford in drag), Miles Gloriosus recognizes the "girl" as "You! the Eunuch!" Erronius mumbles in confusion, "My daughter—a eunuch?!"

While the works of Aristophanes and Plautus amused the Romans, Greeks, and us as well, modern film audiences have also had the opportunity to see freshly written cinematic comedies about the ancient world—musicals, farces, satires, parodies, romantic fantasies, cartoons, animations, full-length features, or comic shorts. Roman history, because of its ubiquity in film throughout the century, has been the subject of many comedies. Buster Keaton's first independently produced feature-length film, *The Three Ages* (1923), was a six-reel parody of *Intolerance*. Cowritten by Clyde Bruckman, the author and director of several classic comedies for Keaton as well as for W. C. Fields and the Three Stooges, the film lampoons Griffith's examination of a timeless theme in different

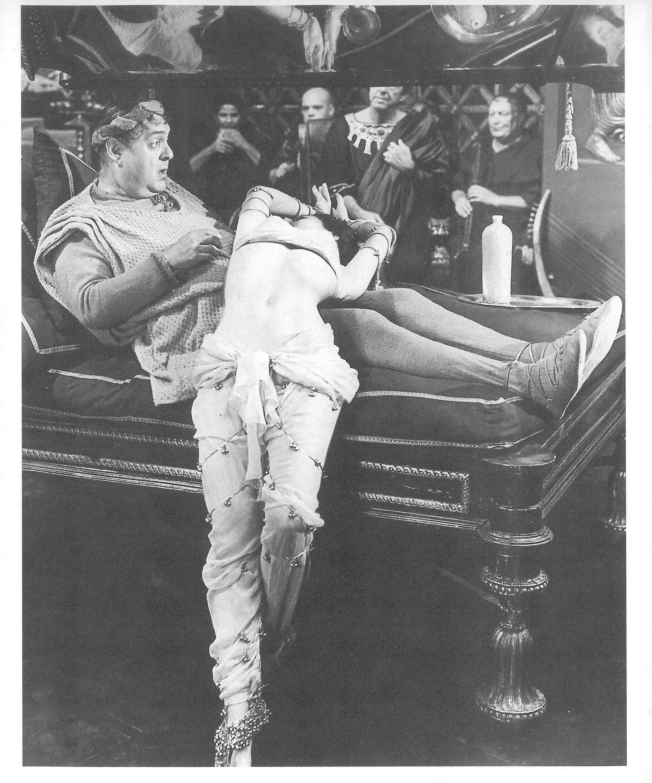

187   Anachronisms, sex, and Zero Mostel's mug help convey the humor of *A Funny Thing Happened on the Way to the Forum*. Here Pseudolus (Mostel) visits the brothel of Lycus (Phil Silvers) in hopes of buying a woman. The huge mirror, the rousing music, and the jingling, gesturing gyrations of Tintinabula (Helen Funai) bring the eyes out of Pseudolus's sockets.

188 Richard Lester's visual gags fill any verbal voids in *A Funny Thing Happened on the Way to the Forum*. Hero (Michael Crawford) needs a cup of mare's sweat to make a sleeping potion, so he takes the mare to the steam room of a Roman bath.

historical periods—here, the theme of love and romance in the stone age, the modern age, and ancient Rome.

The Roman sequences appear in four parts of the film. Anachronisms abound. Keaton wears a wrist-sundial, turns a visit to the soothsayer using Roman-numeraled dice into a crap game with African slaves, tries to park his quadriga (drawn by a horse, a cow, a donkey, and a mule) in front of a No Parking sign, and not only extracts a thorn from a lion's paw à la Androcles but gives it a manicure as well. Only one joke depends on the verbal titles ("Thou rankest high in the Roman army—and thou art the rankest!"). The second half of the film consists mostly of action sequences, including a race in which Keaton negotiates the snowy "sands" of the arena floor by exchanging his chariot wheels for skis and his horses for dogs. At one point he has to change a flat tire—a dog with a sore paw—after which he dangles a cat in front of his team to win the race. Ultimately he rescues his damsel in distress by pole-vaulting on a lance and attempting to drive off in a taxi-litter equipped with a meter.

Universal followed two years later with its "hysterical historical comedy" *Nero* (1925). The first sound comedy about ancient Rome was the Samuel Goldwyn musical *Roman Scandals* (1933), which won renewed attention recently when its costar Gloria Stuart received an Academy Award nomination for her role in *Titanic* (1997). Marx Brothers writing luminaries George S. Kaufman and Nat Perrin contributed to the story, as did Robert Sherwood, and the film starred the multitalented Eddie Cantor. *Roman Scandals* begins in a modern American town called Rome, where Eddie is the watchman at a museum of antiquities. Neglecting his duties, he goes to sleep on the job, his clothes and shoes hanging from the classical statuary. The museum director, leading in a group of visitors, finds the slumberer and yells, "Hey! You can't sleep in here!" Eddie replies, "Well, it *is* a bit noisy." The tone of the film is set.

After singing "Build a Little Home," the first of several production numbers, Eddie is thrown out of modern Rome and begins imagining himself in ancient Rome. Soon the camera is focusing on his sandals and tunic, and Eddie sticks out his thumb to hitch a ride on a passing chariot. He asks a few Roman soldiers directions to the circus:

SOLDIER: Three blocks down.

EDDIE: By the way, which circus is it?

SOLDIER: Maximus.

EDDIE: You're sure it's not Ringling Brothers?

Eddie, soon to be Hellenically nicknamed "Eddie-pus," is sold in the slave market, but he objects that the price on his head is only one hundred "piffics." "Look at me," he protests. "I can cook, I can take care of your children, and if you don't have any children, I can take care of that." Oedipus is bought by a certain whip-bearing Josephus, whom Eddie calls "a good whippersnapper." The one-liners continue as Oedipus is made royal taster for Emperor Valerius and his wife, who bears the masculine name Agrippa. Eddie tastes a glass of wine for the Emperor. "I may be right . . . (drinks) . . . and I may be wrong. . . . (drains the glass) . . . I was wrong; I'd better taste another glass!"

The majority of the sets and costumes in *Roman Scandals* are glamorous, not historically perfect, but after all, this is a comedy. The musical production numbers in particular are not authentic because they were designed and choreographed by Busby Berkeley, whose talents were in Art Deco design. His impressive and dramatic slave market centers around a gigantic column drum, along the sides and in the shadows of which the Goldwyn Girls stand chained to the wall. They are ostensibly naked—the sequence reportedly had to be shot at night in a closed studio—but long blond wigs drape delicately and artfully over their breasts. Later, Oedipus hides in a women's bath. He applies a blackface mud pack to impersonate an Ethiopian slave. He and the chorus then sing "Keep Young and Beautiful" while Berkeley directs the girls in his inimitable geometrical style. Revolving doors between fluted columns reveal the black slaves on one side and the white on the other, and a glass-enclosed steam bath in the center presents the perfect focal point for the dancing, not to mention the ideal hiding place for Oedipus until the steam shrinks him into a midget.

189   Eddie "Oedipus" Cantor disguises himself as an Ethiopian slave with blackface and leads the
Goldwyn Girls through a Busby Berkeley production number in *Roman Scandals* (1933). The
stylized geometry is typical of Berkeley's work, but he uses an ancient Ionic volute motif.

More than twenty years later MGM adapted another Robert Sherwood play, *The
Road to Rome* (1926), into another musical about ancient Rome, *Jupiter's Darling* (1955).
Starring Esther Williams, Howard Keel, Marge and Gower Champion, and George
Sanders, the story takes place as Hannibal advances toward Rome in 216 B.C. But before
historians start reaching for their copies of Livy, they should hear the prologue of the film:
"The history which describes Hannibal's attack on Rome is very confusing; this story will
do nothing to clear it up." The plot revolves around the standard musical-comedy pattern:
boy meets girl, boy loses girl, boy gets girl back. "Boy" in this case is Hannibal (Keel), and
"girl" is Amytis (Williams), the fiancée of the Roman dictator Fabius Maximus (Sanders).
Some of the sets for *Jupiter's Darling* MGM had built two years earlier for *Julius
Caesar*, but Amytis's swimming pool would have cost even Caesar a chariotload of piffics,
to use Eddie Cantor currency. Naturally, Williams has to leave dry land occasionally to
breathe; on one memorable occasion she disrobes while standing on a lovely Greek key design, then plops into her turquoise pool and dances through the water past submerged,

190   Hardly a merman, Hannibal (Howard Keel) gets his first swimming lesson from the Roman Amytis, played by the ubiquitously aquatic Esther Williams, in *Jupiter's Darling* (1955).

chalk-white marble statues. The statues come to life, and a romantic piece of aquatic choreography follows. A few living marble cupids shoot Amytis full of love, whereupon a barrage of orange bubbles fills the water and covers the screen. The statues recalcify, and Amytis returns to the romantic drama at hand.

Elephants, of course, must take center stage in a musical about Hannibal, and indeed, one noteworthy dance sequence of note stars superbly trained—and multicolored—pachyderms. Amytis, who as a Roman would never have seen an elephant before Hannibal's arrival, asks her slave, "What are those animals with five legs?"

It might at first seem startling to see the mighty Hannibal and his Carthaginian army singing songs, but director George Sidney *(Showboat, Bye Bye Birdie)* makes sure to balance their musical talents with military force. The battle at the walls of Rome, with its smokescreens, chariots, elephants, archers, battering rams, and *ballistae,* is as impressive and vivid as almost any in the entire genre. Unfortunately, the historical Hannibal never even approached the city of Rome, let alone besieged it.

Another musical, *Fiddlers Three* (1944), had a plot similar to *Roman Scandals:* when two modern sailors (Tommy Trinder, Sonnie Hale) are struck by lightning, they find themselves in ancient Rome. Many of the gags of this British wartime film depend on specific comparisons between ancient Roman and Second World War Britain. Because of the topical references, *Fiddlers Three* has been compared to an Abbott and Costello film. In the obligatory climactic arena sequence, Nero (Francis L. Sullivan [*The Prodigal, Caesar and Cleopatra*]) throws our heroes to the lions, which prompts their well-timed return to modern times.

O. K. Nerone (1951) is yet another film to use the premise of *Roman Scandals* and *Fiddlers Three*—going back in time to ancient Rome. This Italian production, released immediately after the Neronian *Quo Vadis?* and calculated to ride in the wake of that colossus's chariot wheels, had the advantage of being filmed amid Mussolini's ambitious development of neoclassical buildings at the EUR in Rome. The sexy Silvana Pampanini (Poppaea) fills out the interior shots, but the dubbed soundtrack and the tired jokes come seemingly right out of Joe Miller. The highlight of absurdity in *O. K. Nerone* comes at the end during—you've probably guessed it—the arena sequence, in which the two American sailors teach the ancient gladiators how to play football, though the rest of the film should be penalized fifteen yards for numerous cinematic fouls.

Warner Brothers capitalized on the correlation between the gladiatorial arena and American football with the Bugs Bunny Looney Tune *Roman Legion-Hare* (1955). An opening shot of a road sign, "Slow Chariots Keep Right," pans to a nicely drawn Colosseum. Its program poster reads, "Coliseum Today—Detroit Lions in Season Opener: Undefeated Lions out for first taste of victory." Nero enters the arena—again thanks to the success of the Neronian *Quo Vadis?*—in a twenty-foot-long chariot complete with mid-1950s Cadillac fins, ready to "throw out the first victim." Because victims are scarce, Yosemite Sam, the captain of the guard, is sent out to round up new ones, and the first available victim he comes across is the insolent, carrot-munching leporid who immediately asks, "Ehhh, what's up, Doc?" A clever chase through the lion cages of the arena follows, and this chase culminates in the lions' feeding on Sam and Nero. Nero plays the violin, but it is "Taps" that he plays, and Bugs leaves us with his little Latin and less Greek: "E pluribus uranium."

In a similarly jocular vein was the Three Stooges' short *Matri-Phony* (1942). This Columbia two-reeler is derived in part from the Rodgers and Hart Broadway musical "The Boys from Syracuse," which was in turn made into a film by Universal in 1940. The musical is an adaptation of Plautus's *Menaechmi,* set in ancient Syracuse, whereas this Stooge short is set in the unhealthy-sounding, Greek-sounding land of Erysipelas. Here "Larrycus, Mohicus, and Curly-cue, the biggest chiselers in town," run a pottery shop. As Ben-Hur takes to chariots and Moses to the Red Sea, naturally the Stooges are soon embroiled in a clay fight and taken to the court of the anachronistically bespectacled Emperor Octopus Grabus (Vernon Dent). Borrowing now from Eddie Cantor's *Roman Scandals,* Curly hides in the women's quarters, and Moe becomes the emperor's official "toast-taster," only to find that one particular batch of wine is indeed "the royal mickey."

The flurry of both serious and comedic Italian films inspired by the Roman location shooting of MGM's *Quo Vadis?* included two mid-1950s Italian farces, *Due Notti con Cleopatra* (*Two Nights with Cleopatra,* 1954) and *Mio Figlio Nerone* (released in the United States as *Nero's Big Weekend,* 1956). *Due Notti,* directed by Mario Mattoli, features Alberto Sordi (Caesarino), Italy's answer to Bob Hope, who feigns to be heroic, romantic, and competent but is inevitably cowardly, flirtatious, and inept—though ultimately triumphant. Like Hope, he always has a gag exit line, a sarcastic comment, or a funny facial gesture. Nowadays the film is of interest because it includes an early film appearance by Sophia Loren. She plays both Cleopatra and a look-alike street girl who is used to thwart some palace intrigue.

Sordi is also featured as the Emperor Nero in *Mio Figlio Nerone*. The title ("my son Nero") alludes to Nero's mother, Agrippina, about whom Tacitus tells us much, none of it complimentary. She was the conniving Julio-Claudian blueblood who had the Emperor Claudius poisoned so that her teenage son Nero could ascend to the throne, but as he matured he grew weary and suspicious of her. He attempted to have her killed, most notably by rigging her private barge so that the roof would collapse on her. The line between historical reality and farce is a thin one, however, so director Steno and writer Rodolfo Sonego propel the story via a series of attempted assassinations. Agrippina (Gloria Swanson) tries to kill Seneca (Vittorio De Sica) and Poppaea (Brigitte Bardot), and they along with Nero put snakes in her bed, poison her, rig the ship, and try to drown her.

Italian comedy has always had a predilection toward clowns. From *Cabiria*'s "Monkey" to Roberto Benigni, clowning has always been admired—even memorialized by Fellini in *Clowns* (1970) and *Fellini Satyricon*. Of all the Italian cinematic clowns, none was more prolific than the unsmilingly hilarious Totò (Antonio Clemente), who made several dozen films from the 1930s to the 1960s. In *Totò Contro Maciste* (1961), the Egyptian Totokamen fights Samson Burke playing the muscleman from *Cabiria*. Two years later, in *Totò e Cleopatra* (1963), he plays Totònius. At the film's conclusion the snake dies instead of Cleopatra. Another great Italian clown, Ettore Petrolini, is featured in an earlier Roman farce, *Nerone* (1930).

Generally speaking, the British cinema has been less fond of clowning humor than of such bawdy, verbally witty low humor characteristic of the *Carry On* series produced in the 1960s. *Carry On Cleo* (1964) was the tenth in the series. It does not quite reach the level of the earlier *Carry On* films, but Roman troops marching to "Sinister, dexter, sinister, dexter" and Antony sighing "Oh puer! Oh puer! Oh puer!" bring a chuckle to anyone who took freshman Latin. So do the names of the slave dealers, Marcus et Spencius, and Caesar's bodyguard Bilius. Because it is a British film, there are references to the homeland: the Romans complain about the damp British weather ("Caesar enjoyed the sweet smell of success and eucalyptus"), Caesar addresses the Senate while parodying Winston Churchill, and a famed warrior is attacked by a mob of fans as pseudo-Beatles music plays in the background.

Caesar is a bumbling idiot and often the butt of physical gags. He slips on a bar of soap and tumbles into Cleopatra's bath, his litter bearers carry him catastrophically under a low arch, and in the mandatory send-up of the *Ben-Hur* galley sequence, Caesar ends up "paddling his own canoe." Antony is not much better off. When Cleopatra tells him that "one bite of an asp is enough," "Tony" bites the head off the wiggling snake, makes a face, spits it out, and says "You're right!" And when Cleopatra is unrolled from the carpet she rolls and rolls across the floor until she knocks the banquet table over.

Most of the gags are verbal. A few depend on well-known historical or literary references: "I came, I saw, I conked out!" The puns are wonderfully terrible:

191   The death of Cleopatra in *Carry On Cleo* (1964). When Cleopatra (Amanda Barrie) says "one bite of an asp is enough," Antony ("Tony") bites the head off the wiggling asp, makes a face, spits it out, and says "You're right!" Caesar is played by *Carry On* regular Kenneth Williams.

BRUTUS: I must warn you, Julius: there is unrest in the Senate. There
    have been rumblings!
CAESAR: It's all that spaghetti they eat!

CAESAR: I brought you onions from Spain—
CALPURNIA: I've got some Spanish onions!
CAESAR: cheeses from Holland—
CALPURNIA: I've got Dutch cheeses!
CAESAR: and stones from far off Gaul!
SENECA: She's got Gaul stones!

SOLDIER: I'm Agrippa
CAESAR: And I know one or two holds myself!

But bas-comedy is all that *Carry On Cleo* professes to be.

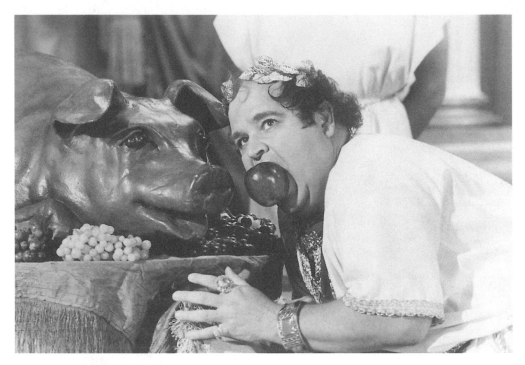

192   Dom DeLuise mugs this comic Neronian portrait in *The History of the World, Part I* (1981).
The theme of Neronian decadence pervades the Roman sequences.

In the United States an old type of historical comedy reemerged during the renascence of "ancient" films that began with *Sinbad and the Eye of the Tiger* (1977). Mel
Brooks, a student of old Hollywood comedy (as opposed to the "old" comedy of Aristophanes), revived the episodic historical comedy when he wrote and directed *The History
of the World, Part I* (1981). The film spans the Stone Age to the French Revolution and includes some thirty minutes set in ancient Rome. Brooks plays "a stand-up philosopher"
who entertains the gluttonous emperor (Dom DeLuise) with jokes like, "The Christians
are so poor, they have only one god!" Typical of Brooks's later films, many gags fall em-
barrassingly flat and/or are needlessly scatological. But there are some fine anachronisms,
as when a gladiator at the VNEMPLOYMENT INSVRANCE office is asked, "Did you kill last week?
Did you try to kill last week?" and when one character says to another, "Nuts! N V T S!"
        Greek myth gets its comical comeuppance in a number of films, beginning as
early as Georges Méliès' *Jupiter's Thunderbolts* (1903), in which a stumpy Jupiter leaps
about vigorously as his thunderbolts explode around him. Alexander Korda closed out the
silent era with *The Private Life of Helen of Troy* (1927). Korda had high hopes for this film.
Carey Wilson's script was based on John Erskine's novel of the same title, and on Sherwood's *The Road to Rome* (as were *Jupiter's Darling* and *Roman Scandals*), and the fine cast

included Maria Corda as the bored, desperate housewife Helen, and Lewis Stone as the meek Menelaus. Unfortunately, the film's modern idiom and superabundance of dialogue (titles) are unsuccessful in the silent medium. Korda was in despair over this, his last major American film, because of its lack of soundtrack. Nonetheless, the light comedy dressed in futuristic-classical costuming and sets received favorable reviews; its climactic chariot race had not yet become trite, for MGM had just released *Ben-Hur* in the previous year.

The Three Stooges poked their eye-gouging fingers into Greek myth in *The Three Stooges Meet Hercules* (1962). This late-career full-length Stooges feature shows the advanced age of Moe, Larry, and Curly Joe, but some parts of the film elicited genuine laughs from skeptical critics. The trio live in Ithaca, "not the ancient one, the New York one," but a neighboring absent-minded professor's time machine goes haywire after the utterly incompetent Stooges connect "the whoseewhatsis to the anawhosis." They land in ancient Ithaca, where Hercules is battling Ulysses. The professor guesses that they have gone back to 900 B.C. (not a particularly good guess). King Odious of Ithaca welcomes the four "Gods" from their "flying chariot," whereupon Curly Joe remembers that he has not eaten "in three thousand years.

At Odious's court Hercules (Samson Burke) immediately dislikes the three imps, but they fool him with the old open-the-door-just-before-he-breaks-it-down trick. The film speeds up as Hercules' momentum carries him across the room and into a cement wall. The more the viewer knows this is coming, the funnier it seems. Hercules finally captures the Stooges, and they are sent to the galleys. "Oh boy! We're gonna do some cookin'," says Curly Joe. The galley sequence is modeled after *Ben-Hur,* of course, but these three bearded slaves have been chained to the oar even longer than General Wallace's "number forty-one." Moe finally slips some twentieth-century tranquilizers into the drinking water, and the hortator falls asleep. Before long Moe has taken the hortator's place and is pounding out the rowing beat in a conga rhythm; everyone dances to the absurdly inappropriate syncopated music, and then an animated map of the Mediterranean shows the ship conga-ing from port to port.

In the last portions of *The Three Stooges Meet Hercules* the absent-minded professor has become a strongman. They reach the island of Rhodes (with scenes from Columbia's *The Colossus of Rhodes*), where they ask directions of an entertaining but confused shepherd (Emil Sitka). The *Rhodes Register* headline reads, "King Theseus Signs Hercules to Throw the Bull." After a fight against the Siamese Cyclops (two heads, one eye each), Hercules fights the nine-headed Hydra while Larry sells programs because "You can't tell one head from another without a program." Finally, a pie fight, with pies supplied by the Greek Humor Man, leads the four back to their flying chariot, and they return via the Crusades to modern times.

In *Hercules in the Vale of Woe,* an Italian mythological farce also released in 1962, another time machine carries two midgets back to ancient times for some unamusing weightlifting with Hercules and Maciste.

Woody Allen often injects one-line comical allusions to Greek mythology and tragedy into his films, and his "Oedipus Wrecks" in the trilogy *New York Stories* (1989) carries an amusing titular pun through a short that focuses on the odd, then divine, relationship between Sheldon Mills (Allen) and his Jewish mother. In *Mighty Aphrodite* (1995) he has one of his best mythological lines ("Achilles only had an Achilles' heel; I have an entire Achilles body!") and takes one step further, actually including a Greek chorus filmed at the ancient Greek theater at Taormina, Sicily. Standing next to them is Jocasta (Olympia Dukakis), who by the film's conclusion is seen sitting with and passionately kissing Oedipus. The blind seer Teiresias (Jack Warden) makes an appearance as well, telling Allen that he "saw" that his wife had a lover: "You had to be blind not to see it!"

Another sequence within a film otherwise not set in antiquity is the Birth of Venus sequence in Terry Gilliam's *The Adventures of Baron Munchausen* (1989). After a large scallop shell opens mechanically—the setting suggests a seventeenth-century theater—a naked Venus (Uma Thurman) is revealed inside and quickly covered by the Graces. Then her husband Hephaestus (Oliver Reed) crushes a lump of coal into a diamond for her. She tells him how sweet he is but then tosses it carelessly into a box of diamonds, quite bored with his one trick.

At least two animated shorts have spoofed Greek myth. In *Neptune's Nonsense* (1936), Felix the Cat visits the underwater palace of the pot-bellied, red-nosed, tilted-crowned Neptune and hears the God of the Sea play "Aloha-e" on his trident. In *Greek Mirthology* (1954), Popeye the Sailor explains to his nephews Peepeye, Pipeye, Poopeye, and Pupeye how the power of spinach was discovered. His great-great-great-great-great-grandfather Hercules—Popeye in sandals and white robes—used to snort garlic to reach his peak strength. But when an ancient Bluto poured chlorophyll on Hercules' garlic, he knocked his defenseless foe into a nearby field. By Jupiter, this field was a spinach patch, and the rest is "hysterical fact." Just before Popeye knocks Bluto "for a row of ashcans" (literally), he rhymes,

> A strange weed this spinach must be.
> It gave me back my vitaliky.

The Old Testament has had its untraditional treatments, too. They begin with the Italian *A Modern Samson* (1907) and an animated *Adam Raises Cain* (1920). In the sound era comes one of the true gems of filmdom, *The Green Pastures* (1936). The film originated in Roark Bradford's stories collected as *Ol' Man Adam an' His Chillun',* which Marc Connelly adapted into a Pulitzer Prize–winning play (1930). When Warner Brothers purchased the film rights, the studio had to pay $100,000 to Connelly, who then became the film's director; at the time this was the largest sum ever paid for the movie rights to a literary work, except for *Ben-Hur,* of course. First Al Jolson and then Paul Robeson were sought for the role of "de Lawd," but Rex Ingram, an actor who had

193   Popeye spoofs antiquity, playing Hercules at a crucial moment in humankind's history— the moment at which this Hellenized Popeye discovers what spinach can do for his "vitaliky." Even Steve Reeves and Arnold Schwarzenegger would have trouble outflexing these zigguratic biceps.

loinclothed his way into film as the cannibal chief in *Tarzan of the Apes,* landed the lead in the all-black cast. Warner Brothers immediately began inventing and publicizing Ingram's past: an M.D. from Northwestern, Phi Beta Kappa, letters in basketball, football, baseball, and track, and a stint at bacteriological research, but all this was typical thirties Hollywood fantasy.

The Green Pastures cannot really be called a farce, for that term implies some disrespect for the subject. *The Green Pastures,* however, shows all due respect for the Bible, even amid the hilarity. Like DeMille's 1923 *The Ten Commandments,* this film transports its setting back to biblical times when a modern character—in this case a Louisiana Sunday school teacher—reads or tells about the Bible. The black dialect and the idiom are stereotyped but poetic, and the humble acting carries the script perfectly. Sample Genesis 1:1: "Yo' got to getcho' minds fixed. There wasn't no Rampart Street; there wasn't no Canal Street; there wasn't no Louisiana; there wasn't nothin' on earth—on occasion da reason dere wasn't no earth; da whole world wasn't nothin' but a mess o' bad weather. Den one day, de Lawd said, 'I think I'll make me some places.'"

Heaven in *The Green Pastures* is a "perpetual fish-fry with ten-cent seegars." All the white-winged angels, led by a gentle Gabriel (Oscar Polk), stand around watching de Lawd "pass miracles." One of these miracles is Earth. When de Lawd literally decides to make man "in his own image," Ingram doubles his role and plays Adam. Then de Lawd asks Adam if he will be all right, and Adam says, "I guess I'll make out once I know de ropes." A little later de Lawd passes by some earthly flowers. He asks them how they are making out, and their squeaky voices reply, "Weze O.K., Lawd." In other charming anachronisms, before the great flood de Lawd is disappointed that his earthlings are not going to church on Sunday. Then he hears one man calling his name. De Lawd is glad until he sees that his supplicant is praying for a good roll in the crap game he is playing. "Prayin' befo' they gamble!" says the shocked deity, "and with frozen dice!"

The flood scene is just as whimsical. First Noah (Eddie Anderson) feels a twitch in his knee, so he suspects that it might rain. When de Lawd visits Noah and instructs him to build an ark, Noah, as pious as he is, tries to convince de Lawd that he will need one or two kegs of liquor "for medicine." Noah has a thirty-foot-long list of livestock that he is to take aboard his "ark"—his clapboard farmhouse supplies the superstructure—but he cannot find any aardvarks. "We'll have to order two o' dem from de Lawd." The animals are then lined up in alphabetical order with identifying signs on their backs or on their cages. Aardvarks, asses, baboons, bears, cows, all the way to the zebras (donkeys with painted stripes!) fill the humble procession into the shanty-boat.

The Moses sequence emphasizes the miracles in *Exodus*. First de Lawd shows to Moses (Frank Wilson in a checkered shirt and trousers) the bush "dat ain't burnt up." When Moses exclaims that "dat was da beatenist," de Lawd assures him it was just a trick and "I'ze gonna make you da best tricker in da whole world." So much for the miracles of the Bible and DeMille's special effects. Pharaoh is thinking up something mean to do, "and there ain't nothin' meaner than killin' babies." But Moses will put a stop to this. He changes his staff into a snake, so Pharaoh calls for the "head tricker in da land of Egypt." Moses frustrates Pharaoh when he makes this charlatan look bad, and then he threatens: "Yo' ain't gonna like it no better when I strike down the oldest boy in every one of yo' people's houses." The Pharaoh replies angrily, "Listen, *I'ze* Pharaoh; *I* do da strikin' down aroun' here."

Babylon makes its appearance, too. Here the wealth and splendor is depicted by the Babylonian king who wears a jeweled tuxedo. But *The Green Pastures* is not all dialect and gentle humor. There are deeply meaningful messages on piety, goodness, and "moisy." If religion ever can be assimilated in bites as sweet as candy, *The Green Pastures* is the finest theological mouthful since "De Lawd made him some places."

Disney's semianimated (stop-action) *Noah's Ark* (1959) deserves mention here as well. The latter's rhyming script blossoms several times into such amusing musical numbers as "The Maiden Cruise of the Good Ship *Noah's Ark*" and "Love One Another." The characters are made of cutouts, corks, thread spools, and other odds and ends, and the Disney technicians (Bill Justice, director) miraculously transform these humdrum articles into living, singing, and dancing giraffes and hippopotamuses.

Mickey Rooney acted in and codirected a dream fantasy based on the Garden of Eden scene in Genesis, *The Private Lives of Adam and Eve* (1961). A bus headed for Reno faces such bad weather that the passengers have to spend the night in a country church; they all have a common dream, and this dream transports them back into Eden. With Mickey Rooney as the Devil, Mamie Van Doren as Eve, and Martin Milner as Adam, the film does not have to go far beyond its casting to evoke some laughs, whether intentional or not.

The renascence in the late 1970s inspired the British Monty Python comedy troupe to follow its successful medieval farce, *Monty Python and the Holy Grail* (1975),

194   Noah (Eddie Anderson) reads his checklist as he loads the animal kingdom onto his Louisiana shanty in *The Green Pastures* (1936). The zebras he eventually loads are donkeys with painted stripes.

with the ancient farce *Life of Brian* (1979). This biting comedy broke new ground in lampooning not just the ancient Romans but their rule in the province of Judea during the early first century A.D. The story follows the life and death of a Jew born in a manger in Bethlehem and crucified by the Romans—but not the figure typically associated with those biographical details. Christ appears only for a few seconds while giving the Sermon on the Mount; religious groups nonetheless picketed and boycotted in an effort to prevent the film's release.

    The opening of the film borrows from both the MGM versions of *Ben-Hur* by following the Star of Bethlehem and the three Wise Men to the manger. The Magi encounter the infant Brian's falsetto-voiced mother (Terry Jones), who thinks that a balm (myrrh) is a dangerous animal. Years later Brian witnesses the Sermon on the Mount, although the noisily argumentative group he stands amid at the back of the crowd think they hear "Blessed are the cheesemakers." The film proceeds from one farcical sketch to the next. False-bearded women come forth to stone a blasphemer, and Brian receives a Latin lesson from a centurion after writing the graffito "Romans Go Home!" (Romani,

195   Graham Chapman about to become a false prophet in *Life of Brian* (1979). Though jovial in spirit and not a direct sendup of Jesus, the film was picketed and boycotted by religious groups. "Blessed are the cheesemakers."

ite domum) ungrammatically as "Romanes eunt domus." During an afternoon at the arena, a slave picks up spilled human organs and hides a ring (with the finger and arm still attached) under his cloak, Brian hawks such Roman delicacies as "wren's livers . . . jaguar's ear lobes, wolf's nipple chips . . . and Tuscany fried bats," a gladiator pursuing a cowardly prisoner has a cardiac arrest and dies, and the anti-Roman People's Front of Judea—not to be confused with the Judean People's Front or the Judean Popular People's Front—has a politically correct meeting in which Stan (Eric Idle) insists on becoming a woman named Loretta.

The People's Front of Judea hates Rome even as they are forced to acknowledge —when someone defiantly asks, "What have the Romans ever done for us?"—the advantages of an aqueduct, sanitation, roads, irrigation, medicine, education, wine, public baths, and public safety, as well as peace. Their night raid into the Roman quarters to kidnap Pilate's wife ends in a quarrel with the Campaign for a Free Galilee, which is carrying out an identical plan. In the ensuing melee, everyone in both factions is knocked out except for Brian, who is led to a prison cell. There he encounters a chained, crazed, wizened prisoner (Michael Palin) who has learned such great respect for the Romans that he loves to be tortured by them. As Brian is then interviewed by Pontius Pilate, Pilate's speech impediment distracts the "rwapscallion Rwoman centurwions" and allows Brian to escape, only to be picked up in an anachronistic, *Star Wars*–like spaceship.

Back on earth, Brian attempts to hide in the market quarter by buying a fake beard, but the vendor, affronted by his hasty acceptance of the price, insists on teaching him how to haggle. Then, in one of the film's cleverest sequences, the crowd in the Quarter of False Prophets at first quibbles with every word out of Brian's mouth, but once the Romans pass by and he tries to escape, the listeners take every one of his words as prophetic and every one of his actions as a miracle. When he vehemently denies that he is the Messiah, a follower (John Cleese) exclaims, "I say you are! And I should know: I've followed a few!"

The "passion" of Brian follows, beginning with the Passover address Pilate makes to the "rwabble," with the able assistance of his Roman friend Biggus Dickus. Biggus reveals his own speech impediment when he offers to help: "I may be of thome aththithtanth if there ith a thudden crithith!" The Roman who organizes the crucifixions treats the prisoners as if they are going to a parade; a Simon figure offers to "shoulder the burden" of one prisoner and ends up being crucified himself; and a Jew already tied to his cross argues for the right to be crucified in a purely Jewish section but is silenced when the centurion in charge says, "Anyone who objects, hands up!" The People's Front of Judea reads Brian a thank-you commendation for his martyrdom, the Judean People's Front suicide squad commits suicide, and when Pilate offers to "rwelease Brwian," everyone on a cross claims, à la *Spartacus,* "I'm Brian!" (including the aforementioned Jew, who exclaims, "I'm Brian . . . and so's my wife!"). The film ends with all the crucified prisoners singing Eric Idle's "Always Look on the Bright Side of Life."

An inferior American imitation of *Life of Brian* was *Wholly Moses* (1980). Dudley Moore plays a tourist in the Holy Land who finds an ancient scroll and reads it into a filmlong flashback. Moore plays Herschel, a Jewish child who is always one step behind Moses, marrying a different one of Jethro's daughters, climbing Mount Sinai just seconds after Moses has finished, and asking Pharaoh to "let my people go" a day or two after Moses has already taken them to freedom. The cast is good, with Dudley Moore between his two most memorable roles, *10* (1979) and *Arthur* (1981), and cameos by Richard Pryor (Pharaoh), John Houseman (the chief angel assigned to Sodom), and John Ritter (the disheartened, liberal Devil). But director Gary Weis and writer Guy Thomas had very little feature-film experience, so even when Moore does his shtick on a chariot ride, there is not much to work with. Nonetheless, almost every disappointing comedy has its moments, and here there is one during Moses' plague, when Moore's father Hyssop (James Coco) has the frustrating job of sweeping leaping frogs into a dustpan.

The ancient Orient had its musical modifications in *Night in Paradise* (1946). This $2 million Universal extravaganza based on George Hellman's novel *Peacock's Feather* involves the fabled Aesop (Turhan Bey), King Croesus of Lydia (Thomas Gomez), Princess Deleri of Persia (Merle Oberon), and Queen Atossa of Phrygia (Gale Sondergaard) in a romantic quadrangle, circa 560 B.C. Aesop visits Croesus as the ambassador from the Greek island of Samos, and he appears at first in a heavy beard, long, silvery hair, a flat nose, and woolly eyebrows. Deleri soon learns to her amorous delight that this is a mere disguise — Aesop believes his wisdom will carry greater force if it has the "experience" of age — and that Aesop is really a handsome young man and, soon afterward, dashing bedside lover. The two are discovered and are brought to Delphi, where they face their deaths. This relatively plain but well-acted story is set amid rather elegant classical settings on Hollywood soundstages. Although the sets are classically styled, they look less like ancient Lydia than like

Miami. But this is Hollywood romance, and historical authenticity has as much claim to the realm of Hollywood romance as does the Circus Maximus to Ringling Brothers.

Egypt has produced its merrymakers, too. Heckle and Jeckle had a brief animated romp through *King Tut's Tomb* (1950). Naturally there had to be a joke about the word *mummy,* and so a sign says, "Do Not Disturb the Mummies—or the Daddies." After the talking magpies have turned the steering wheel of their flying carpet toward King Tut's tomb, they are almost scared out of their safari hats when Tut's ghost comes to life accompanied by an all-mummy marching band and a twelve-hump camel. The Three Stooges' *Mummy's Dummies* (1948) has slightly more psuedohistorical content. Set in the reign of King Rooten-tooten of Egypt, the film starts off with Moe, Larry, and Shemp as proprietors of a chariot-repair shop. They try to find "something in a used chariot for the gentleman" who comes in, but only after they humorously swindle him out of four hundred shekels for a two-wheeled, horse-drawn lemon do they find out that the swindlee was Ranames, the captain of the palace guard. They are, of course, arrested.

Rooten-tooten (Vernon Dent) has a toothache, and Shemp offers to extract "the rear bicuspidor," but he pulls out Moe's tooth by mistake. After much nose-twisting, Rooten-tooten's tooth is successfully extracted, and the Stooges are appointed as royal chamberlains. (Larry: But suppose he wants us to pull out another tooth? Shemp: We'll cross that bridge when we come to it. Larry: Heh, heh, not bad. Moe: Not good [bonk].) The Stooges hear that someone has been stealing tax money, and they find it hidden downstairs in the tomb of King Put-and-Take-It. A fairly tight chase scene develops, highlighted by Shemp's impersonation of a mummy. When he is caught, his pursuer pulls the end of the bandages and twirls Shemp like a top (in fast motion).

One last tongue-in-cheek approach to antiquity came in the earlier scenes of Warner Brothers' *The Story of Mankind* (1957). Irwin Allen produced this star-studded peculiarity based on Hendrick van Loon's best-seller. Allen decided that "history is still something like hearing a joke for the second time. The punch has gone out of it, so we have added a gimmick."[2] The gimmick was a newly invented super-H-bomb that could wipe out the world ("and cause a housing shortage up here," say the angels), and a trial is held in heaven to decide whether the human race is worth saving. The prosecutor is a devilish Mr. Scratch (Vincent Price), and representing humankind is "the spirit of man" (Ronald Colman). The evidence comes from history, and so vignette after vignette of human history appears before the judge (Sir Cedric Hardwicke) and the audience.

Pharaoh Khufu (John Carradine) is the second witness, who apparently did more evil than good in forcing "one million men" to build his pyramid. Fortunately for us and for Irwin Allen's bank account, several scenes of pyramid building from Warner's *Land of the Pharaohs* were available. Moses (Francis X. Bushman) also makes an appearance, as does a battle sequence from Warner's *Helen of Troy.* Plato, Aristotle, and Hippocrates are given a few seconds each, but then we see more "evil ancients": Cleopatra (Virginia Mayo) hugs Julius Caesar while picking his pocket, and Nero (Peter Lorre) is called one of Mr. Scratch's "most talented disciples." The fat, aging Lorre does a decent job in portraying an insane tyrant whose jaded senses feel some remorse for Rome, burning needlessly in the distance. Incidentally, humankind is acquitted at the film's end, no thanks to our ancient entries.

The history of the cinema cannot be written in terms

of intellectual works alone.

—PIERRE LEPROHON, *THE ITALIAN CINEMA*

Punching, wrestling, bending, breaking, riding, running, killing, wounding, hurling, pushing, fighting, stabbing, grunting, yelling, flexing, and bulging, the muscularly heroic gladiators now parade at last out of the arena's dungeons to do battle on their very own blood-stained cinematic sand. The afternoon's spectacle has already shown those somber Romans, Greeks, Christians, and Jews who were trained in the urban schools of pure literature or sincere drama. Gone are the high-salaried stars, the professionals so carefully nurtured with so much money and time—that Judean charioteer, the Nazarene carpenter, the Hebrew kings. The crowd cries for quick action, tons of raw beef and quivering muscles on which their lusting eyes can chomp. They call repeatedly for Hercules, for Goliath, for Samson, for Maciste. By the gods, they will have them!

In 1957, the year *Hercules* was released, only ten costume dramas were produced in Italy. By 1960 there were thirty-seven of these cloak-and-sandal costumers, and in the next four years more than 150 were produced in Italy, or by Italian companies in conjunction with French, Spanish, German, American, Egyptian, or Yugoslavian companies. The *Hercules* phenomenon—the $120,000 film that earned $18 million—mushroomed into a major form of crowd-pleasing entertainment, and before the Italian film industry shifted over to the wild West, 180 films sent Hercules and his amply bicepsed companions to thirteenth-century A.D. China *(Samson and the Seven Miracles of the World)*, to the Navarre of Philip II *(Samson and the Slave Queen)*, to the Inca empire *(Hercules Against the Sons of the Sun)*, to modern Manhattan *(Hercules in New York)*, and in the opposite chronological direction to Ice Age Druids *(Fire*

Monsters Against the Son of Hercules). Any age, any place that already boasted of a hero or desperately needed one was fair game for Italian filmmakers; any innocent young prince or princess, any oppressed people would have their human paragon of strength and justice; any evil despot, any ravaging monster would have its deserved downfall. Might would make right—"might" in its most physical sense, "right" in its most simplistic sense.

When American viewers got a look at many of these films in the early 1960s (and later, on television), reaction was mixed. The critics sharpened their pencils whenever that day's assignment chained them to an encounter with *Amazons of Rome* or *Atlas Against the Cyclops.* Here would be a chance to create some unforgettable metaphors, some beautifully hyphenated slurs. It was not even a question of taste to censure movies such as these; few critics would be searching for truffles in this swine-filled forest of gladiator films. Most of the films were bad; reviewing one was a matter of finding either one or two redeeming qualities or, failing that, the most lavishly cruel vocabulary.

The public and less demanding critics found enjoyment in them. Every era has had its genre of film that has an inexplicable grasp on the public, whether the B-Western or the slasher flick, the kung-fu kickfest or the beach party romance. In the early 1960s it was the muscleman epic. Sometimes moviegoers just want to be unintellectually and inartistically entertained. For many, a Saturday night can offer no better cinematic diversion than a low-budget horror film; for others an Elvis film or the soapiest opera will keep the refrigerator door closed tightly, except during commercial interruptions or Pause button VCR interludes. Such a small and humble niche in the great wall of filmdom is all the muscleman epics wish to punch out for themselves with their mighty fists.

Ricardo Freda, a director of five of these muscleman epics *(Giants of Thessaly, Samson and the Seven Miracles of the World, The Seventh Sword, The Burning of Rome,* and *The Witch's Curse),* explains part of the fascination with the muscleman epic: "What I am interested in is the hero: mankind in times of greatness, in times of war. History is full of possibilities for enthralling scenarios."[1] The hero, of course, was one of the major fascinations of the B-Western and many other genres as well. One can find even Aristotelian *catharsis* in watching a man—be it the Lone Ranger, Steve Reeves, or the high-tech action hero of the nineties—who first suffers physical defeat but then uses his superb physical or mental skills to overcome evil and set all in its proper order.

The means by which the ancient hero overcomes this evil with good is the greatest part of the fascination: performing mighty feats of strength, leading rebellions of slaves or oppressed peoples, outwitting the sinister tyrants, escaping near-death by leaping over one hundred–foot cliffs, and invoking the will of the just gods. All this belongs to a fantasy world, a world that the film viewer will dissociate from his world, a world that he or she can enjoy because it does not have to be believable. Build an ancient palace, no matter how cheap the construction, and dress a few hundred husky, bearded men in cuirasses, greaves, helmets, shields, and swords, put them on horseback or on chariot platforms, and shoot all this by the blue Mediterranean with its beckoning olive trees, and one huge, anatomically majestic hero does not look so absurd when he lifts a tree out of the ground by its roots *(Hercules)*. Belief and sophistication are not in question here. It is only cheap entertainment. Whether one laughs at it or laughs with it, it can be entertaining. Then, of course, some movies must also be made for the children.

The muscleman epics had many common denominators. Most were made in Italy between 1959 and 1965, though their legacy has reappeared each decade—with Arnold Schwarzenegger's film debut in *Hercules in New York* (1970), Lou Ferrigno's two Hercules films of 1983 and 1985, and the syndicated television series *Hercules: The Legendary Journeys* of the 1990s. Most of them used similarly imaginative but plastic sets: the drippy, stalactite-filled cave of the monster, the garish bedroom of the wicked queen, the plain stone walls and wooden tables of the local inn, or the barren throne room of the no-goodnik despot. The bright and shining costumes were almost always supplied by Casa d'Arte Firenze, and a "fencing master" acknowledged in the credits usually directed the wobbling swordsmen's wobbling swords.

It is a rare muscleman epic that lacks a chase sequence, be it on chariot, horseback, or foot. Nor will a wrestling match be omitted, for how else will the hero have a chance to (1) defeat another human giant in hand-to-hand combat and (2) show off his latissimus dorsi? The wrestling match is often complemented by another bout, this one with a hideous, virgin-devouring or Hell-guarding beast. Sword fights are an absolute must, and they generally demonstrate that the fencing master's methods are unsound or his students slow. One of these fights is bound to be on horseback, and another is bound to take place in a local inn. In the latter locale he lifts an eight-foot oak table to use as a shield; when he is rushed by eight or fifteen spindle-legged opponents, the table-shield quickly becomes a club, good for knocking down, or knocking out, all eight or fifteen assailants in one swing. If no table is readily available, the hero tears out a huge wooden beam from the wall or ceiling to use as a battering ram or a lance. When this alternative plan fails, the hero still knows how to rip a column from its place and bring down a ceiling on his adversaries.

Chains come in handy, too. A few whirls around the head keep opponents at a safe distance. Of course, access to chains usually requires temporary imprisonment for the hero, but prison escape only increases his glory and popularity. The escape itself can be an outside or an inside job: friends can make a torch-carrying night raid on the prison, or the incarcerated hero can rouse up all the unjustly convicted criminals in the prison and lead a revolt against the pointy-bearded tyrant who unjustly put them all in there.

Somewhere in his ninety minutes of exploits the hero will come across some sort of machinery. Either his companions can rig a veritable Gatling arrow gun, or his opponents can invent mechanized or at least systematized methods of torture. For example, the hero must master one form of forced combat popular among despots, the duel on a thin platform above sharpened stakes, ferocious beasts, or blazing fire. Meanwhile, the hero's best friend or father must grow an inch or two on the torture rack. Where machines are lacking or

196   This shot from Sergio Leone's *The Colossus of Rhodes* (1961) reveals a hellish mouth-portal and chains à la *Cabiria*. The dark-robed individual underneath the portal's left fang—there he is! The pointy-bearded despot! The Babylonian-ish statue to the right automatically signifies "Orient" in these cloak-and-sandal films.

ineffective by themselves, trickery can be applied. Drugging the hero's drink is a favorite ploy by the pointy-bearded tyrant's pointy-breasted mistress, and the shifty-eyed, high and mitered priest can often maneuver the temporarily unwary hero toward the temple's trap door. The hero himself is not at a loss for tricks, of course; *mens sana in corpore sano*. He knows enough to hide inside an empty wine cask when the tyrant's troops come to the inn to arrest him.

Long nonverbal treks through forests, deserts, and seaside sands appear in most of these sword-and-sandal muscleman epics; they give the viewer a respite from the tense action and sophisticated palace dialogue. Coincidentally, they are easy on the budget as well. The hero usually finds a flaming village along the way, and amid the beaten, stabbed, and bloodied bodies he can often count on finding his aged father or his best friend or his wizened mother or his fiancée's father or his friend's friend or his aged mentor. This tragedy is hard to bear, but the tyrant's troops will pay for it. One or two of these enemy soldiers

197   Pointy-bearded despots often have their own private arenas in the muscleman epics, and here they conduct systematized torture. To the right of this shot from *Gladiators Seven* (1964) is an old favorite—the narrow platform suspended above sharpened stakes. Notice that neither corpse fell on a stake. To the left, another favorite: an inept firing squad consisting of the despot's bowling-pin troops. The spectators in the first few rows have rather poor seats for their drachmas. The entire setup is often used for a muscleman film's "test."

can be sure that they will be bodily picked up and hurled head-on at twelve of their bowling-pin comrades, and another one or two will meet hideous, floating deaths in the palace's *impluvium* (shallow pool). Still another soldier will be thrown off a balcony or cliff or bridge or anything high enough to ensure that his desperate scream will last a full second. Yet this soldier's cacophonous scream will not be heard alone, for the countless punch-induced *ugh*s, *aggh*s, and *bwah*s of his comrades will lead up symphonically to his climactic, descending *yaaaaaaahhhhh*.

　　To make matters worse for the opposition, when the hero tires of throwing soldiers around, he often starts on the huge stones, "stones that no two mortals such as they are today could lift," as Homer wrote. Tree trunks and wine barrels will do, but the pointy-bearded tyrant's soldiers seem to fear the rock-throwing most. In an artistic burst the hero

198   Muscleman heroes are wont to throw things. In this scene from *The Invincible Gladiator* (1961) Richard Harrison tosses his bald opponent (in gladiatorial arm-covering armor), no doubt at a dozen or so of his bowling-pin comrades. Most films of the genre have a shaved-headed character.

199   This time Reg Park hurls a huge, er, um, *thing* at an opponent in *Hercules in the Haunted World* (1961). The drippy stalactite atmosphere is typical of neomythological muscleman films.

200   Now the tables are turned. This time the pointy-bearded despot tosses a few hostages from the ramparts of Thebes in *Hercules Unchained* (1959), the sequel to *Hercules*. The plastic armor, cheap costuming, crude architecture, and gratuitous gruesomeness are hallmarks of the genre. The relief carvings on the gates of Thebes originate with *Cabiria*.

finishes off these endeavors by tossing an oil jar onto a fallen torch. The room explodes into flames, and the hero escapes to his sweetheart in safety. One last shot of the death and destruction, be it Druid village, Roman inn, or mythological palace, rarely fails to reveal one of the strewn dead bearing a huge one-dollar-per-day-for-the-extras smile on his face.

The characters whom the hero befriends, rescues, or opposes are fairly consistent from land to land and from century to century. The chesty hero has a charmingly innocent and chesty girlfriend with a name like Andromeda, Iole, Fulvia, Sylvia, Marcia, or Penelope, and she is adept at virtuously bathing the hero's wounds (generally only flesh wounds on the shoulder) and keeping her plunging-necked tunic from plunging too far. She is usually blond, even if she is Egyptian, Greek, or Armenian. Her counterpart, the evil mistress of the ruling despot, has dark hair, a lizard's eyes, the charm of a snake, and the hots for the hero. Her dark-bearded lover is the despot par excellence. He loves death, oppression, torture, extortion, starvation, usurpation, depravity, slavery, and a sleazy woman. He rarely leaves his palace, for he fears what the stone-throwing hero might do to him on the outside, yet he has total command of his bowling-pin troops. Of course, the sinister member of the

201   One other genre constant —sex. Each sword-and-sandal film worth its weight in celluloid must display a seductress, preferably with much side, back, shoulder, and thigh exposed, as in this scene from *Aphrodite, Goddess of Love* (1958). Lerna (Isabelle Corey) seems to enjoy her work.

film need not necessarily be the king himself. If the king is a weak and unassuming simpleton, his adviser, high priest, or an ambitious son can fill the bill, though this usually necessitates the termination of the unsuspecting king's vital functions.

The hero himself has the pleasure of his male companion's devotion. This companion can be of two sorts: either a mighty, meaty specimen like the hero himself, or a wimpy comedian who cannot lift stones or wine casks but who can instead poke soldiers in the behind with his dagger or bonk them over the head with ceramic jugs. In either case he is handy to have around. He also takes on the responsibility of looking after the hero's innocent girlfriend while the hero goes on one of his escapades, but the companion often is surprised by the despot's soldiers and unwillingly allows himself and the girl to be captured. Fortunately, the innocent girl often has a pipsqueaky little brother who bites his way to freedom and runs to tell the hero that his woman is about to be ravaged by that pointy beard.

The climax of the picture is now at hand. Either the hero himself, his father, his friend, or his woman has been captured by the tyrant, and it is the hero's duty to punch his way out of this paper bag. Often the tyrant congenially offers to free his captive if and only if he can survive "the test." This test can include a chariot race, a wrestling match with some large, semihuman brute, a battle with lions, gorillas, alligators, or the like, combat with a gladiator, or a massive free-for-all with a whole slew of gladiators wielding swords or spears. In the free-for-all the hero finally reveals the aces up his rarely worn, muscle-covering tunic: the enemy charges with a spear, but the hero grabs the spear with both hands, hoists the still-clinging assailant over his back, and kills him with his own spear. Lacking weapons, strangling the opponent with nineteen-inch biceps is the best approach, though full nelsons occasionally break the opponent's neck. In the long run, though, throwing the foe off a balcony or rampart is the most efficient method. At any rate, with the despot disposed of, more often than not a victim of his own crocodiles or tortures, the hero and his beloved wave good-bye to the happily-ever-after, disenthralled townspeople and ride off into a Mediterranean sunset.

The cinematic muscleman began his interminable quests with the 1912 film version of *Quo Vadis?*, which introduced Ursus, the strong and faithful companion of Lygia and her family. He bare-handedly battles a huge bull in the arena, and by killing the bull he saves the naked Lygia, who has been tied to a stake. This scene can be seen as the source of "the test" in the muscleman epics. *Quo Vadis?* also provides "ancient" filmdom with its first wimpy and comical character: Chilon, the bent, ragged, impishly humorous go-between, who set the precedent for *Cabiria*'s Monkey as well as Asclepius in the 1957 *Hercules,* numerous other early-1960s unheroic comedians, and Iolaus in the televised Hercules series. *Cabiria* borrowed its strongman from *Quo Vadis?*, replacing Ursus with Maciste, who was played by Bartolomeo Pagano, a tall, brawny man who had formerly been a dock worker. Pagano and others then went on to film *The Marvelous Maciste* (1915), *Maciste Alpino* (1916), *Maciste Bersagliere* (1916), *Maciste Contro la Morte* (1916), *Maciste Contro Maciste* (1917), *Maciste Supera Maciste* (1917), *Maciste Sonnambulo* (1918), *Maciste in Vacanza* (1920), *Maciste Detective* (1923), *Maciste Imperatore* (1924), *Maciste e la Regina dell'Argento* (1925), *Maciste all'Inferno* (1925), *Maciste nella Gabbia dei Leoni* (1926), *Maciste Contro lo Sceicco* (1926), and still others. Some of these films were set in modern or at least nonancient times, a variation that set the precedent for the later Hercules, Maciste, Samson, and Goliath films set in the Caribbean, South America, China, and elsewhere.

The Montana native Steve Reeves was Pagano's successor a generation later. Reeves, who had won the Mr. World and Mr. Universe contests in the late 1940s, began making films in 1953 and found stardom in the Italian *Hercules* in 1957. Reeves had dark hair, a noble profile, a trim but impressive physique with clear muscular definition in some ways unsurpassed by any of the later strongmen. Reeves never quite mastered the nuances of acting, but he went on to film the sequel *Hercules Unchained* (1959) and then *Goliath and the Barbarians* (1959), *Giant of Marathon* (1959), *The Thief of Bagdad* (1960), *The Last Days of Pompeii* (1960), *Duel of the Titans* (1961), *Morgan the Pirate* (1961), *Last Glory of Troy* (1962), *The Trojan Horse* (1962), *Son of Spartacus* (1962), and a few more. He retired in the late 1960s.

Duel of the Titans, a reasonably faithful film treatment of the founding of Rome by Romulus and Remus—it is no more absurd than Livy's wolf-nursing account—required the services of a second muscleman actor. Enter Gordon Scott, a former drill instructor, military policeman, fireman, and Las Vegas lifeguard who was discovered poolside and invited to revitalize the Tarzan film subgenre in 1955. After six well-received Tarzan features, Scott appeared as Remus opposite Reeves's Romulus and went on to play Maciste, Hercules, and other brawnies in nine films, including *A Queen for Caesar* (1962), *Hero of Babylon* (1963), *Coriolanus: Hero Without a Country* (1962), and the 1965 TV pilot *Hercules and the Princess of Troy.*

202   Many of the musclemen were larger or thicker than Steve Reeves, but none had his definition or proportions. Reeves's sword-and-sandal flicks made a huge impact in the United States and Italy. This shot from *Son of Spartacus* (1962) shows a few more constants of the muscleman genre: the chesty hero (Reeves), his slightly less chesty companion, and his chesty but innocent girlfriend. The three of them will, of course, spearhead a revolt against a tyrant—in this case Crassus.

The proliferation of muscleman epics in 1960–1961 set the table for a number of other beefcakes. Mark Forrest appeared in *Hercules Against the Mongols* (1960) but is best known for reintroducing the Maciste character in *Maciste in the Valley of the King* (1960). The Maciste revival was directed by Carlo Campogalliani, who had already brought back an ancient biblical strongman in *Goliath and the Barbarians* with Steve Reeves (also released as *Son of Samson*). Campogalliani added another long-lost hero to his roster with *Ursus* (1961), resurrecting the strongman from *Quo Vadis?* For the Ursus role he used Ed Fury, who had played a bit part in *South Pacific* (1958). Fury played Ursus in two more films, *Ursus in the Valley of the Lions* (1961) and *Ursus in the Land of Fire* (1963). Fury also portrayed Maciste in *Maciste Against the Sheik* (1962) and was Colossus as well in *Colossus and the Amazons* (1960).

With Hercules, Goliath, Ursus, Maciste, Samson, and Colossus now active, along with Roger Corman's *Atlas* (1960), roles opened up for Kirk Morris, in Mario Mattoli's *Maciste Contro Ercole nella Valle dei Guai* (1961), *Colossus and the Headhunters* (1962), *Samson and the Sea Beasts* (1963), *Maciste at the Court of the Czar* (1963), *Maciste in Hell* (1963), *Hercules, Samson, and Ulysses* (1963), and *Devil of the Desert Against the Son of Hercules* (*Anthar l'invincibile*, 1964); for Brad Harris, in *The Fury of Hercules* (1960), *Goliath Against the Giants* (1962), and *The Last Days of Herculaneum* (1962); for Reg Park, in *Hercules and the Captive Women* (1961), *Hercules in the Haunted World* (1961), and *Hercules, Prisoner of Evil* (also known as *Ursus, the Terror of the Kirghiz,* 1964), and for the powerful Dan Vadis, in *The Rebel Gladiators* (1963), *The Ten Gladiators* (1963), *The Triumph of Hercules* (or *Hercules and the Ten Avengers,* 1964), *Triumph of the Ten Gladiators* (1964), and *Spartacus and the Ten Gladiators* (1964). Harris appeared two decades later with Lou Ferrigno in *Hercules* (1983), and both Vadis and Morris appeared in Ferrigno's *The Seven Magnificent Gladiators* (1983), but otherwise the late-1970s renascence hardly affected the Italian movie industry.

Samson Burke, after appearing in *Vengeance of Ursus* (1961), turned to comedy in the next year with *Totò Contro Maciste* and *The Three Stooges Meet Hercules.* Some of the musclemen took on descriptive pseudonyms. Before he was known to television viewers as *Mission Impossible* strongman Willy Armitage, Peter Lupus debuted as Rock Stevens in one of the Frankie Avalon–Annette Funicello beach-party films (*Muscle Beach Party,* 1964), then used the same alias in *Goliath at the Conquest of Damascus* (1964) and *Hercules and the Tyrants of Babylon* (1964). Sergio Ciani adopted the iron-hard Americanized name Alan Steel while starring in *Samson and the Slave Queen* (1963), *Samson and the Treasure of the Incas* (1964), *Hercules and the Masked Rider* (1963), *Hercules Against Rome* (1964), *Hercules* [or *Maciste*] *Against the Moon Men* (1964), and the all-star feature *Ercole Sansone Maciste e Ursus gli Invincibili* (1964).

All the musclemen of antiquity were summoned to carry these scores of barechested plots in the early 1960s, and it mattered little whom the film was about. "Maciste" might appear as "Goliath," "Samson," "the son of Hercules," "the son of Samson," or "Colossus." *Maciste nella Terra dei Ciclopi* (1961) can also be found under the titles *Atlas Against the Cyclops* and *Monster from the Unknown World,* and *Samson and the Seven Miracles of the World* (1961) is also known as *Maciste at the Court of the Great Khan* and *Goliath and the Golden City.* Very often a film was released in Italy with one title, in France, Germany, or Spain with another, in Britain with still another, in the United States with a fourth, and then, if the distributor changed hands within the United States, with still another title, and each time the film was retitled: Goliath was a name more popular in Germany, while Americans, who cared little for the Italian favorite Maciste, preferred Hercules (or his son). A release like Kirk Morris's *Anthar l'Invincibile* introduced a new character in Italy but then was redubbed and released as *Devil of the Desert Against the Son of Hercules* in the United States and as *Soraya, Reina del Desierto* in Spain. Even

203　Hercules, Maciste, Samson, and Goliath answered the cinematic call in all lands and eras.
Here the hairy hand of Kobrak takes a cup of virgin blood from his "Salmanacian" assistant.
The shark's-tooth epaulettes would make turning the head a little tricky, no? Salmanac is the
mythical home of Kobrak in *Goliath and the Vampires* (1961)—a place, a monster, and a film
that belong to a world other than our own.

"Zorro" entered the fray, when *Samson and the Slave Queen* (1963) was also released as
Zorro vs. Maciste.

　　　Because the release titles were so generic and relatively unimportant, an Italian
title like *Ercole alla Conquista di Atlantide* (1961) could appear in the United States as
*Hercules and the Conquest of Atlantis, Hercules Conquers Atlantis, Hercules and the Captive
Women,* or even *Hercules and the Haunted Women.* Reg Park's *Ercole al Centro della Terra*
(1961) was translated as both *Hercules at the Center of the Earth* and *With Hercules to the
Center of the Earth,* but it also reappeared as *Hercules in the Haunted World, Hercules vs. the
Vampires,* and *The Vampires vs. Hercules.* This variation of titles, along with the accompanying variation in release dates, makes cataloguing these films frustrating today. *Maciste
nella Valle dei Re* (1960) can also be found as *Maciste in the Valley of the Kings, Maciste the
Mighty, Giant of the Valley of the Kings,* and *Son of Samson,* with 1960, 1961, and 1962 release dates. Winning the prize is *Medusa vs. the Son of Hercules* (1962), which is also
known as *Perseo l'Invincibile, Perseus the Invincible, Perseo e Medusa, El Valle de los Hombres
de Piedra, The Valley of the Stone Men,* and *Perseus Against the Monsters.*

Many muscleman films have been termed gladiator films, because they take place in Rome where the arena offered a ready-made setting for their physical tests and heroic exploits. The star of the gladiator films was Richard Harrison, who appeared in *The Invincible Gladiator* (1961), *Messalina Against the Son of Hercules* (*L'Ultimo Gladiatore*, 1963), *The Revolt of the Praetorians* (1963), *Gladiators Seven* (1964), and *Two Gladiators* (1964). Like Harrison's *Giants of Rome* (1963), which concerned marauding Gauls equipped with a giant catapult in 52 B.C., many of these films pretended to involve Roman history, as did *Maciste, Spartan Gladiator* (*The Terror of Rome Against the Son of Hercules,* 1964). There were also clutches of gladiators in *Death in the Arena* (also known as *Maciste the Strongest Gladiator in the World* and *Colossus of the Arena,* 1962), *The Revolt of the Praetorians* (1963), *Challenge of the Gladiators* (1964), *Ten Gladiators* (1963), *A Sword for the Empire* (1965), *The Magnificent Gladiator* (1963), and *Gladiator of Rome* (1962). In Greece there were *The Secret Seven* (*The Invincible Seven,* 1964).

The strongmen also muscled their way into the Old Testament, Greek and Roman mythology, the ancient Orient, the Middle Ages, and the Renaissance. They spread themselves from medieval China to barbaric Britain, from Neronian Rome to imaginary lands, from the peaks of the Alps to the depths of Hades. Sometimes the muscular heroes confronted or fought with each other, the prime examples of this subgenre being *Hercules, Samson, and Ulysses* (1963) and the all-encompassing *Ursus vs. the Universe* (1964). Sometimes they encountered such historical figures as the Roman emperor and glutton Vitellius *(The Terror of Rome Against the Son of Hercules).*

The producers of the muscleman films hoped to attract a ready audience simply by including the name Hercules, Goliath, or Colossus in the film's title, but they often also lured a well-known English-speaking actor to help distinguish their films from the rest. Broderick Crawford appears as the mythological villain Eurytus in *Goliath and the Dragon* (1960); Don Murray plays a Roman named Justinian in *The Viking Queen* (1966); Cornel Wilde plays the title role in *Constantine and the Cross* (1962); Tina Louise plays Sappho in *The Warrior Empress* (1960); Orson Welles plays Saul in *David and Goliath* (1961); Jayne Mansfield plays "the loves" in *The Loves of Hercules* (1960), with her husband Mickey Hargitay playing Hercules; and Anita Ekberg plays Zenobia in *Sign of the Gladiator* (1959). In addition, a nonchalant Louis Jourdan is Lars Porsenna in *Amazons of Rome* (1963), Christopher Lee appears in *Hercules in the Haunted World* (1961), Fernando Rey in *The Last Days of Pompeii* (1959), Robert Morley in *Joseph and His Brethren* (1962), Virginia Mayo in *Revolt of the Mercenaries* (1960), decathlete Bob Mathias in *The Minotaur* (1960), Alan Ladd in *Duel of Champions* (1961), Bruce Cabot in *Goliath and the Barbarians* (1959), Jack Palance and Guy Madison in *Sword of the Conqueror* (1961), Cameron Mitchell in *Caesar the Conqueror* (1963), Jeanne Crain and Vincent Price in *Queen of the Nile* (1961), Edmund Purdom in *Herod the Great* (1958), *The Fury of the Barbarians* (1960), and *The Loves of Salammbô* (1959), and John Drew Barrymore in *The Centurion* (1962), *The Pharaoh's Woman* (1960), and *The Trojan Horse* (1962).

204   Muscleman epics often
employed well-known American
actors in decline. Here a severely
scarred Broderick Crawford plays
the Greek mythological King
Eurytus in *Goliath and the
Dragon* (1960). *Sic transit gloria
cinemae.* The fellow in the
background wears his hair in
ringlets, Assyrian style.

205   *David and Goliath* (1961) featured Orson Welles as Saul, the biblical version of a pointy-
bearded tyrant. Welles's brooding did give the film some depth. Behind him stands an Assyrian
human-headed winged-bull statue—the same type found in *Intolerance, Esther and the King,* and
any other film that tried to suggest an ancient Oriental atmosphere.

The nonmuscular supporting casts become familiar to the frequent watcher of these toga sagas. Mimmo Palmara, Jacques Sernas, Nando Tamberlani, Livio Lorenzon, Ivo Garrani, Massimo Serato, Gino Cervi, Georges Marchal, Gianna Maria Canale, Rossana Podestà, and Massimo Girotti hardly had time to take their sandals off in the early 1960s. Throughout the various *Hercules vs. Goliath and the . . . , The Triumph of . . . , The Sword and . . . , The Revolt of . . . , The Vengeance of . . . ,* and *The Fury of . . . ,* these and other actors became adept at playing the not-so-muscular gladiator (Palmara), the smooth lover (Sernas), the shaved-headed warrior (Lorenzon), the much abused and fought over princess (Podestà), and the stern but troubled statesman (Girotti).

But American audiences never heard their voices. The invisible dubbers in (modern) Rome repeatedly saw to that. It was the dubbers' distant, gravelly voices that pronounced such characteristic lines as "Twelve straight hours on a horse; any more of this and I'll turn into a centaur!" (*The Slave of Rome,* 1960); "You croak like a bird of ill omen!" (*Duel of the Titans,* 1961); "What a waste of a good throne!" (*Hercules and the Captive Women;* see Chapter 3); and the ever-present, "By the Gods!" *Gold for the Caesars* (1963), which places Jeffrey Hunter as an enslaved architect in A.D. 96 Roman Spain and which offers the memorably poetic dubbed motto, "Trust a Roman and you trust a snake!" *Ulysses Against the Son of Hercules,* which has an angry Ulysses deliver this profound translated maxim: "He who eats alone, chokes alone!" Speaking of food, in *The Terror of Rome Against the Son of Hercules* the English voice of the calorie-counting Vitellius dishes out this classic line: "I like food best of all in the world. I wish I had the neck of a giraffe and the stomach of an elephant so I could enjoy it even more!"

Poor dubbing is, of course, impossible to transcribe, but the following passage from *The Secret Seven* (1964) illustrates the standards of non-sequitur and melo- and hyper-dramatic dialogue that characterize the typical sword-and-sandal movie. The plot of the film borrows from the *Seven Samurai* and *The Magnificent Seven*: Leslio (Tony Russell), a Sidonian freelance warrior, starts his own private revolt in the fourth century B.C. against Raberio, a Spartan provincial commander-turned-despot, pointy beard and all; Leslio collects six other able men to carry on the rebellion with him, but he also finds time to fall in love with Lydia, Raberio's mistress. Here the rebel Leslio has sneaked into evil-eyed Raberio's palace and is seen leaving from Lydia's room; after Leslio leaves, the angry despot Raberio catches Lydia trying to escape

> RABERIO: I didn't know you were going away—or should I say "running away"?
>
> LYDIA: I never run away. Why should I? Although I'm tired of waiting for false promises. I'm not so sure I want to get married.
>
> RABERIO: You won't live long enough to marry a beggar. Your little game is over.
>
> LYDIA: That's ridiculous!

RABERIO: Did you think you could fool me? I saw him leave your room, and just now you were trying to escape with him, weren't you? ANSWER ME! [He slaps her despotically.]

LYDIA: [Gasp] Yes—escape you and the hate that surrounds this miserable palace. I would rather die than be with you.

RABERIO: I am sincerely moved by such sentiment. Yours is a love only *death* can dissolve. Since that is your wish, you will be satisfied very soon.

Some muscleman films have dialogue that is better and more coherent than this (*Constantine and the Cross,* for example); a few show excellent color and some fine photography *(Ulysses vs. the Son of Hercules, Duel of the Titans);* a few offer some fine action sequences *(The Giant of Marathon, Carthage in Flames).* Some muscleman films are intentionally light and self-parodying *(My Son, the Hero, Samson and Gideon).* Actually, very few of them are unwatchable. Like reading dime novels, watching sword-and-sandal films has its curious attractions. Intellectual satisfaction and narrative subtlety they do not have. Multidimensional characters and realistic situations they do not have. Sophisticated dialogue and profound meaning they do not have. But they do have colorful costumes and imaginative sets and seductive mistresses and burly humor and Mediterranean scenery and bizarre tortures and nineteen-inch biceps and furious battles and likable heroes and the triumph of good over evil. This is what movies are for, sometimes.

Western civilization grew its roots in the Bronze Age cultures of Mesopotamia and Egypt, matured in classical Greece and Rome, and branched out into medieval, Renaissance, Baroque, and modern European and then American culture. Medieval scholars used Latin, and Christendom watched several different "Holy Roman" empires come and go during the era. Renaissance artists discovered, copied, and imitated the Greco-Roman masters and monuments of literature, sculpture, and architecture. Baroque musicians attempting to re-create the music of ancient Greek tragedy gave birth to opera. The framers of the U.S. Constitution looked to Plutarch, Livy, and Polybius for examples of democratic government. And such twentieth-century titans as Picasso, Sartre, and Stravinsky painted, wrote, and composed important works dependent on ancient Greek myth and literature.

There have been a variety of other influences as well, but the classical tradition has always been a major part of Western civilization. It is then no surprise to find the early years of cinema steeped in the ancient world. Even though too few film historians recognize the "ancient" film as a genre, the impact that this corpus has had on the history of film has been formidable. In 1908 Sidney Olcott's eleven-minute version of *Ben-Hur* blazed the path by prompting the Supreme Court ruling that regularized the legal process of turning a best-selling novel into a feature film. In Italy that same year Arturo Ambrosio turned *The Last Days of Pompeii* into the first great epic of the Golden Age of Italian cinema. *The Last Days of Pompeii* was followed by the most successful European films of their era, Guazzoni's *Quo Vadis?* in 1912 and Pastrone's *Cabiria* in 1914. And *Cabiria* in turn inspired D. W. Griffith to create *Intolerance* (1916), the most ambitious film of the early American silent film era. Griffith's Hollywood competitors responded in the next decade with several more lavish, costly, and successful films set in antiquity, including *Ben-Hur* (1925), MGM's first great film, and Cecil B. DeMille's *The King of Kings* (1927), which for decades remained the most frequently viewed film ever made.

The genre then ranged from 1932's much imitated *The Mummy* to the first Cinema-Scope film (*The Robe* [1953]), the most Oscared film (*Ben-Hur* [1959]), and one of the most expensive and controversial films ever made (*Cleopatra* [1963]). *Cleopatra* was so lavish that it inspired in the next two years not just Samuel Barber's opera *Antony and Cleopatra,* which was commissioned for the new Metropolitan Opera House, but also Las Vegas's first great themed hotel-casino, Caesars Palace. Across the Atlantic, in the wake of Jean Cocteau's poetic *Orpheus* (1949) the next generation of Italian directors produced such timeless works of modern art as *Fellini Satyricon* (1969) and Pasolini's *Medea,* starring Maria Callas (1970).

The 1970s ushered in made-for-television movies, and the ancient genre contributed a half-dozen early entries. The rarely rocked boat of the 1980s was indeed rocked, first by Monty Python's boycotted *Life of Brian* (1979), then by Bob Guccione's X-rated *Caligula* (1980), and finally by Martin Scorsese's iconoclastic *The Last Temptation of Christ* (1988). The 1990s produced *Hercules: The Legendary Journeys,* which became the most popular syndicated television program in the world, and this in turn spawned not just several more television programs set in antiquity but a whole new brood of "ancient" feature films overlapping the turn of the millennium. In the entire history of the cinema, no genre has so consistently produced more successful or more controversial films, nor has any other genre so often been at the avant garde of popular film. Considering how film-makers have been influenced by and have borrowed from one another for one hundred years, it is no surprise that the ancient world is still an important influence in the cinema of the twenty-first century.

From this day on, I would like to be known as "The Big Aristotle," because it

was Aristotle who said, "Excellence is not a singular act but a habit. You are

what you repeatedly do."

— SHAQUILLE O'NEAL

epilogue

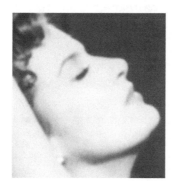

When I began the process of revising this book in the summer of 1999, I was happy to report the successful outcome of my most optimistic projection—that the "ancient genre" would resurface. As I played with this thought, I realized that it would not be out of character for the "ancient genre" to resurface with the same kind of innovative vigor that had characterized the emergences in the silent era and in the 1950s. And as I conclude this version of the book, the genre has exploded into the national consciousness the first few weeks of May 2000. The major television networks had been running trailers for *Gladiator* already for several weeks, and this was during the opening of the greatest home run–hitting baseball season in history and the most carefully contrived playoff television schedule in history for both the National Basketball Association and National Hockey League, not to mention the customary May sweeps month. *Gladiator* was the first summer movie of the new millennium, and after a fine opening weekend (May 5–7) in which it earned $32 million, that Sunday and Monday brought us NBC's *Jason and the Argonauts*.

All weekend long, the commercial, network, and station identification breaks during the NBA playoffs were peppered with promos for *Jason and the Argonauts*. At least once each game in the daily tripleheaders the announcers read copy about the film, and there were one or two hours during those two afternoons in which the viewer saw two or more promos for *Jason and the Argonauts* and one for *Gladiator*. In addition, the Friday edition of *The New York Times* ran a relatively respectful obituary for Steve Reeves, who had died early in the week, and the Sunday edition ran

Thomas Vinciguerra's selection of favorite bits of dialogue from *Samson and Delilah, Demetrius and the Gladiators, Cleopatra, Spartacus,* the Steve Reeves *Hercules,* and many other "ancient" films.[1] The syndicated *Roger Ebert at the Movies* that weekend witnessed one of the greatest disagreements of the post–Gene Siskel era, with Ebert describing *Gladiator* as "shallow and messy" but his guest host proclaiming the film as one the greatest movies she had ever seen—worthy of eight or nine Oscars. On the cover of *TV Guide* that week was Jeremy Sisto, photographed as Jesus for the CBS miniseries *Jesus* to be run the following week. And on that Saturday an appropriately named Fusaichi Pegasus won the 126th running of the Kentucky Derby.

The following Wednesday, Shaquille O'Neal, the Titan-sized center of the Los Angeles Lakers, was named the National Basketball Association's Most Valuable Player, and in his acceptance speech "Shaq"—the same athlete who a few years earlier had visited Greece and responded to a reporter's question, "Did you see the Parthenon?" with "I didn't get a chance to see all the bars!"—offered the elegant quotation from Aristotle that appears as the epigraph to this epilogue.

The classical tradition is indeed alive and well in the twenty-first century, and I assume that *Gladiator* is not an end but a new beginning.

Date	Historical Event/Figure	Film
to c. 1265 B.C.	pre-Trojan War	*Oedipus Rex* (1910, 1912, 1957, 1967 [two]) *The Minotaur* (1910, 1960) *The Golden Fleece* (1918) *Phèdre* (1919, 1968) *Hercules* (1957, 1983, 1997, and other Hercules films) *Antigone* (1961) *Perseus the Invincible* (1962) *Jason and the Argonauts* (1963, 2000) *Medea* (1970) *Clash of the Titans* (1981)
c. 1265 B.C.	Trojan War and aftermath	*Ulysses and the Giant Polyphemus* (1905) *The Return of Ulysses* (1908) *La Caduta di Troia* (1911) *L'Odissea* (1911) *Circe the Enchantress* (1924) *The Private Life of Helen of Troy* (1927) *Loves of Three Queens* (1953) *Helen of Troy* (1955) *Ulysses* (1955) *Last Glory of Troy* (1962) *Electra* (1962) *The Fury of Achilles* (1962) *The Trojan Horse* (1962) *The Trojan Women* (1971) *Iphigenia* (1977) *The Odyssey* (1997)
753 B.C.	Founding of Rome	*Duel of the Titans* (1961) *Romulus and the Sabines* (1961)
c. 650 B.C.	Latin wars	*Duel of Champions* (1961)
c. 612 B.C.	Birth of Sappho	*Saffo* (1919) *The Warrior Empress* (1960)
c. 510 B.C.	Tarquin ousted from Rome	*Hero of Rome* (1963)
c. 491 B.C.	Coriolanus exiled	*Coriolanus: Hero Without a Country* (1962)

Date	Historical Event/Figure	Film
490 B.C.	Battle of Marathon	*The Giant of Marathon* (1959)
480 B.C.	Battle of Thermopylae	*The 300 Spartans* (1962)
c. 476 B.C.	Lars Porsenna	*Amazons of Rome* (1963)
406–367 B.C.	Dionysius I of Syracuse	*Damon and Pythias* (1914, 1962)
399 B.C.	Death of Socrates	*Socrates* (1970)
390 B.C.	Gauls sack Rome	*Brennus, Enemy of Rome* (1960)
356–323 B.C.	Alexander the Great	*Alexander the Great* (1955, 1964-TV)
	Praxiteles	*Goddess of Love* (1958)
		Goliath and the Rebel Slave Girl (1963)
225 B.C.	Colossus of Rhodes	*The Colossus of Rhodes* (1960)
218–201 B.C.	Second Punic War	*Cabiria* (1914)
		Salambo (1914)
		Scipio l'Africano (1937)
		Loves of Salammbô (1959)
		Siege of Syracuse (1959)
		Carthage in Flames (1960)
		Hannibal (1960)
		Scipio Detto Anche l'Africano (1971)
146 B.C.	Sack of Corinth	*The Centurion* (1962)
121 B.C.	Death of Gaius Gracchus	*Cajo Gracco* (1911)
73 B.C.	Revolt of Spartacus	*Spartacus* (1909, 1913, 1914, 1919, 1960)
		Sins of Rome (1954)
		Spartacus and the Ten Gladiators (1964)
	Lucullus in the East	*Rome Against Rome* (1963)
63 B.C.	Consulship of Cicero	*Catilina* (1910)
53 B.C.	Death of Crassus	*Son of Spartacus* (1962)
52 B.C.	Defeat of Vercingetorix	*The Gaul's Honor* (1910)
		The Triumph of the Emperor (1914)
		The Slave of Rome (1960)
		The Giants of Rome (1963)
44 B.C.	Death of Julius Caesar	*Julius Caesar* (1908, 1909, 1914, 1917, 1950, 1953, 1970)
		Brutus (1910)
		Caesar in Egypt (1910)
		Caesar and Cleopatra (1946)
		A Queen for Caesar (1962)
		Caesar the Conqueror (1963)
41–30 B.C.	Antony and Cleopatra	*Cleopatra* (1899, 1908 [two], 1910 [two], 1912, 1913, 1917, 1928, 1934, 1963, 1972, 1999)
		Marcantonio e Cleopatra (1913, 1973)
		Serpent of the Nile (1953)
		Legions of the Nile (1959)
A.D. 14–37	Reign of Emperor Tiberius	*Ben-Hur* (1907, 1925, 1959)
		Salome (1908, 1913, 1918, 1922, 1953)
		The Hour of Execution (1911)
		I, Claudius (1937-inc.)
		The Robe (1953)
		A.D. (1985)
A.D. 37–41	Reign of Emperor Caligula	*I, Claudius* (1937-inc.)

Date	Historical Event/Figure	Film
A.D. 37–41 *(continued)*	Reign of Emperor Caligula	*Demetrius and the Gladiators* (1954) *Caligula* (1980) *A.D.* (1985)
A.D. 41–54	Reign of Emperor Claudius	*Messalina* (1910, 1922, 1951, 1960) *I, Claudius* (1937-inc.) *Messalina Against the Son of Hercules* (1963) *The Viking Queen* (1966) *A.D.* (1985)
A.D. 54–68	Reign of Emperor Nero	*The Sign of the Cross* (1904, 1914, 1932) *Nero and the Burning of Rome* (1908, 1909) *Nero* (1909, 1922, 1925, 1930) *The Way of the Cross* (1909) *Agrippina* (1910) *In the Days of Nero* (1911) *Poppea ed Ottavia* (1911) *Quo Vadis?* (1912, 1924, 1951, 1985) *Nero and Britannicus* (1913) *Nerone e Agrippina* (1913) *Fire Over Rome* (1963) *Ten Gladiators* (1963) *Challenge of the Gladiators* (1964) *Poppaea's Hot Nights* (1969) *A.D.* (1985)
A.D. 69	Reign of Emperor Vitellius	*Terror of Rome vs. Son of Hercules* (1963)
A.D. 79–81	Reign of Emperor Titus and the Eruption of Vesuvius	*Last Days of Pompeii* (1908, 1913, 1926, 1935, 1937, 1955, 1960, 1984) *Seventy-Nine A.D.* (1960)
A.D. 81–96	Reign of Emperor Domitian	*Gold for the Caesars* (1963)
A.D. 98–117	Reign of Emperor Trajan	*In the Days of Trajan* (1913)
A.D. 138–161	Reign of Emperor Antoninus	*Androcles and the Lion* (1952)
A.D. 181–193	Reign of Emperor Commodus and death of Marcus Aurelius	*Two Gladiators* (1962) *The Fall of the Roman Empire* (1964) *A Sword for the Empire* (1965) *Gladiator* (2000)
A.D. 211–217	Reign of Emperor Caracalla	*Gladiator of Rome* (1962)
A.D. 270–275	Reign of Emperor Aurelian	*Sign of the Gladiator* (1959)
A.D. 285–305	Reign of Emperor Diocletian	*Revolt of the Barbarians* (1964)
A.D. 305–312	Rise of Emperor Constantine	*In Hoc Signo Vinces* (1913) *Fabiola* (1916, 1948) *Constantine and the Cross* (1962)
A.D. 410	Alaric sacks Rome	*The Revenge of the Barbarians* (1960)
A.D. 451	Reigns of Marcian and Valentinian III; Attila in Italy	*Attila* (1916) *Attila the Hun* (1954) *Sign of the Pagan* (1955)
A.D. 527–565	Reign of Emperor Justinian	*Theodora* (1908, 1913, 1921, 1954) *Sword of the Conqueror* (1961)

Book	Story	Approximate Historical Date	Film
Genesis	Creation	—	*The Green Pastures* (1936)
			I Patriarchi della Bibbia (1963)
			The Bible . . . In the Beginning (1966)
	Adam and Eve	—	*The Bible* (1921)
			Adam ed Eva (1950)
			Adán y Eva (1956)
			The Private Lives of Adam and Eve (1961)
			Cain and Abel (1910, 1911, 1911)
			I Patriarchi Della Bibbia (1963)
			The Bible . . . In the Beginning (1966)
	Noah	—	*The Deluge* (1911)
			Noah's Ark (1929, 1959)
			The Green Pastures (1936)
			I Patriarchi della Bibbia (1963)
			The Bible . . . In the Beginning (1966)
	Abraham	—	*Abraham's Sacrifice* (1912)
			The Sacrifice of Isaac (1932)
			I Patriarchi della Bibbia (1963)
			The Bible . . . In the Beginning (1966)
			Abraham (1994-TV)
	Lot in Sodom	c. 1900 B.C.	*Sodom und Gomorrah* (1922)
			Lot in Sodom (1933)
			[*Last Days of*] *Sodom and Gomorrah* (1963)
			The Bible . . . In the Beginning (1966)
	Jacob	c. 1700 B.C.	*I Patriarchi della Bibbia* (1963)
			Giacobbe ed Esau (1964)
			The Story of Jacob and Joseph (1975-TV)
			Jacob: A TNT Bible Story (1994-TV)
	Joseph	—	*Joseph in the Land of Egypt* (1914, 1932)
			Joseph and His Coat of Many Colors (1914)
			Joseph and His Brethren (1922, 1930, 1962)
			Her Strange Desire (1930)
			The Story of Jacob and Joseph (1975-TV)
			Joseph (1995-TV)
Exodus	Moses	13th century B.C.	*Moses and the Exodus* (1907)

Book	Story	Approximate Historical Date	Film
Exodus *(continued)*	Moses	13th century B.C.	*Life of Moses* (1909) *Pharaoh; or Israel in Egypt* (1910) *Infancy of Moses* (1911) *The Ten Commandments* (1923) *Moon of Israel* (1924) *The Green Pastures* (1936) *The Ten Commandments* (1956) *Moses, the Lawgiver* (1975-TV) *The Prince of Egypt* (1998)
Judges	Gideon	12th century B.C.	*Samson and Gideon* (1965)
	Samson	11th century B.C.	*Samson and Delilah* (1903, 1911, 1914, 1922) *Samson and Delilah* (1949) *Samson* (1961 and other Samson films) *Samson and Gideon* (1965) *Samson and Delilah* (1984-TV) *Samson and Delilah* (1996-TV)
Samuel	Saul	1000 B.C.	*Saul and David* (1909, 1911, 1912, 1964) *La Mort de Saül* (1913)
	David	975 B.C.	*David and Goliath* (1908, 1961) *David* (1912) *The Shepherd King* (1923) *David and Bathsheba* (1951) *A Story of David* (1960) *The Story of David* (1976-TV) *King David* (1985) *David* (1997-TV)
Kings	Solomon	c. 950 B.C.	*The Judgment of Solomon* (1909) *La Reine de Saba* (1913) *Queen of Sheba* (1921, 1953) *Solomon and Sheba* (1959) *Solomon and Sheba* (1995-TV) *Solomon* (1997-TV)
	Jezebel	c. 850 B.C.	*The Son of the Shunamite* (1911) *Sins of Jezebel* (1953)
Jonah	Jonah	c. 750 B.C.	*Jonah and the Whale* (1960-inc.)
Ruth	Ruth	—	*The Story of Ruth* (1960)
Esther	Esther	c. 475 B.C.	*Esther and Mordecai* (1910) *The Marriage of Esther* (1910) *Esther* (1913) *Esther and the King* (1960)
Daniel	Daniel in Babylon	c. 550 B.C.	*Belshazzar's Feast* (1905, 1913) *Daniel* (1913) *Intolerance* (1916) *Slaves of Babylon* (1953)
Apocrypha	Judith	c. 580 B.C.	*Giudetta e Oloferne* (1906, 1928) *Judith of Bethulia* (1913) *Head of a Tyrant* (1960)
	Maccabees	c. 166 B.C.	*I Maccabei* (1910) *Il Vecchio Testamento* (1962)

1. Mnemosyne: A Survey of the Genre

The epigraph is from *Brutus* 40.42.
1. Walsh, *Sin and Censorship,* 78–80.
2. Quoted in *The Epic That Never Was,* BBC (1965).
3. Shana Alexander, "Christ Never Tried to Please Everybody," *Life,* February 26, 1965, p. 25.

2. Clio: Greek and Roman History

1. "Greatest picture": "The Screen," *New York Times Film Reviews,* July 4, 1921, p. 10.
2. "Spotty Spectacular," *Newsweek,* October 17, 1960, p. 117.
3. Kagan, *Cinema of Stanley Kubrick,* 69.
4. Genini, *Theda Bara,* 40.
5. Sheppard, *Elizabeth,* 323.
6. "Back at the Nile," *Newsweek,* July 8, 1963, p. 78.
7. John Howard Reid, "Cleo's Joe," *Films and Filming,* August 1963, pp. 44–48, and September 1963, pp. 11–16.
8. Sheppard, *Elizabeth,* 335.
9. Ibid., 334.
10. Ibid., 335.
11. "Just One of Those Things," *Time,* June 21, 1963, p. 90.
12. Geist, *Pictures Will Talk,* 336.
13. Taylor, *Elizabeth Taylor,* 101.
14. Leprohon, *Italian Cinema,* 58.
15. Bosley Crowther, "Romans Versus Barbarians," *New York Times Film Reviews,* March 27, 1964, p. 14.

3. Calliope: Greek and Roman Mythology

1. Harryhausen, *Film Fantasy Scrapbook,* 85.
2. "Joe Unchained," *Time,* February 24, 1961, p. 64.
3. Raymond Durgnat, "Orphée," *Films and Filming* 10 (October 1963): 45.

4. Polyhymnia: The Old Testament

The second epigraph is from Essoe and Lee, *DeMille,* 195.
1. Bosley Crowther, "Story of Joseph," *New York Times Film Reviews,* December 1, 1962, p. 17.
2. Koury, *Yes, Mr. DeMille,* 89.

3. Quoted in Essoe and Lee, *DeMille,* 221.

4. "In the Great Tradition," *Newsweek,* November 28, 1949, pp. 70–71.

5. Such a balance can be seen in the so-called Ani Papyrus of the Book of the Dead; see J. A. Thompson, *The Bible and Archaeology* (Grand Rapids, Mich.: Eerdmans, 1972).

6. Essoe and Lee, *DeMille,* 261.

7. Heston and Isbouts, *Charlton Heston's Hollywood,* 66–68.

8. Quotation from "*Solomon and Sheba,*" *Time,* January 11, 1960, p. 64.

5. Erato: The New Testament and Tales of the Christ

1. Higham, *Cecil B. DeMille,* 166.

2. Shana Alexander, "Christ Never Tried to Please Everybody," *Life,* February 26, 1965, p. 25.

3. Quoted in "Calendar Christ," *Time,* February 26, 1965, p. 96.

4. Richard N. Ostling, "Franco Zeffirelli's Classical Christ for Prime Time," *Time,* April 4, 1977, p. 72.

5. Quotation from Babington and Evans, *Biblical Epics,* 152.

6. Quotation from Stanley Kauffmann, "A Pair of Spectacles," *New Republic,* December 28, 1959, p. 27.

7. Robert Coughlan, "The General's Mighty Chariots," *Life,* November 16, 1959, pp. 119, 124.

8. Madsen, *William Wyler,* 43–44.

9. Quoted in Paolella, *Storia del cinema muto,* 27.

10. LeRoy, *Mervyn LeRoy,* 173.

11. Bosley Crowther, "Beads, Beards, and Braids," *New York Times Film Reviews,* May 14, 1955, p. 10.

12. Quirk, *Films of Paul Newman,* 17.

6. Euterpe: Babylon, Egypt, Persia, and the Ancient Orient

1. McBride, *Focus on Howard Hawks,* 22.

2. Bosley Crowther, "Costume Charade," *New York Times Film Reviews,* November 19, 1960, p. 13.

7. Melpomene: Ancient Tragedy and *The Satyricon*

1. Quotation from Stanley Kauffmann, "Love in Old New England," *New Republic,* April 7, 1958, pp. 22–23.

2. Gilbert Highet, "Whose *Satyricon* —Petronius' or Fellini's?" *Horizon,* Autumn 1970, pp. 43–47.

3. Zanelli, *Fellini's Satyricon,* 4–9.

4. "Petronius, 20%; Fellini 80%," *Time,* September 12, 1969, pp. 96–97.

8. Thalia: Ancient Comedy and Satirized Ancients

1. Quotation from Brendan Gill, "Rich Harvest," *New Yorker,* October 22, 1966, pp. 164–165.

2. "Everything, Then Some," *Newsweek,* May 6, 1957, p. 112.

9. Terpsichore: The Muscleman Epics

1. Quoted in Leprohon, *Italian Cinema,* 178; the chapter epigraph is from 175.

Epilogue

1. "'Battle Seems to Become You': The Technicolor Glory That Was Rome," *New York Times,* May 7, 2000.

selected bibliography

Babington, Bruce, and Peter William Evans. *Biblical Epics: Sacred Narrative in the Hollywood Cinema.* Manchester, England: Manchester University Press, 1993.

Basinger, Jeanine. *Anthony Mann.* Boston: Twayne, 1979.

Bliss, Michael. *The Word Made Flesh: Catholicism and Conflict in the Films of Martin Scorsese.* Lanham, Md.: Scarecrow, 1995.

Bondanella, Peter. *The Cinema of Federico Fellini.* Princeton: Princeton University Press, 1992.

Bragg, Melvyn. *Laurence Olivier.* New York: St. Martin's, 1985.

———. *Richard Burton: A Life.* Boston: Little, Brown, 1988.

Brown, Jared. *Zero Mostel: A Biography.* New York: Atheneum, 1989.

Cammarota, M. D. *Il Cinema Peplum.* Rome: Fanucci, 1987.

Canutt, Yakima. *Stunt Man: The Autobiography of Yakima Canutt.* Norman: University of Oklahoma Press, 1979.

Casty, Alan. *The Films of Robert Rossen.* New York: Museum of Modern Art, 1969.

Connors, Martin, and Jim Craddock, eds. *VideoHound's Golden Movie Retriever.* Detroit: Visible Ink, 1999.

Cook, Bruce. *Dalton Trumbo.* New York: Scribner's, 1977.

Douglas, Kirk. *The Ragman's Son: An Autobiography.* New York: Simon and Schuster, 1988.

Durgnat, Raymond. *King Vidor, American.* Berkeley: University of California Press, 1988.

Eames, John Douglas. *The MGM Story: The Complete History of Fifty Roaring Years.* New York: Crown, 1975.

Elley, Dere. *The Epic Film: Myth and History.* London: Routledge, 1984.

Essoe, Gabe, and Raymond Lee. *DeMille: The Man and His Pictures.* South Brunswick, N.J.: A. S. Barnes, 1970.

Evans, Arthur. *Jean Cocteau and His Films of Orphic Identity.* Philadelphia: Art Alliance, 1977.

Fast, Howard. *Being Red.* Boston: Houghton Mifflin, 1990.

Finler, Joel W. *Silent Cinema.* London: B. T. Batsford, 1997.

Finocchiaro Chimirri, Giovanna. *D'Annunzio e il Cinema Cabiria.* Catania: C.U.E.C.M., 1986.

Geist, Kenneth L. *Pictures Will Talk: The Life and Films of Joseph L. Mankiewicz.* New York: Scribner's, 1978.

Genini, Ronald. *Theda Bara: A Biography of the Silent Screen Vamp, with a Filmography.* Jefferson, N.C.: McFarland, 1996.

Gifford, Denis. *BFI Catalogue, 1895–1970.* New York: McGraw-Hill, 1973.

Goldman, Herbert G. *Banjo Eyes: Eddie Cantor and the Birth of Modern Stardom.* New York: Oxford University Press, 1997.

Greene, Naomi. *Pier Paolo Pasolini: Cinema as Heresy.* Princeton: Princeton University Press, 1990.

Harpole, Charles, ed. *History of the American Cinema.* New York: Scribner's, 1990.

Harryhausen, Ray. *Film Fantasy Scrapbook.* 3d ed. San Diego: A. S. Barnes, 1981.

Hayne, Donald, ed. *The Autobiography of Cecil B. DeMille.* London: W. H. Allen, 1960.

Herman, Jan. *A Talent for Trouble: The Life of Hollywood's Most Acclaimed Director, William Wyler.* New York: Putnam, 1995.

Heston, Charlton. *The Actor's Life: Journals, 1956–1976.* New York: Dutton, 1978.

———. *In the Arena: An Autobiography.* New York: Simon and Schuster, 1995.

Heston, Charlton, and Jean-Pierre Isbouts. *Charlton Heston's Hollywood: 50 Years in American Film.* New York: GT, 1998.

Higashi, Sumiko. *Cecil B. DeMille and American Culture: The Silent Era.* Berkeley: University of California Press, 1994.

Higham, Charles. *Cecil B. DeMille.* New York: Scribner's, 1973.

Hirsch, Foster. *The Hollywood Epic.* South Brunswick, N.J.: A. S. Barnes, 1978.

Kagan, Norman. *The Cinema of Stanley Kubrick.* New York: Holt, Rinehart, and Winston, 1972.

Koury, Phil A. *Yes, Mr. DeMille.* New York: Putnam, 1959.

Leprohon, Pierre. *The Italian Cinema.* Trans. Roger Greaves and Oliver Stallybrass. New York: Praeger, 1972.

LeRoy, Mervyn. *Mervyn LeRoy: Take One.* New York: Hawthorn, 1974.

Lobrutto, Vincent. *Stanley Kubrick: A Biography.* New York: D. I. Fine, 1997.

Maddox, Brenda. *Who's Afraid of Elizabeth Taylor?* New York: Lippincott, 1977.

Madsen, Axel. *William Wyler.* New York: Crowell, 1973.

Mann, Anthony. *From Where I Sit—* Aldershot, England: Trouser, 1990.

Maturi, Richard J. *Francis X. Bushman: A Biography and Filmography.* Jefferson, N.C.: McFarland, 1998.

Mayer, David, and Katherine K. Preston. *Playing Out the Empire: Ben-Hur and Other Toga Plays and Films, 1883–1908.* Oxford: Clarendon, 1994.

McBride, Joseph, ed. *Focus on Howard Hawks.* Englewood Cliffs, N.J.: Prentice-Hall, 1972.

McGilligan, Patrick. *Backstory 2: Interviews with Screenwriters of the 1940s and 1950s.* Berkeley: University of California Press, 1991.

Orrison, Katherine. *Lionheart in Hollywood: The Autobiography of Henry Wilcoxon.* Metuchen, N.J.: Scarecrow, 1991.

———. *Written in Stone: Making Cecil B. DeMille's Epic, The Ten Commandments.* Lanham, Md.: Vestal, 1999.

Paolella, Roberto. *Storia del Cinema Muto.* Naples: Giannini, 1956.

Phillips, Gene D. *Exiles in Hollywood: Major European Film Directors in America.* Bethlehem, Pa.: Lehigh University Press, 1998.

Prendergast, Roy M. *Film Music: A Neglected Art.* New York: Norton, 1977.

Quirk, Lawrence J. *The Films of Paul Newman.* New York: The Citadel Press, 1971.

Ragan, David. *Who's Who in Hollywood: The Largest Cast of International Film Personalities Ever Assembled.* New York: Facts on File, 1992.

Robbins, Jhan. *Yul Brynner: The Inscrutable King.* New York: Dodd, Mead, 1987.

Rovin, Jeff. *From the Land Beyond Beyond: The Films of Willis O'Brien and Ray Harryhausen.* New York: Berkeley, 1977.

Sarris, Andrew, ed. *The St. James Film Directors Encyclopedia.* Detroit: Visible Ink, 1998.

Schickel, Richard. *D. W. Griffith: An American Life.* New York: Simon and Schuster, 1984.

Schuster, Mel. *The Contemporary Greek Cinema.* Metuchen, N.J.: Scarecrow, 1979.

Searles, Baird. *EPIC!: History on the Big Screen.* New York: Abrams, 1990.

Sheppard, Dick. *Elizabeth: The Life and Career of Elizabeth Taylor.* Garden City, N.Y.: Doubleday, 1974.

Smith, Gary A. *Epic Films: Casts, Credits, and Commentary on Over 250 Historical Spectacle Movies.* [Jefferson, N.C.]: McFarland, 1991.

Stewart, V. Lorne. *Peter Ustinov and His World: An Authorized Biographical Sketch.* Nashville: Winston-Derek, 1988.

Taylor, Elizabeth. *Elizabeth Taylor.* New York: Harper and Row, 1964.

Thomas, Bob. *Brando: Portrait of the Rebel as an Artist.* New York: Random House, 1973.

———. *Disney's Art of Animation: From Mickey Mouse to Hercules.* 2d ed. New York: Hyperion, 1997.

———. *Thalberg: Life and Legend.* Garden City, N.Y.: Doubleday, 1969.

Thompson, David, and Ian Christie, eds. *Scorsese on Scorsese.* London: Faber, 1989.

Walker, John, ed. *Halliwell's Film Guide 1994.* New York: HarperCollins, 1994.

Walsh, Frank. *Sin and Censorship: The Catholic Church and the Motion Picture Industry.* New Haven: Yale University Press, 1996.

Wanger, Walter, and Joe Hyams, *My Life with Cleopatra*. London: Transworld, 1963.

Winkler, Martin W., ed. *Classics and Cinema*. Lewisburg, Pa.: Bucknell University Press, 1991.

Wyke, Maria. *Projecting the Past: Ancient Rome, Cinema, and History.* New York: Routledge, 1997.

Zanelli, Dario, ed. *Fellini's Satyricon.* New York: Ballantine, 1970.